Deathly Waters and Hungry Mountains
Agrarian Ritual and Class Formation in an Andean Town

Huaquirca, Peru, sits atop an impressive bank of agricultural terraces that rise out of the Antabamba Valley. Above it lies a vast alpine pasture that extends westward towards the Continental Divide. The town itself has eight hundred people, who separate themselves into two classes: notables and commoners. Notables claim rights to this land by enclosing it, whereas commoners do so through collective labour and ritual.

In this unusual book, Peter Gose describes how the commoners of this Andean town use the rituals that accompany their work to develop an understanding of themselves as a labouring class. Beyond marking 'Indian' cultural identity, these rituals regulate the realities of production, property, and political power as they unfold in commoners' lives. Combining a pragmatic approach to ritual with a concern for symbolic detail, Gose's study is particularly innovative in its scope: whereas most recent studies of ritual focus on only one rite, Gose discusses an entire annual cycle of agrarian rituals.

Gose shows that the imagery of death permeates the collective labour of the growing season, in which a loss of human vitality becomes the condition for agricultural regeneration. By contrast, the dry season stresses abundance, consumption, and private property, but legitimates them through sacrifices that recognize political authority. He concludes that many Andean peasant movements of the twentieth century drew on annual cycle rituals and sought to impose them as a quasi-legal framework to curb the lawlessness of local elites. Gose contrasts these movements with the politics of the left-wing party Shining Path, whose violence he sees as a traditional strategy of rural elites to assert their 'racial' distinction.

PETER GOSE is Head, Department of Anthropology, University of Regina.

Anthropological Horizons
Editor: Michael Lambek, University of Toronto

This series, begun in 1991, focuses on theoretically informed ethnographic works addressing issues of mind and body, knowledge and power, equality and inequality, the individual and the collective. Interdisciplinary in its perspective, the series makes a unique contribution in several other academic disciplines: women's studies, history, philosophy, psychology, political science, and sociology.

1 **The Varieties of Sensory Experience**
A Sourcebook in the Anthropology of the Senses
Edited by David Howes

2 **Arctic Homeland**
Kinship, Community, and Development in Northwest Greenland
Mark Nuttall

3 **Knowledge and Practice in Mayotte**
Local Discourses of Islam, Sorcery, and Spirit Possession
Michael Lambek

4 **Deathly Waters and Hungry Mountains**
Agrarian Ritual and Class Formation in an Andean Town
Peter Gose

5 **Paradise**
Class, Commuters, and Ethnicity in Rural Ontario
Stanley R. Barrett

Deathly Waters and Hungry Mountains

Agrarian Ritual and Class Formation in an Andean Town

PETER GOSE

UNIVERSITY OF TORONTO PRESS
Toronto Buffalo London

© University of Toronto Press Incorporated 1994
Toronto Buffalo London
Printed in Canada

ISBN 0-8020-0606-X (cloth)
ISBN 0-8020-7210-0 (paper)

∞

Printed on acid-free paper

Canadian Cataloguing in Publication Data

Gose, Peter
  Deathly waters and hungry mountains

  (Anthropological horizons)
  Includes bibliographical references and index.
  ISBN 0-8020-0606-X (bound)
  ISBN 0-8020-7210-0 (pbk.)

  1. Peasantry – Peru – Huaquirca – Social life and
  customs. 2. Agricultural laborers – Peru –
  Huaquirca – Social life and customs. 3. Agriculture –
  Social aspects – Peru – Huaquirca. 4. Working class –
  Peru – Huaquirca. I. Title. II. Series.

  HD1531.P47G6 1994   305.5′633′0985294   C94-930824-2

University of Toronto Press acknowledges the financial assistance to its
publishing program of the Canada Council and the Ontario Arts Council.

This book has been published with the help of a grant from the Social Science
Federation of Canada, using funds provided by the Social Sciences and
Humanities Research Council of Canada.

Contents

Illustrations

Preface

This book is about the native peasantry of an Andean town, and how they develop a cultural identity, a cosmology, and a political economy through the rituals that accompany their work in the fields. The setting is Huaquirca, a remote agricultural town in southern Peru (see Figure 1), in which 800 people lived at the time of my research there. The main theme of the study is the complex seasonal round of work parties and rituals that takes place in the fields surrounding Huaquirca. These, above all other activities, define 'Indian' cultural identity, and in so doing, link it to the agrarian occupation and world view of a peasantry. In this way of life, the social realities of production, property, and political power largely unfold on a seasonal basis, and are marked by the ritual imagery of death and sacrifice. Through symbolic analysis, I explore how agrarian rituals structure the economic and political practices around them in the annual cycle. Thus, the main goal of this book is to show how the commoners of Huaquirca reflect upon their social condition through a medium that is intrinsic to it: the annual cycle of labour and ritual.

An analytical notion of class is central to this study for several reasons, not the least of which is that it explains why agrarian labour, and its extension into ritual, should be a privileged mode of cultural expression for the commoners of Huaquirca. Education and literacy are available to these people, but it is primarily through the rituals of the annual cycle that they frame their experience and represent their place in the world. Huaquirca's commoners did not arbitrarily 'choose' the annual cycle as a cultural form, since it has an organic connection to their social condition as a peasantry and a labouring class. By looking at how class interacts with cultural expression, I hope

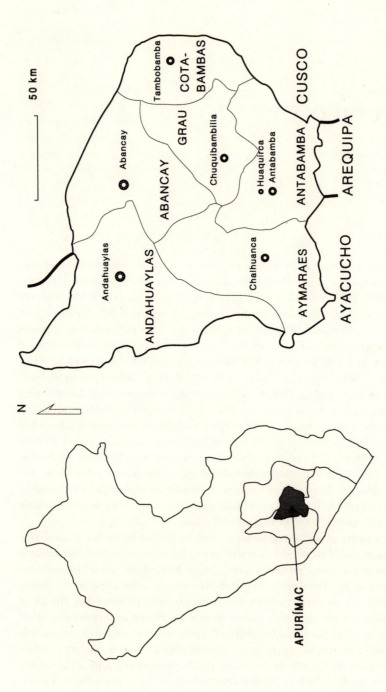

Figure 1 Location of study

to go beyond a simple content analysis of Huaquirca's annual cycle rituals and show that their very form has social significance.

To speak of class in a rural Andean setting inevitably conjures up images of the *hacienda*, a large landed estate worked by servile native labour. Although Huaquirca shared something of the 'feudal' subculture of these estates, it lies in one of the many areas of the southern Peruvian Andes where the *hacienda* never took hold. For the past 400 years, neither has Huaquirca conformed to the alternative stereotype of an 'Indian community' that defends its traditional way of life against the ravages of colonialism. Rather, like most small towns in the Peruvian Andes, Huaquirca combines the 'face-to-face' interaction of a small community in which everybody knows everyone else with a pronounced and occasionally violent differentiation of local society into two groups, which call themselves 'notables' and 'commoners.' Social science literature usually refers to these groups as '*mestizos*' and 'Indians,' respectively, but this introduces many rhetorical distortions that we shall explore presently. Notables amount to less than ten per cent of Huaquirca's population, and commoners more than ninety per cent. These proportions are typical of other small towns in the highlands of southern Peru.

Several criteria differentiate these groups, but perhaps the most basic is that notables do not participate in *ayni*, the reciprocal exchange of labour days by which commoners work their land during the growing season.[1] Rather, notables hire commoners to work on their land or recruit them through asymmetric relations of *mink'a*,[2] in which they compensate their workers with a day's food and drink instead of a comparable day's work in the fields. Notables may work their own land along with the commoners they recruit, but they consider it shameful to reciprocate, and only do so under the most desperate of circumstances. Generally, notables tend to avoid manual labour altogether,[3] and separate their personal activity from their landholdings to pursue commerce, teaching careers, and, above all, local political office, which they virtually monopolize as a group throughout the Peruvian countryside.[4] Thus, the relation between notables and commoners is one of rulers to ruled, one that is exemplified by public works programs in which commoners provide the tributary labour to realize state projects solicited and supervised by notable authorities. Finally, commoners and notables rarely intermarry.[5] The resulting endogamy contributes strongly to the local conviction that the difference between notables and commoners is essentially one of 'race,' namely that commoners are 'Indian' and notables are more 'mixed' (i.e., have more Spanish ancestry).

Yet there is little, if any, biological basis for these notions of 'race,' nor does an opposition between the Indian and the Hispanic adequately describe the cultural differentiation that exists between notables and commoners (see Fuenzalida 1970a: 25–6, 63, 72). Many of Huaquirca's commoners have Spanish surnames and genes bequeathed to them by priests who passed through the area in previous centuries. Others are illegitimate or downwardly mobile offshoots of notable families who lost the means of distinguishing themselves from commoners. In everything from land tenure to religion, the 'traditional' culture of Huaquirca's commoners is as Iberian as it is Andean. Conversely, all but a few of Huaquirca's notables speak perfect Quechua, and, until recently, were active and knowledgeable participants in the most 'Andean' of the town's rituals. There can be little doubt that local notions of race serve to essentialize sociocultural distinctions that are in other respects quite fluid. As a result, we are presented with a basic ethnographic question that this book will attempt to answer: what is the nature of the distinction between notables and commoners?

The standard answer to this question in the literature is that we are dealing with a matter of 'ethnic' difference. Many authorities have argued that the differences between notables and commoners are primarily 'cultural,' and only secondarily economic, or a matter of 'class.' There are many problems with this approach, all of which result from the notion that it is possible to abstract culture from economics, and treat each as an autonomous domain. On the contrary, I will show that one of the most crucial cultural differences between notables and commoners lies in the way they practise and understand the economic process. Far from being a value-free domain of instrumental activity, the economy of Huaquirca is the site of an intense cultural dispute between the two groups. Conversely, there is a strong economic component to the cultural differentiation between notables and commoners, one that a notion of class describes accurately.

Chapter 2 develops this argument by showing how the physical layout of Huaquirca and the surrounding countryside embodies the distinctive and often conflicting ways of claiming property rights that notables and commoners develop while living their lives. Here, the point is not merely to show that notables are richer than commoners, although this is certainly true, but to show that this uneven distribution of property derives from a more basic dispute over what property should be. For notables, property is something that ideally permits an escape from the world of agricultural labour into that of the school or political office. For commoners, however, property is the focus of a life dedicated to agrarian labour and ritual, and is something that should be conditional upon those activities.

In Chapter 3, I describe how both groups dramatize their respective sensibilities in a variety of rituals that occur in July and August, at the end of the dry season. This chapter continues the preceding discussion of social differentiation in Huaquirca, but also initiates a discussion of the annual cycle of labour and ritual, one that continues through the remainder of the book.

Chapter 4 leaves the notables behind, for the most part, to explicate the cultural framework that commoners use to understand and assert their relation with the land. It describes how maize fields are irrigated and sown in September and October, at the beginning of the agricultural year. Here I show how, in the midst of irrigation and sowing, commoners perform rituals that provide a local perspective on the technical, social, and cosmological dimensions of these tasks. Briefly, the ritual imagery of death permeates irrigation and sowing, and prefigures an agricultural regeneration of life in classic Frazerian fashion. I also show that death provides a model of how labour-power is generated within the human body and shared among households through relations of *ayni*, giving rise to a regime of collective production that characterizes the entire growing season. Chapter 5 continues this analysis into the heart of the rainy season by discussing the tasks of weeding and potato sowing, and the community-wide rituals of All Souls' and Christmas.

Chapter 6 describes the period from Carnival to the harvest, when this intense productive effort of cooperating households diminishes and then disappears altogether, to be replaced by a contrasting social emphasis on private appropriation of the crops by individual households. This coincides with a ritual emphasis on sacrifice, in which each household makes offerings to the mountain spirits in thanks for the harvest and in preparation for the coming agricultural year. These sacrifices occur in rituals called *t'inkas* (libations), described in Chapter 7. In these rituals, individual households pay sacrificial tribute to a hierarchy of mountain spirits who appear to personify legitimate proprietorship and political power. I interpret these rites as a local commentary on the acts of appropriation that take place in everyday life at this time of the year, and as part of a cosmology that links political power to agrarian fertility.

Chapter 8 concludes the study. It begins with a synthesis of the previous chapters and summarizes how the annual cycle rituals consolidate a local understanding of production, property, and power. It then shows how the sacrificial rituals of the annual cycle figured in moments of extraordinary political mobilization, such as the land occupations of 1958–64, when commoners wanted to assert the legality of their claims to the land. Not only do these events confirm the connection between sacrifice, property, and political justice that emerged out of the annual cycle, but they show how these rituals have had an impact on the history of twentieth-century Peru. The chapter ends with a discussion of how commoners have struggled to maintain and extend this ritual framework of meaning and right in relation to other political economic and legal discourses in contemporary Peru.

In summary, this study combines Marx and Frazer in an attempt to understand the political economy of an Andean peasantry through their rituals. By using symbolic analysis of agrarian rituals to discuss class formation in the Andes, I hope to narrow the gap between 'class' as a category imposed by the analyst and 'class' as a sensibility implicit in local experience. I also hope to avoid any dichotomous treatment of class and ethnicity, since the rituals I use to discuss class are also powerful expressions of indigenous ethnicity (cf. Urbano 1976: 147–8; Montoya, Silveira, and Lindoso 1979: 153–4). Thus, there is no need to separate cultural identity from class, or symbolism from political economy: both are simultaneously present and interwoven in the annual cycle. Indeed, by showing how these rituals address and shape the political economic structure of rural Andean society, I intend to revindicate 'ethnicity' as something far more substantial than the series of arbitrary markers and racist stereotypes put forward by those who most insist on separating it from 'class' (e.g., van den Berghe and Primov 1977).

Thus, I intend this book to have something of the flavour of a general ethnography, even though it focuses on these specific issues. Without trying to write in the old encyclopedia tradition or to achieve the comprehensive scope of some modern monographs (e.g., Isbell 1978; Allen 1988), I still wish to convey a sense of the 'total way of life' that exists in towns like Huaquirca by cross-cutting the traditional subdisciplinary divisions between symbolic, economic, and political anthropology. In the Introduction that follows, the major themes of this study are discussed in a more analytical manner to better situate them in the relevant ethnographic and theoretical literature.

Acknowledgments

This book would never have been written without the help of many people; in particular, the people of Huaquirca, whom it is about. Without their companionship, patience, and goodwill, my own efforts would have come to very little, and I offer them my sincerest thanks. The eighteen months that I lived in Huaquirca (November 1981 to April 1983) were among the most difficult, intense, and rewarding in my life. Tragically, the area about which I write became embroiled in low-intensity warfare between Shining Path and Peruvian counter-insurgency forces shortly after I left. I have not been back, and suspect that ten years later, Huaquirca may be a rather different place than the one described in this book. Although I do not glorify Huaquirca as it was, neither would I have taken the same time or care to write about a group of people for whom I had less respect.

The first incarnation of this book was as a PhD thesis for the London School of Economics. During 1983–4 in London, I benefited from the camaraderie and constructive criticism of Maurice Bloch, Sophie Day, Pete Gow, Olivia Harris, Penny Harvey, Cecilia McCallum, Johnny Parry, Maria Phylactou, William Rowe, Mike Sallnow, Masa Tanaka, Mark Tate, Rosie Thomas, Christina Toren, Shushila Zeitlin, and many others. Later, at the University of Lethbridge, Charlene Sawatsky entered my thesis onto disk, and after several subsequent drafts, Marcia Calkowski had valuable substantive and editorial suggestions. Deborah Poole also offered detailed commentary on an earlier version of this manuscript. Finally, Michael Lambek and Suzanne Rancourt made it a pleasure to work with the University of Toronto Press. I thank all these people, and absolve them of any responsibility for the shortcomings that remain in this book.

Throughout, Elliott Gose, Kathy Gose, and Frances Slaney covered for me while I wrote innumerable drafts, only to then be asked to read and discuss them with me, which they patiently did. Without their moral support, I might have abandoned this project long ago. To them go my deepest thanks and appreciation.

Parts of Chapters 1 and 2 appeared in *Unruly Order*, edited by D. Poole and C. Paponet-Cantat, and are reprinted with the permission of Westview Press, Boulder, Colorado. Parts of Chapter 3 appeared previously in *American Ethnologist*, and are reprinted here with the permission of the American Anthropological Association.

The town of Huaquirca

Terraces after the harvest

Drinking corn beer during the maize sowing, 1982

Women singing *wanka*, maize sowing, 1982

Funerary clothes washing

Christmas *wayliya*, 1982

Drinking and invocation during a *t'inka*

T'inka offering

Lake Kuchillpo at the foot of Mt Supayco

DEATHLY WATERS AND HUNGRY MOUNTAINS

1

Introduction

The annual cycle of agrarian labour and ritual is central to this study because it is central to the lives of Andean commoners. These people are peasants, not just as a matter of occupational fact, but also as a matter of cultural value. The way in which they work their fields and pastures is fundamental to their sense of who they are, and this expressive dimension of their work regularly spills over into what we might want to call 'ritual.' Growing crops is not just a means to an end for the commoners of Huaquirca, even though they want to eat well and have abundant provisions for the coming year at harvest time. They also grow crops as an end in itself, to make the earth come alive. This concern was communicated to me in a variety of ways, including speech. One day just before Carnival in 1982, the elderly woman with whom I lived announced, 'For us, the earth is a living thing,' and went on to tell me about the offerings she and her husband were going to make to the mountain spirits in the coming days. Directly or indirectly, however, this notion of the living earth informs all of the rites of the annual cycle. As we look at these rites more closely, it will become clear that they often give the well-being of various manifestations of the living earth precedence over that of the individual peasant household as a basic motive for practising agriculture. For a people with these concerns, the annual cycle, in which the earth alternates between periods of fertility and dormancy, becomes an extremely significant form, one that does much to organize their culture as a whole. Indeed, we will see evidence of this in the way that the annual cycle has come to subsume other social facts, such as marriage and death, that have no intrinsic connection to it.

By suggesting that agricultural production in Huaquirca is not an entirely utilitarian pursuit, I do not mean to imply that Andean people are more metaphysically inclined than those of us who live according to the so-called instrumental rationality of capitalist regimes. Our form of production also has its own rites (such as bookkeeping) that, in turn, betray ultimate values such as profit and 'rational calculation,' which are just as metaphysical as Andean notions of the living earth. Two linked possibilities arise from this realization. The first is to expose the fantastic, magico-religious quality of the economic system that passes as our everyday, bedrock reality. This option remains as important now as it was in Marx's day, and may yet amount to more than the surrealist nostalgia of Clifford (1981) and Taussig (1987). A second, but related, possibility is to reveal the everyday, pragmatic quality of what at first appear to be the exotic rituals of other people. Since Evans-Pritchard's (1937) study, this has been a classic ethnographic strategy, one that I will follow here in arguing that Andean annual cycle rituals must be understood in exactly the same way as capitalist bookkeeping: a cultural construction of the economic process that puts into practice certain metaphysical assumptions.

Ritual and the Relations of Production in the Annual Cycle

This study focuses on ritual to discover the cultural notions that inform the political economy of an Andean peasantry. Like most modern writers, I assume that rituals are worth studying because they orient and shape other social practices around them. This is particularly true of the 'regulative' category of rituals distinguished by Tambiah (1985: 136–7). A regulative ritual coincides with other practical acts and directs them. The annual cycle rituals of Huaquirca fall into this category because they closely overlap and interact with agrarian labour processes. Regulative rituals exemplify Leach's (1964: 13) claim that ritual is an aspect of all social action, since they are always joined to larger fields of practice and do not attempt to constitute themselves as a separate type of endeavour.

General theories of ritual in anthropology usually define ritual as a category separate from other mundane actions, thus denying its regulative role. One of the few things that links such diverse but influential writers as Turner (1969), Geertz (1973: chap. 5), and Bloch (1989) is the view that rituals attempt to transcend everyday life. Yet none of the rituals to be discussed here announces such an aim, and all make better sense when interpreted as an outgrowth of 'profane' activities such as labour than they do as acts that try (but fail) to renounce worldly existence. However, these authors are surely right to insist on some distinction between ritual and everyday life, even if it is not a matter of mystical transcendence. I prefer to argue that in generating a symbolism that guides other practices, ritual inevitably stands apart from them to a certain extent. Ritual symbols will always refer beyond themselves and their immediate field of application to previously established notions within a culture. In so doing, rituals do not renounce the world, but on the contrary, draw us further into the cultures from which they spring. By studying rituals, we can therefore hope to locate social action in its relevant cultural context.

There are, nonetheless, certain pitfalls in treating ritual as an interpretive key to other social practices. Such an approach implies that rituals will clearly articulate cultural assumptions that are normally taken for granted in social action. Since Smith's (1889) study, however, we have known that the relation of ritual to articulate belief is problematic and indeterminate. More recently, Lewis (1980) and Bloch (1989) have justly criticized communicative theories of ritual for misrepresenting the largely non-propositional nature of most rituals. All of this presents serious problems for the idea that rituals are a privileged aid to the interpreter. To act as such, ritual must not only supply us with relevant cultural concepts, but do so in a way that is sufficiently discursive to allow translation. Like most rituals, those of the Andean annual cycle rarely take the form of unambiguous declarative statements, and seldom provide a clear-cut message that directs the labour process from without. In other words, the rituals themselves require interpretation and provide no simple explanation of what happens in everyday life, since, as often as not, we must invoke everyday life to explain ritual (cf. Radcliffe-Brown 1952: 163). The regulative function of ritual is problematic, and can be saved only by facing these difficulties squarely, which is why much of this book is taken up with a detailed empirical discussion of what these agrarian rituals might mean and how they might shape other activities. In the concluding chapter, I make the obvious comparison of ritual to law in a final attempt to assess its regulative impact.

Although the agrarian rituals of Huaquirca do not clearly express goals or rules for other activities, they do produce a diffuse imagery that lends colour and tone to the practical acts that accompany them in the annual cycle. In turn, these practical acts implement and predicate the ritual imagery that surrounds them, thereby giving it more precise symbolic meaning (see Gose 1991). Here, ritual is better understood as a moment of practice that is intrinsically incomplete and necessarily resolves itself into other moments, most notably labour. In so doing, however, ritual shapes the social practices that accompany and support it in the annual cycle. Rituals infuse the labour process with a specific cultural texture and sense. They provide the cues that frame and orchestrate the seasonal unfolding of social life. Still, these rituals stop short of overtly directing the labour process, since their meaning is itself dependent upon and supported by the thrust of the practical acts they shape. There can be no absolute distinction between means and ends here, or what is instrumental and what is expressive, precisely because the two are so intertwined and interdependent (see Gose 1988). Rather, we have an interaction between ritual and labour to create a kind of self-directing praxis within which ritual appears to be the shaping element, even though it is itself shaped.

Such a notion of praxis is implicit in the way commoners understand the relation between work and ritual in the annual cycle. Although they sometimes distinguish between 'work' (*llank'ay*) and 'ritual' (*costumbre*), in my experience they do not do so with any rigorous taxonomic intent, and are just as likely to use '*costumbre*' to refer to labour processes, such as irrigation, as they are to refer to acts that we would accept as being 'ritual in the strict sense of the term.' This relative non-distinction between work and ritual has been reported elsewhere (e.g., Firth 1939, 1967) and is precisely what the notion of regulative ritual would lead us to expect. There are very good reasons for this lack of terminological precision, for in many of the cases discussed below, no definitive cultural demarcation between work and ritual appears to exist at the level of practice.

A regulative understanding of ritual can also help us avoid the problems that arise if we go to the opposite extreme and collapse any distinction between labour and ritual. An example of these difficulties can be found in the work of Tylor (1871) and Frazer (1890), who assumed a technological intent behind ritual and went on to interpret it as 'magic': a false science that competes with, and gradually gives way to, causally effective procedures. Malinowski (1925) and Evans-Pritchard (1937) accepted this notion of magic, but argued that it rarely competes with instrumentally effective action, since people invoke magic only when they reach the limits of their technical competence.

All of these approaches assume that labour and ritual are alternative technical means to the same ends, and offer little explanation (beyond uncertainty) of why the two should coincide and interact in annual cycles (cf. Firth 1967: 25).

The answer must surely be that labour and ritual do not always try to do the same things, and that they often coincide because they are complementary. Such an approach was suggested by Lienhardt's (1961: 283) observation that many rituals have little or no magical intent, but serve primarily to formulate the ends towards which practical action is directed. This implies that the mistake of Tylor and Frazer was not to evaluate ritual in terms of the 'rationality' of the means-ends relationship, but rather to assume that it is about means instead of ends. Here, ritual ceases to be pseudo-technique and becomes a way of focusing and expressing the cultural intention that must ultimately guide all labour (see Sahlins 1976). Hence, labour and ritual can be connected as means are to ends, without having to fall back on the idea of 'magic.' Although this means-ends distinction may oversimplify the complex interdependencies between labour and ritual, it accurately identifies their complementarity.

The great merit of regulative interpretations is that they keep ritual within the realm of pragmatic action. In rejecting the idea that ritual is simply bad technique, regulative interpretations do not go to the opposite extreme of portraying it as a purely 'symbolic' or 'performative' act, one that aims at no practical result beyond its own enactment. Regulative rituals aim to change more than just the moods of those who participate in them, and strive for a more lasting and objectified impact on the world. Instead of explaining away the instrumental intentions of ritual, as almost all post-intellectualist theory has done, the idea of regulation helps us to face them squarely. Here, the fundamental insight is that ritual depends on, and interacts with, other kinds of purposive activity, and becomes much more comprehensible once we stop treating it as a type of activity that must be coherent unto itself.

So let us return these rituals to where they belong and have meaning, to where they can tell us something: high in the Andes among working men and women, at the edges of their fields and in the corrals on their grazing lands. From the outline of rural Andean society given in the Preface, we have seen that the practices of *ayni* and *mink'a* play central roles in the differentiation of notables and commoners. One reason why this study focuses on the annual cycle is to clarify the meaning that these relations of production have in the culture of Andean commoners. Most previous research on these relations has assumed that they are primarily 'economic' in nature, although only Mayer (1974: 39) has proclaimed this explicitly. For those influenced by formalist economic anthropology, *ayni* and *mink'a* are dyadic contractual relations that households enter into according to a calculation of their individual interests.[1] In Huaquirca, however, I discovered that these relations of production predominate in specific seasons, and are addressed by the rituals that accompany them in work parties. Therefore, I argue that *ayni* and *mink'a* have normative meanings within a system of livelihood that is ritually and seasonally organized, and refuse to abstract them from this context, as previous writers have done.

The resulting cultural account of Andean relations of production is one of the main ethnographic innovations of this study. By showing that Andean annual cycle rituals actually constitute the economic process, instead of merely stimulating it, as earlier writers such as Malinowski (1935) and Firth (1939) have argued, I also hope to further a more general understanding of economics as culture, following Gudeman (1986). This approach will not satisfy those who believe in the unique truthfulness of Western political economy. My main goal is to understand how the commoners of Huaquirca frame their work in the fields, and only secondarily do I try to compare the results to Western political economic ideas. Accordingly, my field research was based primarily on participant observation, not formal interviewing or household surveys, which tend to be less challenging to the analytical categories of the observer.

Let us begin by discussing what differentiates *ayni* and *mink'a* from each other, since as Malengreau (1980: 518) perceptively notes, it is not always easy to distinguish the two. Both involve the participation of many people in a work party sponsored by a host who provides food and drink during the working day. In *mink'a*, food and drink are considered sufficient remuneration, whereas in *ayni* they are not, and the hosts must return a day's labour to those who helped them. As a result, *ayni* is a symmetric and egalitarian relationship[2] that does not allow a permanent separation between workers and proprietors, while *mink'a* is asymmetric and potentially exploitative, since it makes no attempt to relativize the relation between worker and proprietor. Mediating these two basic relations are two additional practices known as *yanapa* and *jornal,* which may align with either *ayni* or *mink'a* depending on how they are developed (see Figure 2). *Jornal* takes place when a proprietor compensates labourers with a wage (often nominal) plus food and drink during the working day. In *jornal*, the wage can be part of a definitive short-term remuneration of labour (as in *mink'a*), or it may act as a kind of security until the host can return a day's labour to the worker according to the *ayni* model (see Fioravanti 1973: 123–4; Skar 1982: 215). *Yanapa* translates as 'help,' and it occurs when someone works for food and drink in the short term, but hopes to establish an informal moral claim on the host to reciprocate at some future date. The claim of the worker on the host is not binding in cases of *yanapa* mainly because the host does not formally solicit the help of the worker before the work party, as is the case in *ayni*. The worker shows up uninvited and thus initiates the relationship, which may resolve itself along the lines of *ayni* or *mink'a* depending on whether the host returns a day's labour in the future. To simplify the apparent complexity of this situation, all of these relations of production involve the feeding of workers (cf. Malengreau 1974: 185),[3] and what is at stake is whether this becomes the basis of a hierarchical and exploitative relationship or acts only as short-term remuneration until the host can return a day's labour.

I would argue that Andean relations of production revolve around a basic opposition between *ayni* and *mink'a*.[4] At a fundamental level, this is an opposition between symmetry and asymmetry, egalitarianism and hierarchy. Just as *mink'a* underwrites notable rule in the small towns of the Peruvian Andes, so *ayni* emphasizes labour as an egalitarian social bond among commoners, one that contributes greatly to commoners' sense of themselves as a class. Even when unequal landholdings among commoners rule out a strictly balanced exchange of labour days according to the *ayni* model, they avoid the hierarchical implications of *mink'a* by representing asymmetric cooperation as a matter of *yanapa*. This shows that *ayni* and *mink'a* are not neutral means of labour recruitment to be used according to the technical requirements of individual households, outside of any structured social context, as writers in the formalist tradition imply. Rather, they presuppose and contribute to the formation of classes, and make sense only in this context.

At a second level, *ayni* and *mink'a* contrast in their respective emphases on production and consumption in the remuneration of labour. A noteworthy feature of *ayni* is its built-in productivist bias. Although the sponsors of an *ayni*-based work party always offer their labourers food

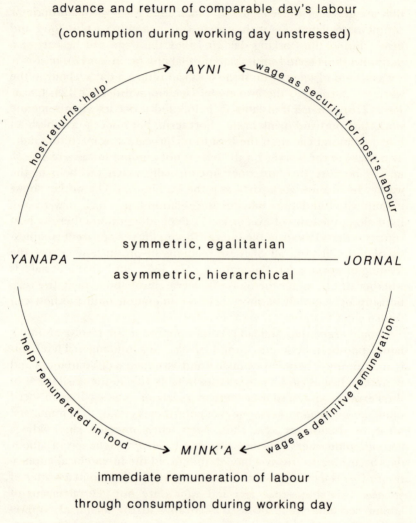

advance and return of comparable day's labour

(consumption during working day unstressed)

AYNI

host returns 'help'

wage as security for host's labour

YANAPA —————— symmetric, egalitarian —————— JORNAL

asymmetric, hierarchical

'help' remunerated in food

wage as definitve remuneration

MINK'A

immediate remuneration of labour

through consumption during working day

Figure 2   Andean relations of production

and drink during the working day, and nobody would consider working for more than a few hours without ample provisions of corn beer, such consumption is not definitive payment. True reciprocation in relations of *ayni* comes about only when the hosts return an equivalent day's labour to all of those who participated in their work party. The distinctive feature of *ayni* is that it can only work itself out through an ongoing process of production that consists of many temporally separated work parties sponsored by individual households. Thus, *ayni* can appear as an exchange of working days, particularly male working days (cf. Malengreau 1980: 510), even though it is arguably the prospect of consuming corn beer made by women that is decisive in recruiting people for a work party, and not the accumulation of 'credits' in a labour-exchange system. *Mink'a*, on the other hand, does not require the host to return an equivalent day's labour to the worker, and stresses remuneration through consumption instead. It makes explicit what *ayni* tends to suppress, namely that people work to eat and drink during the working day.

This contrast between deferred labour and immediate consumption as modes of remuneration underscores the class-bound nature of these relations of production. *Ayni* emphasizes labour as the basis of commoner equality and class identity, whereas *mink'a* stresses the patron's greater capacity to feed, and the labourer's need, as the basis of a hierarchical relationship. In the rural Andes, feeding people is an expression of power and proprietorship, unlike in our society, where it is part of the marginalized domain of 'housework,' which exists on the fringes of the supposedly more socialized domain of commodity exchange. Therefore, the patron's position in the community is based on the woman's position in the household, which is, above all, that of a feeder-proprietor. Thus, we arrive at a third level of contrast between *ayni* and *mink'a*, whereby the former stresses the exchange of like-gender labours, and the latter presupposes an exchange of unlike-gender labours (cf. Skar 1982: 216), in which those of women rank higher than those of men.

In Huaquirca, I discovered a fourth, seasonal dimension of contrast between *ayni* and *mink'a*, one that also arises from their respective emphases on production and proprietorship. Like all agriculturalists, the commoners of Huaquirca experience a seasonal delay in return on their productive expenditure. There is one phase of the agricultural cycle in which the crops are an object of production, and a second phase in which they are an object of consumption and appropriation.

In Huaquirca, relations of *ayni* prevail during the period when crops are growing in the ground and are the object of an intense productive effort. The productivist emphasis in *ayni* is appropriate to the concerns and requirements of the growing season, and its symmetric, egalitarian nature gives this productive effort a collective character. Once the crops begin to reach maturity and consumability after Carnival, however, the *ayni*-based regime of collective production has served its purpose. The order of the day shifts to securing and storing the fruits of this collective labour as private property. Each household harvests its own land, largely in isolation from the rest. What little cooperation that does occur among households at this time of the year takes place through relations of *mink'a* during the harvest, and stems from the fact that some households have more land than they can harvest with their own labour, whereas others do not have enough land to fully occupy their members. This is the only agricultural task in which commoners openly proclaim that they practise *mink'a* with each other: to do so during the growing season would be to join the notables in denying the ethic of collective production that prevails at that time of the year, and is so central to commoner's sense of themselves as a labouring class. However, now that the crops have become an object of private consumption and appropriation by individual households, and disparities in property holding so clearly underwrite the modicum of cooperation that still takes place, *mink'a*'s hierarchical formula of food for labour suddenly becomes uniquely appropriate.

These seasonal associations of *ayni* and *mink'a* are also what establish their connection with particular rites of the annual cycle. Other researchers have noted important seasonal variations in Andean ritual imagery that might well be used to interpret the variations in social practice to which they correspond. For example, Isbell (1978: 163–4) notes that the ritual imagery of the rainy season features sickness, death, and scarcity, whereas that of the dry season depicts abundance and renewal. Bastien (1978: 63) observes a similar movement between themes of life and death in the cycle of agrarian ritual. Although these are little more than passing observations, Harris (1982) has shown in detail how the imagery of death pervades the entire growing season. In a brief but extremely insightful study of Andean pastoralists, Wallis (1980: 252–5) shows that their year consists of a seasonally conceived opposition between a period of dependence and cooperation among households, and one of independence and separation. This opposition affects relations of kinship, affinity, marriage, and those that apply between human souls (Wallis 1980; cf. Rasnake 1988: 178). The seasonal opposition between *ayni* and *mink'a* that I shall explore corresponds very neatly to the pattern described by Wallis, and expands upon it in many ways. Although I will undertake a more extensive study of the annual cycle than any of these authors, their conclusions have nonetheless provided a remarkably solid point of departure, for which I am most grateful.

In Chapters 4 and 5, which cover the phase of the annual cycle dedicated to collective production, I show how the ritual imagery of death addresses and develops the emphasis on symmetry and labour that is distinctive to *ayni*. Life, in local thought, is defined by an asymmetric relation between two souls, one which is 'big' and corporeal, and another that is 'small' and energetic. Death negates this relation between souls, first by separating them, and then by reducing the 'big' soul to the size of its 'small' counterpart. This process of bodily shrinkage releases energy in the form of rainfall, which, in turn, creates the growing season. Like the dead, the living also deplete their bodies when they work together in relations of *ayni*. Indeed, the rituals of the growing season suggest that the living undergo a deathly reduction of souls to symmetry to generate the labour that they exchange in *ayni*. Such a negation of the body corresponds to *ayni*'s denial of consumption. It also explains the overlap between *ayni* relations and those of Christian spiritual kinship (*compadrazgo*) in Andean culture, since both are anti-carnal. Not only do *ayni* and death converge around the substantive concerns of the growing season, but they are both part of a larger discourse about consumption, bodies, and souls.

In Chapters 6 and 7, I show how this pattern of cooperation under the sign of death begins to break down by Carnival. As the productive death of the growing season is transformed by the maturation of the crops into a regeneration of life, the emphasis shifts from the depletion of the body in work to building it back up again through consumption. This consumption raises the issue of appropriation, which initially appears as generalized theft and sorcery, in stark contrast to the morality of Christian cooperation that pervades the growing season. Here, then, we glimpse a relation of moral contradiction between periods of collective production and private appropriation within Huaquirca's annual cycle. Yet the elaborate *t'inka* rites discussed in Chapter 7 lend an element of legitimacy to this phase of consumption and appropriation by offsetting it with sacrificial tribute to the state.

The calculated loss of these sacrifices involves the recognition of higher powers, and thus implements a hierarchical morality; but it also amounts to a substitution of offering for self, one that buys a limited autonomy that will break down with the resumption of the growing season and its deathly generation of labour. Here, sacrifice provides a basic model of social cohesion within the hierarchical political unit, and a particularly acute way of looking at relations of class and power within it. In its emphasis on feeding and hierarchy, sacrifice corresponds perfectly to *mink'a* as a relation of production, and the concern to consume and appropriate the crops that prevails during the dry season. Once again, we are dealing with an integral complex of practice and representation.

The seasonal distinctions of the annual cycle have further implications for the regulative approach to ritual discussed above. Rather than address 'society' as an abstract, Durkheimian whole, the rituals of the annual cycle each structure a specific range of activities (cf. Firth 1967: 24). As Bourdieu argues (1977: chap. 3), social practice never unfolds all at once, but rather sequentially from one qualitatively distinct moment to the next. Sequentiality does not mean that experience is entirely detotalized and fragmented, as Bourdieu and most postmodernists imply, but it does deny that ritual can structure experience absolutely and permanently. Indeed, most societies produce a multiplicity of rituals because the regulative effect of each is localized and of limited duration. It is only in a plural, heterogeneous, and decentred form that 'ritual' can structure social action. Thus, it is methodologically preferable to study an entire sequence of rituals, each with its own specific character and pragmatic context, than it is to focus on only one and mistake it for a paradigmatic case of ritual in general (cf. Firth 1967: 5). Unlike most contributors to the boom in ritual studies over the last twenty years, I will attempt to document and explain the structured diversity of rituals within a single locale.

When considered as a whole, the annual cycle shows both continuity and disjunction between the two seasons that make it up. The continuity is evident at many levels, from the premises that death and sacrifice share as organizing themes to the even more fundamental orientation of social activity towards the crops throughout the year. Clearly, the seasonal disjunctions of the annual cycle occur very much within a context of unity. Far from muffling seasonal differences, however, this unity only serves to accentuate them, since neither regime can avoid defining itself against the other. Thus, there exists a situation of contradiction, 'non-identity under the aspect of identity' (Adorno 1973: 5). This is seen most clearly in the way *ayni* and *mink'a* emphasize labour and consumption as opposing aspects of what is effectively the same format of the work party. However, the same contradiction exists in the seasonal alternation between periods of collective production and private appropriation, in which the social dispositions appropriate in one phase become entirely inappropriate in the next, although both imply and presuppose each other.

This contradiction in the annual cycle between a productive process that is collective, and an appropriation process that is private both reflects and contributes to the fact that Andean commoners have existed in class societies for millennia. It is as labourers, and not as proprietors, that Andean commoners have most developed a sense of themselves as a distinctive social group. Certainly, commoners have retained and occasionally advanced certain notions of communal property that will be explored below. However, these notions of communal property amount to little more than private agricultural use-rights validated by *ayni* within the community, and by the community paying a collective labour tribute to the state. This property is communal only in the way it is worked and legitimated, not at the level of rights to the product. Labour remains the ideological source of what little communality exists here. The appropriation process itself, as it exists in the annual cycle, is hardly an expression of commoner solidarity and takes place under many signs of ethnic otherness: the notables, the mountain spirits, and the state. And since this ethnic otherness also embodies proprietorship and political power, there is little choice but to see it as a matter of class as well.

Thus, there is a significant sense in which commoners behave like notables when they use the proprietary format of *mink'a* to recruit those with less land to help them during the harvest. Far from subscribing to a univocal ethos of reciprocity, as Núñez del Prado (1972: 136–7) has claimed, commoners often take advantage of each other where matters of property are concerned; furthermore, there are no effective moral sanctions to prevent this. Indeed, it is precisely because commoner group identity is so firmly based on *ayni* labour, to the virtual exclusion of the rest of the agricultural process, that it displays a blind spot on the topic of property. This is the price commoners have paid for developing a very real solidarity as labourers, a feature common to labouring subcultures the world over.

None of these observations would be possible if Andean annual cycle rituals did not address the issues of production, appropriation, and political power around which classes are usually said to form, and raise them to the level of culturally constructed experience. Agrarian ritual is nothing less than the cultural form out of which a sense of class emerges in the Andes. Thus it becomes possible to speak of class as a lived reality and a social fact in the Andes, and traditional Andean culture as an embryonic form of class consciousness, in the manner suggested by Albó (1979: 519). Although Nash (1979) and Platt (1983) have shown that class consciousness emerges through the rituals of traditional Andean culture, what they failed to explain is why it should take this form.[5] By providing the groundwork that links ritual and political economy in the annual cycle, I shall undertake a more ambitious analysis than that provided by these authors, which will show that there is nothing romantic or fanciful about the way they have treated these rites as a kind of class consciousness. Rather, the question is whether it is enough to describe these rituals as mere 'consciousness' when they do so much to create the reality of class in the first place.

Class and 'Indianness'

This discussion of the annual cycle shows how difficult it is to distinguish ethnic identity from class identity among Andean commoners. The same rites that Urbano (1976: 147–8) puts forward as the basis of an ethnic identity also address the issues of production, property, and political power around which social classes form. It seems that commoners' class and ethnic identity derive from a common, or at least overlapping, set of practices, and need not be treated in a dichotomous manner as a result. But the vast majority of the existing literature on the Andes assumes that class and ethnicity can and should be analytically separated. Broadly speaking, there are two main positions: one eliminates class entirely, presenting ethnicity as the only legitimate way of looking at social difference in the rural Andes, and the other assumes that class and ethnicity are both present, but irreducible to each other. Both of these views run counter to what will be argued throughout the remainder of this chapter.

The writers who most clearly advocate an ethnic characterization of Andean commoners to the exclusion of class are Ossio (1978a) and Skar (1982). Ossio argues that commoners and notables are distinct sociocultural groups based on marriage and inheritance rules (Ossio 1978a: 22), even though they cannot be clearly differentiated according to cultural traits such as language, dress and music, nor in terms of income or occupation (Ossio 1978a: 7). He further suggests that the commoners' main complaint against notables is that they are aliens who disrupt the local cultural order, not that they exploit commoner labour, and concludes that commoners define their opposition to notables in an ethnic, not a class-like, manner (Ossio 1978a: 22; cf. van den Berghe and Primov 1977: 187). Skar (1982: 76) argues that commoners are ethnics primarily because they call themselves *runa*, 'people' in an exclusive, tribal sense, and do not identify with universalist notions of class. However, he also writes that they display little ethnic consciousness (Skar 1982: 77), a claim that many would dispute, but if true, would invalidate his ethnic interpretation on precisely the same grounds as he rejected the notion of class.

What unites these writers is the assumption that social groups are what they define themselves to be, and that commoners are not a class because they do not see themselves as such. E.P. Thompson (1963: 11) has argued along very similar lines: 'class is defined by men as they live their own history, and in the end, this is its only definition.' I accept this emphasis on self-definition, even though it can lead to a simplistic voluntarism whereby the 'consciousness' of a social group defines its identity in abstraction from interaction with other social groups under specific material and historical conditions. What I find problematic is the claim that class does not figure in how commoners define themselves. One way to resolve this issue is by looking at the social vocabulary of the rural Andes. After all, if people really do construct their social identities around such notions as 'class' and 'ethnicity,' this ought to be evident in how they speak about themselves and others. Of course, this is not to suggest that social differentiation is caused entirely by the use of linguistic categories. Chapter 2 will show that there is a massive extra-linguistic basis for the sense of difference that underlies the social vocabulary of towns like Huaquirca, and that class and ethnicity are never a matter of how people define themselves in speech alone. Neither can we assume that social differentiation is simply given to language as a completed object to describe, for linguistic categories and usages (ranging from accents to insults) also contribute to social differentiation and are a part of it. At this stage, the point is simply to approach, but not exhaust, questions of class and ethnicity through the various ways that Andean people talk about themselves and others.

In this account, I write of 'commoners' and 'notables' because these

are the best translations of the terms most commonly used by the people of Huaquirca to refer the two social groups recognized in their
town: *comuneros* (commoners) and *vecinos notables* (notable residents),
often *vecinos* for short. These terms are Spanish in origin and refer to
the Iberian village institutions (e.g., the *cabildo*) that were transplanted
into the New World. With time, however, these institutions underwent
local modification, assuming a form that will be described in Chapter
2. In the process, the terms in question were assimilated into Quechua
as '*comuneru*' and '*vecinu*,' where they now occupy a central place in
the social lexicon. Now, both commoners and notables use these terms
in referring to themselves or others. Neither term has any insulting
connotations, which contributes to their general usage, making them
the closest approximation of a neutral social vocabulary.

Briefly, 'commoner' denotes both a person of undistinguished origins and a holder of rights over common land. Each of these senses of
'commoner' brings out a dimension of contrast with 'notable,' since
the latter is by definition a distinguished person, but also a holder of
'private' land separate from the commons. This second aspect of notable social identity is further developed in another terminological
opposition that pertains to the legal context of civic obligation, in
which commoners are people who pay labour-tribute to the state, and
notables are 'proprietors' (*propietarios*), who, in theory at least, pay a
monetary tax instead. Although 'proprietor' is a more specific, con-
text-bound term than 'notable resident,' both refer to the same group
of people, who are constantly defined by their opposition to another
group of people known as 'commoners.'

An alternative, and less frequently used, social terminology revolves
around a concept of 'race.' Much local talk supposes that Andean society is made up of 'Indians,' '*mestizos*,' and 'whites.' Each race is thought
to be defined by a substance, 'blood,' which is common to all of its
members, creates a solidarity among them, and specifies their conduct. For example, I was once told by a man who considered himself a
mestizo: 'We have two bloods which run in our veins, one which is
Indian, noble and hard-working, another which is Spanish, lazy and
overbearing.' This clearly displays the idea that there is a substantive,
racial basis for specific kinds of conduct, even if it is uncertain which
complex will prevail in *mestizos* at any given time, because of their
'mixed' racial identity.

What these 'racial' terms refer to remains a question, since there are
no clear-cut phenotypical divisions in rural Andean society to which

they could correspond, and their biological reference is largely suspended in use (cf. Fuenzalida 1970a: 26). Virtually everyone who has studied the matter agrees that the notion of 'race' involved here is used metaphorically to describe social hierarchy, so that the more powerful one is, the 'whiter' one is considered to be, irrespective of actual skin colour. Conversely, when the object is to offend or belittle, nothing works better than '*indio*' or the closely related '*cholo*' (often combined in the epithet '*cholo indio*' for emphasis). These insults make statements of relative status across the entire social spectrum, and do not, as has often been reported, denote readily identifiable social groups.[6] Yet even though they lack sociological reality, there can be no denying that these 'racial' categories are an integral and effective part of the Andean social imagination.

What I find interesting about these 'racial' terms is that they evoke a point in history when it might have been possible to draw clear-cut biological and cultural boundaries, namely the moment of the Spanish conquest. 'Racial' vocabulary suggests that a primordial encounter between the Hispanic and the Indian is still going on, and uses this image of conquest as a mythical vehicle to help form modern social relations. This is a phenomenon I join Peter Gow (personal communication) in calling 'the myth of the conquest.' Like all myths, the myth of the conquest is partly true, in that modern Andean society does owe something of its form and content to the conquest. However, since both parties to that original encounter have been so thoroughly transformed by each other in their subsequent interaction, we must conclude that this conquest model obscures at least as much history as it explains. Yet these 'racial' terms are constantly used to negotiate the indeterminacy of modern Andean social relations in an outpouring of perlocutionary acts, all of which evoke the Spanish conquest as a primordial act of creative and clarifying violence.

What this totemistic notion of race captures, in a way that no academic analysis of class and ethnicity ever could, is the aura of violence that surrounded notable rule in towns like Huaquirca. This violence was manifest in a style of extra-legal domination known as *gamonalismo*, which is comparable to mafia activities in Sicily (Block 1974), and the Mexican *cacique* complex (Friedrich 1965). Poole (1988) summarizes the basic elements of *gamonalismo* as follows: a fusion of local economic and political power in the person of a small resident landowner (*gamonal*), whose intimate familiarity with 'Indian' culture on the one hand, and systematic violation of it on the other, upheld a servile agrarian social order characterized by low levels of technical innovation and productive investment. It is only through the 'mixed' identity attributed to the *gamonal* by this racist folk model that we can understand his wildly oscillating behaviour towards the 'Indian,' so well described by Poole, in which he switches from a sympathetic and sincere participation in agrarian ritual at one moment to an intimidating destruction of commoner livelihood in the next. These dual impulses of attraction and violation are precisely codified in the idea expressed to me by several notables that the origins of racial mixture (*mestizaje*) go back to the forced consummation of the lust of the Spanish conquistador for the beautiful Inca princess (*ñusta*) in a scenario of primordial rape that is one of the more significant components of the myth of the conquest as a whole.

Historically and culturally, this form of local rule can only be understood in the context of the infamous servile institution of the large landed estate or *hacienda*. Indeed, the stereotypical *gamonal* was, and is still, thought to be an owner of large landed property. Yet there were vast areas of the southern Peruvian Andes, including the region in which Huaquirca is situated, that never supported *haciendas*, although they spawned generation after generation of small-time *gamonales*. These areas were left virtually untouched by the Peruvian agrarian reform of 1969–75, and continue to be the repositories of the 'feudal' political culture that was supposed to have been swept away with the expropriation of the *haciendas*. Since *gamonalismo* is the social basis and ultimate referent of the conventional racist discourse that defines 'Indians,' '*mestizos*,' and 'whites,' we must be sceptical when the same terms appear in the anthropological literature, and are said to denote different 'ethnic groups' in some abstract cultural space where the *gamonal* is no longer visible. Equally, however, we must refuse to follow Taussig (1987) into a pornographic obsession with this violent mythohistory, lest we end up glorifying it and making it seem absolute, when it is only one social discourse among many. If we are to adopt a less essentialized view of Andean social identities, and wish to end our complicity with local notions of 'race,' we must begin to recognize the full range of terms that people are already using in towns like Huaquirca.

The limited efficacy of the myth of the conquest is demonstrated by the fact that commoners in small Andean towns do not call themselves '*indios*' (Indians). They take the term as an insult, sometimes even as 'fighting words,' and if it is a part of their identity, it is only the most negative part. Occasionally, commoners may identify other people as 'Indians,' but this is rare. For example, I once asked my adoptive commoner 'father' in Huaquirca whether the Amazonian natives (*ch'un-chos*) he had once met in Cusco were 'Indians,' and he replied no, that they were good people! Although this response confirms that '*indio*' is a derogatory term, it does not affirm that people called '*indios*' necessarily exist. Thus, the myth of the conquest is meaningful primarily to those who seek power and distinction within Andean society, and an alternative, less competitive set of values is also present.

While notions of 'race' are more important to notables, even they will make considerable efforts to avoid addressing or even referring to commoners as 'Indians,' by using terms such as 'peasant' (*campesino*) and 'native' (*indígena*). Arguably, these are nothing more than euphemisms for 'Indian,' and involve most of the same assumptions, but they do show an intent to avoid overt insult. Furthermore, most notables do not explicitly endorse the myth of the conquest as a code of social conduct. Nowadays, the term *gamonal* is normally used to stigmatize the actions of others, particularly in moments of recrimination and rivalry that inevitably accompany the ongoing jockeying for power among notables. At the time this research was carried out, notable rule in small towns like Huaquirca was being reconstructed around left-nationalist ideologies, and was no longer a simple caricature of colonial domination, even if it still retained some of its broader outlines. Finally, although notables occasionally represent themselves as *mestizos*, as in the discourse on 'blood' above, they do so far less frequently than the social science literature on the Andes. Therefore, we have to guard against overemphasizing notable preoccupations with 'race,' without going to the opposite extreme of denying that they exist at all.

Many investigators have stressed the use of *runa* (person, people) as the predominant self-appellation of commoners in small Andean towns, particularly those in the Cusco area.[7] Perhaps the exclusive and almost tribal sense of humanity implicit in the word *runa* appeals to ethnicity theory. To fully understand what *runa* means here, we have to turn to its counter concept, *misti*, one of the first words an anthropologist (or any other foreigner) is likely to hear on entering a small town in the Peruvian Andes. This is a Quechua corruption of the Spanish *mestizo*, but is used to describe people with blonde hair and blue eyes even more readily than those with 'mixed blood' (cf. Mayer 1970: 118). It refers, above all, to those who are politically and economically dominant in a town or region (cf. Montoya 1982: 273, 276). 'Powerful other' might be the best translation of the term. The reference of *misti* to powerful foreigners was made dramatically clear to me by one informant's derivation of the word from the English 'mister.' It is rare for people to identify themselves as *mistis*, and the word is usually spoken with a certain venom that becomes explicit in insults like *q'ala misti* (naked *misti*) or *q'ala khuchi* (naked pig). In some areas, the term *q'ala* (naked one), along with the image of shamelessness that it denotes, supplants *misti* entirely, and also applies to those who were born into an 'Indian' background, but rejected it.[8] These terms denote a fundamental lack of the kind of sociability that characterizes *runa* as true human beings.

In this couplet of *runa/misti*, it seems that commoners have developed a powerful antidote that allows them to resist colonial notions of 'race,' and to indulge in their own form of chauvinism. Certainly, I have heard *runa* used this way in Huaquirca, but not as a matter of routine. It was far more common to encounter *runa* as part of complex nouns like *qheshwaruna* (valley people) and *punaruna* (alpine people). Admittedly these terms refer only to commoners, and never to notables, though the latter may also live in the valley and have flocks in the alpine zone. However, these uses of *runa* focus less on confrontation with *mistis* than on the different categories of commoner as defined by mode of livelihood. The same could be said of the couplet *hacindaruna/llaqtaruna* (*hacienda* people/townspeople) that characterized areas where large landed estates encompassed or existed around small rural towns and 'free' native communities: the classic configuration of Andean feudalism that continued up to the expropriation of the latifundia in the agrarian reform of 1969–75. Even though these latter, less confrontational uses do not rule out *runa* as the focus of a separatist ethnic identity, it is significant that the term *comunero* plays this role far more frequently in Huaquirca, along with its other meanings.

This list could be expanded, and would look slightly different if it were based on another region, or included terms of address (see Montoya 1982: 274–5); nonetheless, it contains the major categories of social discourse throughout the Andean region. For the record, it is important to note the absence of any local terms that could be readily translated as 'class' or 'ethnicity.' The Spanish terms *clase* and *clase social* are simply not a part of everyday speech, and while I did hear an urban communist militant use the Quechua term *allpa llank'aq runakuna* ('earth-working people') to refer to commoners, the phrase is hardly prevalent in the countryside. There were a few times when I heard commoners use phrases such as 'we the poor' (*nosotros los pobres*) to refer to themselves, which is probably as close an approximation to the notion of class as can be found in their speech. Similarly, the Spanish words *etnicidad* and *cultura* were never invoked in my presence to account for social differentiation in Huaquirca, although attitudes towards *costumbre* (ritual) were often mentioned by commoners in this regard (cf. Montoya, Silveira, and Lindoso 1979: 153). In sum, despite certain near-convergences, there are no ready-made lexicalized notions in use that would plausibly translate as 'class' or 'ethnicity': both are only approximations of a complex set of linguistic, cultural, and social practices, interpretations that cannot claim to represent local consciousness verbatim.

Clearly, there are many ways of talking about social differentiation in rural Andean towns, not all of which can be called 'ethnic.' Furthermore, some ostensibly 'ethnic' terms such as *misti*, and all of those based on the notion of race, have such strong connotations of 'class' that it is pointless to suggest that they belong to one domain and not the other. Much more significant is the permutability of terms on the same side of the various categorical oppositions (e.g., *indio/mestizo, comunero/vecino, comunero/propietario*, and *runa/misti*). Each pair seems to emphasize a different aspect of the same felt distinction instead of designating a different social alignment. Thus, with data that are entirely separate from those of the annual cycle, the same conclusion emerges, namely that it is impossible to uphold any rigorous distinction between class and ethnicity in the rural Andes.

Let us now turn to the second major position on class and ethnicity in the literature, namely that both are simultaneously present, but irreducible to each other. This has been most directly expressed as a matter of principle by van den Berghe (1974a: 123) and van den Berghe and Primov (1977: 2). In practice, however, van den Beghe and Primov (1977: 255–6, 259) do at times speak of a near-identity of class and ethnicity, and the exercise of class domination through a cultural medium. These formulations are less dichotomous, and much closer to the position I take. Similarly, Flores (1974: 182) distinguishes class and ethnicity, but does not treat them as mutually exclusive, although he clearly prefers an ethnic characterization on the grounds that there is allegedly no significant economic difference between notables and commoners (1974: 186–7), a claim that can be disputed by the very data he provides (Flores 1974: 188–9). In another variant of this position, Isbell (1978: 67) suggests that commoners and notables are distinct ethnic groups, but that each may have secondary internal class differences. This pluralist model fails to explain why economic upward mobility cannot be pursued by 'Indians' in most areas of the Andes, and requires that they change their ethnic self-presentation (cf. van den Berghe and Primov 1977: 169–70). Alternatively, some hard-core Marxists (e.g., Montoya, Silveira, and Lindoso 1979: 159–60) join modernization theory in arguing that class and ethnicity are both present in the Andes, but the former is superseding the latter. Finally, Rasnake (1988: 45) suggests that although relations between commoners and notables are predicated on economic and political power, this does not fully explain the nature of these groups, and must be supplemented by an analysis of cultural symbolism.

All but the last two studies represent ethnicity as a more important social fact than class in the modern Andean countryside, and even Rasnake (1988: 45) joins the rest in thinking that something important is lost when ethnicity is 'reduced' to class, namely culture. This fear of economic reductionism is justifiable. One need only turn to the Mesoamerican literature to discover that many ethnographers (e.g., Favre 1971, 1980; Friedlander 1975; Warren 1978; and Deverre 1980) are indeed eager to represent 'Indian' ethnic identities as a simple reflex of colonial and/or capitalist domination. Whereas Andean ethnicity theorists have tended to argue that Indianness has little or nothing to do with class, this second group of authors has opted for virtually the opposite stance, that Indianness is alienation, nothing but a symptom of exploitation and oppression. Indeed, it is only against this background that it is possible to understand why Ossio (1978a: 8, 13–4) felt the need to point out that if the Andean community were a mere epiphenomenon of colonialism, it would have disappeared long ago, and that it has legitimacy for commoners, in part because it allows them to successfully impose some of their agenda on notables. This is an extremely important line of argument that has been developed in more recent ethnic interpretations (e.g., Necker 1982: 255–8; Labrousse 1985; Rasnake 1988), which concede that Indian identity does involve oppression and exploitation, but insist that this is only half the story, since it also generates resistance and alternative social projects. My own research in Huaquirca was originally informed by this position, and I still have considerable sympathy for it.

Yet it is ironic that these attempts to valorize 'Indianness' as ethnicity have disfigured our understanding of native cultures almost as badly as the economism they intended to cure. Ethnic interpretations concede so much to an economistic understanding of the social order that the relation between the two is more one of complicity than opposition. This is evident in the way students of Andean ethnic relations have capitulated to the idea that economics is separate from culture, and largely beyond its influence.[9] All too often, this means that the 'ethnic' character of Western political economy goes totally unrecognized, and masquerades as a neutral, unmarked backdrop against which the 'ethnicity' of non-Western peoples can be thrown into relief. For example, ethnicity theory (in its Weberian guise) presupposes that ethnic groups will share the market and the state as a common framework of social action, and locates their differences outside of this sphere in the ancillary and somewhat folkloristic realm of 'culture.' No doubt this is a superficially plausible abstract description of the situation in many developed capitalist countries, but it rules out precisely what is going on in the Andean countryside: a dispute over which 'ethnic' model of political economy is to prevail as the hegemonic framework of social action. In short, by excluding political economy from the purview of cultural struggle, ethnicity theory trivializes the phenomenon of Indianness as it exists in the Andes.

It is equally important that class interpretations of rural Andean society investigate local political economic traditions instead of assuming the applicability of Western theories. The reason we should turn to the rites of the annual cycle for an understanding of Andean relations of production is quite straightforward: there is no better place to look for the meaning of acts of production and appropriation than in the rituals that surround and accompany them. Local understandings must be sought out and given the highest analytical privilege because, as E.P. Thompson (1978a: 147–8) argues, class is something that actually happens in human relationships: we know about it through the ways that people interpret and express their experience, and not because we possess an *a priori* analytical formula from which we can deduce its existence.[10] If class is real, it is because it is objectified in culture and history, and does not happen just in the eye of the beholder.

Yet for reasons of ethnographic clarity, I will state what I mean by 'class,' since it is the only way of monitoring the gap that inevitably exits between natives' and observers' categories. When speaking of class, we necessarily engage in cultural translation, something that Thompson tends to overlook in his understandable eagerness to pre-

vent our analytical categories from short-circuiting any real investigation into the different ways that class may be culturally constructed.
The word 'class' must still have a meaning for us, even if that meaning
is only an approximate equivalent of the reality we are trying to understand. I assume, then, for purposes of translation, that class is about
political economy, and implies a polarization between one social group
identified with labour, and another identified with appropriation and
political power.

This definition does not mean that class is 'caused' by the brute facts
of political economy, since they are always culturally mediated, and,
therefore, cannot be an unconditional point of departure in a causal
chain. The 'facts' of Andean political economy are not so basic and
self-evident that they can simply be collected without first having to
come to grips with the cultural form they take. Furthermore, as Bourdieu (1984) has shown, the very nature of class presupposes different
points of view within the same society, different ways of making social
claims, and, therefore, different ways of portraying the social whole,
including what its relevant 'structural' features might be. We cannot
assume the universality of any particular version of political economy
when studying class, let alone that any one version provides a 'true'
causal account of it, for dispute over these matters is built into the very
nature of class as a social phenomenon. Without evidence of political
economic pluralism, it is difficult to argue that a society has polarized
into classes. The reason for providing an analytical definition of class,
then, is not to solve these disputes with a 'correct' answer, but simply to
identify what they are about.

Again, the fact that the annual cycle embodies both a cultural identity and an extra-official system of meaning through which commoners
claim economic and political rights is key to the rebuttal of economistic views of class and derived positions like Indianness-as-alienation.
What is crucial here is that commoners do not just accept the prevailing system of right, or try to claim a larger quantity of property within
it, but have developed an alternative definition of property that is
grounded in their condition as a labouring class. Instead of just following notable strategies of appropriation (to be discussed at length in
Chapter 2), commoners claim rights for themselves, and recognize
those of others, through a practice that is unique to them: the mutual
aid relation of *ayni* during the growing season. Thus, class formation
involves more than just the uneven distribution of quantities of property; it also hinges on conflict over the very ways in which property

rights are defined and claimed in the first place (cf. Thompson 1975: 261; 1976: 337, 358). This, among other things, is what makes class 'a cultural as much as an economic formation' (Thompson 1963: 13).

By focusing on how rights are defined and claimed in different ways, it is possible to move the discussion from structural definitions of class to the more directly political question of whose terms of reference manage to define the social whole, that is, the question of hegemony and class struggle. Both notables and commoners derive their strategies of claiming rights from broader frameworks of meaning that are grounded in their particular manner of existing in society. For notables, the educated discourse of schoolteachers and politicians has increasingly become the vehicle of their power as a class; whereas for commoners, agrarian labour and ritual play this role. These discourses are not just contemplative 'native models' of Andean society. They are actual strategies that intervene in it and shape it by organizing and disputing different areas of experience within it, right down to the physical layout of towns like Huaquirca, as we shall see in Chapter 2. Far from defining an abstract, quasi-topographic social space full of empty class positions of the sort produced by objectivist theories of class (e.g., Wright 1985: 10), these discourses embody particular points of view, and proceed to organize the social whole from them. As a result, the social life of Huaquirca cannot be reduced to the invariant structure of a mode of production, nor can notables and commoners be treated as mere inversions of each other in relation to some such principle of order, since each has developed a social discourse that is at least partially incommensurate with that of the other. By constantly returning to how various property rights are defined and contested, not just distributed within a given framework, this study aims to cross the great divide between 'class-in-itself' and 'class-for-itself.' This dichotomy is created by a purely economic understanding of class, and can only be spanned by breaking with the naturalistic fallacy it rests upon, namely the idea that there is a precultural 'social being' that determines 'social consciousness' (cf. Sahlins 1976).

By posing the question of class through Andean cultural categories and practices, I intend to avoid this economic reductionism. However, I also intend to avoid ethnic reductionism by showing that Andean culture regulates political and economic life, and is not mere folklore. Instead of separating the ritual themes of marriage, death, and sacrifice from the political economic practices they accompany and represent in the annual cycle, this study will underline the significance of their fusion. Towards that end, I propose a more flexible method, one that does not impose a metaphysical separation between economics and culture, and allows for the symbolic construction of social practice, as well as the pragmatic construction of symbolic meaning. Thus, this ethnography intends to address both a specialized topic and more general interpretive issues.

2

'Race,' Property, and Community

Huaquirca lies at the end of a secondary road that departs from the Lima-Cusco highway near Chalhuanca, and gingerly picks its way over the alpine zone (*puna*) and down into the Antabamba Valley (see Figure 3). This road was completed in 1967. An average of two trucks per week make the sixty-kilometre journey to the town of Antabamba (capital of the Province of Antabamba), generally taking between six and ten hours to do so. In 1978, the road was extended across the valley to Huaquirca, passing through the town of Matara. About twice a month, a truck will make this journey to the end of the road, creeping down the switchbacks to the Antabamba River, then scaling the opposite flank of the valley until it arrives in Huaquirca, pursued by throngs of excited children.

Like all of the agricultural towns in the upper Antabamba Valley, Huaquirca sits near the top of an impressive bank of terraces etched into the valley wall. These terraces begin at the river bottom, around 3000 m above sea level, and climb like several hundred gigantic steps to the level of the town, at 3480 m, and in some areas, slightly higher. This is the altitude limit for the intensive maize agriculture that takes place on the terraces, but the valley wall continues to rise steeply into a belt of sectoral fallow potato fields between 3800 and 4200 m above sea level. Only here does the eroded valley wall begin to give way to gentler glacial land forms. The hillside above 4200 m is sparsely covered with coarse *ichu* grass, and quickly gives way to rocky peaks at 4500 m. From atop these peaks, one can see a vast alpine zone, the *puna*, that rolls and plunges off into the distance, varying in altitude from 4000 to 5000 m. Huaquirca marks the first place where it is low enough to grow

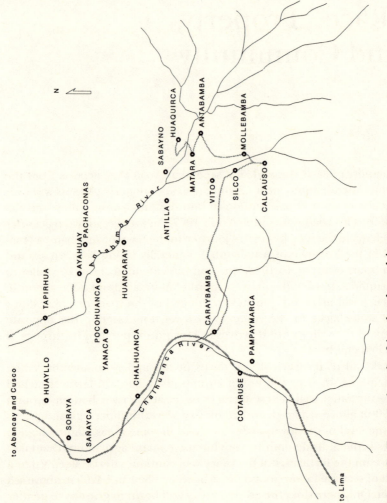

Figure 3   Towns and roads of Antabamba and Aymaraes

maize on the Antabamba River, as it flows from the Continental Divide across the eastern slope of the Andes and into the Amazon. From Huaquirca downstream, there are agricultural towns. A few nucleated settlements of up to fifteen houses exist in the expanse of *puna* above and beyond Huaquirca, but most people there live in widely dispersed homesteads, each with several corrals and a customary grazing territory for the llamas and alpacas that are the principal means of livelihood in this zone.

As a district, the minimal territorial unit of government in Peru, Huaquirca includes a certain amount of the *puna* above it, but the exact boundaries are neither certain, nor a matter of great concern (see Figure 4). Residents of the *puna* rarely feel the presence of the state directly, and have far more in common with each other than they do with people in valley towns like Huaquirca, to whom they may be nominally linked by administrative units like the district. The only other ethnographic work that has been done in this area focused on the *puna* people (Concha 1971, 1975). Although my main concern will be with the agriculturalists of the valley, I will discuss the significance of their distinction from the *puna* people, and their interaction with them. In this chapter, I will describe social relations in the District of Huaquirca by passing over the landscape just described in greater detail, and showing how they have become embodied in it.

The Town

The centre of Huaquirca is defined by a ponderous early colonial church that dwarfs all other buildings with its immense bulk. The three neighbourhoods (*barrios*) of which Huaquirca is composed all border on the church and the plaza in front of it (see Figure 5). There are good historical reasons for the visual centrality of this church. In the 1570s, three pre-existing settlements (one of which corresponds approximately to one of the modern neighbourhoods) were consolidated to form Huaquirca as it is now known, through the colonial policy of *reducción*. Many residents think that the church's massive walls incorporate squared stones from the abandoned pre-Columbian dwellings that can still be seen in the neighbourhood of Champine. Thus, there is a sense in which this church symbolizes the social order that took form during the colonial period. Indeed, the Parish of Huaquirca was the *de facto* local presence of the state well into the eighteenth century. From it, secular forms of municipal government slowly

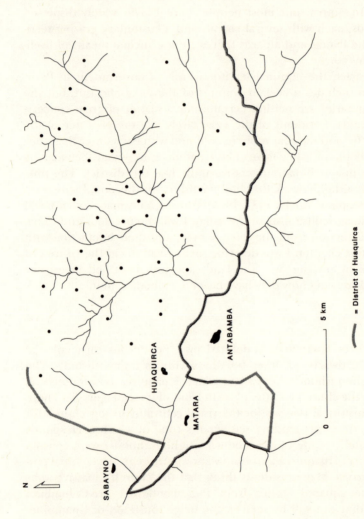

Figure 4 District of Huaquirca

N

SABAYNO

MATARA

HUAQUIRCA

ANTABAMBA

5 km

0

= District of Huaquirca

. = dispersed herding settlements

emerged by the end of the colonial period. With the declaration of the republic in 1821, the church found itself in crisis throughout the Province of Aymaraes[1] (of which the Antabamba Valley was then a part), as the state withdrew its subsidy of the clergy. With time, the clergy left the area. The church began to decompose, and continues to do so today. Its tile roof has fallen into disarray, and the frescos painted on its plastered interior walls have smudged and run under the constant attrition of leakage. The gold-leaf embossing on its high altar has long since been sacked. The ornately carved woodwork has sagged or fallen, to be collected in heaps at the back of the church, along with an assortment of limbs, torsos, and heads from what were once the images of saints, and several lengths of plastic pipe for the mains of the town's drinking water system. No priest has lived in the town since the mid-nineteenth century, and now only four or five masses per year are celebrated in the church, when the priest from Antabamba is invited across the valley to do so.

The church's main entrance faces onto the plaza, and is separated from it by a steel pipe railing and a few cement steps. The plaza is about the size of a soccer field, and is occasionally used as such. Another side of the plaza abuts onto the neighbourhood of Ñapaña, and is separated from it by a cement wall and steps. Rows of two-storey mud-brick buildings form the other two sides of the plaza. There are three shops open regularly in the plaza. These are owned by people who were once itinerant salesmen from the Departments of Puno and Cusco. They travelled by foot with their wares on their backs and were called 'dusters' (*polveros*), but found that they could make a modest living in this region of low commercial turnover as vendors of kerosene, sugar, flour, cane alcohol, coca leaves, and vinyl shoes, and as buyers of sheep and alpaca wool. The rest of the houses on the plaza are either occupied by families or abandoned. Next to the church are several public buildings, a telephone office that is occasionally open, the two-storey municipal offices of the District of Huaquirca, and one of the town's two elementary schools.

In the early morning, notable men holding or aspiring to hold political power in the district will meet in the plaza to chat informally or argue in Spanish before breakfast. Commoners with a matter to raise stand patiently a few paces away, waiting for a lull in the conversation to address the appropriate official, usually in Quechua. Other notable men may comb the streets around the plaza during the growing season, seeking to recruit commoners to work in their fields. Older commoners dressed in ragged coats held together in a loose patchwork may give way to an approaching notable on the narrow sidewalks, stepping into the muddy street, even doffing their misshapen felt hats. Women and children pass into the plaza to see if any of the shops baked bread the night before, and to buy cane alcohol and coca leaves for work parties they may be sponsoring that day. By 9:00 in the morning, most activity in the plaza ceases, as children go to school, and adults begin to prepare for the day's work. During the day, the only people likely to occupy the plaza are small children playing or men getting conspicuously drunk in the shops. In the late afternoon, children return from school, adults return from the fields, and another round of errands brings people to the plaza before dinner. Thus, the plaza is only occasionally anything more than a zone of transit. If the church and plaza were once the founding pillar of Huaquirca, they have now become a kind of no-man's-land, and to know this town is to know its three outlying neighbourhoods (see Figure 5), their reputations, and their interrelations.

Behind the church, going uphill, is the neighbourhood traditionally called Huachacayllo, now called the Barrio Alto (Upper Neighbourhood). Two main streets run uphill through this neighbourhood, and several smaller tracks connect them along contours at various elevations. Within this framework, loose, rambling clusters of houses occur almost randomly across the hillside, and they are connected more by networks of paths than by these main avenues. Interspersed with the clusters of houses are areas of unoccupied hillside, covered with low undergrowth and eucalyptus trees, which gradually predominate in the upper reaches of the neighbourhood.

The houses are rectangular, rarely more than five by ten metres in floor area, or one storey in height. Their mud-brick walls are broken only by a low framed wooden door, which will be secured with a padlock when the residents are not in. Of the seventy-five houses in this neighbourhood, there were equal numbers with thatch, tile, and tin roofs during the period 1981–3. Of these roof materials, thatch is the only one that is locally available: it is also the least prestigious. Tiles are a higher status material, but must be bought across the valley in Matara. Tin is trucked in from Abancay at a much greater cost, but is the material of preference. The privacy of the house relative to the exterior world is not generally carried over into further internal partitioning: most houses in this neighbourhood consist of one large room, and those that are divided rarely have more than two rooms. Cooking,

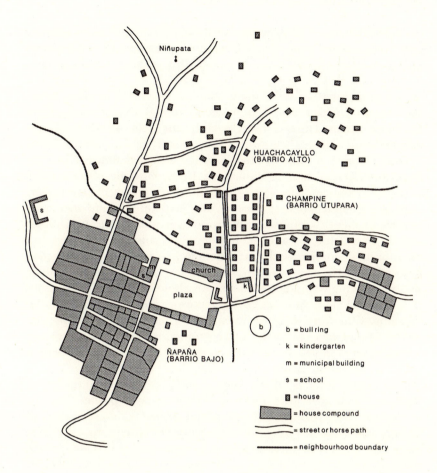

Figure 5   Neighbourhoods of Huaquirca

eating, socializing, and sleeping usually take place in a single, all-purpose room, amidst tools, jugs of fermenting corn beer (Spanish *chicha*, Quechua *laqto*), sheepskins and blankets (for sleeping), cooking ware, and the guinea pigs that are always kept indoors. Food is generally stored in a makeshift attic under the peaked roof. The only public building in Huachacayllo is a small, tin-roofed chapel used in the Christmas rituals. The two shops that sell cane alcohol and coca leaves are rarely open, since their owners are primarily agriculturalists.

Only commoners live in Huachacayllo, and it is unusual to hear Spanish spoken in the neighbourhood. In the morning, the hillside is alive with people moving along the paths that connect the level clearings around which houses cluster. Men in tattered commoner garb may sit in these clearings mending tools, or wander the neighbourhood with a bottle of cane alcohol, trying to solicit help from other men for an upcoming work party. Women in frayed synthetic sweaters and multiple layers of woollen skirts (*polleras*) may sit outside their homes spinning wool, or feed their household's chickens or pigs, but they generally stay indoors cooking during the early hours of the morning. Children often busy about on errands, such as cutting fodder for the guinea pigs. During the growing season, Huachacayllo is largely deserted during the day. It returns to life only at dusk as people come back from the fields, either to quietly eat a small meal and go to sleep, or to continue drinking, singing, and playing flutes at the house of whoever may have sponsored one of the day's work parties.

Huachacayllo is commonly considered to be the 'most Indian' of Huaquirca's three neighbourhoods by those who live in the other two. Since Huachaca is a common surname in the neighbourhood, people often speculate that in the pre-Columbian past, there was an elder (*kuraka*) named Huachaca who led his people (*ayllu*) to the site in question and settled them there, thus creating Huachacayllo. Although there is every reason to believe that this neighbourhood, and particularly its name, are of considerably more recent origin than this,[2] prevailing local notions to the contrary serve to further underline the indigenous ancestry attributed to Huachacayllo's inhabitants. The residents of Huachacayllo have also been described as '*punáticos*' (residents of the alpine zone, herders) by a native of Huaquirca (Centeno 1949: 5). In all but a few cases, however, the residents of Huachacayllo have never been anything other than agriculturalists. Since most valley people consider those who live in the *puna* to be less civilized and more 'Indian' than themselves, the attribution of a pastoral background to the residents of Huachacayllo is little more than another way of asserting their 'Indianness.' The modern alternative designation of the area as the Upper Neighbourhood also promotes this association with the *puna* by singling out elevation as its most salient feature.

The neighbourhood of Champine borders on both the plaza and Huachacayllo, but is much less sprawling than the latter, although it also has about seventy-five houses. One of Champine's two major streets divides it from Huachacayllo, and is oriented with the slope of the hill. The other leads out of town on a contour of the hillside, towards Mt Utupara, which provides the neighbourhood with its modern alternative name (Barrio Utupara). Champine's settlement density is much greater than Huachacayllo's, leaving few open areas of natural vegetation. Houses are even oriented parallel to each other in a semi-grid pattern in some areas. Approximately forty of the houses in Champine have tin roofs: the roofs of the remaining thirty-five houses are split almost equally between tile and thatch. There are several two-storey houses, and many more that are divided into two or more rooms. Most houses still share a common yard with others, but in contrast to Huachacayllo, most of these yards are at least partly enclosed by dry-stone or mud-brick walls. Informal pathways pass around these enclosures more often than through them. Other houses exist independently of any cluster, with their own enclosed yards, into which no common paths enter. Champine has no shops, but does include the town's graveyard, its bullring, its kindergarten, and a medical post that has never been opened because the state cannot persuade competent personnel to work there.

Commoners are the only inhabitants of Champine, but it is not as poor a neighbourhood as Huachacayllo, as the greater proportion of tin roofs and two-storey houses suggests. This is further reflected in the clothes of its inhabitants, which are predominantly store-bought, not homespun or endlessly repaired cast-offs. Again, Quechua is spoken in the home, and only rarely is Spanish heard on the street, though most inhabitants are quite able to speak it. The same pattern of daily activity described for Huachacayllo also prevails in Champine, since its residents are all agriculturalists. Yet the neighbourhood has a significantly different feel to it. In part, this is due to the concentration of the Aiquipa family in Champine. The Aiquipas appear to have been indigenous rulers in the area, and the Spaniards retained in this capacity throughout the colonial period. In the eighteenth century, an official

named Zola y Castillo granted them title to a large extension of terraced land just upstream from Champine (Tamayo 1947: 58). Modern
inhabitants of Huaquirca universally consider Champine to be the oldest of the town's three neighbourhoods, partly because it contains the
archaeological remains from which the church is said to have been
constructed. Equally important to Champine's putative antiquity, however, is its contemporary association with the Aiquipa family and their
illustrious past, whether or not that included residence here.[3]

Ñapaña, or the Lower Neighbourhood, is the only one of Huaquirca's three *barrios* to be laid out on a grid pattern. Its parallel and per-
pendicular streets usually feature cement sidewalks, drainage ditches,
and streetlights. They form an orderly public matrix into which rectangular house compounds, separated from the street by high mud-brick
walls or two-storey buildings, aggregate in blocks. Ñapaña is generally
thought of as the neighbourhood of the notables or *mistis*, even
though they account for only twenty of its sixty households. In fact,
some of the town's poorest commoners also live in this neighbourhood, but because it has been so thoroughly shaped by the fortress-like
house compounds of the notables, and because the notables refuse to
live anywhere else in town, Ñapaña effectively is a *misti* neighbourhood. There can be little doubt that this grid pattern is a physical
reflection of notable dominance, whether or not we join Flores (1973:
46, 1974: 184) and Brush (1977b: 26) in seeing it more abstractly as a
cultural trait that defines the 'ethnic' identity of the Andean *mestizo*.

The heightened formal separation of public from private space in
Ñapaña gives the streets over to a restricted but regular set of activities.
Dogs and pigs run free, constantly searching for refuse, and fighting
each other for it. Children play in the dirt and on the sidewalks. It is
here that notable children now learn Quechua, since Spanish has
become the language of the home in the past two or three generations. Teenagers and unmarried people from notable backgrounds
flirt on the street corners in the afternoon, and meet clandestinely at
night. Groups of notable men congregate on the corners to talk in the
morning, while commoners willing to work for a day's food and drink
stand by with their tools. Notable women bustle by wearing single-lay-
ered skirts or pants, and straw hats over their short, unbraided hair.
Since Huaquirca's two schools are located in Ñapaña, there is also a
routine movement of children and teachers through the neighbourhood in the morning, at noon, and in the afternoon. The teachers distinguish themselves from other notables and well-dressed commoners

by not wearing hats to work. The road and paths to other towns in the Antabamba Valley also enter town through Ñapaña. During my residence in Ñapaña, four shops were open sporadically there, but only those located in the plaza did regular business.

The portals (*puertas de calle*) through which one passes in going from the street into a house compound in Ñapaña are made of heavy eucalyptus wood that can be bolted shut from the inside, or padlocked from the outside: people who wish to enter knock or call out first. From the portal, the compound opens out onto a yard (*kancha*) that is usually paved with flagstones, and equipped with a deep cement sink and tap with running water. Here, clothes can dry on lines, relatively safe from theft. The yard is also a general work area and zone of transit among the various rooms or semi-independent outbuildings arranged along the periphery of the compound's four walls: a kitchen; a larder; a storeroom for tools, saddles, etc.; a dining room; a sitting room; and bedrooms (see Figure 6). None of these rooms are directly connected to each other by means of internal doors; to pass from one to the other means to pass through the yard onto which all doors face, with their respective padlocks. The walls that separate one compound from another are up to three metres tall, and include niches for chickens to roost and lay eggs in, safe from theft. During my stay in Ñapaña, one of the few remaining yards still shared by more than one household was partitioned when one family decided that it was losing animals due to the existing arrangement. The protection of property therefore is an important factor in the enclosed, four-square layout of Ñapaña, and this is partly confirmed by the breakdown of the grid pattern on certain peripheral areas of the neighbourhood inhabited by commoners. Commoners as poor and ragged as any in Huachacayllo may nonetheless inhabit the enclosed interstices between notable compounds. Conversely, there are some wealthy commoners in Champine, where no real compounds exist. Finally, what most typifies the notables is not their property consciousness, since everybody at least locks the door to their house, but their systematic spatial segregation of activities within the compound (cf. Stein 1961: 70).

The multiplicity of functionally specialized rooms in the notable house compound effectively sorts life out into an implicit folk-dichotomy of the instrumental and the expressive. In the kitchen, larder, storerooms, and yard, one deals with the necessities of life, such as cooking, washing, preparing for work in the fields, and mending tools. These are the rooms in the *misti* house compound within which the

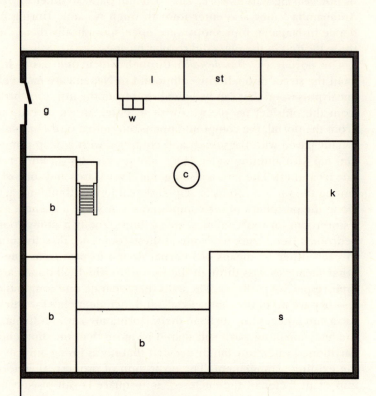

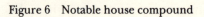

b = bedroom

c = chili plants

g = gates

k = kitchen

l = larder

s = salon

st = storage room

w = water

Figure 6   Notable house compound

commoners move, either as day labourers or as more permanent domestic servants. An even more degraded space is the yard, where the dung of assorted animals sadly accumulates, and must be walked through. It is here that uncouth commoners are served their meals and demand drink after their day's work on the notables' land. Even the rooms associated with the household economy are tainted by the presence of commoner domestic servants, and the instrumental tasks they perform. The bedrooms are the only ones used on a daily basis that begin to transcend all of this. Here, pictures of the national football team, naked blonde women, and faraway places adorn the walls, and one finds sewing machines, books, old newspapers and magazines acquired in a lifetime of trips to Abancay, Cusco, Arequipa, or Lima. Bedrooms are often located on the second floor, out of the wind-blown dust, and at night pressurized kerosene lamps burn for a few hours behind glass windows and wooden shutters, while the notables sew, read, drink, or otherwise finish off the day.

Only on special occasions are the dining rooms and salons used. Like the bedrooms, these usually have plank floors, but feature the additional refinement of plaster walls painted in pastel colours, which are sparsely decorated with family portraits, calendars, and religious and political iconography. Battery-operated record or cassette players are stored in these rooms, and are invariably used in the select, but infrequent, gatherings that take place there, along with the guitars and mandolins that so many notable men play so well. Above all else, these rooms exist for banquets (featuring pork among many other courses, and an assortment of wines, liquors, and beer) in honour of a *fiesta* or the visit of a relative from the city. Notables acknowledge the significance of these gatherings by engaging in their characteristically florid style of formal public speaking, but they measure the success of the event by whether people forget their mundane cares and squabbles with each other in the struggle for local power by getting drunk, making music, and telling stories of bygone days. The banquet is arguably the quintessential expression of what it means to be a refined person (*gente culta*) in Huaquirca. Conversation takes place in Spanish, but Quechua is used in occasional witticisms and orders to the servants, who, as a rule, are the only commoners allowed to enter these rooms.

Again, it is not so much raw quantity of wealth that separates notables from commoners as the aesthetic of segregation and refinement through which they enjoy it. What makes a notable banquet different from the drunken aftermath of a commoner work party in a single-room, all-purpose dwelling of Huachacayllo is, above all, the meticulousness with which it is spatially isolated from other aspects of life in the house compound. For the notables, this relative non-differentiation of space in the houses of Huachacayllo borders on anathema, for it systematically negates the most fundamental categorical divisions that they live by. This gives rise to a sense of motivated opposition between Huachacayllo and Ñapaña, which was expressed when they were renamed as the Upper Neighbourhood and Lower Neighbourhood respectively. Whereas notables in other Andean towns tend to gravitate towards the 'civilized centre' of church and plaza in a concentric opposition to a periphery of commoners,[4] class opposition in Huaquirca is spatially expressed as an opposition of low to high. The meaning of these contrasting class strategies for the organization of space will be further developed and clarified when we turn to the agricultural property holdings of both notables and commoners.

Fields and Pastures

All of the households whose living space has just been described depend on access to fields and pastures. Not only are there different kinds of land tenure in different zones on the mountainside, each with its own mode of transmission, but there are alternative and even contradictory definitions of property in each zone. Local notions of property sometimes conflict because they are elaborated through two different frameworks of meaning (cf. Thompson 1975: 261, 1976: 337, 358), one that is grounded in the class position of the notables, and the other in that of the commoners. National law only adds the distinct interests of the Peruvian state into an already complex local situation, but it is largely tangential, and will not be discussed extensively here. 'Custom' and the various conflicts within it are what is most salient.

Landholdings in the terraced valley or *qheshwa* zone below town are crucial to the independent existence of a household. They not only provide maize and beans as staples, but also the raw material for corn beer, without which it would be impossible for a household to sponsor the work parties that are so basic to interaction as a social unit. All but a few of the viable households in Huaquirca possess between 0.67 and 0.75 ha of valley land,[5] usually distributed among two to five parcels in different locations.[6] Whether the produce from this land in a normal year is adequate for domestic consumption depends on the success of the complementary potato harvest, monetary income, and, of course, family size. Thus, there is a considerable range in the standard of living of households owning comparable amounts of valley land. Only two households in Huaquirca own more than one hectare of valley land, and in both cases it is only slightly more. For many commoners, it is a struggle to get enough valley land to run a viable household, whereas for most notables this is an easily attained point of departure in the developmental cycle of domestic groups. However, the fact that nobody accumulates valley land beyond these minimal levels in Huaquirca[7] indicates that land ownership defines only one threshold of social differentiation, effectively that between servitude and forming an independent household.

Rights to terraced valley land are acquired mainly through inheritance, purchase, or rental. On marriage, a couple usually receives a kind of inheritance called a *dote* or *dotación* from each parental household. When both parental households contribute property of equal value, the young couple lives neolocally, and forms a separate household. Because terraced land is rarely accumulated beyond domestic needs, however, the parental households can never part with enough to establish the young couple in this regard.[8] Thus, inheritance must always be supplemented by some other mode of access to valley land, usually rental or purchase. Although rental and purchase prices of land are well below what one would expect in a capitalist market,[9] sources of cash income are restricted enough that poorer young commoners are unable to meet them. As a result, many seek servile incorporation into a notable or wealthy commoner household, as a herder of cattle (*vaquero*) or camelids (*llamero*). A period of service is set before the justice of the peace in Huaquirca, for terms including a token cash payment,[10] part of which is advanced, and a monthly supply of provisions (*qhoqaw*) to supplement whatever staples the herder might produce (cf. Concha 1971: 65). Several widowers and a few landless families perennially exist on the margins of the community under these conditions, with their older children affiliated to notable households as domestic servants. As herders, it is very difficult for a young couple to accumulate additional property to form a household of their own, and petty theft from their patrons is virtually institutionalized (cf. Stein 1961: 42, 229).[11] When notables address their herders as '*hijito*' and '*hijita*' ('little son,' and 'little daughter'), they do so with a certain paternalistic tolerance that accurately expresses the dependent incorporation of these servants into their domestic economy. A similar dynamic exists in commoner extended families, where the incorporation of a young couple into one of their parental households usually involves an exploitation comparable to servitude,[12] and negates the equality of parents-in-law implied by neolocality. Finally, there are commoners who have just enough land to form their own household, but have to work in *mink'a* (i.e., for a day's food and drink) for notables to make provisions last. Widowers and the recently married form the majority of this group. Even in this mild form, servitude is predicated on the frustration of the developmental cycle of commoner domestic groups.

Although the only use of terraced valley land in Huaquirca today is to provide a household with enough maize to exist as an independent economic unit, such land is nevertheless divided into two folk-categories: land that is 'private' (*privado*) and land that is 'of the community' (*de la comunidad*). According to local custom, individual units of 'private' property are defined by stone fences that enclose them along their outer perimeter. By contrast, lands 'of the community' are not individually fenced, but form large blocks of hundreds of units that share a common outer fence where they border on roads, paths, and other points of access. The distinction between these two categories of land does not pertain to agricultural use rights, in which they are identical. Both involve exclusive household rights to the produce of a given parcel of land, and both are subject to collective regulation of the timing of the harvest and sale.[13] However, these forms of enclosure do define different grazing rights to the stubble left in the fields after the harvest: 'private' lands involve exclusive right, whereas lands 'of the community' allow every owner's animals free range within the collective enclosure. These rights and restrictions are wholly without foundation in national law, but represent instead the outcome of struggle and negotiation over 'customary' practice.

Notables were the driving force behind the creation of 'private' land on the terraces, and this imparts a class significance to these folk-categories of property. 'Private' land is concentrated in the areas known as Pomache and Qochawaña, where most notable holdings are located, and also characterizes Lucrepampa, owned in its entirety by various Aiquipa households (see Figure 7). However, 'private' land may occur in isolation anywhere a notable owns property in sectors of communally enclosed land. There appears to be no restriction on the enclosure of land: several notables told me that one simply builds a fence around one's parcel and calls it 'private.' Although not all parcels of

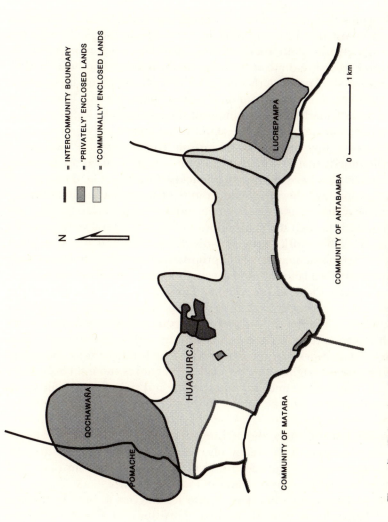

N

= INTERCOMMUNITY BOUNDARY

= 'PRIVATELY' ENCLOSED LANDS

= 'COMMUNALLY' ENCLOSED LANDS

POMACHE

QOCHAWAÑA

HUAQUIRCA

LUCREPAMPA

COMMUNITY OF MATARA

COMMUNITY OF ANTABAMBA

0   1 km

Figure 7   'Private' and 'communal' land in Huaquirca

land owned by notables are enclosed, the great majority are. Correspondingly, I know of no commoner family other than the Aiquipas who have separated their land from neighbouring parcels with a fence.

It seems that the aesthetic of separation that governs the notable house compound is also at work in the fields. In the fields, however, commoners find these statements of separation much more threatening, and several told me of how their older relatives had been forcibly dispossessed of particularly choice parcels of valley land by notables, who went on to enclose them on a 'private' basis. It is as if these fences were a particularly sharp reminder of the injustices by which the land was taken, and an ongoing threat of further attacks.

I suspect that an additional reason commoners find enclosure threatening is that it negates reciprocal labour (*ayni*) as a method of recognizing property rights. On unenclosed parcels of land that are 'of the community,' the proprietary rights of individual households are every bit as strong as they are on enclosed 'private' lands, but they are recognized through the conventions of the agricultural work party. To sponsor such a work party, and distribute food and drink to guest workers, is to assume the role of proprietor. Conversely, to attend such a work party as a labourer, and accept food and drink from the hosts, is to recognize them as proprietors. Therefore, the institution of the work party constantly reconfirms the property rights of individual households, and for commoners, no further public statement of ownership is required. To claim ownership through enclosure, then, is to deny that the work party is an adequate vehicle for claiming and recognizing property rights. 'Private' enclosure ignores and even negates an entire quasi-legal framework of meaning and right that is built up by commoners through the culture of the work party. Commoners, therefore, describe enclosure as a kind of aggression, something that is tantamount to lawlessness, and an integral part of the theft of their lands. As we move out of the valley into the alpine zone (*puna*), the link between enclosure and dispossession, familiar to us from European history, will become even clearer in local experience.

All of Huaquirca's households also have access to land in the sectoral fallow fields (*laymis*), located above town at altitudes between 3800 and 4200 m above sea level. The first year a *laymi* field is open, it is planted with potatoes. The second year it is sown with other Andean tubers (mainly *oqas* and *ullukus*), *quinua*, beans (*habas*), wheat or barley. After the second year, the *laymi* sits fallow for seven years, and is then reopened. Thus, in any given year, one sector of these fields will be producing potatoes, an adjacent sector will be producing the variety of second-year crops, and seven others will be lying fallow. At the end of that same agricultural year, people will break ground in a third sector in preparation for the year to come, and leave to fallow the sector in which second-year crops were grown, thus advancing a cycle that takes nine years to complete (see Figure 8). There are four *laymi* systems within the territory of Huaquirca, one large system immediately above town, and three small systems that are used mainly by the pastoralists in the lower reaches of the *puna*. For both valley agriculturalists and alpine pastoralists, cultivation of these fields represents a supplement to their main source of livelihood.

All residents of Huaquirca are entitled to a plot (*chaqmana*) in every *laymi* sector. Once assigned, plots are generally used by a household until its dissolution, at which point they will be reassigned by the president of the Peasant Community of Huaquirca, an institution that will be discussed later in this chapter. When an older couple incorporates one of their married children into an extended family, rights to particular *laymi* plots may be passed on from one generation to the next. At current population levels, however, land is not scarce in the *laymis* (cf. Skar 1982: 157), and any given sector under cultivation has less than half of its total area open.This situation has probably prevailed only since the 1950s, when a grass with a tough creeping root, known as *grama* or *kikuyu*, was introduced as a miracle fodder. Among its many disastrous consequences for Andean agriculture, this grass made opening new plots in fallow sectors at least four times as labour intensive as before. As a result, the area under cultivation has shrunk, and only a few households with little valley land bother opening more than the average of 0.50 to 0.67 ha (divided among first- and second-year crops) that most households plant in the *laymis*. In both of my years in Huaquirca, people ran out of products from this zone four months before the harvest was due, and missed them severely. Yet they still did not open larger *laymi* plots, which indicates just how severely this grass has curtailed agricultural use of the lower *puna*.

The only positive effect that *kikuyu* grass had on the area was that it slightly improved fallow *laymi* plots as pastureland for cattle. All but a few of the poorest households in Huaquirca keep cattle, and for most, it is their principal source of cash income.[14] Although the odd sale

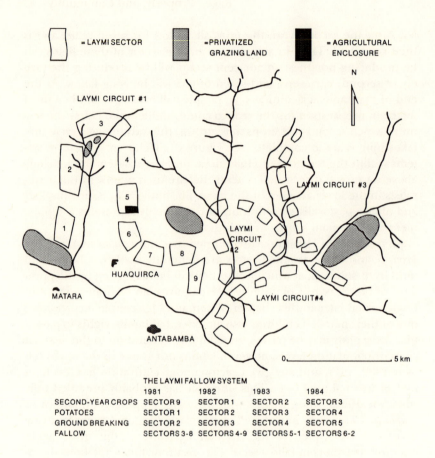

Figure 8   Agricultural and pastoral uses of the lower *puna*

may be made within the community, most sales are made to the cattle buyers who come on horseback over the Continental Divide from the town of Cotahuasi in the Department of Arequipa. When these cattle buyers are in the area, they stay with notables who have become their friends over many years of buying and selling. Since the notables tend to have the largest herds, and the greatest need of money in their way of life, the association is a natural one. Commoners sell their cattle much more sporadically, to buy fields, sponsor a *fiesta*, or meet unforeseen medical expenses, generally keeping them more as a form of saving than to generate cash on a regular basis. Once they have obtained cattle in Huaquirca and Antabamba, the buyers take them back to Cotahuasi, where they possess large tracts of irrigated land for growing alfalfa, which fattens the animals after their journey over the mountains. The cattle are then sold to mining camps on the Pacific coast, such as Marcona. This is one of the last remnants of a vast network of commerce that sprung up in the 1880s linking the remote areas of the highlands to the nascent capitalism on the coast. With the completion of the Lima-Cusco highway in 1942 (see Montoya 1980: 107), most of this commerce has been restructured around motor transport, which has tended to marginalize areas off the beaten track, including the Antabamba Valley. It is nonetheless of the greatest significance that in its developmental cycle, a household in Huaquirca must supply a market need for beef before it has the money to get enough valley land for its own 'subsistence economy.'[15]

Cattle are kept in the seven fallow *laymi* sectors from mid-September, when the sowing begins, through to the harvest, when they are brought down to the terraces to browse on the stubble. Since the presence of cattle in fallow areas of the lower *puna* corresponds to the agricultural season in the valley, when there is a great deal of work to be done there, it is not always possible to have someone looking after them, despite the very real danger of theft. Commoner households often designate an older child to keep an eye on the cattle, but this usually conflicts with commitments to school or agricultural work. There are few commoner households with more than ten head of cattle, either because of theft or as a precaution against it. The only extended time that commoners spend with their cattle, drinking milk, making cheese, and relaxing, is for a few weeks beginning in late January, when agricultural work in the valley declines. At this time, whole commoner households move up to their *vaquerías:* flexible, non-exclusive grazing territories centred around small thatched huts. Notable households, on the other hand, have servants (*vaqueros*) to look after their cattle throughout the agricultural year, and thus escape the problem of insufficient domestic labour to look after household property that plagues the commoners (cf. Stein 1961: 56), above all in relation to cattle.

Because grazing sites are located in the *laymi* circuits above the town, occupancy is limited to a maximum of seven years (i.e., the fallow period). Although individual households tend to return to the same areas to rebuild their huts, this does not lead to exclusive rights over particular territories, nor to their oversaturation, since people are looking for areas of rich pasture when they contemplate a move, and they disperse accordingly. For commoners, however, proximity to town to allow surveillance of the animals is at least as important a consideration as the quality of the pasture. Thus, the sectors of the main *laymi* circuit immediately above the town are more intensively used for grazing than those sectors farther away, or the three smaller *laymi* circuits in the *puna*. Correspondingly, the notables tend to locate their *vaquerías* farther afield, where the pasture is best, because their *vaqueros* save them the trouble of looking after their animals personally.

Inevitably there have been conflicts between the agricultural and pastoral uses of the lower *puna*, most of which have an additional class significance. For example, the *kikuyu* grass disaster, which has tipped the balance in favour of grazing, was the unintended result of certain *hacendados'* preoccupation with raising cattle as a way of making money in the Departments of Apurímac and Cusco (Montoya 1980: 305). Its devastating effect on *laymi* cultivation cannot be divorced from these considerations. As one commoner ruefully remarked to me, 'This grass is the worst *gamonal* we have here.' Another area of conflict is the encroachment of cattle on the unenclosed *laymis* from adjacent fallow sectors. To prevent this, guardians (*kamayoq*) for each sector under cultivation are appointed from within the community each year to live in a hut among the fields from December to June, to keep cattle out. Animals caught grazing in plots under crop are impounded until their owners pay a fine. However necessary and reasonable such a system may seem, owners of impounded cattle rarely pay their fine without a struggle. During my stay in Huaquirca, a notable of the old school, then in his seventies, even went as far as attacking the *kamayoq* with a machete for impounding his cattle. Even though the fine was well within the notable's means, he was furious that other people's crops should take precedence over his animals. This attitude on the part of some notables culminated in their enclosure and/or appropriation of large tracts of land for grazing in some smaller and more distant *laymis* in the alpine zone (cf. Skar 1982: 157). Commoners still tell of how these lands used to be cultivated, and of the cruelty with which particular notables seized land that was under crop, and put their cattle out to feed on it. The three notable households in Huaquirca with the most cattle in 1982 (two with more than 100 head, one with over eighty) all appropriated estates of twenty to fifty hectares from what had previously been *laymi* land subject to communal tenure (see Figure 8). Yet some notable households with only fifteen head of cattle owned small estates of grazing land, and one even had an enclosed agricultural property in this zone (see Figure 8) (see also Skar 1982: 158; Ossio 1983: 49–50).[16] Other notables with herds as large as sixty head still use temporary grazing sites on *laymi* land and respect communal tenure there. Thus, enclosure is less a functional correlate of wealth than a particular strategy for pursuing it, one that is based on a violation of that which is 'of the community.'

Above the *laymis* is the high *puna* (4200–5000 metres above sea level), where pastoralists herd llamas, alpacas, and sheep from dispersed settlements. As mentioned earlier, pastoralists form a separate social group, with whom the commoners of the valley will not intermarry out of a feeling that they are more 'Indian' (Concha 1971: 22, 27; Tomoeda 1985: 282). Each household of pastoralists is centred around a principal residence called an *estancia* or *hatun wasi*, which includes several corrals and exclusive rights to a grazing territory around the residence, usually including a swamp (see Palacios Ríos 1977: 77). The tendency for clusters of adjacent *estancias* to be owned by people with the same surname is due to the predominance of virilocality tied to a transmission of rights to this land through the male line (Palacios Ríos 1977: 77), although uxorilocal and neolocal residence may occur with different forms of transmission (cf. Concha 1971: 23). Although unused and abandoned pastures do exist, and can be used when necessary, ancestral (generally patrilineal) right to an abandoned *estancia* can be asserted at any point (cf. Concha 1971: 23). In addition, each household must have access to a supplementary grazing area that is generally used during the rainy season, when natural pasture is most abundant. These supplementary territories have smaller houses, and access to them is generally regulated in a more flexible, bilateral manner than to the principal estates.

Valley people say that pastoralists are 'more Indian' than themselves because they lack nucleated settlements and have a propensity to become curers, oracular mediums, or rainmakers. This stereotype also includes the notion that pastoralists are so far removed from mainstream Peru that they have little need or understanding of money, and bury it under the floors of their huts out of pure avarice or ignorance. The reality is that the pastoral economy is far more monetized than the valley economy. Pastoralists receive a significant income from the sale of alpaca and sheep wool, and have long used their llamas as pack animals in return for a share of the maize harvest that they transport from the fields to the towns in the valley (see Chapter 6 and Concha 1971, 1975), and in very profitable combinations of trade and barter over long distances (Custred 1974). This did not escape the notice of notables in Huaquirca and other towns of the upper Antabamba Valley, who began to acquire *estancias* in the high *puna* from the 1920s onward, according to some of my older informants. The wool they sheared from their animals in February, along with any they managed to seize from neighbouring commoners, underwrote a whole cycle of muleteer commerce that was probably inspired by the llama herders of the *puna*.

In April, the notable muleteers set out with their wool on a month-long return trip to Arequipa, coming home with their mules laden with books, wines, hardware, and even sewing machines: commodities that defined the civilized life. Any remaining cash could initiate a new round of commerce after the harvest in June. Apples and chili peppers would be obtained during a trip to the coastal valleys and brought back to the Antabamba Valley, along with the finest wines from foreign lands, which the notables were proud to serve to each other in those days. The journey continued to Cusco, where the chili peppers were sold. The profits were used to buy coca leaves in the high jungle of the Province of La Concepción in Cusco, which the muleteers would take back to the Antabamba Valley. Some continued on to the town of Coracora in Parinacochas, Ayacucho, to make additional transactions, and return home just in time for the sowing in mid-September. By the 1950s, woolbuyers had arrived in the Antabamba Valley as a result of the completion of the Lima-Cusco highway in 1942. This sent the commercial activities of the notables into decline, since there was now a more convenient means of selling their wool, and obtaining the commodities they desired. Nonetheless, there is considerable nostalgia among the notables for the passing of muleteer commerce, for in it they actively immersed themselves in both metropolitan refinement and the myths and rituals of the *puna*. This allowed them to be at once more 'white' and more authentically 'Indian' than valley commoners, and to portray themselves as the bearers of a distinctively '*mestizo*' subculture that made them privileged mediators between two worlds.

Such nostalgia aside, the high *puna* land associated with Huaquirca was, by all accounts, the scene of some brutal dispossessions and enclosures during the 1940s and 1950s. Not only were notables of Huaquirca involved, but those from other towns in the upper Antabamba Valley also tried to obtain some of the excellent grazing land that could be found there. One contemporary account (Tamayo 1947: 58–63) portrays the enclosure of small estates in the *puna* as a precedent for the creation of 'private' enclosure of terraced valley land, in a generalized scramble for rights to grazing land of any sort. In the early 1940s, the neighbouring town of Sabayno began to press a claim to some land in the principal *laymi* circuit above Huaquirca, putting additional pressure on a collective resource already being eroded from within. In those days, Huaquirca was still an annex of the District of Sabayno and, therefore, subordinate to it politically. By incorporating themselves as a *Comunidad Indígena* (an institution to be described below), the residents of Sabayno hoped to extend the traditional boundaries of their land at Huaquirca's expense. To meet this threat, both commoners and notables took to their horses and staged a highly theatrical tour of Huaquirca's boundaries, confronting a similar party from Sabayno in the process. This spurred the residents of Huaquirca to break away from the administrative jurisdiction of the District of Sabayno, and form a separate District of Huaquirca in 1945. Orlove (1980: 120) rightly links district formation to the notable quest for power at the local level, since it involves the creation of new political posts and patronage opportunities. Here, however, it had the additional effect of settling the boundary dispute with Sabayno in favour of Huaquirca, and halted the expropriation of pastureland within its territory by notables living in other towns of the valley.[17] These results reflect the participation and interest of commoners in the initiative.

When the creation of a separate District of Huaquirca proved insufficient to curb the land-grabbing of the notables still resident in Huaquirca during the 1950s, commoners organized to register the entire territory described here as a *Comunidad Indígena* (now *Comunidad Campesina* or Peasant Community) in 1957, under existing legislation meant to curb the illicit appropriation of land. Legally, this made all but a small proportion of land with title predating 1920 (mainly that held by the Aiquipas) corporate property of the Comunidad Indígena de Huaquirca, and should, in theory, have ended the inheritance, sale, and rental of such land. In reality, it was and still is impossible to apply this law strictly.[18] However, the commoners' demonstrated ability to recur to the law stopped the notables from expropriating any more land, and stabilized communal tenure in the limited areas where it still applied, without in any way jeopardizing exclusive and alienable rights to the most central resources of both valley and alpine economies.

A final burst of political activity occurred in 1960, when many of Huaquirca's commoners joined in the land occupation movement that was sweeping all of southern Peru. Elsewhere, these land occupations aimed to regain lands illegally appropriated by neighbouring *haciendas*. In Huaquirca, however, the occupations were directed at the 'private' terraced valley holdings of the Aiquipa family in Lucrepampa, which were apparently being enclosed and possibly enlarged at the time. By enclosing their land, the Aiquipas violated the notion of 'communal' property that was sacrosanct to other commoners, and reiterated their claim to native aristocratic status. This, along with the fact that land scarcity was reaching a peak in the late 1950s, made the Aiquipas, and not the local notables, the primary targets of the movement. It seems that some of their lands were not being cultivated, and were occupied by needy commoner families. I came to know the principal leader of that movement, one of the very few commoners who held political office during my stay in Huaquirca (as a United Left alderman). He told me how the police came and took him to jail in Abancay for two months. This intimidated other commoners and the movement quickly fell apart, but twenty years later, he thought that they could have succeeded if they had been more tenacious. Assured of my political sympathies, he was nonetheless reluctant to discuss the matter further with me, perhaps because my adoptive 'father' (his cousin) had married into the Aiquipa family and still supported them in this old dispute. As a result, I met with little success in trying to reconstruct the performative and symbolic dimensions of the land occupation movement in Huaquirca, much as the matter interested me.

Clearly, agrarian property rights in Huaquirca have been continuously renegotiated in an atmosphere of struggle and legal pluralism, in which no one perspective has been entirely dominant. However, I do not join Smith (1989) in his contention that these struggles boil down to a series of opportunistic economic claims advanced through arbitrary and ephemeral cultural vehicles. In Huaquirca, the basic issue was whether property rights were to be recognized through work parties on unenclosed land, according to commoner practice, or whether they would be proclaimed through enclosure, as the notables and Aiquipas did. Both work parties and the folk classification of land based on enclosure have a long genealogy in Andean culture and cannot be dismissed as ad hoc constructs. They are the focus of moral and legal sensibilities that have built up over time, and to deny this is to deny the tenacity of commoner resistance, among other things.

Perhaps the surest indication that property concepts in Huaquirca are categorical, and not improvisational, is that they occasionally override empirical observation. There can be no doubt, for example, that the alpine pastoralists above Huaquirca have exclusive and alienable rights to their grazing territories. Yet valley commoners would sometimes insist to me that these lands are 'of the community,' presumably because in their experience, only notables would attempt to assert exclusive rights to grazing land. Similarly, when discussing the notables' dispossession of certain pastoralists, or their appropriation of *laymi* land, valley commoners would insist that the notables went on to enclose the land in question, although upon subsequent investigation I usually discovered that the land remained unfenced. Again, it appears that we are dealing with a categorical imperative: land that is somehow no longer 'of the community' is by definition enclosed.

Spanish customary land tenure is undoubtedly the source of the folk distinction between 'private' and 'communal' land in Huaquirca. Identical categories of land are defined by enclosure and grazing rights to the harvest stubble in the Province of Zamorra, from which many *conquistadores* came (Arguedas 1968: 33–9). In the New World, it was colonial policy to promote communal grazing rights to agricultural stubble and uncultivated areas, and to forbid enclosure of the latter, according to ancient Castilian practice (Chevalier 1963: 86–8). Iberian land tenure patterns took hold and persisted in Huaquirca, perhaps because of the unusually high number of poor Spaniards who settled the area as peasants during the colonial period (see Mörner 1978: 29). However, fragmentary evidence suggests that similar patterns are widespread throughout the southern Peruvian Andes.[19] It is ironic that the commoners of Huaquirca are so faithful to Spanish land tenure customs, despite the 'Indian' ethnicity that is attributed to them.[20]

More significant still, however, are the notables' deviations from these property customs. Although they undoubtedly gained considerable economic benefits from appropriating large areas of pastureland, these benefits alone are insufficient to explain enclosure, particularly in the valley. As Arguedas (1968: 38, 258) argues, generalized access to pastures favours those with the most livestock; therefore, it could be argued that the notables' decision to enclose their terraced valley land and have exclusive grazing rights to its stubble was economically irrational. The same could also be said of the enormous effort it would take to enclose a large grazing territory to protect it from the insignificant amounts of fodder that might be lost through the occasional encroachment of other people's animals in a zone where exclusive right is recognized. These costs are the reason, despite prevailing notions to the contrary, most notables did not actually bother to enclose their alpine lands. In short, enclosure does not make sense except as a costly statement of separation from that which is 'of the community,' or as a theatrical violation of communal right, both of which define notable identity in a negative and transgressive (but not 'ethnic') manner. Thus, enclosure could be seen as a continuation of the notables' repudiation of *ayni*, the generalized exchange of labour, food, and drink across household boundaries, by which commoners implicitly affirm each other's property rights. To proclaim one's property rights through enclosure is to deny the efficacy of this labour theory of property, and to threaten the rights claimed through it. By their own testimony, the notables frequently made good on this threat. Notable property holdings presuppose servitude not simply because they are too extensive to be attended solely by the labour of their owners, but primarily because they are claimed through a kind of semiotic aggression against the framework of meaning and right that inheres to all of that which is 'of the community.'

Community and District

We have already touched on some reasons why the District of Huaquirca and the Peasant Community of Huaquirca came into being, and even on the social forces that prevent them from fulfilling their legal function, without actually describing these institutions in any detail. In this section, I will continue to argue that these institutions are primarily an outgrowth of local class relations, and that most of their relevant features are either banned or unspecified by national law.

The District of Huaquirca has its quarters in a building on the plaza, which consists of an office for the mayor, a room containing a typewriter and the town's records (mostly births, deaths, and minutes from various meetings), and on the floor above them, a large hall for meetings. During periods of formal democracy, such as the one during which this research was conducted, people may vote for aldermen and a mayor, who form the district council. Under more authoritarian regimes, the mayor is appointed by the ruling party or junta, and the aldermen are simply dispensed with. There are two additional positions that are always appointed, no matter what kind of government is in power: the justice of the peace, who resolves minor disputes, and the governor, who acts as the official liaison with the ruling party or clique. These positions are accompanied by what can only be described as a gesture towards a salary, but then none are full-time occupations. The district council has a small operating budget, most of which is spent on sending members to Abancay to solicit public works at the departmental and national levels of government. These works are the main accomplishment that a council can hope to present to its electorate when seeking another term of office. Thus, district councils are subject to effective control and manipulation by the programs that higher levels of government have to offer.[21] In short, the district has little authority or autonomy, but this has not discouraged the notables of towns like Huaquirca from all but completely monopolizing its positions.[22]

Orlove (1980: 113, 125–6) has tried to explain the notables' political domination as a result of their control over the district level of government. However, I find it difficult to reduce the class power of notables, which is considerable, to their control of a weak local state. After all, the notables committed their various acts of *gamonalismo* without using the law or the police. Until recently, those who ran afoul of a prominent notable could expect incarceration, a public flogging, or an informally administered beating, with little chance of recourse to a higher level of justice, much as certain *hacendados* would mutilate peasants who failed to kneel before them (Arguedas 1968: 336; Favre 1970: 130). Other 'abuses' for which the notables were famous include outright seizures of wool, animals, or land, and forced recruitment of domestic servants (see also Orlove 1980: 125) or day labourers to work their personal holdings. To be sure, it was as governor, mayor, or justice of the peace that the most 'abusive' of the notables committed their most flagrant acts of *gamonalismo*. It is also true that the political mobilization of the commoners during the period 1945–60, which established links to the central state unmediated by the notables, sent the *gamonales* of Huaquirca into decline. Yet the fact that I could witness most of these 'abuses' still taking place during the period 1981–3 shows that *gamonalismo* is not an entirely spent force. That it has little to do with holding office became clear to me when I asked a commoner why he was working in *mink'a* for a notable who had just been defeated in elections for mayor, when he knew full well that the favour would never be reciprocated. The reply was: 'We work for don Julio because he is a boss.' Since only notables can consistently use the hierarchical relation of *mink'a* as a way of getting their agricultural work done (cf. Malengreau 1980: 515; Orlove 1980: 118), it must indeed be because they are bosses, even when they are not holding office. A similar logic underlies the way that notables may pay commoners less than a fair price for their produce or animals (e.g., Flores 1974: 188–9; Montoya 1980: 212–14), or enjoy a constant influx of 'gifts' in food to placate them (Stein 1961: 167). Consequently, I would argue that the notable monopoly on district office is more a result than a cause of their class power.

This sort of local rule in many ways paralleled the existence of the large landed estate or *hacienda*: sometimes its source, sometimes a necessary condition of its existence, and other times its direct competitor in the exploitation of commoners' labour. Certainly the fact that so many *haciendas* were founded or enlarged upon the illegal appropriation of land (cf. Hobsbawm 1974: 124–6) can be understood only against the background of this kind of state, which it undoubtedly also helped to create (cf. Mariátegui 1971: 23). In any case, there is a widespread feeling among commoners that notables administrate the district as a personal enterprise for their own benefit (cf. Malengreau 1974: 202). Orlove (1980: 113, 126) may be technically correct to distinguish between local 'elites' and *hacendados*, but he implies an overly rigid separation of property from sovereignty in a situation where *haciendas* were run like fiefdoms beyond the law (Mariátegui 1971: 62–3), and the local state was run like à *hacienda*. Much more fundamental is how the unity of property and sovereignty under *gamonalismo* was constituted by the violation of that which is 'of the community' and 'Indian,' in a constant reenactment of the myth of the conquest. This phenomenon can be better understood in juxtaposition with its more civilized reflection in attempts by the central state and progressive notables to 'modernize' the highlands through public works built by the labour tribute of commoners (*faena*).

From pre-Columbian times through most of the colonial period, labour tribute to the state guaranteed its recognition of communal land tenure for those classified as *indios tributarios*.[23] Even though this tribute was officially dropped in 1810, only to be reinstated and dropped in a bewildering succession of legal forms, it never disappeared in practice.[24] The modern era of this ancient relationship began in 1920, when the Leguía regime offered legal recognition (and, in 1925, registration) of communal land to protect it from the sort of *gamonal* predation described earlier, in a constitutional package that also included *conscripción vial*, a labour draft for road construction (Grondín 1978: 54–5). Although the latter was supposed to be a universal civic obligation, it applied only to 'Indians' (Chevalier 1970: 193), and was widely perceived at the time as a revival of colonial labour tribute (Davies 1974: 82–4). With the fall of Leguía in 1930, amid riots and the burning of files (Davies 1974: 85), *conscripción vial* officially ended. But the same practices were surreptitiously revived to complete the major highways through the southern Peruvian Andes during the period 1935–42 (see Montoya, Silveira, and Lindoso 1979: 36). With virtually every passing government, the agencies and programs based on *faena* change, but the formula remains the same: the state provides materials and technical knowledge, and the district officials provide the labour of commoners. If modern commoners are no longer known juridically as *indios tributarios*, this is still very much their status in practice, and after *ayni* (the generalized exchange of labour for food and drink on lands 'of the community'), *faena* is one of the most diagnostic features of commoners' social position (cf. Stein 1961: 227; Montoya 1980: 202–3).

It is generally as supervisors, whether or not they hold district office, that notables participate in *faena*, although in recent years they may occasionally do token stints of manual labour (see Grondín 1978: 123; Isbell 1978: 177). Most, however, including all of the schoolteachers, simply declare themselves individual proprietors (*propietarios*) resident within the district, since membership in the Peasant Community has never been compulsory. Theoretically, they pay a small fine that would be the equivalent of a municipal tax, were it systematically collected. This money is supposed to hire a substitute labourer for the proprietor, but since all commoners over the age of seventeen already have their own obligation to fulfil,[25] there is effectively nobody to hire. As a result, when fines are collected, they are generally used to buy alcohol for the commoners (see also Stein 1961: 111; Doughty 1967: 678–81; Isbell 1978: 176), whose quota of work is increased to compensate for the absence of the notables (cf. Montoya, Silveira, and Lindoso 1979: 83). However, even this residual commoner claim to festivity during *faena*, one that has long been a part of Andean sensibilities (Murra 1978: 149), is being eroded and most of the *faenas* I attended lacked drink altogether. From here, it is a short step to reports of notables renting out the labour of 'their' commoners to private individuals (Davies 1974: 13; Flores 1974: 190). This sort of 'abuse,' like most within the complex of *gamonalismo*, can only be measured against the civic norm it transgresses. Since that norm also presupposes that commoners are a servile labour force, it might seem that there is little sense in condemning the excesses of the *gamonales*. However, this is not the political conclusion that the commoners of Huaquirca have drawn.

Despite questioning several commoners on the subject, I never heard one complaint about *faena* obligations. Perhaps this is because they were amounting to only about ten days per year during my stay in Huaquirca. What seems more likely, however, is that labour tribute remains a way of maintaining or, when necessary, asserting a 'pact of reciprocity' with the state, in which it recognizes communal land tenure (Isbell 1978: 171; Platt 1982: 139, 145). Since the state is still tacitly dependent on this labour tribute, it cannot completely disregard the land claims made through it. Nonetheless, the modern state stops well short of the Inca moral economy, in which the state provided food, drink, and music for its tributaries. The main issue is the land, and the political mobilizations of the period 1945–60 show that not only did the commoners of Huaquirca perceive the state as a potential ally in the struggle to curb *gamonalismo*, but that they were actually able to make it work as such. Therefore, we may pardon the commoners of towns like Huaquirca for seeing in *faena* something more than their instituted subordination to district notables (Stein 1961: 96, 188–9), or their 'calculated exploitation' (Grondín 1978). For they have managed to turn *faena* labour into an affirmation of a different kind of property and a different kind of sovereignty than that resulting from the endless transgressions of the *gamonales*.

Furthermore, when we turn to the various projects realized through *faena* in Huaquirca, several conceptions of civil society are at work, not a monolithic or coherent scheme of domination. One can point to the schools and municipal buildings as collectively built edifices of notable power, but it was also in these schools that Spanish and literacy were first made available to commoners. These skills were quickly used to

confront *gamonalismo*, even if they also led to ambivalence over traditional commoner culture, and rejection of it in many cases (see Montoya 1982: 296). Running water and electricity are the services
installed by *faena* that seem most clearly oriented towards the notable
way of life and vision of progress. Both are integral parts of the notable
house compound, though the electricity seldom works. In Huachacayllo and Champine, several houses tend to share a common faucet, and
there are no streetlights beyond the main thoroughfares. Although
these services were installed and are maintained through the labour of
commoners, they cannot enjoy them because of the rates charged.
This is a common pattern in other Andean towns (see Grondín 1978:
119, 229–30). During my stay in Huaquirca, and for some years before,
construction of cement reservoirs and irrigation canals was the main
priority. Although there is good reason to be sceptical about the need
for these works,[26] what they do seem to reflect is an almost guilty
resolve to offer programs that will benefit commoners. Other tasks
undertaken by *faena* include the construction, improvement, and
maintenance of roads, paths, bridges, and fences. As with schools (see
Grondín 1978: 122), one could argue that the main effect of roads has
been to decapitalize the countryside, but surely this is not an inherent
feature of the roads, and might be changed by their future uses.

There is much evidence to indicate that the commoners of Huaquirca have managed to distinguish between those aspects of communal organization that serve their interests and those that do not. Prior
to the formation of the Peasant Community of Huaquirca in 1957,
there had been a long tradition of communal government based on a
Spanish model inherited from the colonial period (Arguedas 1968:
194). Its pillars were eight 'staff-holders' (*varayoq*, in reference to these
emblems of their authority), all commoners, who recruited labour for
the *faenas*, and enforced prevailing definitions of public order as a
kind of informal police. These eight functionaries were placed at the
disposal of notable authorities in the following proportions: five to the
governor, two to the mayor, and one to the justice of the peace. They
had to recruit labour for the agricultural tasks of the notable over-
lords, which were included in the working definition of *faena* at the
time.[27] The notable authorities were also notorious for their tours
through the alpine zone, in which they seized alpaca wool from each
estancia, and sometimes commandeered domestic servants, always
accompanied by their corresponding staff-holders (see also Montoya
1980: 258–62). In short, this system of communal authority was fully

implicated in *gamonalismo*, and there are graphic accounts of the frustration that some commoners felt in being accomplices to it (e.g., Arguedas 1968: 334). With the passage of the Law of Yanaconaje in 1947, which was designed to abolish unpaid labour, the commoners of Huaquirca found a pretext to discontinue the staff-holder system. This was a political triumph that can only be measured by the continuing existence of this system in areas where notables were not subject to pressure from below. Not surprisingly, older notables of Huaquirca still look back with nostalgia on the staff-holder as a symbol of the time when commoners 'still had respect.'

Yet not every traditional aspect of communal government was thrown out. One post that persisted was that of *kamayoq*, who as we have seen, guards the *laymi* sectors under cultivation from grazing cattle. Given the strategic importance of the land they guard, and the conflicts that the *kamayoqs* have had with 'abusive' notables over their animals, they clearly serve an important collective interest. Every commoner is obliged to serve as *kamayoq* for one agricultural season at some point in his life. Another post that has been retained is that of water judge on each of Huaquirca's seven irrigation canals. These officials are nominated from among each canal's users annually, when they gather for canal cleaning during the second half of August. In the early 1970s, the government agency SINAMOS attempted to abolish this system, and replace it with one in which users would pay money for irrigation water to provide wages for those who maintain the canals. This plan was vigorously and effectively resisted by the commoners of Huaquirca, who lacked the money to make such payments, and were unwilling to let control of the canals pass out of their hands. The experience of other areas suggests that they were wise to refuse this proposal (see Grondín 1978: 119; Montoya, Silveira, and Lindoso 1979: 77–80; Montoya 1980: 111). Thus, I join Montoya (1980: 263) in concluding that communal organization is partly about commoner self-determination, even if it also involves oppression and servitude (cf. Stein 1961: 233).

Education and Migration

In the early 1960s, the population of Huaquirca may have been as large as 1400, but since that time it has been declining at a rate of more than one per cent per year, and was reckoned at 832 in the 1981 census. This is typical of the entire Province of Antabamba, which has one of the highest rates of population decline in the southern Peruvian Andes. The main reason for this decline is the migration of people between the ages of fifteen and forty to the cities, most notably Cusco and Lima, to obtain education and work. Migration to urban centres is now an integral feature of Huaquirca's social life, one that affects every other aspect of local social organization.

There can be no doubt that migration to urban centres has stabilized the domestic economies described earlier in this chapter. All households require access to terraced valley land, which is still scarce, and was even more so during the middle decades of this century, when local population levels were at their highest. Tamayo (1947) describes much smaller parcels of land than currently exist, which suggests that pressure to subdivide land on inheritance has eased due to migration. Larger parcels of land have been consolidated through purchase and rental from migrants, acts that are now almost obligatory in the formation of any household in Huaquirca. In short, the developmental cycle of domestic groups in this town has become structurally dependent on population decline through migration.

Migrants from Huaquirca do not, as a rule, maintain extensive economic ties with their town of origin. Unlike the situation described for the Huancayo region by Smith (1989), where migrants and villagers form complex household coalitions to pursue diverse economic activities, Huaquirca is simply too far away from any opportunities for wage labour and marketing to make such strategies viable. Some households do receive occasional remittances from members working outside Huaquirca, and when migrants return to visit their families in Huaquirca, they seldom leave without taking a sack of produce with them. However, these transfers are too infrequent to have any real economic significance. Perhaps the only important exception to this generalization concerns the education of students in urban secondary schools and universities. Until the last few decades, only notable families sent their children out of Huaquirca to be educated, but now, many of the town's more prosperous commoners do as well. Parents typically finance their children's education by selling cattle, since this is the only local agrarian activity that can raise the money required. Those notable households that include schoolteachers also spend significant proportions of their salaried income on education. The result is a net drain of capital from the country to the city, since few of these educated children ever return to Huaquirca.

Migration from Huaquirca seldom results directly from dire poverty or dispossession, although the situation may have been different when the town's population peaked during the 1960s. Nowadays, the very poor cannot even afford a fare out of town on the back of a truck, and are much more likely to become servants to notables than they are to migrate. Rather, most migrants come from the ranks of more accommodated commoner and notable families. They typically have more education than the members of their families who remain behind in Huaquirca; often, this appears to have been part of a deliberate strategy whereby some children are selected to migrate and others to stay. For commoner families, schooling is an especially important part of this process, since it provides not only literacy but also basic proficiency in Spanish, both of which are crucial to the prospects of migrants. The massive migration of commoners to the cities of Peru is due as much to the general availability of primary education as it is to poverty.

In the 1940s, the Peruvian state expanded its primary education system into towns like Huaquirca, which had many consequences in addition to increased migration to the cities. Indeed, the first generation of commoners to be educated in Huaquirca did not migrate, but put their skills to work locally in the political mobilizations of 1945–60. Many commoners describe how education 'woke them up' to the abuses of Huaquirca's *gamonales*, and allowed them to do such things as read law books. There can be little doubt that educated leaders played an important role in all of the commoner struggles over land and community organization described earlier. Even today, migration can be something of a political act for commoners, since it is the only way they can escape their local status as 'Indians' and tributaries. In Lima, for example, provincial distinctions between notables and commoners count for little, and considerable upward mobility is possible for commoners whose speech does not betray them as *serranos* (highlanders). A case in point concerns two brothers born to a commoner family in Huaquirca. One gained an education and became a university professor in Lima, whereas the other stayed in Huaquirca and became a notorious drunkard. The first brother passes for 'white,' even among the notables of Huaquirca, whereas the second brother is often described as 'Indian.' However, such a transformation in status absolutely requires migration. One of Huaquirca's first schoolteachers was a man from the aristocratic Aiquipa family, who was in his eighties at the time this research was carried out. Although this remarkable man taught many of the town's notables and had a better education than most of their parents, he was never accepted as their social equal and few were prepared to recognize his contribution.

Notables in small Andean towns have always valued education highly, perhaps even more so during the earlier part of this century than they do now (cf. Arguedas 1968: 337; Montoya, Silveira, and Lindoso 1979: 40; Montoya 1980: 304). However, the possibility of a teaching career in the country has existed only since the expansion of the rural education system during the 1940s. The notables of Huaquirca are particularly strong believers in education, and proudly point to a deaf old man in their number who is the first university student ever to have been produced by the Province of Antabamba. Many others followed shortly thereafter, and Huaquirca produced enough doctors, lawyers, judges, colonels, and academics to fancy itself 'the intellectual capital of the Province of Antabamba.' Naturally, these people pursued their careers in the cities, and many lost interest in visiting the town where they were born. Even the deaf old university student insisted to me that 'Huaquirca is a garbage dump,' and leaving it became little short of an ideology among those who followed him into higher education. Those who returned to teach school, on the other hand, are sometimes regarded as failures.

Nonetheless, the demand for teaching posts in Huaquirca is extremely high, and it can take years to be transferred from another town. Some speculate that it is easier to get a post in the departmental capital of Abancay than it is in Huaquirca. In contrast to many other areas, eleven of the town's thirteen teachers were born locally; the other two married into notable families, had children, and are long-time residents. Of those notable adults under the age of forty at the time of my fieldwork in Huaquirca, eleven of sixteen were teachers, and every notable household of this generation included at least one teacher in its focal couple. The status of notable and occupation of teacher have all but converged (cf. Primov 1980: 153), and this is a powerful force for the expansion of education. With a maximum of 220 students divided among two elementary schools, a kindergarten, and thirteen teachers (for a student/teacher ratio of no more than 17:1), the process is already well advanced. As I left Huaquirca, negotiations for a secondary school seemed to have been successfully completed. None of the notables would consider sending their own children there, despite the considerable cost of maintaining and educating them in the city, but there was great interest in who would get the teaching posts.

Perhaps the most important reason that the only notables left in Huaquirca are all teachers is that this occupation allows them to take advantage of the significant holdings of land and livestock that they inherited from their *gamonal* parents, while also enjoying the benefits of a salary. Thus, the economic gap between notables and commoners has continued to widen, but with little visible effect,[28] since most of the money that the teachers earn goes towards educating their own children, which is often facilitated by purchasing a home in the city. Nonetheless, refinement of the inner sanctums of the notable house compound continues. My stay in Huaquirca coincided with that of an itinerant carpenter from Abancay, who had planned to stay in the area for only six months, but decided after sixteen months that he had to disappoint the still–escalating notable demand for more cultivated surroundings by leaving.

A teaching career provides notables with more than just the means to continue their pursuit of refinement: it also embodies in praxis the ideal of being a cultivated person. Previous generations of *gamonales* aspired to distinction, as seen not only in the homes they built and the products they consumed but also in their almost slavish veneration of formal education. Yet their pursuit of distinction through violation of that which is 'of the community' ultimately gave them only notoriety, and thus became self-defeating. Simply put, *gamonal* violence did not embody the ideal of refinement in the way that teaching now does. Thus, the sons and daughters of Huaquirca's *gamonales* have sought to distance themselves from their parents while still pursuing the same strategies of refinement and distinction, as schoolteachers. These people were among my best informants on the topic of *gamonalismo*, since they grew up with it, and repudiated it in a particularly intense form, which for many still involves left politics.

By the time of my fieldwork in Huaquirca, condemnation of the *gamonales* was universal and mandatory. In 1982, even the more conservative notables were outraged when the sons and nephews of an old *gamonal* publicly assaulted a wealthy commoner for allowing his dancing horse to make the old man stumble on a sidewalk in Ñapaña. Three of the offenders served sentences of a few days each in the Antabamba jail, which would have been unthinkable in the past. Although such violent acts of 'racial' domination are now considered to be in poor taste, this does not mean that group boundaries and identities are breaking down, but, on the contrary, that their maintenance has become less problematic. Even the exceptions prove the rule. Three young leftist notables would occasionally join forces on weekends to plough their various family fields cooperatively, without recruiting commoners as day labourers (*mink'ays*). One even claimed that in so doing, they practice *ayni* among themselves. Yet the irony of this statement is that even in flaunting the notables' taboo against cooperative manual labour, they still maintained separation from commoners and their *ayni* networks. Like it or not, the progressive young notables of Huaquirca are heirs to the property and 'race' of their *gamonal* parents.

3

Aesthetics and Politics in the Rituals of the Dry Season

From the previous chapter, we have seen that the material, social, and political organization of the town of Huaquirca is the outcome of confrontation and interaction between notables and commoners. Far from being the unproblematic material embodiment of a homogeneous social structure, the town of Huaquirca has been shaped by a struggle between two very different social groups. In this chapter, we shall begin to look at how their alternative social projects are publicly articulated through the town's ritual life. Yet only the first of the rituals to be considered here, the Celebrations of the Fatherland (*Fiestas Patrias*), straightforwardly asserts a particular vision of social order, that of the notable schoolteachers who organize it. The next ritual we shall consider, that of house rethatching, is practised only by commoners, and operates in a decidedly non-discursive, practical mode. This provides an immediate contrast with the more ideological orientation of the Celebrations of the Fatherland, and one of the goals of this chapter is to discuss what that difference is about. Finally, we will turn to the festivities of Santiago, the Virgin of the Assumption, and Santa Rosa, which surround the Celebrations of the Fatherland and house rethatching in the annual cycle. These *fiestas* are celebrated and sponsored by both notables and commoners, and this gives their aesthetic organization and thematic content something of a hybrid character. In summary, this chapter will continue to discuss the cultural differences between notables and commoners by focusing on several events that take place towards the end of the dry season, and in so doing, will initiate the discussion of the annual cycle that will occupy the remainder of this book.

Celebrations of the Fatherland

The *Fiestas Patrias* (or Celebrations of the Fatherland) of Peru take place on 28 and 29 July. In 1982, notable women and their servants swept pig and horse dung from the streets of Ñapaña early on the morning of 28 July. Rumour had it that there was a fine in effect for those allowing their animals to run loose on that day. Once the streets were swept, Peruvian flags were hung from most of the balconies and windows of the two-storey buildings of Ñapaña. The main event of the day began about 10:30 in the morning in the plaza, where most of the townspeople congregated to watch a spectacle put on by the local elementary schools, which had spent the previous month in earnest rehearsal. Commoners and less important notables took their seats on the long bank of steps leading down to the plaza from the church, whereas a row of wooden chairs was set up in front for the more illustrious notables, including the town's current political authorities. The event began with the student parade (*desfile escolar*): an extended session of marching in goose-step around the plaza to military music played roughly by some older students on drums and brass instruments. In 1982, 220 children took part in this performance, a number that would surpass even the most optimistic estimates of elementary school enrolment in the town. There were also six men from the adult literacy (*Educación Laboral Básica*) class who took part. The march was performed in brigade-like units formed according to school year and sex. All of the students made a particular effort to assemble as many elements of the (theoretically) obligatory grey school uniform as they could. Several teachers used long pointing sticks to regulate the internal organization of the brigades and to maintain the spacing between them. Yet the gravity of the spectacle was constantly undermined by roving dogs and toddlers wandering out of the audience to engage in enthusiastic, but meandering bouts of goose-stepping.

After about an hour, when the marching finally came to a halt, each brigade took turns performing folkloristic dances and nationalist dramas, and reciting patriotic speeches in a flowery Castilian that was most untypical of the children's everyday parlance. The dramas included a depiction of San Martín's exploits in the liberation of Peru from colonial rule, and several more static, allegorical pieces. In one such performance, the whitest of the notable girls in Huaquirca, dressed in the national colours of red and white, stood on a chair staring off into space and saying nothing while a series of very brown commoner boys came to swear allegiance and undying devotion to her, as a personification of the Fatherland. Occasionally, these performances were interrupted by bands of pigs chasing each other through the plaza and shrieking, which many of the assembled commoners found amusing, along with the flawed choreography and forgotten lines of the skits. The audience was generally more tolerant of the patriotic speeches and poetry recitals, a peculiar feature of which involved arm movements resembling the breast-stroke and the crawl that the children had obviously been taught to emphasize what they were saying, and to make it more expressive. A similar speech from a commoner man in the adult literacy program was met with boredom verging on hostility from the audience, who all but drowned him out with their chatter, despite pleas for silence from one schoolteacher. The morning ended with a long patriotic speech by one of the schoolteachers. It reviewed the military history of Independence; listed the so-called 'precursors' of the republican uprising, dwelling particularly on the Tupac Amaru revolt of 1780–1; and moved into the present with the conclusion that the republic has meant a certain freedom, but one that is constantly threatened by capitalism and imperialism. The speech ended with a reminder of the need to defend the nation's borders, citing the recent example of Argentina in the Falkland Islands. Immediately following the speech, several other notables came up to shake hands with and congratulate the speaker.

Next, the brigades regrouped for a final tour around the plaza, each being applauded as it passed by the spectators. By this point, a commoner from the adult literacy class had managed to get drunk, and aiming his goose-steps at the posterior of a classmate ahead of him all the while, he loudly proclaimed, as he passed by the seated notables, that the only reason he came out for the event was a bribe of cane alcohol that he had received from the instructor. This was met with uproarious laughter by the commoners on the steps, and many notables as well. In the afternoon, there were two soccer matches, one between the commoner neighbourhoods of Huachacayllo and Champine, and a second between the notables of Ñapaña and a selection drawn from the two commoner teams. As usual, Ñapaña won its game.

The *Fiestas Patrias* are of considerable interest for the way they build an image of the nation through a militarized presentation of the local school system. By treating the Fatherland as a school writ large, this ceremony creates several politically important rhetorical effects. First of all, the school is portrayed as the privileged, even unique, source from which the nation derives its order. Of course this portrayal must be qualified since it is not the everyday routine of the school that is displayed during the *Fiestas Patrias*, but a particularly militarized transformation of it. Thus, the nation is understood as a school only to the extent that the school is understood as an army, something that was particularly stressed under the Velasco regime (1968–75) according to one informant. In many ways, the partial fusion of school and army is appropriate, since historically these have been virtually the only institutions that have drawn commoners into the national life of Peru. The fact remains, however, that in rural towns like Huaquirca, it is the schools, and not the army, that are called upon to provide the appropriate image of the nation as a society in order during this celebration.

A major spin-off of this basic metaphorical representation of the nation as a school is the sense that education provides the fundamental medium of social relations within the Fatherland. It follows that the literate discourse of the notable schoolteacher is to be understood as an unmarked category, an expression of the national norm, rather than their local power as a class. No doubt the folkloristic dancing and soccer matches are supposed to be a mitigating concession to popular culture, but the fact is that both are learned in school, and have little or no place outside it. By implication, the alternative political discourses that commoners have developed (such as those explored in Chapter 7) are 'ethnically' marked, and do not contribute to the life of the nation. In extending the benefits of education to commoner children, however, the school also promises them true citizenship. Thus, the school represents something of a 'mission of civilization' in these Andean backwaters, a sentiment that several teachers confided to me during my research. In these ways, the *Fiestas Patrias* represent an aggressive declaration of notable hegemony, that they are the part that stands for the whole, and provides its terms of reference.

There is, of course, a certain sociological truth to these various thinly veiled proclamations. As Gramsci (1971) argued, every relation of rule is in part an educative relationship, and various modern authors suggest that education is an integral component of modern nationalism (e.g., Geertz 1973; Anderson 1983; Gellner 1983). There can be little doubt that education is a prerequisite for participation in what is generally recognized as the national life of Peru. This is probably why commoners feel compelled to attend the event in the numbers that they do, and suffer its implicitly belittling message. Above all else, the fact that commoner parents tolerate and even indulge the participation of their children in this event suggests that they take seriously the idea that schooling may determine their future opportunities.

However, none of these considerations change the fact that Peru is not a school writ large, and that the Celebrations of the Fatherland are not so much an accurate 'model of' Peruvian society as they are an ideological 'model for' it. In their laughter and irreverent remarks, adult commoners show an uncanny ability to deflate this spectacle and its implicit messages into farcical unreality. How far does this scepticism extend? Although it generally stops short of the children, even their mistakes and miscues were laughed at. It is from their own perspective as adults that commoners are least complicit in the image of the Fatherland depicted in this ceremony. To be sure, one commoner from the adult literacy program was co-opted into delivering a patriotic speech, but one can readily confirm the level of audience disenchantment by comparing the outright boredom and derision with which it was met to the delighted laughter that greeted his companion's confession that only a liberal bribe of alcohol had induced him to take part in the event. Scepticism was expressed even more directly to me when in the midst of the event, a young commoner gently suggested that I should not bother taking photographs because it simply wasn't worth the film. In summary, commoners show an ambivalence about the spectacle as a whole: on the one hand, they have little doubt that it is irrelevant to their own reality, but on the other, they cannot be sure that it does not have something important to offer to their children.

This atmosphere of pervasive doubt contributes directly to what is probably the single most important dynamic in the aesthetic organization of the celebration: purposive, explicit, and fully denotative 'representation' of an anti-colonial revolt that took place in the 1820s. By constructing a narrative of how Peru became a republic, one that starts with the litany of 'precursors' to independence and culminates in the exploits of Bolívar and San Martín, the discourse of the schoolteacher creates a nationalist teleology in which the modern state appears as an unproblematic outgrowth of the people and their past. What disappears in the process are all the thorny issues of 'race' and class that have given Peru a 'national question.' Instead the oratory of the schoolteacher takes the nation as an unquestionable given, and attempts to portray it in a sacralizing manner. We are dealing with a tradition of sacred narrative here, as proved by the popular outrage that greeted Bonilla and Spalding (1971), professional historians who argued that Peruvian independence was not achieved through a heroic people's struggle. Such a message can have no place in the triumphal genre of speech-making practised by students and teachers in this ritual.

Yet through their didactic and expository form, the Celebrations of the Fatherland tacitly admit that the meaning of the modern republic is uncertain. There is an interesting paradox here. As the ritual tries to concretize the meaning of the historical events in question by enacting them and placing them in a propositional framework, it increasingly comes to rely on the abstract predicates of 'nation,' 'independence,' and 'freedom.' However, these terms do not designate ready-made realities in people's lives, and have little power to clarify the events they are supposed to explain. It is ironic that the more the celebration approaches ideology, in the sense of trying to make explicit and systematic propositions, the more incoherent it becomes at the most basic representational level. Finally, the only thing this nationalist rhetoric can refer to with any certainty is the ritual experience it is embedded in. Instead of providing a model of an external national reality, the Celebrations of the Fatherland have little choice but to simulate the nation they refer to. This should come as no surprise if one accepts the idea that nations are imagined communities, which can be apprehended only in a symbolic form, through rituals such as this one (cf. Anderson 1983; Kertzer 1988). The fact remains, however, that this imagining takes place in a class-specific ritual form. The oratory deployed in the Celebrations of the Fatherland is a distinctive feature of the notables' cultural repertoire. To the extent that the representational aims of the ritual break down, this socially charged way of speaking emerges as the true medium and content of the Fatherland. This development, in turn, underwrites the notion that notables are the local representatives of something called 'the national culture,' into which commoners are integrated less completely or not at all.

Of course most of these observations apply to nationalist discourse in general, and not just that of Peru. However, the peculiarly pseudo-propositional nature of nationalist discourse becomes apparent when it is juxtaposed with the agrarian rites of the annual cycle performed by commoners. These agrarian rituals do not take place primarily in a verbal mode, let alone an ideological one. In fact, they do not appear to attempt any sort of representation at all, but merely provide an open-ended imagery. At first glance, nothing could contrast more with the discursive orientation of the Celebrations of the Fatherland. After all, these rituals are the artifacts of a peasantry, not a group of school-teachers. Yet these rituals situate their imagery in the midst of the other agrarian activities that compose the annual cycle, and in so doing, they allow it to 'reflect and refract' local practice in a way that is both concrete and subtle. Ironically, this non-discursive approach allows them to achieve a far greater level of referentiality than the short-circuited performances of the *Fiestas Patrias*. To see how this is so, let us now turn to the first agrarian rite of the annual cycle, that of house rethatching.

House Rethatching

In Huaquirca, there are about forty-five houses with thatched roofs. We have already seen that such roofs generally indicate poverty in the rural Andes. Since a thatched roof generally lasts at least ten years in Huaquirca, it is uncommon to see more than five rethatched during a given year, although this would have been different a few decades ago, when all of the houses of Huachacayllo and Champinè were said to have had thatched roofs (Centeno 1949: 5). The significance of house rethatching is not statistical, but arises instead from the particular per-spective on domestic life that it creates, one that is firmly grounded in the annual cycle of labour and ritual, and, therefore, reflects the life activity of commoners as a whole, not just the poorest and most 'tradi-tional' of their number who still live in thatched houses.

House rethatching takes place in Huaquirca from August to mid-September (cf. Isbell 1978: 168), which is after the harvest and before the sowing. This is an interstitial period between one agricultural year and the next, or more precisely a time when households must undergo a change away from the phase of private appropriation centred on the harvest, towards a period of collective production that begins with the sowing. The house itself is a crucial site in this transition. During the harvest, crops are brought in from the fields and stored in the attics of people's houses. If houses are generally associated with consumption, privacy, and exclusiveness (see Stein 1961: 70, 74-5, 79, 136), this is especially true of their roofs, which are the repository of the privately appropriated harvest. The rethatching of roofs both confirms and challenges this emphasis on domestic appropriation. Before the roof can be renewed as a container of domestic property, it must first be stripped bare by a large work party, the first to assemble since the end of the rainy season in March. Removal of the old straw roof dramatically prefigures how work parties will encroach upon and deplete the household's provisions during the growing season. Thus, the house rethatching straddles and expresses a seasonal transition from private appropriation to collective production in relations between households in the annual cycle (see Figure 9 for an overview of the annual cycle).

The first task in house rethatching is to cut coarse straw on the high slopes of the alpine zone above town. A week beforehand, the woman whose house is to be rethatched makes a batch of corn beer that will be ready for the main work party. At the same time, her husband visits between six and ten of his closer friends or affinal relatives, and solicits their help by offering a few swallows of cane alcohol and a handful of coca leaves. On the appointed day, these men assemble for breakfast at the house in question and then go up to the alpine zone, sickles in hand, where they advance up the hillside in rows, cutting coarse straw (*ichu*). The sponsor of the work party will have already prepared a small cloth bundle containing a quarter-litre bottle of cane alcohol, some toasted maize kernels, and cheese, which he will discreetly hide somewhere in the path of the cutters as they advance up the hill. Whoever finds it stops work immediately and sits down to conspicuously enjoy the contents by himself; he is proclaimed the 'son-in-law' (Quechua *qatay*) of the house-owners for the duration of the rethatching.[1] On finishing this treat, the 'son-in-law' returns to town, leaving the other men to continue cutting hay until it is reckoned that they have enough to complete the job. Huge, bulky mounds of straw are lashed onto an assortment of pack animals that will transport it down to the village. So ends the first day.

On the second day, the actual thatching of the house begins. Early in the morning, a general invitation to come and work may be shouted from a strategically high location in the neighbourhood where the rethatching is to take place. Those who have already agreed to work that day will arrive at the house early in the morning for a hot meal. Many more people will participate on the second day, however, simply because the event takes place in town and may attract anyone with nothing better to do. The younger men start by removing the old thatch and making any necessary repairs to the rafters. Meanwhile, the women (who may comprise up to one-third of those present, as they do during an agricultural work party) twist coarse ropes from the piles of newly cut hay, a task in which they are aided by a few older men. These ropes are used to lash a matting of thin parallel boughs in place

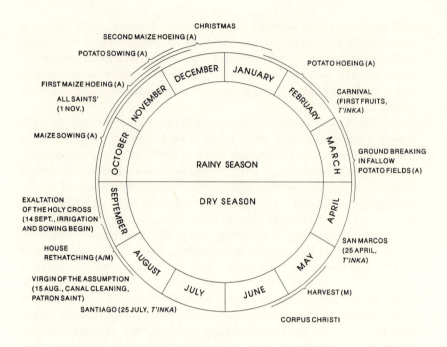

CHRISTMAS
SECOND MAIZE HOEING (A)
POTATO SOWING (A)

FIRST MAIZE HOEING (A)
ALL SAINTS'
(1 NOV.)

MAIZE SOWING (A)

EXALTATION
OF THE HOLY CROSS
(14 SEPT., IRRIGATION
AND SOWING BEGIN)

HOUSE
RETHATCHING (A/M)

VIRGIN OF THE ASSUMPTION
(15 AUG., CANAL CLEANING,
PATRON SAINT)

SANTIAGO (25 JULY, T'INKA)

POTATO HOEING (A)

CARNIVAL
(FIRST FRUITS,
T'INKA)

GROUND BREAKING
IN FALLOW
POTATO FIELDS (A)

SAN MARCOS
(25 APRIL,
T'INKA)

HARVEST (M)

CORPUS CHRISTI

DECEMBER JANUARY
NOVEMBER FEBRUARY
OCTOBER MARCH
SEPTEMBER APRIL
AUGUST MAY
JULY JUNE

RAINY SEASON

DRY SEASON

(A) = TASK PERFORMED BY *AYNI*
(M) = TASK PERFORMED BY *MINK'A*

Figure 9   Annual cycle of labour and ritual in Huaquirca

over the rafters of the roof, and at right angles to them. Onto this matting, men arrange and secure the thatch with additional rope. Two 'foremen' (Quechua *kamayoq*) are appointed to supervise the operation, one for each slope of the roof; this is a somewhat decorative detail, since everyone already knows what needs to be done, even when there are thirty or more people working. Corn beer (of the variety called *laqto*) is served in abundance every few hours by the woman of the sponsoring household and her close female friends and affinal relatives, who may also contribute corn beer to the cause. The man of the sponsoring household also distributes cane alcohol periodically. Food and drink are the only remuneration for those who work, which suggests that house rethatching involves the work-for-food relation of *mink'a* (cf. Stein 1961: 107, 109; Fonseca 1974: 99–104).[2] By mid-afternoon, the 'son-in-law' designated the day before has arrived with a full bottle of cane alcohol and a small wooden cross that he has made in the meantime, which will be put on the crest line of the roof when the rethatching is finished.[3]

By nightfall, whether or not the job is done, a serious drinking session will be in progress. At this point, those who have worked out of public-spiritedness begin to slip away, but those closer to the sponsoring household will stay to the end, sometimes passing out in the process. As the evening wears on, a few of the men present may make a figure of a fox out of the remaining hay and straw rope (see also Morote Best 1956a: 18). This is followed by a mock remarriage of each member of the sponsoring couple to someone of the opposite sex chosen impromptu from the company present. These 'remarriages' are performed with no small degree of farce by a man given the title of 'priest' (Spanish *cura*), who on at least one occasion was nominated for this role by virtue of being the drunkest man present. He may, I was told, even be outfitted with a makeshift habit. The drunken revelry in which all of this takes place may well continue into the next day.

This is how people rethatch roofs in Huaquirca. Although there is a good deal of banter, chat, and laughter during the house rethatching, I heard only a few fragmentary comments about its ritual details, and this seems to be the closest anyone comes to discussing what it all might mean. When I tried to engage commoners in this sort of discussion, both during and after the event, their initial (and often final) response was to classify the house rethatching as a '*costumbre*' (custom, ritual). Following Bourdieu (1977), one might conclude that this reluctance to verbalize and interpret is a defining feature of practice. I assume, however, that some symbolic processes are at work here, and will make an interpretive effort to find out what they are, while trying to respect their resolutely implicit nature, which Bourdieu (1977) rightly emphasizes. The alternative is to assume that there are no cultural meanings to be discovered, a null hypothesis that runs the grave risk of mistaking our own ignorance for the 'practical sense' of Andean people, and makes it impossible to explain why they should continue to practice and enjoy this *costumbre*.

The surest indication that house rethatching is not an unreflective instrumental act is that it incorporates so many 'alerting' details, such as the 'son-in-law,' the cross, the fox, and the mock remarriage. Each of these ritual details refers beyond the immediacy of house rethatching to pre-established notions that can help us locate this act in the broader context of Andean culture.

Let us begin with the figure of the 'son-in-law.' Many ethnographers have noted the categorical nature of Quechua affinal terminology (see Quispe 1969: 14; Fonseca 1974: 99; Ossio 1980: 212, 250), and have observed that the term 'son-in-law' may designate a simple 'outsider' to the kin group of the speaker as much as it does an actual affine (cf. Earls 1970: 74; Mayer 1977: 74; Isbell 1978: 174). Thus, the application of 'son-in-law' to the man who finds the bundle of food and alcohol while cutting hay is only one of the many cases in which the term's reference to marriage is suspended. Here, it might be even better to say that the packet of consumables substitutes for the marriageable daughter as the link in the relationship. What is the significance of defining the 'son-in-law' in this figurative manner? To answer this question, let us examine two figures that are closely related to the 'son-in-law' and are constructed along similar lines: the mountain spirit and the day-labourer (*mink'ay*).

The Andean alpine zone, even more than the agricultural valleys below it, is dominated by mountain peaks, each with its corresponding spirit. These mountain spirits generally take the human form of rich and powerful notables, and are sacrificially 'fed' or 'paid' in the *t'inka* rites that come to the fore during the phase of the year dedicated to private appropriation and consumption (see Figure 9 and Chapter 7). These sacrificial offerings are often spoken of as dishes or servings of food (*platos*). When a mountain spirit wants to initiate a more intensive and prosperous relationship with a household, however, his demands can no longer be confined to food, and focus on the ritualist's daughter as a sexual partner (see Gose 1986: 302–3). In these cases, the mountain spirit virtually becomes a 'son-in-law,' whereas in the house rethatching, the 'son-in-law' is recruited through a packet of consumables that, like the 'servings' for the mountain spirits, constitutes a low-level substitute for a marriageable daughter. Thus, wife-taker and mountain spirit are each seen in terms of the other to a significant extent (see also Harris 1982: 65).

One reason this conceptual merging occurs is that both the mountain spirit and the 'son-in-law' receive offerings that legitimate private appropriation by individual households during the growing season. By redistributing its property through sacrifice and marriage, a household proves that private appropriation is compatible with a larger good, which these figures come to represent. I will show in Chapter 7 how sacrifices to the mountain spirits legitimate the conversion of crops into the private property of individual households during the dry season. However, it is also noteworthy that in many parts of the Andes, people try to coordinate marriage with the dry season, before or during the time of house rethatching.[4] At a time when agricultural cooperation lies dormant, and the emphasis has been on property for months, marriage is a uniquely appropriate form of interhousehold sharing. We have already seen that the parents of both the bride and the groom usually contribute property to the formation of a new household, which lives neolocally. The house rethatching, on the other hand, depicts marriage differently, as the surrender of a 'daughter,' by a sponsoring household, to a 'son-in-law' recruited from among those who work for it. By representing marriage as the loss of a daughter in a virilocal system based on the 'exchange' of women, the rite suggests that the sponsors are making a sacrifice to a wife-taker of higher rank at precisely the moment when they are actually benefiting from the labour of others in what appear to be relations of *mink'a*.

Indeed, the packet of food and alcohol that defines the 'son-in-law' would also be apt remuneration for a day's work in the fields under *mink'a*, where feeding signifies the superiority of patron to worker (cf. Fonseca 1974: 103–4). This contrasts with *ayni*, the more egalitarian, generalized exchange of working days and food among households that takes place during the growing season, and suggests that the 'son-in-law' works for his 'parents-in-law' as a propertyless, inmarrying peon: a pattern typical of uxorilocal marriage in the Andes.[5] My own experience working the fields in Huaquirca taught me much about the 'son-in-law' as day-labourer (*mink'ay*). Because I did not have any land of my own and, therefore, could not work for others on the truly reciprocal basis of *ayni*, the most plausible motive that people could construct for my presence in the fields was that I was looking for a woman. Accordingly, I began to be treated with the diminished respect befitting an inmarrying man. The teasing began on a cautious, almost experimental note, but soon became institutionalized, and, significantly, people began to refer to me as 'the town's son-in-law' ('*el qatay del pueblo*'). Only well into my fieldwork did I discover, in an entirely separate context, that young men actually do show up uninvited to work in the fields of the parents of a woman they may be interested in. Apparently, this is how my actions were being interpreted, and not always in jest. In several work parties I, alone among all the participants, was offered a packet of consumables identical to that which defines the 'son-in-law' of the house rethatching. This extra food and drink was probably intended to fend off any claims I might have been about to make on people's daughters. In so doing, however, it emphatically reiterated that my labour was being remunerated with food, according to the hierarchical formula of *mink'a*.[6]

In sum, there is considerable ambiguity about the way the 'son-in-law' is defined by this package of consumables: in relation to his 'parents-in-law,' it is uncertain whether he stands as a superordinate wife-taker or as a subordinate labourer. This uncertainty is mainly the result of the metaphorical operation by which the package of consumables is portrayed as a daughter, a situation that allows the sponsors to have the best of both worlds. On the one hand, the 'marriage' in question allows them to renew and legitimate their property; on the other hand, they do not really give a daughter and dowry away, only a *mink'a* payment. Yet the same ambiguity is present outside this ritual in everyday life, where sons-in-law act both as legitimating co-proprietors and as labourers who can be endlessly exploited through *mink'a*. Interestingly enough, this status ambiguity is contained entirely within the proprietorial social values appropriate to the dry season: the 'son-in-law' may be either inferior or superior, but not an equal on the model of an *ayni* partner during the growing season. When we turn to the sequential development of the 'son-in-law' in this rite, however, his association with the proprietorial concerns of the dry season becomes less absolute.

Before he emerges as such by finding the package of consumables, the 'son-in-law' is just another friend of the sponsors, helping them in a work party of the sort that routinely takes place among *ayni* partners during the growing season. In abandoning cooperative work for a form of consumption that is equated with conjugality, the 'son-in-law' effectively recapitulates the movement of the annual cycle from Carnival through the harvest. As in real life, the matrimonial claim of the 'son-in-law' is very much an outgrowth of a previous period of work in the fields. The 'conjugal' encounter that defines the 'son-in-law' occurs in the place of work in the alpine zone: only on the following day does he appear at their house in town. Commoners of valley towns like Huaquirca generally see the fields and the alpine zone as places appropriate for uncommitted sexual encounters, whereas matrimonial relations take place in houses in town (see Isbell 1978: 59; Harris 1980: 78). Thus, the two different appearances of the 'son-in-law' in this rite correspond to two different modes or stages of conjugality. Furthermore, just as marriage is conceptually associated with the dry season, so these uncommitted encounters in the wild are associated with the growing season. These encounters were institutionalized in nocturnal dances for the unmarried called *qhashwas* or *aylas*, which used to be held in the fields following canal cleaning to mark the resumption of the growing season in Huaquirca and many parts of Ayacucho. Such dances apparently still take place in the Bolivian altiplano between All Souls' Day and Lent (Buechler and Buechler 1971: 76–7; Carter 1977: 181), that is, during the height of the growing season. It is very much in this undomesticated mode, appropriate to the growing season, that we first encounter the 'son-in-law,' and only when he appears in town on the second day has he really undergone the matrimonial transformation (itself partly seasonal) from wild outsider to tamed insider. Only then, moreover, is he able to legitimate the proprietorial concerns of his 'parents-in-law' by placing a cross on the crest line of their roof.

When I asked people why the cross was put on the crest line of the roof, the only detailed answer I got was that it was put there to ward off 'flying heads' (Spanish *cabezas voleadoras*, Quechua *uma phawa* or *qepqe*). These heads ostensibly detach themselves from the bodies of living people, especially at night, and fly through the air with their jaws clacking. This is an old and widespread image in the Andes (see Guaman Poma 1615: 282; Morote Best 1953), one that is often attributed to witchcraft. In Huaquirca, however, I was told that incest, particularly that between father and daughter, is what generates these phantasms (elsewhere incest between *compadres* is singled out, see Stein 1961: 134–5). Flying heads are said to beg for assistance, knowing that on death they will become *condenados*, souls that must spend an extended period of purgatory in this world, during which they will terrorize the living. The cross protects the domestic group from this most dreaded father/daughter form of incest and its consequences, much as does the 'son-in-law' who donates it. This suggests that the 'son-in-law's' main value to the sponsors is not as an exploitable labourer (*mink'ay*), but rather as someone who, by consuming the bundle of food and alcohol equated with their daughter, prevents the illicit, incestuous consumption of this same entity by the male sponsor. Indeed, the more voraciously the 'son-in-law' consumes on the first day, the more surely he can legitimate his 'parents-in-law' with a cross on the second day. But of course, the sponsors are not giving a daughter away in this rite at all, only a payment befitting a *mink'ay*. Thus, the blessing of the house through the cross donated by the 'son-in-law' turns out to be more apparent than real, and subject to further revision.

In Andean culture, crosses are also intimately associated with crops,[7] mainly because the festivities of the Exaltation (14 September) and the Finding (3 May) of the Holy Cross coincide with the sowing and the harvesting of maize. Crosses are also used to guard planted fields during the growing season. Typically, crosses are taken from the church and out to the fields on 14 September, particularly to fields in the alpine zone, and are brought back into town on 3 May, decorated with the produce they have been protecting, to be blessed in church. This is a kind of 'second-fruits' ceremony that supplements Carnival and immediately precedes the harvest, anticipating and connoting its abundance. Since the straw for the roof also follows this downward movement from the alpine zone into town, and is 'harvested' with sickles like the crops a few months before, it would seem that the cross underscores the metonymic connection between harvest and roof that results from the storage of the former in the latter. Indeed, people in many parts of the Andes make this connection explicit by hanging a basket or a cross decorated with produce and wildflowers from the ridgepole during house rethatching,[8] so that the cross signifies abundance beneath the roof.

These two aspects of the cross, as a sign of agricultural abundance and as a mitigating force against incest, are directly linked by the widespread Andean belief that incest causes crop failures in a community where it may occur (Stein 1961: 35; Burchard 1980: 600; Valderrama and Escalante 1980: 260), a notion that may even be extended to adultery (Flores 1973: 51). To ensure abundance, the cross must also prevent incest. Yet it was not always thus, since in Laymi myth, 'the time before the incest taboo was one of plenty, in which all their favourite food grew ready-prepared for them, and clothing was produced miraculously from the earth, a veritable golden age in which work was unnecessary' (Harris 1980: 79). The cross evidently represents a particular sort of abundance, that which is legitimate and has been obtained through work, and not that which is wild, spontaneous, or incestuous. As a result, the cross not only signifies the abundance and private appropriation of the harvest but also provides a safeguard against unacceptable excess in that direction, and so becomes a force for the resumption of the growing season, in which cooperative labour is given a Christian flavour by the overlap of relations of *ayni* and those of *compadrazgo*. Thus, in providing his 'parents-in-law' with a cross for the peak of their roof, the 'son-in-law' is also pushing them towards a phase of renewed collectivity centred around work on the crops, which are themselves signified by the cross. This is particularly so in the context of the rite, where there is an element of doubt over whether the 'son-in-law' and his cross really legitimate the sponsors as proprietors, a doubt that further underlines the necessity of agricultural cooperation.

The cross atop a thatched roof cannot help having an additional connotation. Directly above many Andean towns, including Huaquirca, there is a mountain known as the Cerro Calvario (Mount Calvary), on whose peak, appropriately enough, a cross is placed. Such crosses are often called *calvarios* (Isbell 1978: 146), and may be among the ones brought down for blessing before the harvest. Crosses of wood or straw also adorn the summits on which other mountain spirits dwell and, in certain contexts, seem to represent them (see Quispe 1969: 89; Isbell 1978: 59, 138). There is, therefore, more than a passing similarity between houses and mountains, particularly during the dry season, when the bricks of mud and straw correspond to the bare fields strewn with chaff after the harvest, while both roof and summit are covered with dry yellow hay, and crowned with a cross. Indeed, the two share a reciprocal metaphorical structuring, whereby the house may be thought to have a spirit that requires sacrifices on the model of the mountain,[9] while the latter is seen as but the outer shell of an abode (more a palace or a *hacienda* than a house) in which the mountain spirit lives in luxury (see Arguedas 1956: 236; Earls 1969: 68; Isbell 1978: 59). Like houses, the mountain spirits come to the fore during the proprietorial phase of the year and are the beneficiaries of its most elaborate rites, the *t'inkas*, which are occasionally incorporated into the act of house rethatching (see Tschopik 1951: 192; Aranguren Paz 1975: 122).

These associations between house and mountain do not revolve solely around the proprietorial concerns of the dry season, however, for as we saw earlier, the cross that connects them guards against excessive and illegitimate appropriation of the sort signified by incest. It is no accident that the cross is provided by the 'son-in-law' during house rethatching, and at this point we may return to the link between this figure and the mountain spirit discussed previously. Despite the mountain spirits' incestuous tendencies (Earls 1969: 67), and their overwhelming association with power and private appropriation, they nonetheless have a 'Christian' side, and exert a pressure towards sharing through this connection with affines, one that legitimates property. Although both house and mountain are places where wealth accumulates during the dry season, this only sets the stage for the expenditures of the growing season, during which the house returns a goodly proportion of its reserves to the fields in the form of seed and corn beer, and the mountains empty themselves of the water built up through the libations (*t'inkas*) that people have offered them during the dry season, to make the crops grow.

Of all the images in the house rethatching, that of the fox seems least related to the act as a labour process, yet it is also the one that returns most surely to the materiality of the roof by being made from its leftover rope and hay. Because of this substantive connection, the fox deserves special consideration as a vehicle for understanding the roof itself, the object of the entire event. Above all else, Andean people see the fox as a creature of appetite and gluttony, a stereotype that is confirmed by its destructive attacks on domesticated animals and even planted fields (see Stein 1961: 33; Tomoeda 1982: 278). We might conclude that the image of the fox transfers these same qualities to the roof, as a repository of the privately appropriated harvest, and that the two share a common opposition to the productive order. Yet in a widespread Andean myth, the fox's proclivity for excessive consumption explains the origins of agriculture. One day, the fox managed to talk the condor into taking him to a celestial banquet, where his gluttony caused the condor, that paragon of good manners, to abandon him. Thanks to some small *papachiuchi* birds, the fox secured a rope to begin his descent to earth. But in the process he insulted some passing parrots, who cut the rope above him. So the fox fell to earth and burst 'like a rotten orange,' but all manner of crops arose out of the ground from the celestial nectars he had consumed (see Tomoeda 1982: 277–8). This mythical origin of cultivated plants is underlined in how their spirit (*sawasiray*) and their empirical wild prototypes often take the prefix *atoq*, which means 'fox' in Quechua (see Valderrama and Escalante 1978: 132; Tomoeda 1982: 291). Thus, although domesticated plants appear to be derived from the fox, he remains a wild outsider to agricultural production, and can only be incorporated into it by dying.

Even in the annual initiation of agricultural production, as opposed to its mythical origins, the conduct of the fox and the nature of his gastric contents are of no small importance. Some Andean people believe that the quality of the rainy season, and the overall success of the agricultural year, can be foretold by the strength of the fox's cry during the months of October and November (Zuidema 1983: 49). Others believe that if the fox defecates potato skins or goes uphill during the sowing, the alpine zone will have a particularly abundant harvest, but if he defecates maize husks or goes downhill during the sowing, the valley will enjoy agricultural bounty (Platt 1986: 233). In a sense, the presence of a fox in house rethatching rites, which come immediately before the resumption of sowing in the annual cycle, reenacts this mythical origin of the crops on an annual basis. In both cases, gluttonous concentration and consumption of the crops must give way to a productive dispersal marked by death (see Tomoeda 1982: 282, 294–5): in myth, the bursting of the fox on his return to earth, and in the annual cycle, the return of the seed concentrated in the rooftop back into the ground during a growing season dominated by death imagery (see Chapters 4 and 5; Harris 1982). Although in the house rethatching proper it is not the seed but the sponsoring couple who are 'dispersed' in mock remarriage to other people, there may be a veiled reference to death here, since Andean views of the afterlife often specify that on death, people remarry to someone who was not their spouse in life (see Valderrama and Escalante 1980: 262). This reformation of the conjugal bond makes the imagery of death (and the wild) particularly appropriate to *ayni*'s generalized exchange of gender-specific labours across household boundaries.

However, it is more than just contiguity in the annual cycle that links house rethatching and sowing, since both are concerned with the theme of 'domestication.' Both the house rethatching and the mythical origins of agriculture involve ascent, an interlude of anti-social consumption (by 'son-in-law' and fox), and a descent that leads to a socialization and incorporation of the wild (into domestic space and agricultural production). Although 'son-in-law' and fox appear to be moving on a common trajectory, the meanings of high and low turn out to be opposed in each case. The gluttonous consumption of the 'son-in-law' in the alpine zone constitutes a departure from collective production, whereas that of the fox represents a departure from the polite consumption of the condor (or perhaps the mountain spirit in that guise). Similarly, the arrival of the 'son-in-law' in town legitimates the property of his 'parents-in-law,' whereas the descent of the fox initiates agricultural production. The seasonal associations of up and down are opposed in these two cases. The meaning of domestication also differs: the 'son-in-law' represents a feral productive force that must be tamed by marriage, whereas the fox represents a wild consumer who must be introduced into the productive order. Thus, it seems that 'son-in-law' and fox represent opposing facets of the same process, namely the transition into the growing season. If this is so, the fox would express the position of the 'parents-in-law'[10] or sponsors of the house rethatching, those unruly and exploitative proprietors/consumers who, as we shall see, also resist unto death their incorporation into the productive order.

The construction of the straw fox precipitates the final image of affinity in this rite: the mock remarriages of the sponsoring couple by the drunken 'priest.' The satirical flavour of this performance is best appreciated against the background expectations created by the very name of house rethatching: *wasichakuy*. On strictly analytical grounds, *wasichakuy* should translate as 'house-making.' In practice, however, it denotes not only house rethatching, but also the founding of a new household in marriage (see Cusihuamán 1976). There is thus a sense in which rethatching a roof has connotations of marriage, and the imagery of the rite plays with the expectation that the two acts should somehow coincide. Far from being a sincere attempt to enact both meanings of *wasichakuy*, however, this performance exploits the dark side of what it would mean if the two actually were to correspond.

By the time the mock remarriage takes place, only close friends who share and cooperate extensively with the sponsoring couple are likely to be present. The act seems to flirt with the actual sharing of spouses that takes place in parts of the Andes where *ayni* is not institutionalized during the growing season (see Bolton 1974a: 162). With the practice of *ayni* at such a low ebb during the dry season, it is understandable that there should be a playful acknowledgment that one domestic group should not renew its house (as an emblem of its property hold-ing in general) through the labour of others without undergoing a fig-urative dissolution, much like that of the fox in its fall to earth. In this sense, house rethatching anticipates the growing season, and under-lines its necessity with a gesture towards the more radical form of shar-ing that will be required if the focus of activity cannot be shifted from house to fields. Rather than facilitate a transition into the collective production of the growing season, however, the mock remarriages are more a way of avoiding it, and staying within the conjugal framework of private appropriation. Unlike the *qhashwa* dances that used to take place at this time of the year, these mock remarriages do not displace conjugality from house to fields, nor do they transform it into a pro-ductive force of the wild. They are simply a figurative transgression.

Even in areas where spouse-sharing actually does take place, the par-ticipants are looked upon as wild and unruly (Bolton 1974a: 166–7), and we have already seen that in some places, adultery is thought to have the same disastrous consequences for agriculture as incest (Flores 1973: 51). In a sense, the mock remarriage could be seen as a gesture towards incest, since those present at this stage are likely to share bonds of *compadrazgo* as an outgrowth of their close cooperation. Sex between *compadres* is considered highly incestuous, and in some areas it is even said to produce the same results as father/daughter incest: 'flying heads' (Stein 1961: 126, 134–5). In these places, it is not the 'son-in-law' but the *compadres* who bring the cross for the roof (Stein 1961: 126; Aranguren Paz 1975: 122). Since the cry of the fox has been said to announce the arrival of 'flying heads' (Guaman Poma 1615: 282), the materialization of this animal just before the mock remarriages might also suggest their incestuousness.

As the final image of this rite, the mock remarriage leaves us with a profoundly unresolved situation. Like virtually everything else about the house rethatching, it affirms the necessity of community interven-tion in the renewal and legitimation of individual households and their property. Yet it also displays an acute scepticism about marriage as a solution to this problem, largely by reducing it to a figurative oper-ation. In real life, marriage is virtually the only form of sharing that is appropriate during the dry season. Marriage is also one of the few strands of continuity between the growing season and the dry season, since short-term exchanges of labour can underwrite a longer term claim to a spouse (and land) within the community. Thus, marriage can attenuate the contradiction between domestic appropriation and collective production, and becomes an obvious mediation between these otherwise irreconcilable regimes of social action. However, this rite displays a single-minded dedication to undermining just this aspect of marriage, by exaggerating its defects. The 'marriage' that creates the figure of the 'son-in-law' is nothing more than a cynical, exploitative joke by the sponsors, whereas the mock remarriage at the end of the rite suggests incest among people who really should be behaving as *compadres*. As a result, the contradictions of the annual cycle are underlined precisely at a point where they might have been most convincingly resolved.

Through the inadequacy of these hypothetical marriages, we catch a negative glimpse of what proper communal regulation of domestic life ought to consist of. It should uphold relations of *compadrazgo* instead of subverting them, and subordinate an individual carnal union to a broader notion of spiritual community. In the Andes, this notion of community is particularly bound up with the practice of *ayni*, which comes to the fore in the growing season, immediately after the house rethatching. *Ayni* shifts people's concerns away from marriage and towards agriculture, and the spatial focus of their lives away from the house and into the fields. Although the house rethatching foreshadows the growing season by drawing people together in large work parties, it fails to relocate them in the fields; thus it is inconclusive as a seasonal transition.

In summary, the thatched house, like the annual cycle of labour and ritual in which its maintenance is situated, exists in a state of permanent contradiction. It is only by bringing in straw from the wild *puna*, through a process marked by the scarcely controllable disruptiveness of affinity, that a contained domestic space can be created. Abundance requires this influx of the wild and the avoidance of incest, yet abundance and the wild are themselves incestuous in nature. Thus, the thatched roof is like the crops in that it is the object of cooperative action, and like the adobe walls of the house below it, in that it is obstinately private and resists renewal. Specific instances of contradiction within this rite could be further enumerated, but they all seem to revolve around the more basic conflict between appropriation and sharing.

The same does not hold true for houses with more permanent roofs of tile or tin, especially those in the fortress-like house compounds of the notables, whose strict class endogamy and refusal to share their labour with commoners is reflected in these materials. Of course, most

commoners now live under tile or tin roofs, and still manage to intermarry and share their labour with those who live in thatched houses,
so the significance of the materials cannot be pushed too far in this
regard. Furthermore, I was told that many ritual details of house
rethatching may be adapted to the installation of a tile roof, although I
never saw this happen. Still, the relative permanence of tile and tin
roofs removes the house and its maintenance even further from the
annual cycle and its tension between periods of collective production
and private appropriation. The result is that the house aligns almost
exclusively with proprietorial concerns, a development that corresponds to the notions of 'progress' that have led so many people in
Huaquirca to reject the life of a commoner and migrate to the coast.
In other words, roofs are not just indicators of relative wealth and status, but they also represent different views of how domestic life should
be regulated by the broader community.

By now it should be clear that the house rethatching allows, and
even demands, a different sort of symbolic analysis than was possible
with the Celebrations of the Fatherland. It is true that both rituals
have to be understood pragmatically, for what their performance
could possibly mean to those who enact and witness them. Still, an
important difference emerges because the imagery of the house
rethatching, which at first glance seems much more obscure than that
of the *Fiestas Patrias*, actually addresses many practical concerns for
commoners, and does not involve a massive breach between ritual and
everyday life as does the national celebration. The house rethatching
is a practical task that has a definite place in a seasonal round of other
practical tasks. Its meaning depends on this structured context, which
participants make little or no attempt to transcend or supplement
through articulate speech. Although the act generates an imagery that
refers beyond itself, it does so more by actions than words. Because the
house rethatching is a labour process and a ritual, it can signify in a
grounded manner, and does not need to invoke elaborately verbalized
connections for those that are not objectified in the performance
itself. In the process, the house rethatching draws on a culture history
that is far more developed and consolidated than the historical discourse of Peruvian nationalism, and makes its presence felt through
symbolic connections that pervade everyday life: something that no
recitation of the exploits of 'great men' can accomplish. In short,
unlike the Celebrations of the Fatherland, the house rethatching does
not have to take place in an ideological mode.

The difference between these two performances suggests that 'ritual' does not have an essential or homogeneous character that is autonomous from the social position of those who deploy it. Rather, we have two different ritual discourses grounded in two different class positions and sensibilities. The rituals that surround house rethatching in the annual cycle have a hybrid form: both notables and commoners sponsor and participate in them, but neither monopolizes them or fully imposes their distinctive sensibilities upon them. Thus, these events represent an important aesthetic 'grey zone' in which certain kinds of dispute, negotiation, and compromise can take place.

Santiago

The first of these 'hybrid' events is the observance of Santiago on 25 July. In 1982, it consisted of an afternoon of horse-races and sprinting matches across the length of the plaza, and much milling about while drinking cane alcohol. The sponsor of Santiago bought twenty bottles of cane alcohol in a shop the day before, and also provided a small amount of corn beer. This alcohol was not enough to satiate those present, many of whom brought their own bottles to augment what was provided for them. Unlike every other public celebration I saw in Huaquirca, this event has only one sponsor (*carguyoq*) and not two, or at least this was the case in 1982. His activity consisted mainly of distributing the cane alcohol among the various informal clusters of people drinking in different areas, pouring each person a swallow as he moved from group to group. Commoner women sat around large vessels of corn beer, well to one side of the starting line for the races. Commoner men quickly got drunk in a shop by the starting line, where they were joined by some younger notables who wanted the races to start fairly, and to talk horses with any commoners who were interested. The older notables gathered at the opposite end of the plaza by the finish line, not drinking quite as much. By around 5:00 in the afternoon, the cold, people's empty pockets, and drunkenness began to take their toll, and the event broke up. The event was not so different from the days that many commoners spend sitting around in the yard and drinking at this time of the year, when there is no agricultural work to be done. Perhaps the main difference between Santiago and one of these more informal drinking sessions is the larger number of people involved, the races, and the availability of free alcohol.

In the Antabamba Valley, Santiago also marks the beginning of the third and final round of *t'inkas*, rites whose main purpose is to ensure the well-being and fertility of livestock. Whereas Santiago is a public event that takes place in the plaza, the *t'inkas* bring together an ego-centric network of friends and relatives on the grazing land of a household, as does the house rethatching in town. The *t'inkas* of Carnival and San Marcos take place in the grazing lands of the *puna*, but those of Santiago occur on the agricultural terraces below town, where the animals graze at this time of the year. The location of the *t'inkas* of Santiago, together with the fact that they may continue to be performed well into the second week of August, makes them something of a prelude to the growing season. Further discussion of these most complex rites will be postponed until Chapter 7, however, since in many ways they represent the culmination of the entire annual cycle.

The Virgin of the Assumption

The Virgin of the Assumption (15 August) is Huaquirca's patron saint, and was, until the 1970s, given the most extravagant celebration held in Huaquirca at any time of the year, complete with five consecutive days of bullfighting. It has recently declined into a more moderate affair, with most of the celebrations confined to 15 August. On this day, there is a mass, followed by a procession of an image of the Virgin, and a smaller but comparable image that is said to represent her sister (much to the horror of the visiting priest from Antabamba). There is no longer any bullfighting associated with this event, but on the afternoon of 15 August, teams from each of Huaquirca's three neighbourhoods stage a soccer tournament in the plaza. The main festivities take place at the homes of the two principal sponsors (*carguyoq*, or more precisely, *alferados*) of the event, who provide a banquet on the evening of 15 August, and up to a week of drinking and dancing to the music of hired violinists and harpists.

There are several minor sponsorships connected to the event, which involve the preparation of 'altars.' These serve as stopping points in the procession of the saintly images around the plaza, and dispensation points for corn beer and cane alcohol provided by the sponsor. These 'altars' consist of a wooden table backed by a massive two-dimensional facade, five metres long and five metres high, made of a lashed wood and wicker frame draped with long bolts of colourful silk and velvet, which is, in turn, pierced by myriads of imitation peacock feathers. In 1982, there were six 'altars' of this sort, and appropriately their sponsors were called *altareros*. These sponsors were all poor commoners, who lacked the means to take on a more costly *cargo*. In the recent past, the Virgin of the Assumption had two additional sponsorships: *terceros* provided a day of bullfighting each and *capitanes* provided the military bands of cornets, fifes, and drums that played day and night (see Centeno 1949: 10). These aspects of the celebration disappeared in the early 1970s, or better, were transferred to the celebrations of Santa Rosa (30 August). As the festivities of the Virgin have become more simplified, competition between the two major sponsors or *alferados* has become their most noteworthy feature.

Each sponsoring household tries to attract more people to their home than their rival, provide better musicians, more drink, a better banquet (the ideal here being the *banquete de las doce potajes*, or banquet of the twelve courses), and make their celebration last longer. In 1982, the event had both a commoner and a notable *alferado*, which further emphasized the antagonistic nature of this competition. However, the commoner sponsor managed to 'win' in the celebration of the Virgin because his opposite number had to cut the festivities short to resume teaching school in a neighbouring town. The cost of sponsoring such an event is very high, and it is customary for an *alferado* to solicit contributions from godchildren, affines, and kin. These contributions may be in money, kind, or services, and are duly recorded in a notebook to commemorate the occasion. Even the poorest commoner godchildren of a sponsor will be expected to contribute something, even if it is only firewood. This donation of firewood is called *llant'akuy*. It figures conspicuously in preparations for this event, but is difficult to explain except as a gesture of solidarity with the sponsor, since only a small amount of the wood is actually used for cooking and the rest accumulates in great stacks around the yard of the sponsor, adding to the general impression of abundance. During the festivities, guests may make donations of money or alcohol as a matter of politeness and loyalty: these too will be scrupulously recorded in the sponsors' notebook. Sometimes these contributions are represented as *ayni* that will eventually have to be repaid. A sponsor who wishes to display monetary donations ostentatiously may slip bills into the band of his or her hat and parade about among the assembled guests, or even out into the streets of the town.

It is difficult to say when the festivities of the Virgin come to a halt. In 1982, drinking and dancing continued at the home of the commoner sponsor through the afternoon of 22 August, although every day fewer people attended. By the end, the event was scarcely distinguishable from the more intimate drinking sessions that commoners regularly take part in during the dry season.

Santa Rosa

The celebration of Santa Rosa (30 August) is not a long-standing tradition in Huaquirca, but was initiated by a group of young notables during the early 1970s. In almost every detail, these festivities are modelled on those of the Virgin of the Assumption. Santa Rosa has two principal sponsors (*alferados*), who draw on a personal network of carnal and spiritual kin to provide a mass and procession, banquets, musicians, and up to a week of drinking. It also has several *altareros*, who provide exactly the same services as their counterparts during the celebrations of the Virgin of the Assumption. Even the inter-neighbourhood soccer tournament was repeated on 30 August, with the same outcome (a Ñapaña victory).

It is not clear how and why people began to observe Santa Rosa in Huaquirca. One informant suggested that the group of notables responsible had trouble gaining access to the principal sponsorships of the Virgin of the Assumption, and decided to stage an alternative event instead of trying to compete directly. This would explain why these events are nearly identical in their content. The irony is, however, that the festivities of Santa Rosa quickly came to upstage those of the Virgin of the Assumption. Santa Rosa now includes the bullfighting and military bands of cornets, fifes, and drums that were, until recently, a central part of the celebrations of the Virgin.[11] Of the two events, Santa Rosa had arguably become the more 'traditional,' even though it was barely a decade old. The original group of notables still controlled one of its two main sponsorships, but the other had fallen into the hands of a commoner. Santa Rosa had become integrated into the ritual life of the town as a whole, and its *cargos* were sought by all.

However, it would be wrong to treat the celebrations of Santa Rosa as an exact replica of the traditional festivities of the Virgin of the Assumption. During Santa Rosa, the two *alferados* provide a day of bullfighting and a military band each, whereas these duties used to fall to separate sponsors during the Virgin of the Assumption: *terceros* provided the bullfighting and *capitanes* provided the military bands (see Centeno 1949: 10). Thus, there has been a consolidation around the two major sponsors of what were once distinct ceremonial obligations. Most people with whom I discussed the matter attributed this transformation to the fact that fewer people have the resources to participate in the system of sponsorships. As the *alferados* assume duties that previously fell to other people, their costs also increase, although most people agree that the banquets they serve rarely match the standard of days gone by. This means that fewer people are willing to attempt these *cargos* for fear of failing to meet their obligations, as happened to an *alferado* (a commoner) in 1982. Only the most prosperous commoners can hope to hold their own at this level, so it is little wonder that most of the ritual emphasis in commoner life lies not on the *cargo* system, but on work in the fields. The difficulty of successfully passing one of these consolidated sponsorships only accentuates competition between *alferados*, which is an even more central dynamic in Santa Rosa than it is in the Virgin of the Assumption.

The festivities of the Virgin contrast with those of Santa Rosa in that the former is the patron saint of Huaquirca, whereas the latter is identified with Lima, both liturgically and in the popular mind. Notables, in particular, feel that the celebration of Santa Rosa is more cosmopolitan than that of the Virgin, though their content is otherwise identical. This feeling is confirmed by the way many of their relatives who have migrated to Lima return to Huaquirca for a visit during Santa Rosa. Throughout Ñapaña, there are many private banquets in honour of their return, many of which rival in sumptuousness those put on by the *alferados*. Taken together, the festivities of the Virgin and Santa Rosa establish an interaction between the local and the national that is typical of the domain of 'folklore' in modern nation-states. Certain elements that signify 'local colour' (e.g., bullfighting and religious processions) are subsumed under a generic pattern of festivity that is essentially secular, and abstracted from any specific contextual relation to everyday life.

In 1982, the celebration of Santa Rosa was already under way by the night of 27 August, with military bands playing throughout town all night, and much public drinking. After peaking on 30 August and 1 September, the festivities came to an end on 3 September, a week after they had started. The following day, a town council took place to transfer the sponsorships of the Virgin and Santa Rosa for the coming year, and to appoint guardians for the potato fields.[12] This is perhaps the only agrarian concern that is directly linked to these festivities.

Canal Cleaning

The first concrete step toward initiating the growing season is the community labour draft for cleaning irrigation ditches, called the *yarqa faena*. This involves four days' work, which take place between the celebrations of the Virgin of the Assumption on 15 August, and Santa Rosa on 30 August. In 1982, the irrigation ditch cleaning began on 23 August, a day after the festivities of the Virgin had finally ended, and finished on 26 August, a day before the festivities of Santa Rosa began. Despite such close association with these two events, the irrigation ditch cleaning finds little recognition in them, and is scarcely more than an interruption in this protracted period of consumption, drunkenness, and diversion.

Huaquirca has seven irrigation canals (see Figure 10). In 1982, work began on the highest of the canals, Huaylla-Huaylla: approximately half of the commoners cleaned the canal, while the other half excavated a reservoir to be filled by this same canal, as a state-sponsored public works project. On the second day, everyone cleaned Totora canal, which at seven kilometres in length is the town's longest canal, and the only one that all commoners, and not just those who own parcels irrigated by it, are obliged to maintain. People say that Totora canal 'is for the whole town,' probably because it passes through town along the division between the neighbourhoods of Ñapaña and Huachacayllo, and also because this is where people went to haul drinking water and to wash clothes in the days before running water. On the third day of the *yarqa faena*, those owning land irrigated by the Wañaqota and Chuqchuka canals went to clean them, as did those owning land serviced by the Pomache, Santo Domingo, and Taype Larqo canals on the fourth day. Those who did not work on the reservoir connected to the Huaylla-Huaylla canal on the first day were obliged to do so during any of the following days on which they were not cleaning a canal. After the four days' work on the irrigation system, there was a fifth day of work on the roads to smooth them for people arriving by truck for the festivities of Santa Rosa. In this way, work on the canals mixes with other kinds of labour tribute, and does not form a special category of its own.

The cleaning of the canals is noteworthy for the calculated egalitarianism displayed in the organization of the work process. Men arrive with picks and shovels at the source of the canal, and spread themselves in a long line down the canal, leading away from the source.

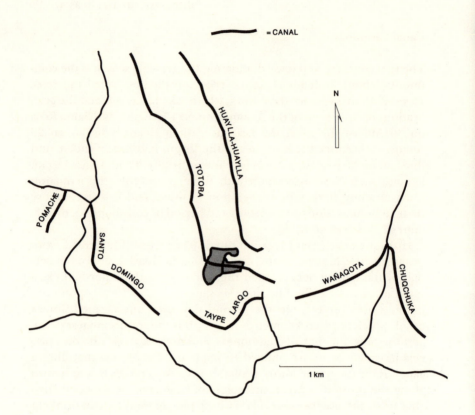

= CANAL

N

POMACHE

SANTO

DOMINGO

TOTORA

HUAYLLA-HUAYLLA

TAYPE LARQO

WAÑAQOTA

CHUQCHUKA

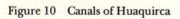

1 km

Figure 10   Canals of Huaquirca

Men with picks and men with shovels carefully intersperse, and although each man is responsible for cleaning a space of two to three metres, the man with the pick usually works over an area twice that size in cooperation with a man using a shovel, who follows, removing what has been loosened. Once finished, the men wait where they are until all of those behind them have finished and gone to the head of the line to assume new positions and start work again. Only the last worker in line must move on. In this way, each worker makes an equal contribution. Usually, it takes longer to walk to a new position than it does to clean it on arrival: thus, people spend more time waiting and walking than they do working. The line is always in a process of leapfrogging itself, and people are always passing by. With each change of position, the workers tease and insult each other, or indulge in various kinds of horseplay. In fact, men may alter their position in the line to socialize with somebody else, which would not be allowed if equal contributions to the execution of the task were rigidly enforced. This combination of formality and informality reflects well the intermediate position that canal cleaning occupies between mutual aid among commoners and their labour obligations to the state.

A meeting or *cabildo* is called in the middle of the longer canals, or at the beginning or end of the shorter canals. Its purpose is to nominate a water judge (Spanish *juez de aguas*, Quechua *unu kamayoq*) whose duty it is to maintain the secondary canals that bring water from the main canals to the particular fields that are to receive water on a given day, and to make the appropriate diversions early in the morning so that the water will already be there when the work party arrives. All canals have the same fixed order of access to irrigation water: those fields closest to the source get water first and those farthest away last. Only rarely does the judge make decisions about who should receive water.[13] If people are caught jumping their turn, the judge is supposed to refuse them access to water for the rest of the agricultural year. Any offenses are most likely to occur after the second (and final) irrigation, when this sanction will not be effective if carried out. Every commoner who owns a piece of land irrigated by a canal is expected to serve as its water judge once in his lifetime. Notables never serve, since this is one aspect of the communal labour service that they systematically avoid. All of the water judges appointed in 1982 were middle-aged, and thus served at approximately the halfway point in their agricultural careers. Sometimes they immediately volunteered for the duty, and other times, those who had already served needed to coerce them. In either case, the moral basis of recruitment was clearly the number of years that the person had used the canal without serving as its water judge.

With the help of several other people, the first act of the newly appointed water judge is to gather grass (both *kikuyu* and the coarse *ichu* that is used for thatch, if possible), ferns (*raki-raki*), carnations (*claveles*), and the elongated leaves of a bush that grows in the valley (which I did not identify). These plants are brought to the end of the canal and sorted into sprigs that the judge places in the hatbands of the irrigators as they finish work, a practice that is common in Ayacucho (see Arguedas 1956: 247; Isbell 1978: 144; Ossio 1978b: 386). Perhaps it is significant that two of Huaquirca's canals, both of which originate in the *puna*, bear the name of wild grasses: Huaylla-Huaylla ('much straw') and Totora ('reed'). Here, it seems that bringing water down from the alpine zone could parallel the downward movement of wild thatch in the house rethatching. Yet there is an additional upward movement of wild plants from deep in the valley (particularly ferns) to meet the descending water (cf. Ossio 1978b: 386). This also appears to enter into the concept of irrigation, since *raki-raki*, the fern, is in this context clearly related to the notion of *raki* ('a portion') which refers to an allotment of irrigation water (see Montoya, Silveira, and Lindoso 1979: 76), and suggests an abundance of these allotments by reduplication. This same upward movement of wild plants can be seen in the collection of firewood from the valley bottom for the sponsors of the festivities of the Virgin and Santa Rosa. Thus, irrigation seems to be represented as an encounter between upward- and downward-moving forces embodied in wild plants.[14] More generally, these details further suggest that agriculture is based on an incorporation of the wild, a notion that we first encountered in the house rethatching.

Unlike the house rethatching, however, canal cleaning presents us with only one such image, not an elaborated series of them. Far from clarifying the cultural meaning of canal cleaning, this poverty of reference simply leaves it indeterminate. What is probably most significant about canal cleaning is how it is suspended between the celebrations of the Virgin and Santa Rosa, which establish competitive duality as an overarching form, both in the rivalry of sponsors and in the events themselves. In Chapter 4 I will show that there is, indeed, a relation between this competitive duality of formally identical elements, the practice of *ayni* cooperation in an agrarian context and the production of water, which stimulates germination and growth of the crops. For the moment, these celebrations and canal cleaning are merely juxtaposed, and lack any symbolic connection.

There is evidence, however, that the *yarqa faena* in Huaquirca was once a more ritualized and festive act than it is now. At the beginning of one day's work on the canals, a few older commoners remarked wistfully to me that in the past, water judges had performed a libation of the canal source (*t'inka de toma*) as part of their responsibility to the community, and that this was a 'beautiful custom' that should not have been abandoned. Although I was not able to learn what this act consisted of, libation of the canals is part of the elaborate festivities that accompany irrigation ditch cleaning in the neighbouring Department of Ayacucho (see Arguedas 1956: 257; Ossio 1978b: 383). In Huaquirca, the *yarqa faena* was also the occasion for *qhashwas*, nocturnal dances that were supposed to end with sex between unmarried men and women. This was the only motive that commoners could devise for my participation in the *yarqa faena* of 1982, since I owned no land on the canals.

I was told that during the *qhashwas*, the mountain spirits (*apus*) used to come down with the intention of seducing and impregnating young women from the valley. This movement from high to low follows that of the water in the canals, and is underscored by the name *qhashwa*, which suggests *qheshwa*, or valley land. Comparable dances go by the name of *ayla* in Ayacucho, and were also part of canal cleaning festivities until recently (see Arguedas 1956: 259–62; Montoya, Silveira, and Lindoso 1979: 212; Montoya 1980: 314–15). In Puquio, canal cleaning festivities feature a category of dancers known as *llamichus* (a pejorative name for pastoralists), who are said to be offspring of the mountain spirits, and actively promote the *ayla* (Montoya 1980: 314–15). As we have already seen, valley-dwellers tend to associate the *puna* with undomesticated sexuality, and so they describe illegitimate children as 'of the mountain' (see Earls 1970: 87–8). Several ethnographers have extended these observations to argue that canal cleaning represents an agricultural fertilization of *pachamama* (as 'earth mother') by water from the mountain spirits, which'symbolizes' their sperm.[15] In Huaquirca, however, what people describe is the impregnation of women, not an agrarian 'goddess.' This is part of a more general emphasis on undomesticated sexuality as a productive force during the growing season,[16] as I have proposed in the analysis of house rethatching. One aspect of this general theme may have been the performative transfer of undomesticated fecundity from young women to the fields. Equally important, however, is that these women draw young men and mountain spirits into the productive order of the growing season.

It is unlikely that canal cleaning in Huaquirca was ever as festive as it is in the valley towns of Ayacucho. Still, the nearby town of Molle-bamba (see Figure 3) has elaborate canal cleaning celebrations,[17] which suggests that deritualization of this task in Huaquirca was neither inevitable nor a matter of distance from the Ayacucho culture area where the act is most elaborated. The relative instrumentality of the *yarqa faena* in Huaquirca is more a result of how it is lumped with other *faena* tasks to be completed before Santa Rosa (reservoir construction, maintenance of roads and the church, cleaning the bullring) than any original lack of meaning. At the various *cabildos* in which water judges were nominated, the governor was also present, naming those who had missed days of *faena* at previous times of the year (*faltadores*), and assigning them compensatory tasks. Rather than promote a sense of cosmological specificity about the canal cleaning, this sort of substitution presents all *faena* as a kind of homogeneous abstract labour, and this leads to deritualization. Even on those rare occasions (e.g., during the cleaning of Totora canal in 1982) when fines collected from the notables finance the purchase of rum for commoner tributaries, their labour does not necessarily become festive. In areas where canal cleaning is highly ritualized, drinking may be prohibited during the work itself (see Isbell 1978: 139), but what is not lost sight of, either in the *faena* or the celebrations that follow it, is that the canals are the focus of what is taking place.

Deritualization of canal cleaning in Huaquirca is nonetheless a complex matter. Although some older commoners lament the passing of canal cleaning rituals, this may well be a consequence of the more general commoner strategy of using *faena* labour to make claims on the state. By acquiescing to the official view of canal cleaning as part of an abstract labour obligation, and relaxing the ritual controls that might assert an alternative cultural definition of this act, commoners may have decided that their first priority was to retain effective administrative control of the canals on a day-to-day basis. The greater ceremonial elaboration of canal cleaning in Ayacucho, in contrast, rarely implies greater commoner control over irrigation once the canals have been opened. As we saw earlier, Huaquirca's system of water judges and *faena* obligations actually favours commoners in that it does not oblige them to pay for water, and they control its distribution far more completely than in other areas.

As for ritual, I will argue (in Chapter 7) that concern with irrigation, and water in general, has been transferred to the *t'inka* rites, since their very name denotes libation and the restitution of fluids to the earth. The last round of these rites begins on Santiago (25 July) in Huaquirca, and continues well into August, so it is not far removed from the cleaning of the canals. In Ayacucho, these rites are called *herranzas* in reference to the branding of cattle. Although they take place separately from the canal cleaning festivities, they occur either at the same time (Arguedas 1956: 243; Ossio 1978b: 379) or slightly beforehand (Isbell 1978: 151). The parallelism between canal cleaning and the *herranza* in Ayacucho is underscored by the way they feature the same burnt and interred offerings, libations, and sacrifices (see Arguedas 1956: 244–63; Isbell 1978: 139–51; Ossio 1978b: 382–7). Therefore, it is a simple matter for the *t'inkas* to subsume offerings for water, and I would argue that this is what happens as one moves from Ayacucho to Cusco, and the name of these rites changes from *herranza* to *t'inka*, with a corresponding decline in canal cleaning festivities.

None of these considerations changes the fact that canal cleaning in Huaquirca has undergone a ritual impoverishment within living memory, and that this process has been directly related to the revival and expansion of labour draft programs by the republican state. Once we cease to see canal cleaning as an isolated act, and put it in the context of a larger ritual cycle and of state-community relations, its deritualization looks less like a loss of 'tradition' and more like a strategic compromise.

Summary

Taken together, the house rethatching and canal cleaning show both some interesting substantive convergences and a radical divergence in their ability to incorporate festivity and symbolic detail. On the one hand, the two are united by the context of private appropriation established by the *t'inkas*, and show various degrees of dependent incorporation into these master rites of the dry season. House rethatching and canal cleaning also share thematic connections through their common concern with the 'domestication' of wild plants, and the fertile meeting of high and low, both of which clearly foreshadow the resumption of the growing season. On the other hand, the two acts are poles apart in the sort of aesthetic synthesis they bring about. The house rethatching is in many ways a model of how labour can be directed by ritual, and find its place in a broader totality by referring to other acts and ideas. Canal cleaning, however, has been largely purged of this symbolic self-direction, and is almost untouched by the celebrations of the Virgin and Santa Rosa that occur on either side of it. The only possible link that these festivities have with canal cleaning lies in the excessive collection of firewood, which might be part of the influx of wild plants into domestic space common to the house rethatching and canal cleaning.

The events commoners are most able to control and shape through their rituals are those organized through informal networks of inter-household cooperation. Since these networks contract during the dry season, it is not surprising that commoners leave a weak imprint on many events described in this chapter. As we will see in the chapters that follow, the situation is dramatically different when we enter into the growing season. Notable sensibilities predominate and appear to exert an increasing influence within all of the more institutionalized 'public events' discussed here: Santiago, Celebrations of the Father-land, Virgin of the Assumption, canal cleaning, and Santa Rosa. Although it would be wrong to say that commoners have renounced all interest in these events, their poverty (in absolute terms and relative to the notables) puts them at a considerable disadvantage when sponsoring public celebrations, as does their cultural background when dealing with the state. Theirs is a culture of agricultural work above all else, and so it is to agricultural work that we now must turn.

4

Sowing, Death, and *Ayni*

By the early days of September, the cold nights of the Andean dry season have begun to moderate, and frosts are unusual in valley towns like Huaquirca. The arrival of spring is confirmed when the first wildflowers and shoots of *kikuyu* grass appear. People attempt to uproot and burn this grass so that it does not stifle the growth of the maize they will soon plant. The Antabamba Valley fills with a thin blue smoke during these days. Along the canals and on uncultivated areas of the lower hillside, broom bushes (*retama*) are in brilliant yellow flower, while cattle and horses search listlessly for the last bits of fodder in the valley before their owners lead them to higher and greener pastures.

Irrigation begins on the two canals that originate in the *puna*: Huaylla-Huaylla and Totora. I was told several months in advance that planting should begin on 14 September (Exaltation of the Holy Cross), but in 1982 it was not until 15 September that irrigation began in preparation for sowing. The highest parcel of land serviced by each canal is normally the first to be irrigated, and with each passing day, the next-lowest parcel of land has its turn, until the fields at the end of the canal have been irrigated.[1] The remaining canals may not come into use until early October, and generally people are in no great rush to sow their land. Those near the top of the terraced zone are more vulnerable to an early frost in March that might kill their plants before they are fully grown. It is only fair that they should have the right to plant before those with land in the lower and warmer parts of the valley. However, they are also more vulnerable to a late frost that would kill their sprouted maize in the ground. Therefore, some do not take their turn as early as they might. Since each household has several different plots located on different canals, and in different positions on them, this risk is relatively evenly shared. People do not irrigate at night[2] (except in times of drought), and they may often await the arrival of regular rainfall in late October or early November to sow their fields '*de temporal*,' that is, without irrigation, using available rainfall to moisten the soil for seed germination. There is much speculation about when and how the rains will begin, and when it would be most advantageous to plant.[3] Thus, re-entry into agricultural production is protracted, and puts little strain on Huaquirca's irrigation facilities. Commoners assemble in a few large agricultural work parties each day, instead of many smaller ones, as they do when the agricultural calendar becomes more hectic.

Irrigation

A day of irrigation begins at dawn, when the water judge diverts his canal to the particular field where the work party will take place. By 9:00 in the morning, men will begin to arrive at the house of the owners of the field in question to eat the one meal of the working day. As in all agricultural work parties, this meal centres on a dish known as *picante*, a thick stew of potatoes, maize, and any greens that may be available. Some men remain after the meal to help transport various items to the fields, but the majority leave to attend to their own affairs for an hour or so. By 10:30 in the morning, the men begin to converge on the field where the work is to be done, picks in hand. Some who have not eaten at the hosts' that morning may also arrive. All domestic holdings of valley land in Huaquirca consist of several terraces, and irrigation begins with the lowest terrace in the parcel and works uphill. First, the men excavate (or repair) a canal that flows along the back of each terrace, at the foot of the retaining wall for the terrace above it. From this principal canal, they cut a series of branching secondary canals along a diagonal across the width of the terrace. These secondary canals are successively bifurcated to ensure an even dispersal of water over the entire surface of the field, and men use their picks to break up any mounds of soil that are not immediately inundated (see Figure 11). A rich and powerful smell arises from the ground as the water permeates the soil, and the dung and chaff that have mixed into it over the dry season.

Although it is pleasantly warm during the day at this time of the year, nighttime temperatures may be little above freezing, which means that

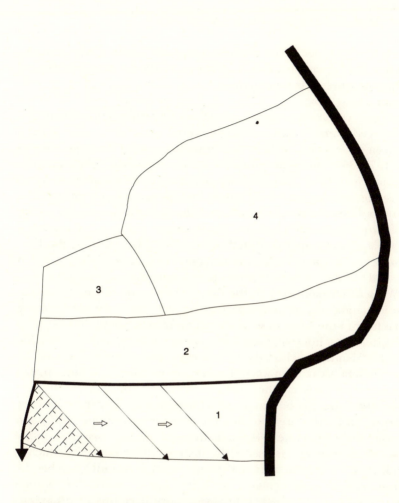

numbers   = position of terrace in irrigation sequence

████████ = branch taken from main canal

───────── = retaining wall canal

─────── = diagonal secondary canal

╱╱╱╱ = inverted 'y' ramifications

Figure 11 Method of irrigation

the irrigation water is still very cold, and chills the feet of the men who work in rubber sandals. This is a remnant of the extreme temperature contrasts between day and night during the dry season, which are only beginning to move towards the relative equilibrium of the rainy season. Men constantly express fear of contracting sickness from their prolonged contact with the water. This is part of a more general Andean notion that the first rains bring sickness (cf. Earls and Silverblatt 1978: 304), and that running water is categorically 'cold' and dangerous (Stein 1961: 295). In Huaquirca, I was often admonished not to consume '*agua cruda*' (cold water, literally 'raw water'). Stein (1961: 83) mentions the specific conviction that malaria can be contracted from working in cold water, and in this regard it is significant that one of Huaquirca's canals is named Chuqchuka, from *chuqchu,* the Quechua term for malaria. The verb *chuqchuy* also means 'to shiver,' and by the end of a day's irrigation, this is precisely what many men are doing.

Women normally work in the fields, but they do not participate in the irrigation, except by preparing the morning meal and bringing corn beer to the fields to serve the men. Around noon, the woman of the sponsoring household and perhaps one or two other women (who may be friends, godchildren, or affines) arrive in the fields. This signals the first break from work. The men sit on the grass at the edge of the field where it is dry, the women serve them corn beer, and the men distribute cane alcohol, as in all agricultural work parties in Huaquirca. During this break (called the *samakuy* 'to rest one's self') and the one that takes place in the mid-afternoon (*chawpi samay* 'rest of the mid-point'), women also serve the men a drink called *pito,* which is made by stirring toasted maize flour into corn beer until it reaches the consistency of liquid cement. *Pito* is not easy to drink, nor do men seem to enjoy it the way they do normal corn beer. It is almost as if its stickiness and turgidity had some medicinal value, although nobody ever elaborated on this to me except to say: 'Drink, without nausea.' During the periods of work following each of these breaks, the irrigation proceeds uphill terrace by terrace, until finally the highest is completed, and people go home for the day. The water is left to sink into the soil during the next day, but the day after, sowing takes place.

Maize Sowing

The maize sowing (*sara tarpuy*) is carried out using either a light plough drawn by a team of two yoked bulls or the traditional Andean footplough (*chakitaqlla*). Occasionally the two techniques are combined in the same work party, but this is rare. The footplough is used in about eighty per cent of the fields in Huaquirca, sometimes because the terraces are too narrow for a yoke and plough to be used efficiently. Still, the yoke and plough could be used far more widely than it is. Few people own a team of bulls, but it is always possible to borrow one in return for a few days' labour or for each of two households to contribute a bull to form a team, strategies that are rarely used in Huaquirca despite the undeniable saving of work that would result. In Huaquirca, commoners' reluctance to use draught animals corresponds to their positive valorization of participation in *ayni* networks. Notables use a yoke and plough far more frequently, precisely because it minimizes their dependence on commoners' labour. For the sake of brevity, I will describe only sowing by footplough here.

Like all other agricultural tasks, maize sowing begins with a meal at the house of the owners of the field. Between 10:30 and 11:00 in the morning, people arrive at the parcel of land and begin to work in teams, which usually consist of four men with footploughs, along with a woman (generally a *comadre* of the owners) or an older man who sows. There will always be at least two such teams, even if, as in the smallest work parties I attended, they include only two or three footploughs each, instead of the normal four. When more people are present, there may be four or even six teams, but their number is always even. The teams form pairs that work competitively on the same terrace. Each team starts at opposite ends of the downhill retaining wall of the terrace and moves towards the imaginary dividing line at the mid-point of the terrace. They slowly ascend the terrace in horizontal strips, working back and forth between the end and mid-point of the terrace, until the first one to finish moves on to the next-highest terrace of the parcel (as in irrigation). The result is a kind of uphill race between pairs of sowing teams, which will last until the parcel has been completely sown.

The task of the sowers connected to these teams is to distribute a few seeds into the compact bursts of soil sent up by every plunge of the footploughs. Different colours of maize seed are sown on different parts of the parcel, while broad beans (*habas*) are intermixed in some areas, and segregated from the maize in others.[4] There are undoubtedly good technical reasons for distributing seeds in this manner, but when I asked people about it, they did not speak of nitrogen cycles, but rather of *sawasira* and *pitusira*, the principles of plant growth, the

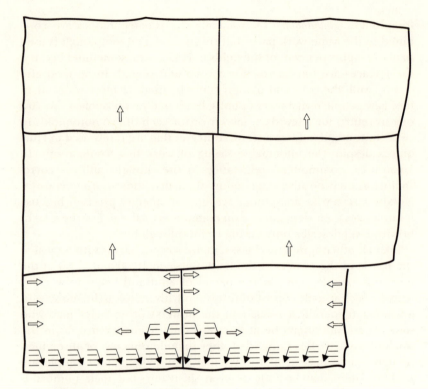

⇨ = movement of sowing teams

| = imaginary mid-point of terrace

☰ = group of four ascending footplough plunges

▼ = long downward footplough plunge

Figure 12 Method of sowing

spirit or power of agricultural products in general (cf. Roel Pineda 1965: 27; Wallis 1980: 251), and maize in particular.[5] The idea most frequently expressed about *sawasira* and *pitusira* in Huaquirca is that 'the two are a single thing, the maize that is growing in front of us.' On two different occasions, people used the model of human souls when trying to explain to me the idea of maize as the living unity of *sawasira* and *pitusira*. They told me that *sawasira* 'has affinity with' the human *ánimo*, which provides energy, and that *pitusira* 'has affinity with' the human *alma*, which provides embodiment. However, the distinction between *sawasira* and *pitusira* was also described to me as that between the grain and the cob of maize, and that between white maize and yellow maize, or maize and beans (*habas*). The last two versions would appear to confer a kind of generative significance on the various ways that sowers intersperse these different seeds in the fields. Thus, the life of the fields results from the distribution of complementary categories of seeds, comparable to the complementary souls that define human life.

Most women do not participate in the work party as sowers, and only arrive in the fields before the first break, which they initiate by bringing corn beer in large, heavy pottery vessels on their backs. After the first break, most of them will comb the already-sown sectors of the parcel with small picks, *allachos* (a kind of single-pointed pick), or simply with crooked wooden sticks, breaking up clods of earth, digging out and removing any tufts of *kikuyu* grass, and covering any exposed seeds. The first break in the work, or *samakuy*, is very relaxed and sociable. People go to the edge of the field where the women have laid out the jugs of corn beer. Men sit in a long line, side by side, talking to those next to them. Women sit in a loosely circular cluster around the jugs, talking and drinking, and pouring corn beer from the jugs into cups made of bull's horn or plastic. They take turns serving it to the men, pacing up and down the long line taking away empty cups, urging the men to drink more, or finish quicker so that someone else can be served. The man of the sponsoring household, or one of his godsons (who are all expected to be present at the work party), will circulate with a bottle of cane alcohol, serving all present, both male and female. The men may consume several cups of corn beer, and again they are obliged to consume one cup of turgid *pito*. These breaks can last for up to two hours if there are many people present and the work is going well. People festoon their hatbands with flowers of many colours that the women and children have collected on their way to the fields. Particularly esteemed is the *hamank'ay*, a large, white, daffo-dil-like flower that grows wild on the hillside.

During the first break, a performance called the 'libation of the seed' (*t'inka de semilla*) takes place. After they have had a few cups or horns of corn beer, the men begin to ask among themselves who will serve as 'son-in-law' (*qatay*), nominating various candidates until one finally accepts. On his appointment, the 'son-in-law,' and sometimes the owners of the field with him, will go and pour a small amount of corn beer on the sacks of seed by the edge of the field, into which bot-tles of cane alcohol have invariably been nested. This initiates a divina-tion among the men that bears the same name as the break itself: *samakuy*. One by one, as they are ready, men approach the sack with a cup or a horn, and scoop a small pile of seeds out onto the ground nearby. When all have done this, the 'son-in-law' proceeds to 'count' each pile, removing the seeds pair by pair, and replacing them in the sack. No overall tally is kept, and the only result that matters is whether one seed or two are left at the end of the process. If it is one, the 'son-in-law' pronounces 'he does not save himself,'[6] and the man in ques-tion, usually with a dejected look on his face, must go collect 'fertilizer' (*wanu*). This consists of moist black earth and decaying twigs found under bushes at the edge of the field, which the man dumps in a pile close to the bags of seed on his return. When I failed to 'save myself,' people would tease me with remarks like 'lack of exertion,' which amounted to a negative *ex post facto* judgment of the goodwill and live-liness of my work within the competitive context of the sowing teams. Those whose result is a pair, on the other hand, 'save themselves,' and sit back contentedly to drink more corn beer, their efforts vindicated. When everyone has completed this divination, the 'son-in-law' then recites the creed over the sack of seed, hands together in a praying position, handling the Latin with greater or lesser panache (see Stein [1961: 314] for a description of similar prayers over sown fields).

The next act in about half the sowings I observed was the passing of a 'lake' (*qocha*) among the entire group present. This consists of a cup or horn full of corn beer into which the woman of the sponsoring household puts two seeds of maize. Everyone is obliged to take a sip and pass it on. Twice I was told that the seeds in the 'lake' should ger-minate immediately once the corn beer has been drained, although nobody ever seemed to worry when they did not. In one case, two 'lakes' were circulated in opposite directions within the group, one containing maize seeds and the other a pair of bean (*haba*) seeds.

The 'libation of the seed' concludes with a ceremonial planting that immediately follows the preceding acts. In the fold of a woven bag for coca leaves (*ch'uspa*), the 'son-in-law' assembles a *coca k'intu* (three unblemished leaves of coca arranged on top of each other, dark face up), two seeds of maize (taken from the 'lake' when there is one), and a red carnation. He then passes this bundle on to the woman of the household that owns the field. One of the men who has not 'saved himself' takes a footplough and plunges it into the mound of 'fertilizer' that he and others have collected. As he pulls back on the handle, the woman slips the contents of the *ch'uspa* into the hole, and withdraws the bag.

At the end of the first break, most of the women who are not sowing with a team of footploughs, particularly those who are single, assemble at the edge of a terrace in a compact group, and face the opposite side of the valley, looking up at the mountains, to sing a song known as a *wanka*.[7] The women sing with one of their many *polleras* (layers of skirts) held up to their mouth with the right hand, as if to filter the song through it. The *wanka* at the end of the first break is in honour of the 'son-in-law,' thanking him for his goodwill and kindness towards his 'parents-in-law.' At the end of the second break from work (*chawpi samay* or mid-point rest), these same women do a *wanka* for the *comadres* who are usually off sowing with the teams of men. Among other things, they tell the *comadres* that their hearts are sweet like a carnation (the same wildflower that figures in the ceremonial planting at the end of the 'libation of the seed'). The defining trait of a *wanka* is that it ends each stanza with a high-rising exclamation: '*wuuu!*'

If there is still daylight left by the time the sowing is finished, and sometimes even if there is not, a final short session of drinking, conversation, and resting will precede the journey home. On the way back to town, the men perform a combined song and march that are together known as the *wayliya* (Quechua: 'joy,' 'happiness'), probably because of the lyrics:

wayliya, wayliya, wayliya, wayliya

wayliya-hiya, wayliya

They sing in a variety of tones, ranging from the thick, low, and urgent to full voice. The men sing one stanza while facing each other and not moving. For the next stanza, they whistle the tune and stamp their feet in a marching step, during which the women sometimes join in with improvised lyrics about the events of the working day, or anything else that occurs to them. Thus, the return to town becomes a protracted affair, and there are always those who decide that they are ready to take their leave and go home ahead of the rest. Invariably, the group waits just before entering town so that stragglers may catch up, and finally it proceeds, amassed and in full-throated *wayliya*, for maximum impact on potential witnesses. People will come out of their houses to watch an especially impressive entry. Participants in an enthusiastic work party will slowly pass through town on their way to the house of the sponsors, where they will continue to drink cane alcohol and sing the *wayliya* for a few hours more before everyone retires, usually very drunk.

Should groups returning from two different sowings encounter each other on a path outside town, there will be a standoff, with each group of men singing and stomping the *wayliya* in compact unison. These standoffs do not occur often, since there is rarely more than one work party per day on any given canal at this time of the year. I never witnessed one, but when they do occur, people said that it is because the men are drunk, but still in an energetic, competitive frame of mind from work, and want to fight. And fight they do, often with great fury and considerable bloodshed. I knew a young man who had his arm broken in one of these encounters. Although he made it known that he would appreciate the opportunity for revenge against his assailant, he also took a stoic attitude about his injury as the inevitable consequence of this fighting. Indeed, this violence is largely impersonal, something that arises from the spirit in which men work, as my informants suggested. The fighting lasts a short while, and then ends, with each group re-forming and continuing the *wayliya* into town, just like any other enthusiastic work party.

This completes the simple description of irrigation and sowing, but we are clearly far from an adequate comprehension of the full sense and meaning of these acts. Despite the obvious sequential and referential complexity of the 'libation of the seed,' for example, I never heard anyone discuss what it might 'mean.' Still, the care and attention that are put into these acts show that they are more than a matter of insignificant routine. Therefore, we must assume that there is meaning here, even if it is largely non-discursive. Fortunately, the ritual details of irrigation and sowing introduce many images and ideas that would otherwise lie beyond the immediate context of these acts. I think we can legitimately assume that the commoners of Huaquirca use this imagery to 'reflect and refract' these acts, and give them a definite cultural sense. Still, the referential quality of these ritual details is open-ended enough to allow many points of interpretive departure, and specify none. It is not obvious, for example, that death metaphorically structures irrigation and sowing, although this is my primary interpretative claim. At this stage, I can show only that the ritual details of these acts refer to death, as a preliminary justification for a more detailed discussion, which will demonstrate at length how the imagery of death pervades irrigation and sowing.

First, men's performance in the competition between sowing teams is discussed in terms of 'salvation' (or lack thereof): this suggests that work is metaphorically understood as death and spiritual judgment. The implication is that men die a little as they release energy from their bodies in vigorous work. We will see below that in Huaquirca, people define death as the irrecoverable loss of an animating soul, the *ánimo*. A loss of energy that is almost as intense may occur in agricultural labour, and this is the result that commoners aim for when they discuss work in terms of 'salvation.' Because commoners regard energy as something generated by the *ánimo*, it follows that they can evaluate work in spiritual terms. When viewed as an expenditure of vitality on behalf of other people, work in relations of *ayni* creates a powerful sense of moral connection. Thus, I once heard a commoner emotionally commend another simply by saying that he 'had the tenderness to work' for other people. Although this notion of 'salvation' through work is unorthodox, its Christian inspiration is undeniable. In the discussion of house rethatching, we saw that people use spiritual kinship terms in *ayni*-based work parties, and this further enhances the sense of spiritual community through work that is implicit in this notion of 'salvation.' Despite these social referents, 'salvation' remains a matter of death, in local terms, a separation of energy from embodiment. It is fitting that those who fail to 'save themselves' must fetch *wanu* (guano, fertilizer). This word is derived from the Quechua *wañuy* ('death' or 'to die'), and refers to decaying organic material. Women often told me in the fields that every living plant 'has *ánimo*, but when it dies, is just vegetal matter.' Like a dead body, *wanu* is a negative by-product of 'salvation,' a carnal form from which life has been removed. Those who fail to 'save themselves' must associate with this degraded organic residual, which aptly represents their sluggishness in work. Thus, the divination sorts men out into lazy and energetic workers according to the model of separation between body and soul on death, and agricultural labour becomes a kind of spiritual judgment.

A second deathly theme emerges from the 'son-in-law's' prayer over the seeds. Similar prayers are said in Latin over the graves on All Souls' Day in Huaquirca, which suggests a metaphorical view of the sowing as a collective observance for the dead. Such an idea could be corroborated by the endless discovery of pre-Columbian burials in the terraces during the sowing in Huaquirca. In the pre-Columbian Andes, the living treated the dead as a sort of seed to be buried, and in many parts of the Andes today, people still treat human burial as a kind of sowing.[8] But the most significant evidence from the acts just described is that people in Huaquirca use the model of human souls to understand seeds and their distribution in the fields when they invoke the *sawa-sira/pitusira* couplet. Because plants have souls comparable to those of people, the sowing of seeds becomes a kind of collective, regenerative burial.

I suspect that these two metaphorical themes, 'work as death and spiritual judgment' and 'sowing as burial,' form a single complex in which people and maize become consubstantial. This linkage explains why seeds are an appropriate medium to divine men's 'salvation.' The Quechua term *samakuy* also develops the unity of these themes by referring to the first rest from work, the seed divination, and something in a state of interment or burial.[9] I do not intend the evidence just given to do anything more than suggest, at this stage, that there are references to death in the sowing and that a fuller knowledge of death in the Andes might help to unpack the cryptic imagery of the sowing. As Sapir (1977: 10, 12) argues, we cannot perceive the aptness, or even the existence of a metaphor without considerable commonplace knowledge of the terms involved, particularly the vehicle or structuring term (in this case, death). By describing the rites and ideas that surround death in Huaquirca, I will make good the claim that it metaphorically structures irrigation and sowing. In the process, I will refer back to the many details of these acts that remain unexplained, and show that they make sense when seen through death. Thus, the remainder of this chapter will argue that death is an integral part of the productive activities just described.

Death

Deaths can and do occur at any time of the year in Huaquirca. Like Buechler (1980: 39), however, I noticed that they were more frequent during the rainy season. From a simple occurrence, death develops into a series of emotional and conceptual separations through funerary rites, concepts of the person, and the afterlife. In most contexts, it is enough to say that someone died of old age, sickness, a wound, or in childbirth, without subjecting these circumstances to metaphysical speculation. Once death has occurred, however, reference to soul concepts becomes almost inevitable, even though their number and precise character are not a matter of universal agreement (cf. Carter 1968: 246). Soul concepts also enter into the diagnosis of disease and witchcraft, and their treatment.[10]

Of the various soul concepts used in Huaquirca, the couplet *alma* and *ánimo* appears with the most frequency, and seems to be the basis for other concepts. Death rites and stories of the afterlife primarily concern the *alma*. According to almost all of the accounts I heard, the *alma* records the body form and moral character of the person as they were developed in life. The *ánimo* maintains the life and health of the individual, and is responsible for vitality, animation, consciousness, courage, and sensory capacities. An interdependence between *alma* and *ánimo* exists, since the physical and moral development of the *alma* presupposes its animation, just as the vital force of the *ánimo* cannot take form except in relation with an impulse towards embodiment (the *alma*).[11] Nonetheless, there is an intrinsic asymmetry in this relationship since it takes place within the body, which has a decided affinity with the *alma*. The *ánimo*'s relative indifference to the body is expressed in its proclivity to leave the body when a person is startled, a condition known as 'fright' (Quechua: *mancharisqa*). A final indication of the dominance of the *alma* within this couplet is the use of 'major soul' (*alma mayor*) and 'minor soul' (*alma menor*) as respective synonyms of *alma* and *ánimo*. In certain accounts, both *alma* and *ánimo* can be subdivided or multiplied. For example, a woman from Huaquirca told me that men have three *almas*, each with a separate destiny in the afterlife, whereas women have seven.[12] Carter (1968: 246–7) shows how various aspects of the *ánimo* can be separated as distinct entities, or aggregated, depending on the individual and purposes at hand. There is also a counter-tendency towards the fusion of the duality or multiplicity of souls, one that is implicit in the merely quantitative distinction between *alma mayor* and *alma menor*, and explicit in the non-differentiated concept of *espíritu*, a kind of generic term applicable to any souls of the living or dead.

When someone is about to die, it is said that the *alma* wanders to all of the places it frequented in life (cf. Stein 1961: 308). Many people in Huaquirca swore to me that they had seen *almas* on the roads and in the fields, far away from the sick, bedridden bodies of their host. Apparently, these *almas* look exactly like the person they are connected to, and can be distinguished only by their utter inability to perceive or interact with the living. Deafness to the greetings of the living is the most common way these *almas* are detected as such.[13] Since the *ánimo* is supposed to maintain the senses, it is logical that these *almas* wandering in a state of separation would be oblivious to the presence of others. Such a scenario was proposed in the diagnosis of the mayor of Huaquirca during a serious illness: 'The big one [*alma mayor*] is already gone, only the small one [*alma menor*] remains.' In this line of thinking, death results when, in the absence of the *alma*, the *ánimo* dissipates or leaves the body as a blue fly (*chiririnka*), which again emphasizes its smallness and relative non-correspondence to the human body. *Aya* is the Quechua word for 'cadaver,' but as one of my best informants insisted, it also refers to the *alma* before burial. The intimate relation between *alma* and body remains;[14] therefore many Andean people feel that an autopsy defiles the *alma* (see Valderrama and Escalante 1980: 263; Allen 1988: 123–4). As we will see, the main object of death rites is to break this link and send the *alma* on to the afterlife. However those accounts that give people three *almas* always reserve one for the buried cadaver (the '*alma del centro*,' see Valderrama and Escalante 1980: 252).

In Huaquirca the *almas* that remain in the graveyards of this world are sometimes thought to act as agents of death: the *apaq* ('those who bring') or *apaqata*, ghostly figures dressed in black cowls. At night, they may arise collectively from the graveyard, each with a lit candle in hand. With a rapid, ethereal gliding motion, they go to the home of someone destined to die that night. They file past the front door of the house where their victim languishes, then return to the graveyard and extinguish their candles as they re-enter the tomb. Their appearance marks certain death, and I heard several accounts from people who had fled in terror before the advance of the *apaq* on paths at night, only to discover that they had other victims in mind. Zuidema and Quispe (1968: 359) report manifestations similar to the *apaq*. In these cases, Andean people attribute a causal role to notions of the soul in death, as opposed to a merely descriptive role.

People can die at any time of the day, but the incessant tolling of church bells that publicly announces death does not begin until early on the following morning, as if the death took place at night. Kin of the deceased immediately dress in black and go into mourning (*luto*), putting all everyday activities aside. Affines take charge of all of the arrangements for the funeral, and sponsor most of its costs. If the deceased is elderly, and has sons- and daughters-in-law, most of the burden will fall on them, and they continually address each other as 'son-in-law companion' and 'daughter-in-law companion' ('*qatay masi*' and '*qhachun masi*,' i.e., through the egocentric position of the deceased). I was told that affines must be in charge 'since we are apart.' As we shall see in more detail below, consanguines of the deceased are felt to have an almost physical connection to the corpse, one that puts them in a state of considerable ritual danger until the *alma* is banished from the community. Affines are apart because they do not share this link and can, therefore, oversee the process of separation that must take place. The dark side of this is that affines are expected to be the ringleaders in any squabbles over inheritance and are suspected of manoeuvring if they grieve too openly.[15] Death is the one ritual context in Huaquirca where actual sons- and daughters-in-law must provide services to their affines, and other non-kin cannot take their place, as in the house rethatching and sowing.[16]

When someone dies, male affines mobilize immediately to wash and arrange the corpse, and cover it with a black poncho. They do not bury the body for several days, both as a matter of tradition, and to let distant kin come to pay their last respects. During this time, an extended wake (*velorio*) takes place. Two candles of unequal diameter (connoting big soul and little soul) burn near the head of the corpse, and are constantly renewed throughout the wake, which friends and relatives attend, especially at night. Nonetheless, only consanguines attempt to forego sleep throughout the entire wake, which may last up to five days. Mourners drink small amounts of cane alcohol at these gatherings, but smoke many cigarettes and chew many coca leaves as defensive measures against being 'seized' by the deceased.[17] At frequent intervals, kin will begin to sniffle or openly weep, the women among them breaking into the *aya taki*, a tearful and sobbing song, but this rarely reaches an overwhelming level during the wake.

People commonly play a game called 'five' or 'fived' (*pisqa* or *pisqasqa*, probably referring to the five days' wake traditional to the Andes) during wakes in the *puna* of Huaquirca, and in the neighbouring town of Matara (it is rarely played in Huaquirca itself). It is played at night, and has many variants in the southern Peruvian Andes (see

Valderrama and Escalante 1980: 237). The players are men, either friends or affines of the deceased, but never consanguines or women. I did not see the version that is sometimes played in Huaquirca, but was told that a black cloth is laid on the floor and several dried beans (*habas*) are placed on top of it. From a standing position, each player drops to one knee, putting his full weight on a bean placed upright underneath it, in an attempt to split it into its two halves. If the bean splits, the player 'wins,' but if not, he 'loses,' and must recite hymns for the soul and/or buy cane alcohol for the wake. In the *puna* of Huaquirca and in Matara, six beans are broken in half, and the resulting twelve cotyledons are thrown like dice onto the black cloth. If more than half land flat side up, the player 'wins,' and if less, he 'loses,' with the same consequences mentioned above. Centeno (1960: 103) describes another variant for the town of Antabamba, where maize seeds that have been painted black on one side are thrown onto the mat, and then removed pair by pair, with the result of a pair indicating an unproblematic journey to the afterlife for the *alma*, and a single seed the necessity of various 'magical acts' by the living to help it.

After breakfast on the morning of the burial, close male friends of the family (Spanish *querendores*, Quechua *khuyaq*: 'those who care'), particularly male affines, assemble at the house of the deceased for two tasks: digging the grave and washing the dead person's clothes. Female *querendores* arrive later, around mid-morning, to prepare the meal that will be served to members of the community who come to the house after the burial. Around 9:00 in the morning, after a few preliminary swallows of cane alcohol, one group of men departs to dig the grave. About 10:30 in the morning, another group of men supervised by a 'son-in-law' sets off to a stream two kilometres from town to wash the clothes. This timing ensures that the burial proper and the clothes washing will take place more or less simultaneously, a fact of some significance, since both of these rites have the goal of initiating the *alma*'s journey to the afterlife, and would seem, by virtue of their own separation in space, to advance the process of separation already begun with physiological death.

Although many men may go to dig the grave, only two can work at once, so the work advances vigorously in turns, while those who wait talk and rest by the side of the grave. One man breaks ground with a pick while another forms the sides and corners of the rectangular grave with a metal bar, and after a few minutes, the two retire for a third man to shovel out the loose soil. Huaquirca's cemetery is small, and has been well used over the centuries. The excavation of a new grave invariably turns up bones from previous burials. Care is nonetheless taken to avoid areas marked with a cross, which indicates that the occupant of the grave is still remembered (cf. Harris 1982: 51). Occasionally, the pick breaks a skull or another bone, but this does not cause concern, even though the men attempt to avoid it. The graves are about one metre deep, and the orientation of skeletons in them varies in different sectors in the graveyard: either parallel or at right angles to the Antabamba River. Some graves, mainly those of the notables, contain coffins. When encountered, the men make every effort to avoid breaking the wood of the coffin. Near the centre of the graveyard is a cement mausoleum with several coffin-sized niches, which only the notables use. People say that in the past, both the notables and the *kurakas* (i.e., the Aiquipas) paid the priest to be buried in the church, and it is true that there are funerary niches, coffins, and assorted bones to be found there. These coffin burials attempt to preserve the individuality of the deceased from the communal anonymity of the cemetery, which is so concretely expressed by the mixing and remixing of bones as successive graves are dug on the same spot. As in life, when they refuse to marry commoners, the notables retain a substantial separation from the rest of the community on death. Two rest periods punctuate the excavation of a grave, during which the men retreat to the gate of the cemetery to drink corn beer and cane alcohol. These breaks define three periods of work, on the model of an agricultural working day, although grave digging takes only two hours to complete.

By noon, or slightly before, people begin to congregate at the house of the deceased, or at the graveyard. The corpse is put in a coffin or a black poncho, taken down to the cemetery and lowered into the grave by male affines and *querendores*. Quickly, they inter the body, with everyone but the wailing kin scrambling to toss handfuls of dirt into the grave. At this point, the *alma* is most desperate to 'seize' someone to take to the afterlife, which explains the haste in filling the grave.[18] This act completed, two small wreaths of wildflowers (usually yellow broom and white *hamank'ay*) are assembled and put at the head and the foot of the grave. A small chamber of tiles may be inset at the head of the grave and covered with a sheet of tin, into which two candles of unequal diameter are placed and lit, as during the wake. Almost as if to make sure that the corpse stays down, heavy rocks and a cross are planted on top of the grave.[19] The mourners take turns praying over the grave, and then retire to the path just outside the entrance to the cemetery to drink and await the return of the men from the clothes washing. Many bring bottles of cane alcohol that they hand over to the deceased's affines, who serve them to the assembled company. Other affines record these contributions in a notebook, much as do the sponsors of a dry season *fiesta*. To provide drink in this manner is called 'doing *ayni* with the *alma*.'[20] The female affines of the deceased also distribute corn beer that they have made for this occasion. People pour libations on the ground for the benefit of the *alma*, often mentioning Qoropuna and Solimana, two immense mountains in the Department of Arequipa that are thought to be the abode of the dead and the afterlife throughout most of the southern Peruvian Andes.[21]

Meanwhile, the *p'acha t'aqsana* or clothes washing has been taking place. This happens in a creek named Wañaqota, which flows into the Antabamba River upstream from Huaquirca, or sometimes in a canal that is taken from this creek, shares its name, and flows back towards town (see Figure 10). As in the digging of the grave, clothes washing is done in three sessions of work broken by two rest periods, based on the model of a working day in the fields. In everyday life, women wash clothes: thus, it is noteworthy that men should do so here. The men do not scrub the clothes by hand as women would do, but lay the garments and sleeping skins in the stream and trample them by foot. In the last session of work, the 'son-in-law' makes a fire to burn the most ragged clothing of the deceased (which has not been washed), and with it, a small selection of the deceased's favourite foods. In the past, a black dog was sometimes killed here, to accompany the *alma* on its journey, as is still the case in the neighbouring Province of Cotabambas (Valderrama and Escalante 1980: 258–9). Occasionally a cord called *lloqe*, made of black and white strands of yarn that are spun from right to left, is strung over the stream during clothes washing, or tied around the left wrist of each washer. Once the clothes are washed and put out to dry, the men take a final rest. Then they tie the clothes in a bundle that hangs from the middle of a pole that two men carry into town. The washers return to town at a brisk trot, since the 'son-in-law' cuts a thorny switch to whip his charges onward. Nobody looks back for fear that they will feel compelled to follow the *alma* on its journey to the afterlife, a journey that continues away from town along the same path on which the washers are now returning.

When the clothes washers arrive at the cemetery on the edge of town, panting for breath, the burial has been completed, but people remain at the gate of the graveyard, drinking and waiting for their return. The clothes washers stop several metres from the mourners and receive a few swallows of cane alcohol, but they do not draw near. Slowly, everyone moves on to the house of the deceased, but the washers do not mingle with the rest, under the threat of the 'son-in-law's' switch. On arrival, the washers hand over the clothes to the family of the deceased, who save them for the vigils that take place on All Saints' Eve. Food is served to the washers before anyone else. Over one hundred people can be present for the meal that is prepared by female affines and *querendores*. The guests take turns consoling the consanguines of the deceased, who frequently break into weeping or the *aya taki*. Bit by bit, people leave during the afternoon, and finally the scene returns to the tranquillity of the wake, which focuses on the two lit candles, now that the body is buried. The following morning, some affines of the deceased will return to the grave to look for footprints of people or livestock, which indicate what sort of being the *alma* will attempt to take with it into the afterlife, for the survivors expect this as a matter of course. When the period of mourning finally ends, often several days after the burial, a 'son-in-law' washes the tear-stained faces of the consanguines and spouse of the deceased.

This completes the description of death ritual in Huaquirca. A relentless emphasis on duality and separation is perhaps its most noteworthy feature. Not only is death represented as a separation of *alma* from *ánimo*, but when it comes time to separate the dead from the living, the *alma* is dispatched to the afterlife through the simultaneous ceremonies of burial and clothes washing. This dual send-off advances the separation process of death, when the *alma* is dislodged from the cadaver and sent on its way. Although the living remain attached to the dead, these rituals initiate their separation.

Before continuing into accounts of the afterlife, it is worth establishing some linkages between the rituals of sowing and death. These domains are organized in a remarkably parallel fashion, and each consistently provides a structure for the other. On the one hand, grave digging and clothes washing are divided into three periods of work and two periods of drinking, just like a working day in the fields, though they only take two hours each to complete. In this way, these mortuary rituals are implicitly equated with agricultural work. On the other hand, the distribution of seeds in the fields is orchestrated according to a model of generative duality (*sawasira/pitusira*), which is ultimately modelled on the relation between human souls (*ánimo/*

alma). In this way the growth of the crops is linked to human soul concepts that are prominent in mortuary ritual.

This connection between seeds and souls becomes even more apparent in the divinations that take place during sowing and wakes. Both divinations use seeds to learn the fate and disposition of human souls. Indeed, the wake divinations simply extend the notion of 'salvation' that was developed in the sowing divinations by indicating the soul's progress in the afterlife. Yet what is most noteworthy about sowing and wake divinations is how they interchange terms of reference: work in the competitive context of the sowing teams is posed in terms of 'salvation,' whereas during the wake, the fate of the soul is treated in terms of 'winning.' This counter-reference underlines the formal similarity between the two divinations, but clearly we are dealing with more than a simple homology between two distinct 'semantic domains.' The very aptness of seeds as a medium for divining the fate of human souls in work and the afterlife already presupposes a connection between the two that is further developed in how *sawasira* and *pitusira* are modelled on *ánimo* and *alma*, and the emphasis on pairing, splitting, and blackening in the divinations, which is based on the separation of souls at death. Not only do people modify seeds to make them correspond to ideas about human souls, but they do so to learn about the spiritual disposition of the living and the dead. This interaction of seeds and souls goes beyond formal homology, and suggests that they are not separate 'domains' for participants in these rituals.

Even more striking is the correspondence of detail and formal organization between the couplet of irrigation and sowing, and that of clothes washing and burial. First, both couplets involve one aquatic term and another that is buried in the earth. The parallel relation between clothes washing and irrigation is particularly evident. Both acts exclude women from contexts in which they normally participate, and both appear to involve a degree of supernatural danger, as expressed by the drinking of *pito* and the quarantining of the washers. In both cases, water seems to be the source of this danger, and the men seek to limit contact with it to their feet, even though they must adopt a highly unorthodox clothes-washing style to do so. A connection between these acts is further suggested by the homonyms *p'acha* (clothes) and *pacha* (earth), whereby *p'acha t'aqsana* (clothes washing) might be subject to a double entendre as *pacha t'aqsana* (earth washing, i.e., irrigation).[22] These homologies between irrigation and clothes washing have their counterpart in the relation between sowing and burial: we have already seen that sowing is treated as burial, and the dead as seed. The result is that the couplet of clothes washing and burial shares an elaborate formal correspondence with the couplet of irrigation and sowing.

Behind all of these correspondences of detail and formal organization lies a substantive connection between the domains of human death and agriculture. This connection focuses on the cosmological distribution of water, and will emerge when we turn to local understandings of the afterlife.

Accounts of the Afterlife

As in its wanderings before death, the *alma* may be sighted by the living on its westward journey into the afterlife, and will be utterly oblivious to their presence. After a long trek across the *puna* and over the high peaks of the Continental Divide, the soul begins its descent onto the western slope of the Andes, and reaches its first significant landmark: Campanayoq. This is a huge bell-shaped stone that is supposed to toll as the soul passes by, announcing its arrival to points ahead. Next, the soul comes to a large arid plain known as 'Dog Town' (Alqollaqta), which is strewn with large stone figures that resemble dogs, and are said to be their souls. Anyone who has mistreated dogs in life is likely to be severely bitten, or even totally devoured there (see Valderrama and Escalante 1980: 258), a punishment that further suggests that the journeying *alma* is still in some sense corporeal, as well as animate. When the notable muleteers used to pass through Alqollaqta on the way to Arequipa, they would save bones for many days, if need be, to put at the feet of these large stone dogs, in the hope that it would ease their passage on death.

Just beyond Alqollaqta lies the second obstacle of the *alma*: the 'Dirty River' (Map'a Mayo), which springs from the foot of Qoropuna, mountain of the dead. For the living, the Map'a Mayo is a small but turbulent stream. Some accounts I heard in Huaquirca stressed that it runs turbulent year-round (and hence is 'dirty'), as if it had its origin in a land of constant rain. According to one of these accounts, the water of this stream is dirty because the water is turbulent and 'wild' (*bravo*), like a puma. Other accounts I heard held that the Map'a Mayo is the only river in the world that runs clear during the rainy season and muddy during the dry season, which suggests a reversal of seasons between the worlds of the living and the dead (cf. Harris 1982: 45). I was also told that the Map'a Mayo occasionally expels apples and oranges from the subterranean orchards of Qoropuna. For a journeying *alma*, however, the Map'a Mayo expands out of all living proportion into a vast, seething ocean that is immensely intimidating, and impossible to cross without help.[23] It seems that this change in the perception of the Map'a Mayo is an integral part of the loss of subjective capacities on death, which has already been seen in the deafness and muteness of the *alma*.

There are two theories of how the *alma* crosses the Map'a Mayo. The less common of the two in Huaquirca is the most common elsewhere in the Andes: that the *alma* rides across on the back of a black dog.[24] More widespread in Huaquirca is the idea that the *alma* crosses the Map'a Mayo on a suspension bridge made from a *lloqe* cord (of interwoven strands of black and white wool) of the sort we have already encountered in the clothes washing.[25] Notable muleteers placed these miniature suspension bridges across the Map'a Mayo on their journeys to Arequipa.

Two things are common to both versions of how the *alma* crosses the Map'a Mayo: an elaboration of black/white symbolism (dogs and strands of wool), and their duplication or foreshadowing during the clothes washing. On the one hand, black seems to signify death. The clothes of mourning are black, blackened maize seeds are used in wake divinations, and it is a black dog that delivers the *alma* to the foot of the mountain of the dead. On the other hand, many accounts of death in the Andes pose an inversion of night and day between the respective worlds of the dead and the living,[26] so black/white symbolism may represent these worlds in themselves less clearly than it does the formal contrast between them, as part of the general emphasis on separation in death rites. In any case, the traditional killing of a black dog at Wañaqota, the site of the clothes washing, and the suspension of a *lloqe* cord there, clearly anticipate the *alma*'s needs for crossing the Map'a Mayo. During one clothes washing I participated in, the men actually teased some people passing by Wañaqota that they were crossing the Map'a Mayo back into the land of the living, implicitly equating the two streams. It is as if Wañaqota and the Map'a Mayo were somehow the same place, one that is nearby for the living, but far away for the dead. This difference is proportional to how the Map'a Mayo is a small stream for the living, but grows into a vast ocean for the dead, who lose their sense of proportion when they lose their *ánimo*.[27]

According to one account, the *alma*'s ascent of Qoropuna takes it through 'Cat Town' (Michillaqta), 'Chicken Town' (Wallpallaqta), 'Guinea-Pig Town' (Qowillaqta), and 'Pot Town' (Mank'allaqta), where each of these beings punishes the *alma* for any mistreatment it may have given them in life (cf. Valderrama and Escalante 1980: 258–60). The *alma*'s inability to dominate these beings as it did in life is a further indication of its undoing, a process that began with its loss of speech and hearing and, in the same way, is traceable to the loss of *ánimo*. However, most accounts of the afterlife I heard in Huaquirca simply had the *alma* climbing a long, zigzagging path through the snow to the top of Qoropuna,[28] where a lake lies in the midst of three peaks. Here, a kind of judgment is passed by either God or St John the Baptist,[29] depending on the account. It is tempting to interpret this crossing of the Map'a Mayo and judgment by St John the Baptist as a kind of baptism into the afterlife, especially since the *alma* has been reduced to the helpless state of an infant.

Several versions agreed that once inside Qoropuna, the dead remarry to someone who was not their spouse in life, live in houses, and work in fields. In one clothes washing I attended, however, this latter idea was openly mocked: 'How is an *alma* going to hold a pick, then?' Some stories I heard emphasized the physical defects of the dead, such as swollen eyes. Elsewhere, the dead are described as miniature beings (Casaverde 1970: 208), and the land of the dead as a place of shrunken proportions (Harris 1982: 62–3). Other details of the afterlife stress its inversion of the patterns of this life; for example, in the reversal of power relations between notables and commoners (see Stein 1961: 312–13; Ortiz 1973: 14; Valderrama and Escalante 1980: 260), along the lines of day and night, and the seasons.

Qoropuna has a companion named Solimana, and the two mountains are always mentioned as a couplet in the libations poured for the *alma* after its burial. Nonetheless, most accounts that I heard did not give Solimana any particular role in the afterlife. Two accounts, however, did mention Qoropuna as the domicile of 'saved' *almas* and Solimana as the abode of 'criminal and wrongdoer' *almas*. These same accounts stressed that Qoropuna is covered with yellow snow, whereas the snow on Solimana is white. Thus, the snow on these mountains indicates the spiritual condition of the *almas* inside them. Perhaps this snow is even derived from the dead. A likely model for this process is the freeze-drying of potatoes, whereby internal moisture gravitates to the surface and condenses as frost. Allen (1988: 172) reports the idea that the dead exist as freeze-dried potatoes (*ch'uño*) in the afterlife, and suggests that this process is equivalent to mummification (cf. Murra 1978: 34). In the Antabamba Valley, this interpretation is further suggested by the way a particular variety of potato used for making *moraya* (white freeze-dried potato) is given the name *waña* (Tamayo 1947: 39), which means 'dead' or 'dry.'[30]

Synthesis

The snow colours of these two mountains correspond to the colours of the main flowers used in death rites: broom and *ayaq zapatillan* are yellow (Carter 1968: 244; Arguedas 1976: 149), and the *hamank'ay* is white. The affinity between the dead and flowers has been noted elsewhere (Zuidema and Quispe 1968: 369; Isbell 1976: 50; Harris 1982: 48, 54), but in this context, it is specifically the water extracted from the dead and expelled as snow that corresponds to them, a fact that might suggest that this frigid water is predestined to be incorporated by plants. This notion is confirmed by the colour-coding of the souls of cultivated plants: *sawasira* is white maize and *pitusira* is yellow maize. Furthermore, each of these souls is embodied in Sawasiray and Pitusiray, the twin peaks of a single mountain near Calca in the Department of Cusco (see Figure 13), which is generally regarded as the spiritual source and guardian of maize throughout the southern Peruvian Andes (see Valderrama and Escalante 1975: 179–80). Not only do the spirits of maize form a complementary pair of yellow and white like the mountains of the dead, but they are also localized in a pair of mountains. However, Sawasiray and Pitusiray are located on the humid eastern slope of the Andes, immediately above the jungle, whereas Qoropuna and Solimana lie on the dry western slope. This introduces an important contrast between the mountains of the dead and the mountains of maize, which otherwise show parallel organization.

A single hydraulic cycle unites these two pairs of mountains, whereby death in the west produces the water that leads to the germination and growth of maize in the east. It is through the Map'a Mayo that Qoropuna expels water eastward, and back into the world of the living (see Figure 14). Several people in Huaquirca told me that the Map'a Mayo disappears underground a short distance from its source in Qoropuna, and that its waters divide thereafter. My suspicion (although I never had it directly confirmed) is that the Map'a Mayo's unruly waters are thought to feed the various 'wild lakes' (*lagunas bravas*) that informants identified in the region. One 'wild lake' reported

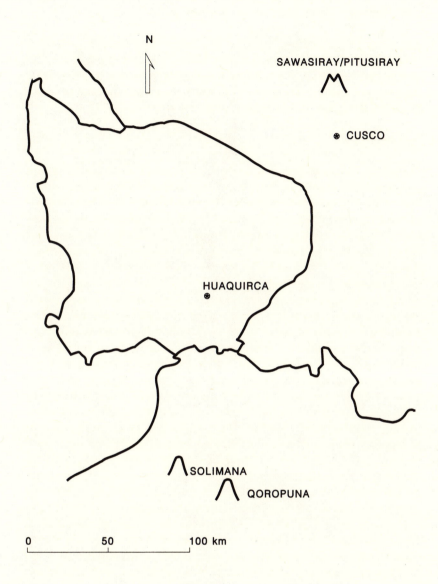

Figure 13   Mountains of maize and mountains of the dead

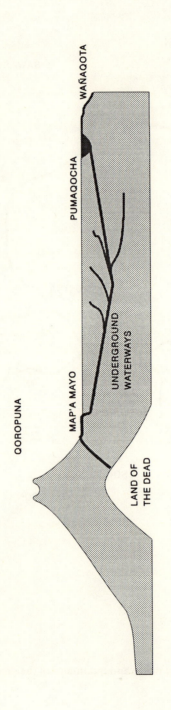

QOROPUNA

MAP'A MAYO

PUMAQOCHA

WAÑAQOTA

UNDERGROUND WATERWAYS

LAND OF THE DEAD

Figure 14   Expulsion of water from Qoropuna

by Stein (1961: 305) retains its connection to the dead by bearing the name Awkish Qocha (Lake of the Ancients). The 'wild lake' of Huaquirca is known as Pumaqocha (Puma Lake), as are many other such lakes throughout the Andes (Earls and Silverblatt 1978: 315). People said that Pumaqocha causes lightning, hail, and storms when anyone tries to catch the large, whiskered trout that live in it, and that it controls weather in the locality.[31] Like all 'wild lakes' in the region, an especially volatile feline called an *uturunku*[32] inhabits its depths, imparting similar qualities to the water, only sallying forth when it wants to cause a storm. We have already seen that the turbulence of the Map'a Mayo may also be attributed to a puma, and this is probably because the two bodies of water are assumed to share a subterranean link and an ultimate origin in the land of the dead.[33] Through these underground connections, the land of the dead supplies the living with water in the various localities they inhabit.

Abundant references to fire, heat, and thirst in the experience of the dead underwrite this expulsion of water from Qoropuna back into the land of the living. First, the clothes washing is marked by a polarization of fire and water in which the ragged clothes and favourite foods of the deceased are burned, whereas the clothes retained by the living are washed. This opposition of fire and water adds a new dimension to the emphasis on separation in death, and perhaps suggests that the *alma* undergoes a reduction by burning that is comparable to this treatment of its food and dress.[34] Descriptions of the land of the dead as a place of chili pepper cultivation (Harris 1982: 62) and a myth in which Qoropuna serves burning food to the Inca (Roel Pineda 1965: 25) further associate the afterlife with heat and burning. Geographically, Qoropuna is associated with heat and dryness because of its location on the arid western slope of the Andes. Thus, a gourd may be tied to the wrist of the cadaver so that the soul may drink (Stein 1961: 282), and avid thirst is said to characterize the *alma*'s journey to the afterlife (Zuidema and Quispe 1968: 360). Prohibitions against salt and chili consumption during mourning (Harris 1982: 52) might help to prevent a contagion of burning dehydration among the living through their attachment to the deceased. Similar prohibitions of dried meat (*charki*), salt, and chili in times of drought (Yaranga 1979: 703) underline that this process of desiccation should be taking place in the world of the dead, to provide this world with water. The same ideas inform the allegation that a brick-maker from Puno residing in the Antabamba Valley caused the drought of 1982–3 by burning bones of the pre-Columbian dead (*gentiles*). Cremation is not widely practised in the Andes, probably because it violates the idea that the dead should be dried out in the underworld, to provide the living with water.

The intense heat of Qoropuna seems to dry and shrink the dead. This tendency is particularly evident in those accounts that describe the shrunken proportions of the land of the dead, and the dead themselves as miniature versions of living people. With this heat-induced diminution of the dead comes a corresponding decline in their subjective capacities and perhaps their activity level, but otherwise their world is very much like ours. The by-product of this transformation is water (cf. Bastien 1985: 597, 601), which is expelled back into the land of the living through a small but turbulent stream, the Map'a Mayo. In losing these waters, the dead also lose much of their sensory capacities, their animation, and the growth that they achieved in life. All of these characteristics are attributed in local thought to the *ánimo*, which is precisely what the *alma* lacks on death. Vitality has no place in the land of the dead, and departs from it through the active waters of the Map'a Mayo. Therefore, it appears that this stream originates in an ongoing separation of *ánimo* from *alma* in Qoropuna, a process that begins with death in this world, but extends well into the afterlife.

If water is what the dead give back to the realm of life, then it is understandable that the Map'a Mayo should present such a dramatic obstacle to the *alma* on its journey to Qoropuna. In water, the *alma* is confronted with a product of its own decomposition, a pure vital force (cf. Ossio 1978b: 381) turned alien and antagonistic, which it can no longer embody as *ánimo*. The separating role of this water has been noted by Harris (1982: 55), and can be explained by its connection with vitality: once across, the soul is literally on the far side of life.[35] This is why a contrasting imagery of black and white occurs around the Map'a Mayo. Its raging, energetic water resists embodiment in a human form, and threatens to overpower the intimidated *alma*, which can no longer act for itself. Therefore, it is up to the living, who still incorporate *ánimo* and can keep the Map'a Mayo in perspective, to help the soul across. What the *alma* experiences at the Map'a Mayo is the crisis of death in a particularly acute form, one in which it faces life as an alien and overwhelming substance.

The water expelled from Qoropuna contains a vitality that has escaped human embodiment, and can no longer assume the humanized form of *ánimo*. Unlike humans, however, plants can absorb this water, and convert it into a source of life and growth. Water is the key cosmological link between the realm of death and the realm of agriculture. As the soul is reduced by heat in the afterlife, the animating water that it once embodied is driven back into the land of the living, where it is absorbed by plants. Thus, plants are the initial beneficiaries of human death, and are dependent upon it for their own life.

As life forms, people and plants are both united and divided by their reliance on water as an animating force. Although water is the common denominator of life for both, the very fact that it can be recycled from people to plants (and back again) suggests that it is embodied in one form at the expense of the other. This zero-sum game is one powerful reason why the ritual imagery of death permeates the tasks of irrigation and sowing that mark the resumption of the growing season. At another level, however, human life is sustained by the crops, and through them the living manage to recapture the energy released by the dead. By 'interring' seed, the living manage to partially recuperate the by-products of the physical and spiritual breakdown of the dead in a regenerative agricultural synthesis. Agriculture is a central but complex mediation between the living and the dead because it simultaneously renews and extinguishes human life.

There is an Andean concept that unites deathly separation and agricultural synthesis into a single process: *pallqa*. This word denotes the simultaneous bifurcation and confluence of running water (see Earls and Silverblatt 1978: 312). Because Andean people often hold that there are underground rivers that flow in a direction opposite to their aboveground counterparts (see Allen 1988: 52), the bi-directional flow of water posited by the concept of *pallqa* becomes less of a paradox. Here, unity and separation fuse in a single esoteric concept that perfectly captures the flow of water between death and life, people and plants. A related image is that of the twin peaks of Sawasiray and Pitusiray, the mountain spirits in charge of maize, which are often represented by two cobs of maize joined at the base (see Chapter 7). In earlier times, such siamese twin cobs were called *aya apa choclo*: 'cobs of the dead' (see González Holguín 1608: 31). It is as if they stand midway between the separation of death and the synthesis of the crops, and incorporate aspects of both.

However, it is not just the dead who sustain local agriculture. The role of the living is also crucial, but as we saw, their work is metaphorically represented as death and spiritual judgment in the rituals of irrigation and sowing. Now that we have traced the connection of the dead to agriculture, we can turn to how these notions of death structure the labour of the living. Therefore, let us return to the previously elusive details of irrigation and the sowing, and complete their analysis.

We have already noted the correspondence of the irrigation to the clothes washing in funerary rites, but it is now possible to explain the sense of danger about both tasks by connecting it with the symbolic origin of water from the land of the dead. It seems likely that irrigators fear their contact with water because the *chuqchu* (malaria, shivering) it induces is all too similar to the deathly breakdown that gives rise to water.[36] In the past, when commoners from Apurímac and Ayacucho journeyed to the coastal valleys associated with the land of the dead, they often came back with fatal cases of malaria (Montoya 1980: 274). So even though contact with irrigation water falls well short of the absolute antagonism that the *alma* experiences before the Map'a Mayo, the fear that it will produce *chuqchu* amounts to something of the same thing. Yet it would clearly be wrong to simply equate this water with death, first because it is expelled from Qoropuna, and second because it is the catalyst that will activate the growth of the maize (the interaction of *sawasira* and *pitusira*). Rather, it should be seen as a wholly disembodied vital force, pure *ánimo*, which is extracted from the reduction of the *alma* by heat in Qoropuna, and expelled from the land of the dead as an alien substance. It is the hostility of this water to embodiment that makes it dangerous and corrosive, and shivering is an indication of its unincorporable vitality. Thus, in life as in death, water is 'the enemy of our *alma*,' as the Macha of Bolivia put it (Platt 1986: 247).

Pito is an appropriate antidote to this water in several ways. As corn beer made turgid by the addition of considerable quantities of toasted maize flour, *pito* all but cries out for dilution. This toasted maize flour can absorb the cold, energetic water expelled from the land of the dead in the way that maize seeds are meant to do, but the bodies and souls of men are not. Therefore, *pito* acts as a buffer. It not only restores an equilibrium of wet and dry, but also of hot and cold, and thus reunites these polar separations caused by death. This interpretation is further supported by the linguistic derivation of *pitusira* from *pito*, since the former is sometimes considered the *alma* of maize, and would, therefore, be an appropriate vehicle to absorb the disembodied *ánimo* of water. Besides the flour that is added to make the drink, *pito* denotes a pair or the pairing of like things (González Holguín 1608: 293; Lira 1944: 758), which recalls the integrating effect that this drink has on *alma* and *ánimo* in the face of the separated and separating nature of water.[37]

Yet water remains an almost pure form of vitality both in spite of and because of its connection to death, and this is why women are systematically kept away from it in irrigation and funerary clothes washing. Contact with the dead is supposed to affect women's fertility in a negative manner, and cause monstrous births (Harris 1982: 65). Similarly, contact with water during menstruation is held to cause the birth of defective individuals (Bolton and Bolton 1976: 660), or a bloating that induces sterility or death (Bourque and Warren 1981: 112). The problem with water is not just that it can impregnate women, but that it does so destructively or at least improperly. Water is meant to awaken life in the crops, not in women. Again, we see that cultivated plants form an important mediation between the living and the dead, one that allows the living to productively harness the energy released by the dead. Thus, water and maize appear to be two basic components of life, pure vitality and pure embodiment, whose degree of contrast is far greater than that between *alma* and *ánimo*. Once water has been absorbed and transformed by plants, however, it is no longer a threat, and can even be consumed, provided that it is cooked first. Nowhere are the subtleties of this transformation more apparent than in the production of corn beer for agricultural work parties, and the various ways it is distributed in this context.

Women are the exclusive producers of corn beer (*aqha*) in Huaquirca. They start by grinding dried kernels of corn with stones (*batanes*) and add water to make a dough during the latter stages of the grinding process. When preparing *laqto*, the variety of corn beer preferred by commoners, women spit into this dough as they grind it, which presumably helps break its carbohydrates down into sugars, to the benefit of the fermentation process. Once the dough is sufficiently fine-grained, the women divide it into pieces, drop them in various tins, dilute them with water, and boil the mixture vigorously for many hours. Sometimes the women will add sugar to the wort for extra strength. When the wort has cooled, they pour it into large pottery jugs that contain sediment from a previous brew, which will leaven the new batch. Then they cover the jugs and leave the brew to ferment for three days to a week, depending on the time of the year.

Once fermented, corn beer still contains the vitalizing powers of irrigation water, and may even be attributed the power to cause the instant germination of maize seeds, as in the 'lake' (*qocha*) from which everyone drinks during the 'libation of the seed.' Corn beer is also treated as a catalyst of life in relation to women, since it is apparently represented as sperm in certain contexts (see Allen 1988: 174). Unlike irrigation water, however, it is not said to cause monstrous births, and women consume it as readily as men. Therefore, corn beer appears to be a more mediated substance, one that bears both vitality and the impulse towards embodiment. Nonetheless, vitality predominates, and corn beer is sometimes represented as a fuel, as when a commoner remarked to me that his 'motor doesn't work without gasoline' while downing a cup. Men regularly remarked to me that one drinks corn beer 'to animate one's self' in work (cf. Doughty 1967: 677), and it always did seem to have that effect. The same is said of the cane alcohol and coca that are given out in work parties, and may be called '*el ánimo*' (Montoya 1980: 251) in an even more explicit reference to this soul or quality. In all of these cases, corn beer seems to add vitality in a simple, mechanical fashion, which boosts the *ánimo* or energy principle that is contained within the body.

As with irrigation water, however, the life-awakening properties of corn beer derive from an intimate relation with death. By 'animating' the men in their work, corn beer promotes the productive expenditure of energy that is represented as 'salvation' in the sowing divinations. Work is modelled on death. As the men sweat in their labour, so they prove their spiritual worthiness. Here, it seems that the outpouring of productive energy from the body of the living worker is entirely parallel to the outpouring of water from the *almas* in the land of the dead. Beyond inspiring the men to work up a sweat, corn beer also induces them to urinate copiously, an image that is sometimes used to depict the way Qoropuna provides this world with water (see Roel Pineda 1965: 25). Both the living and the dead expel aquatic energy at the expense of the body, which is converted or consumed to produce the desired 'animation.' This suggests that corn beer does not mechanically add vitality to the body as much as it generates energy from a reductive internal transformation. The animating effect of corn beer is profoundly linked to the notion of work as death and spiritual judgment because it is based on the same deathly separation of energy from embodiment.

Fermentation is the key to understanding how corn beer causes this 'animating' but deathly separation in the worker. In the sowing, water and maize are combined to create germination and growth, but in the production of corn beer, they are combined through fermentation, a process that is closely allied to the decomposition of death (cf. Lévi-Strauss 1964: 158–60). Those who drink corn beer undergo a kind of fermentation process themselves, in which labour power is released like alcohol during a process of 'salvation' that leaves an organic residual (*wanu*): the body transformed by death. The divinations of the sowing identify men with the by-products of this polarization, and in so doing, differentiate them. However, the 'death' ensuing from the consumption of corn beer is clearly a metaphorical one, which is marked by a less intense process of separation. Energy release in the worker 'animated' by corn beer is more subtle and directed than the shivering that results from contact with irrigation water. This is because corn beer is a more complex and mediated substance that tempers the pure vitality of water with the embodying virtues of maize. As a result, the energy released by the consumption of corn beer is not as unruly as the turbulent waters of the Map'a Mayo, and is channelled into the institutionalized form of *ayni*. This transformation is neatly demonstrated by the names given to various ways of serving corn beer.

The most frequent form, in which a woman serves a man a single cup or horn, is called *maña*. This is derived from *mañay*, which refers to the procedure of formal request in *ayni*, whereby a host solicits help for a work party with a few swallows of cane alcohol and a good deal of cajolery, often in an exaggerated high whining tone (cf. Mayer 1974: 46–50, 1977: 63–7; Flores and Nájar 1980: 487–90). Another definition of *maña*, 'what should be lent, that which should be requested' (Lira 1944: 628), focuses even more clearly on the *ayni* to be advanced or reciprocated. According to one woman in Huaquirca with whom I discussed the subject, *maña* means 'something which lacks its pair.' More than a simple drink, then, *maña* establishes the lack of, and need to return, an equivalent thing, which initially is the labour power of the man who drinks it (the 'animating' effect of corn beer), and ultimately is the reduplication of the process on another day, or the return of the *ayni*. Thus, the consumption of single servings of corn beer, known as *maña*, expresses relations of *ayni* and drives them forward.

Another mode of serving corn beer is called *yanantin*, and consists of a woman serving two cups to a man, who then passes one of them on to a second man of his choice. The literal meaning of *yanantin* might be 'helper and helped united to form a single category' (Platt 1986: 245), much as *yanapa* (help) is *ayni* without a strict calculation of labour debts and credits. Nonetheless, *yanantin* refers almost exclusively to a pair of categorically equal things (cf. Platt 1986: 245), such as the two cups of corn beer in this case. The two possible meanings of the word are complementary here, since the identical pair is the formula for *ayni* ('like for like'), and can, therefore, incorporate the reference to mutual aid implicit in the literal sense of *yanantin*. In turn, both meanings of *yanantin* connect with the idea of 'salvation,' which is designated by the result of a pair in the *samakuy* divination, and refers to the vigour of a man's work. *Yanantin* realizes the pair posited, but not yet achieved, in the serving of *maña*. However, this couplet is no longer that of a woman serving and a man receiving, but rather a continuation from this initial act to a second act of serving among two men, a transformation of gender difference towards symmetry and identity that characterizes other manifestations of *yanantin* (cf. Platt 1986: 248, 252). The symmetry achieved by the reduplication of the act of serving in *yanantin* shares with *ayni* the repetition of the same service. Although *yanantin* can be served in any work party during the growing season, it is not an everyday occurrence, but one that marks particular enthusiasm or accomplishment in work, which again connects it closely to the notion of 'salvation' as the intense expenditure of energy during production.

Thus, men drink under the sign of *ayni* just as they work under the sign of death, and both of these domains turn out to share the same formula of symmetric duality. The two processes largely imply each other, since *ayni* labour is generated by a deathly equalization of soul sizes, and that equalization of souls is orchestrated by the symmetric model of *ayni*. To achieve 'salvation' in work, a man must expend a tremendous amount of embodied energy. He generates this energy by drinking corn beer, which 'animates' his body but also depletes and reduces it, in a process modelled on the fate of the *alma* on death. In work, the *alma* or 'big soul' shrinks, and approaches an equalization with the *ánimo* or 'little soul.' This transformation of souls towards symmetry is what allows 'salvation' to be achieved as an intense release of productive energy in work. The consumption of corn beer not only sets this process off by modifying the relation between *alma* and *ánimo* in the body, but also captures the energy that results for the social process of *ayni* by bearing the labels *maña* and *yanantin*. Thus, the connection between death and *ayni* labour is a substantive one that is mediated by the consumption of corn beer, and this connection underwrites their shared formula of symmetric duality.

Much has been made of *ayni*, the advance and return of like for like, as a cosmological principle (e.g., Núñez del Prado 1972: 136, 150–1; Earls and Silverblatt 1978: 309; Custred 1979: 392). Without endorsing the romantic excesses of some analysts, I agree that the principle of *ayni* does inform the parallel contributions of the living and the dead to agriculture, and the cyclical movements of sun and water between their respective worlds, which Bastien (1978: 53) aptly compares to the stroke of a pendulum. Specifically, when people 'do *ayni*' with the dead by providing alcohol at the burial, the dead repay them with water during the rainy season. Indeed, I would argue that this relation with the dead explains why libations figure so prominently in Andean ritual as a whole. Urton (1981: 26) has even argued that drinking may be a way of 'calling water,' in which saturation of the drinker's body helps bring about a similar saturation of the earth. The living and the dead practise another form of *ayni* when they provide labour power and water as like forms of energy that become embodied in the crops as an object of 'salvation.' In this way, the 'work as death' theme developed in relations of *ayni* among the living becomes a prelude to their doing *ayni* with the dead. For it is only through this broader collaboration that the conditions of agriculture can truly be secured.

Having said this much, however, we must return to the initial asymmetry that led us to understand sowing on the model of death, and that continues to deny a fully reciprocal relation between them. Although human death and the growth of the crops share a complex set of metaphorical interconnections, the intelligibility of this relationship derives primarily from local reflections on death, which are far more elaborated than those on the sowing. The fact that work in the sowing is evaluated in terms of 'salvation' is a key piece of semantic evidence, which tells us where to look for a fuller understanding. In the metaphorical relation that results, it is death that establishes non-identity and movement (in the separation of the *alma*, its journey, and the return of water) that allows the sowing to create a new synthesis. An equally pervasive asymmetry remains to be explored in the organization of domestic labour.

Just as there is an asymmetry between souls in the body, so there is an asymmetry between women and men in the household. To put it crudely and schematically, women are to men as the *alma* is to the *ánimo*. Like the *alma*, women are primarily identified with embodiment, and like the *ánimo*, men are primarily identified with energy. Furthermore, the reductive transformation of souls towards symmetry in work parallels the gender transformation effected by the serving of *yanantin*, in which the asymmetry of woman and man is converted into the symmetry of two men. Women disappear not only in the serving of *yanantin*, but also in the divinations of the sowing and the wake. They do so in these contexts for the same reasons they do in the irrigation and the funerary clothes washing: to preserve themselves from inappropriate contact with the deathly dissolution of the body, and to safeguard their embodying capacities. Similarly, women may appear not to participate in *ayni*,[38] and thus to avoid the deathly equalization of souls in productive labour. One day when I was working in the fields, however, a man took me aside and solemnly told me that although it may look as if women do not work as hard or as often as men in agriculture, there would be no work parties at all if women did not first prepare corn beer for everyone. Thus, I was let in on the 'secret' of women's relative invisibility in the contexts described here, which is their outright control over consumption, and other processes that affirm the life and growth of the body.

In Huaquirca, as elsewhere, women control and manage the domestic food supply, with a right that borders on absolute ownership.[39] To this right accrues the duty of preparing food and drink, but this is itself a form of power. In Huaquirca, it is unthinkable for a man to make corn beer,[40] and this makes it impossible for a single man to run a household, for no matter how many days' 'credit' he accumulates working in *ayni* for other people, he cannot sponsor a work party of his own without corn beer (see also Núñez del Prado 1975b: 625–6; Allen 1988: 83). Single women, on the other hand, can and do sponsor work parties by simply providing corn beer to the men who work in them; they make no pretence of returning a day's labour. Nothing could better demonstrate that women personify the proprietorial aspect of the household. It is an expression of women's power, not marginality, that they do not join in male-dominated rituals of labour, death, and equality.

The exchange of female labour embodied in corn beer for male field labour could easily be construed as an example of *mink'a* hierarchy (cf. Şkar 1982: 248), but in Huaquirca it is not proclaimed as such. On the contrary, notions of *maña* and *yanantin* frame the serving and consumption of corn beer, and represent it as an aspect of *ayni*. Otherwise, *ayni* would have to suppress the issue of consumption altogether, and become an equal exchange of labour days among men, as happens in some areas (e.g., Malengreau 1980: 510), and as is also suggested by the elimination of women in the *yanantin* transformation.

But this productivist male symmetry is little more than wishful thinking. It would be more precise to say that the relative equalization of
men that takes place in *ayni* results not from suppression of the
female-dominated framework of domestic appropriation, but rather
from how men circulate and substitute for each other within it. This
takes us back to *ayni* as something more than mere labour exchange
among commoners, namely a socialized recognition of property (see
Chapter 2).

There is a certain intimacy in the use of the conjugal model as a
basis for interhousehold cooperation. One example is that corn beer
fermentation requires that women spit into the dough from which the
brew is made, a fact that some notables dwell on with disgust in their
more general repudiation of commoner life and its semiotics.[41] Yet
there is an unmistakably sexual dimension to this use of conjugal principles in cooperation that we have already glimpsed in the mock
remarriages of the house rethatching and the *qhashwa* dances discussed in the previous chapter. This dimension is further developed by
the predication of *ayni* on spouse-sharing in areas where interhousehold cooperation is unusual (Bolton 1974a: 162), and reports of an
overt sexual connotation to men and women working together in the
fields in areas where *ayni* is common (Skar 1982: 129, 232). In the previous chapter, we also saw how young men come uninvited to work on
the land of the parents of a woman in whom they may be interested
(which casts a new light on the figure of the 'son-in-law' in the sowing). All of this shows that cooperative work takes place within a framework of conjugal appropriation, and is grounded in desires that
correspond to it. In common with 'work as death,' however, 'work as
desire' breaks down the boundaries of the particular self and the particular conjugal unit and recombines their elements into new entities
synthesized along the lines of the old. The remarriage of the *alma* to a
new partner on arrival in Qoropuna is a case in point, which shows
that death carries on where *ayni* in this world leaves off. Yet there is an
asymmetry in these recombinations, since seeds, women, and other
forces of embodiment attract and predominate. Perhaps this is why
Qoropuna, the mountain of the dead, is sometimes described as a
young woman (Roel Pineda 1965: 25, note that in Quechua, *qoro*
means young woman).

It is not surprising that in many parts of the Andes there are prohibitions against men distributing seed during the sowing (Isbell 1978: 57;
Lund Skar 1979: 454), although this is not so in Huaquirca. Female

control of seeds, apart from its proprietorial significance, is in many ways the positive side of women's exclusion from contact with the corpse, the waters of funerary clothes washing, and irrigation. It seems that women are quarantined from these processes of deathly separation to accentuate their embodying capacities. By controlling seeds, however, women can harness this potentially destructive energy, and the men who deal with it. Just as *ayni* in this world takes place through the framework of conjugal appropriation, so the *ayni* that takes place between the living and the dead, in the parallel release of energy from the 'animated' male body in work, and turbulent water from the desiccated *alma,* comes about through their mutual subordination to the seed.[42]

This is an image of male-female cooperation that the sowing itself provides us with, in the *wankas* sung by single women for the *qatay* ('son-in-law') and *comadres.* Both play directive roles, the 'son-in-law' by orchestrating the themes of work as death and sowing as burial, and the *comadres* by distributing the seeds that will bring the field back to life. The complementarity that exists between these two roles should now be evident. But this complementarity does not imply that the two figures are somehow 'equal.' Despite the minimal ritual elaboration of their role, the *comadres* encompass and prevail. It is they who distribute the seed that absorbs the deathly labour power generated by the 'son-in-law' and his male cohorts. The hierarchical dimension of this relationship is unmistakable, and is the background against which the egalitarianism of *ayni* must be understood as a mixed blessing, in which it is not always possible to distinguish brotherhood from death.

5

From All Saints' to Christmas

By All Saints' Day (1 November), most of the terraced land below Huaquirca has been sown with maize, even if some people may still be
holding out for increased natural rainfall. Slightly before All Saints',
the first fields sown in mid-September are due for the next agricultural
task, the *mallma* or second irrigation (as opposed to the *qarpay*, which
precedes the sowing). Shortly after follows the first hoeing, or *hallma*.
Not only is the sowing nearing completion, but agricultural tasks are
starting to overlap, a situation that will prevail throughout the peak of
the growing season. Rainfall becomes more intense and frequent, and
the temperature contrasts between night and day diminish further.
This thermal equalization of night and day, abundance of rainfall, and
proliferation of agricultural work can be seen as an intensification of
the *ayni* between living and dead that was initiated with the sowing.
Appropriately enough, people say that the *almas* return to this world
from Qoropuna for the feasts of All Saints' and the Day of the Dead
(2 November).

All Saints' and the Day of the Dead

The first sign that something is to happen on these days comes on 31
October, when blasts of gunpowder are let off in the fields associated
with the sponsorship of Christmas festivities (*Taytaq* and *Mamaq*). In
some places, it is said that these explosions announce the arrival of the
dead (Bastien 1978: 178). Nonetheless, the following day (All Saints')
is spent working in the fields, like any other at this time of the year. At
night, however, those who have had a death in the family during the

previous year assemble an 'altar.' This consists of a small table onto which the clothes of the deceased that were washed during the funeral are placed, along with a photograph or other personal memorabilia, a selection of choice foods, and two lit candles of unequal diameter (see also Bastien 1978: 179–80; Buechler 1980: 80; Harris 1982: 56). This altar becomes the object of an all-night vigil similar to the one that takes place on death, with the exception that no games of chance are played, and few, if any, of the non-consanguines of the deceased attend.

During the night, a figure known as the *Paqpako* does the rounds of all the houses where vigils are taking place. *Paqpako* refers to an owl (sometimes called *paqo-paqo*) that announces an imminent human death with its cry. This was an important *cargo* in Huaquirca until recent years,[1] and still carries with it a field for the sponsor. The *Paqpako* dresses in a loose black cowl, and performs a special song and dance that are meant to condole the mourners in each household performing a vigil. Yet he invariably steals part of the food offerings that are put out for the returning *almas* during his performance and, in this sense, ridicules the continuing attachment of the living to the dead. After visiting all of the houses in mourning, he retires to the graveyard to dance on the graves until dawn, drinking with an entourage of friends, and placing an arc of eucalyptus boughs over the cemetery gate. Through this series of actions in the graveyard, the *Paqpako* is said to provide for the returning dead who have nobody left to remember them, and thus prevents their displeasure from befalling the community (see also Montoya 1980: 251).

Nobody works on the Day of the Dead. Those with kin who have been dead for some time may prepare a mid-day meal consisting of the deceased's favourite dishes. An extra place is set at the table and served with food for the returning soul. Some people express the idea that the *almas* return as flies on these days (cf. Bastien 1978: 179); therefore, it is forbidden to kill them. Thus, it is a matter of satisfaction for the kin to see a fly hover over or alight on the serving that has been put out for the returning *alma*. In the early afternoon, everyone goes to the cemetery to put wreaths of flowers on the graves of people they wish to remember. Bunches of large white *hamank'ays* (which I was told are 'especially for the dead') accompany or substitute for the wreaths, but are never woven into them. Elsewhere, food may be put on the graves to attract and nourish the dead (Hartman 1973: 180–4; Flores 1979: 64). Certain men in the community who have been trained as sacristans are eagerly sought after to say prayers in Latin over the graves, for which they are lavishly rewarded in cane alcohol. Everyone else pours libations of corn beer or cane alcohol on the graves. The event quickly devolves into extreme drunkenness, and by mid-afternoon, if heavy rains have not already driven people indoors, the mourners begin reeling home, either to pass out or continue their vigils. Generally, a priest from the neighbouring town of Antabamba comes to celebrate mass in the afternoon, and people were very upset when he did not in 1982. At the back of the church in Huaquirca is a crude adobe altar with various niches in it, each containing a skull, which is said to be dedicated to the Day of the Dead (see also Harris 1982: 61).

On the Day of the Dead it is customary to eat *phatawa* in Huaquirca. This dish is prepared by boiling whole cobs of dried maize in water. It contrasts with the normal mode of cooking dried maize, in which grains are stripped from the cob before boiling to produce a dish called *mote*. *Phatawa* has a hard, chewy texture: the grains never entirely rehydrate because they still adhere to the cob. Some people eat *phatawa* throughout November, and it is occasionally served at funerals as well, but it is the classic and often exclusive dish that is served at sundown on the Day of the Dead,[2] and it is generally confined to this occasion. It is during this second night of vigil, I was told, that the *alma* departs again for Qoropuna, but its journey does not appear to involve the same tribulations as the one following death. By the morning of 3 November, most people are back at work in the fields, and only those who have been conducting a vigil for someone who died during the past year are likely to stay at home.

All Saints' and the Day of the Dead recapitulate many aspects of individual death, but with some important differences. First, the washed clothes take the place of the cadaver during the vigil, as if they had the power to attract the *alma* back from Qoropuna towards its former condition in life. The same could be said of the food offerings on the 'altar' and the mid-day meal served for the *alma*. Whereas the living burned the *alma*'s clothes and food to banish it from this world and initiate its journey into the afterlife, they now seem to reconsider and even reverse this process by again extending these items to the *alma* to induce its return. The idea that the *alma* returns as a fly, on the other hand, is evidence of the transformation that it has undergone in the afterlife. Since it is sometimes said that the *ánimo* leaves the body as a blue fly (*chiririnka*) on death, it would now appear that the *alma* has been reduced to the same size and condition in Qoropuna (see Arguedas 1956: 266). The asymmetry that existed between *alma* and *ánimo* (or in other terms, major *alma* and minor *alma*) reduces to a symmetry of flies in the separation of death, much as the asymmetry between women and men is reduced to a symmetric pair of men by the *yanantin* transformation (cf. Platt 1986: 248, 252). Nonetheless, these flies are still *almas*: they have a kind of nostalgia for life, and return for the food and clothing that accompanies it. They never completely lose their affinity for physical and social incorporation that characterized their life, any more than they are completely forgotten by their kin. It is this state of affairs that leads both living and dead back to the mutual attachment of the mourning period, and undoes the separation previously achieved in funerary rites.

Another aspect of this regressive process is eating *phatawa*, maize cooked in a manner that refuses to separate grain from cob, *sawasira* from *pitusira*. This cooking technique seems designed to restore the living unity of a fresh ear of maize that has not yet been dried in the sun and frost of the dry season. It is precisely this refusal of separation, however, that prevents a real restoration of life. *Phatawa* is cooked and, therefore, cannot serve as seed, yet it remains hard and dry inside, so neither does it conform to local culinary codes. The productive consumption of maize, whether as food or seed, demands the destruction of the formal unity of a dried ear. Similarly, 'salvation,' or the proper expenditure of productive energy in the sowing, demands that death first be accepted. It seems that just as All Saints' and the Day of the Dead deny or undo the separation of the living and the dead, they also deny the separation between grain (*sawasira*) and cob (*pitusira*) in maize. The parallelism and substantive interconnection between these two 'domains' continues.

The *Paqpako* challenges this renewed attachment to dead kin. Although he links all of the vigils in his round, the *Paqpako* also steals the food that continues to link the *alma* to its living kin, and maintains its corporeal individuality. In so doing, he begins to break the bonds of kinship between the living and the dead, and makes a mockery of their mutual attachment (like affines among the Laymi, see Harris 1982: 60). With his black cowl, the *Paqpako* resembles the *apaq* who arise collectively from their tombs to cause death (see Chapter 4), and this is corroborated by his very name, which refers to the owl whose cry announces death. By dancing on the tombs, the *Paqpako* presents death and its collectivization as a cause for celebration, not mourning.

Finally, his message is clear: there can be no consolation, let alone renewal, by means of grief.

This function of the *Paqpako* fits well with Harris' (1982: 55–6) argument that the observances of All Saints' and the Day of the Dead de-individuate death and give it a more collective orientation. There is an additional dimension to this in Huaquirca, where the sowing that has been taking place for a month and a half on individual parcels of land, and very much under the sign of death, is now coming to a close, and is also collectivized by these rites. Indeed, this emphasis on overcoming attachment to individual dead is so strong in Huaquirca that it leads to a denial of the Laymi belief that the dead remain in this world until Carnival to make the crops grow (see Harris 1982: 58–62). This became clear to me one day in November during a rest period at a hoeing work party, when a man was pouring libations for someone who had just died and his ancestors, as he explained to me that the dead 'are for us, a second God, only just below Jesus Christ,' and that one should always ask advice from 'the most capable' among them. Having by then worked out a cruder version of the analysis presented in the previous chapter, I took the opportunity to ask, 'Do the dead make the crops grow then?' to which he replied with a knowing smile, 'No, we don't believe that.' Perhaps this encounter shows little more than the futility of a questioning procedure that asks people to make 'beliefs' out of their ritual imagery,[3] but it is also true that this imagery does not suggest that it is the dead, as integral beings, who renew the life of the crops. On the contrary, it is the breakdown of the *alma*, and its release of energy in the anonymous form of water, that leads to the germination and growth of the seeds, a point that Harris (1982: 60) acknowledges in noting that it is only gradually that the deceased becomes incorporated into the collective energies that produce the crops. Since the *almas* never appear to achieve complete de-individuation, however, there is inevitably a certain ambiguity here.

Finally, there is no simple or unidirectional transition from individuality to collectivity that takes place in these rites, although this is the desired outcome. For it is equally, if not more profoundly, recognized that individualized attachments between the living and the dead remain, and create the generalized regression to a state of mourning on these days that calls the counter-tendency towards collectivization into being. This is effectively the same tension between failure and success in the attainment of 'salvation' that is present in the sowing. In the case of Huaquirca, at least, it is wrong to presume that this dilemma is resolved by the observances of All Saints' and the Day of the Dead, since they lack any conclusive gestures, and simply fade back into more agricultural work. I will argue below that it is only in the Christmas festivities that the deathly preoccupations of the sowing, All Saints', and the Day of the Dead are convincingly resolved.

Second Irrigation

Even though it rains frequently by November, it is generally necessary to irrigate those fields sown in September a second time to ensure crop growth; in some years, even the last plots to be sown require a second irrigation. Depending on climatic conditions, this second irrigation will take place a month to six weeks after the sowing, when the maize seedlings are about ten centimetres high. With plants growing in the field, it is impossible to irrigate as thoroughly as before the sowing, and the men take great care not to uproot the seedlings with their picks, or excessively strong flows of water. This second irrigation is made even more difficult by the use of footploughs in the sowing, which leaves the plants growing in a scattered pattern. In contrast, a feature of sowing by bull-drawn plough is that once a terrace has been completed, the plough cuts long diagonal furrows down the terrace that displace seeds to either side, thus creating a channel for subsequent irrigation. Work parties in the second irrigation tend to be small, seldom consisting of more than four or five men. There will also be one or two women to serve corn beer, but as in the first irrigation, they do not work in the fields or come in contact with the water. The small size of these work parties is due, in part, to the unintensive nature of the irrigation. It is also due to the fact that agricultural tasks are now beginning to accumulate and overlap. The same number of people are distributed among many more work parties. In 1982, heavy rains arrived early, and the second irrigation was carried out on only a few of the first parcels to be sown, so I was unable to participate in this task.

First Hoeing

The first hoeing, or *hallma*, generally follows the second irrigation by a few days, but when the second irrigation is omitted, hoeing takes place four to six weeks after the sowing. Therefore, this task is already under way by late October, and will continue to mid-December. The aim of the first hoeing is both to remove weeds and to pile up soil at the base of the young plants for protection against the wind. This is done with a hoe (*lampa*), which is used only by men. It consists of a steel shovel blade with a collar into which is fixed a handle about 80–100 cm long that doubles back over the blade at a very closed angle of about thirty degrees. To operate the tool, the men bend deeply at the knees and lean forward from the waist, working in a position verging on a crouch. Despite the irregular pattern of plant distribution, hoeing proceeds in an orderly fashion, with up to five men working across a single terrace advancing in adjacent parallel columns, and returning in the opposite direction. Starting from a full arm's reach, a hoer drags soil back towards his body, depositing it around the stalks of nearby plants with deft flicks of the wrist to either side. Men take care to alternate the side of their body from which they launch each successive drag of the hoe. They advance along the terrace in a kind of herringbone pattern, one drag to the left, one drag to the right, etc.: motions that form a column of hoed ground about a metre wide. Although there is a certain degree of competition among the men to see who can advance the fastest, they also converse, and the working day does not become an explicit race between opposing teams, as in the sowing. Each informal group of hoers keeps to its own terrace, and does not divide it in half with another group against which it competes. In the neighbouring town of Antabamba, men take care to advance evenly across the terrace in a collective front, without leaders or stragglers. Although the themes of competitive individuality versus collectivity are handled differently from town to town in the Antabamba Valley, it seems that there is a general tendency away from competition in this task, perhaps because of the collectivization initiated by All Saints' and the Day of the Dead. The smallest number of men that I saw in a *hallma* was six, but the average was usually about ten to twelve.

Women's work in the *hallma* is remarkably similar to what they do in both the sowing and the second hoeing. Again, most women arrive late, carrying the corn beer that precipitates the first break from work (*samakuy*). Usually, there are only half the number of women present as men, so their absolute number ranges from two to six. When there are only two or three women, they often do not participate in the cultivation of the field at all. When there are more, they will invariably take up small picks or *allachos* to weed the parcel. They concentrate on removing tufts of *kikuyu* grass, which are so detrimental to the growth of the maize, but they also remove other weeds by hand, and toss them to the margins of the field or collecting points in the middle of the terrace. Although men dislodge most of the weeds with their hoes, or bury them with soil, there is always the danger that they will grow back unless they are removed. Thus, the women tease and ridicule the men for not being thorough, and the men respond with charges that women only do 'light' work.

Under no circumstances did I ever see a woman use a hoe or footplough, which are semiotic pillars of male identity comparable in importance to the grinding stones (*batanes*) and jugs (*puñus*) that women use to make corn beer, which as we have already seen, form a domain of heightened male exclusion. The rapt manner in which men may take their hoes and footploughs apart and reassemble them during breaks from work, and pour libations on them, suggests that their involvement with them goes well beyond the instrumental. The tools that women use in the fields may all be used by men in other contexts, and have nothing of this carefully fomented mystique about them. Furthermore, the emphasis that men put on lateral alternation in successive drags of the hoe seems to recall the concern with lateral symmetry in the concept of *yanantin* (see Platt 1986: 245-8), and the 'like for like' formula of *ayni*. Admittedly, this method of work does not explicitly denote relations of *ayni* as did the names of the various ways of serving corn beer mentioned in the previous chapter. It does add an additional expressive dimension to the use of the hoe, however, one that contributes to the tendency of men in valley towns to identify themselves with the principle of *ayni* as it is developed in agricultural labour. Older men will do weeding, however, if there are not enough hoes to go around, or enough women to complete the task.

The first break from work in the hoeing has nothing like the elaborate ritual performances that take place during the sowing. Again, the men sit in lines that extend away from the area where the women pour corn beer into cups from the vessels or skin bags used to transport it to the fields. Occasionally, I saw men bring young seedlings that had been accidentally uprooted by the hoeing, along with some edible weeds that are collected from the fields for stews (i.e., *picante*), and pour a small libation over them, saying something as simple as '¡*sara*!' (maize!), but this is hardly a regular practice. What does begin in a standardized way with the *hallma* is flute playing by men during breaks from work and in the evenings.

These flutes are known as *quenas*, and were once made of cane, but are now universally made of plastic tubing. Usually, only one or two men will play at any one time, even though several may have flutes with them. People commented that the music sounds best when played by a pair of flutes. Once again, there is an emphasis on the identical pair (*yanantin*), as a comment from one man to another that I heard during a break from work illustrates: 'Brother, do you know why I like you so much? It is because we play exactly the same!' The *hallma* (first hoeing) and *kutipa* (second hoeing) both feature particular *quena* tunes that are at once mournful and extremely beautiful, and are sometimes accompanied with improvised lyrics by the women. This stops well short of the elaborate musical coding of the various phases of the rainy season described by Buechler (1980: 40–1, 358), Harris (1982: 58), and Urton (1981: 30–2). It is significant, however, that such music should resume in customary association with a task that follows All Saints'. The magical relation of flute music to rainfall that Harris (1982: 58) suggests is given an interesting twist in Huaquirca by the playing of *quenas* in the *t'inkas* ('libations') of the dry season, not just in these tasks that coincide with the onset of the heavy rains. Instead of expressing the literal presence of the dead, *quena* music could be seen as a way of soliciting rainfall. Men endlessly told me that they play *quenas* to seduce women, not to attract rainfall. In their view, flute music is an object of female desire, perhaps something that counter-balances their own desire for corn beer. If so, the breaks from work in which corn beer and flute music circulate against each other would express a more reciprocal form of gender complementarity ('lack for lack' verging on 'like for like') than the hierarchical relation of unproclaimed *mink'a* discussed in the previous chapter, where the power of corn beer was absolute.

Potato Sowing

Potato sowing (*papa tarpuy*) usually begins in the sectoral fallow fields (*laymis*) above town by mid-November to early December. Many people told me that they sow tubers only when the moon is waxing (*pura*), and in both 1981 and 1982, the task was abruptly curtailed once the moon began to wane (*waña*), although a few notables carried on into this phase. Most of those who had not managed to sow their plots waited until the waxing phase of the next cycle. Elsewhere, a more elaborate version of this scheme applies to all cultivated plants, not just tubers, and people explicitly connect the waxing of the moon to the growth of plants (Brush 1977b: 102). Since both the first and second hoeing are coming due in the terraced fields below town at this time, and can be advanced or postponed to accommodate the dependence of tuber sowing on the lunar cycle, the moon does not create any appreciable problems in the scheduling of agricultural work.

Potato sowing always takes place in the sector of the *laymi* system where ground was broken the previous March. This process will be described in the following chapter. It results in a series of vertically oriented furrows and ridges that are created by cutting a strip of sods to form a furrow, and inverting them on a standing row to form a ridge. In this way, wild vegetation is also smothered and ploughed under. With the arrival of *kikuyu* grass in the 1950s, breaking ground has become considerably more strenuous, and it is all the more necessary to do it well, since the subterranean root of the plant must dry out thoroughly if it is to die. In the lower plots of a given *laymi* sector, a *kikuyu* removal session, or *grameo*, may precede the sowing. In the *grameo*, people advance slowly up the ridges and furrows in an even front, breaking up what remains of the old sods, and removing dead and living tufts of *kikuyu*. Higher up the slope, in areas less heavily infested with *kikuyu*, the *grameo* takes place at the same time as the sowing, and falls to the younger men in the work party due to its strenuous nature. Advancing competitively up the ridges, they lift their picks high over their heads and strike the overturned sods hard with the flat of the blade, dislodging soil from the dried roots. This is by far the hardest agricultural work that I encountered in Huaquirca, and I have no reason to doubt people's claims that *kikuyu* led to a fourfold increase in the time spent to open a plot and reduced the amount of *laymi* land under cultivation.

Behind the men who bash the sods with their picks come the sowing teams. These consist of a man with a footplough and a woman with a supply of small seed potatoes held in one of her multiple skirts (*polleras*). The man, who is usually elderly, sinks his footplough easily into the already loosened soil and pulls back on the handle just enough to open a small space into which the woman drops a potato as the man removes the plough to repeat the procedure thirty to forty centimetres up the ridge. Often there will be only two or three older men with footploughs and five or six women to sow with them, in which case the women take turns working with the men, waiting at the bottom of a ridge until they are next in line. The younger men, who move ahead at a faster pace than the sowing teams, return to the ridges that have already been sown, once they have built up a backlog of prepared ground, and go over them a second time, further breaking up the soil and shaping the ridges with the flat of their picks.

Unlike any other agricultural task in Huaquirca, potato sowing work parties may cover the holdings of more than one household in the course of a single day. This is especially feasible when the sowing has been preceded by a *grameo*, or in the higher areas where there is little *kikuyu*. It is also easy to sow multiple *laymi* plots in their second year of cultivation, since they require little ground preparation. When *oqas* and *ullukus* (Andean tubers) are sown as a second-year crop, this is also coordinated with the waxing moon, but when the choice is *habas* (broad beans) or grains such as *quinua*, wheat, or barley, the phase of the moon is not important. Before the arrival of *kikuyu*, it is likely that the sowing of potatoes also took place in the small work parties of eight people or less that are typical for the second-year crops. Generally, twelve to eighteen people comprise a potato sowing work party nowadays, about a third of whom will be women. They work on as many as four people's holdings, completing them either wholly or in part. This is the only task in the annual cycle where it is usual for a work party to cultivate more than one household's land in a single day.

The first break from work in the potato sowing (also in *oqa* and *ulluku* sowings) features a *samakuy* divination similar to that of the maize sowing, but with some important differences in detail. After drinking some corn beer, a 'son-in-law' (*qatay*) is nominated. He takes a sack of potatoes and pours part of its contents onto a cloth (*lliqlla*) that has been placed on the ground. Next, he may nest bottles of cane alcohol into the pile of potatoes, and arrange wildflowers around the edge of the cloth, as people come forth to pour small libations of corn beer on the seed. Once these libations have been poured, first the men, and then the women, approach the pile of potatoes and scoop some up in their cups, which they then empty on the ground in front of where they are sitting. When all have removed some potatoes, the 'son-in-law' begins to 'count' each individual's pile, removing potatoes pair by pair and returning them to the cloth. This time, however, 'salvation' consists of a result of three instead of two. Those who do not 'save themselves' in this manner must allow the 'son-in-law' to cut a tatter or loose thread from their clothing as '*wanu*' (fertilizer), and this is stored in a fold of the cloth on which the pile of seed rests. Meanwhile, the 'son-in-law' rearranges the wildflowers and assembles an offering in the fold of a *ch'uspa* (woven bag for storing coca leaves) whose basal layer consists of a *coca k'intu* (three unblemished leaves of coca super-imposed with their dark side up), followed by the tatters of clothing, wildflowers, and three potatoes in that order. A cup of corn beer called a 'lake' (*qocha*) is passed around, and everyone present drinks from it. The 'son-in-law' then pronounces a credo over the pile of seed, and the woman of the sponsoring household plants the offering he has prepared. Women also distribute flowers and sing *wankas* during the potato sowing, with no differences that I could detect from those sung during the maize sowing on the terraces.

The principal differences between the *samakuy* divinations of potato and maize sowings concern female participation, whether the number two or three represents 'salvation,' and the nature of the 'fertilizer' provided by those who fail to attain this state. Let us construct an analysis of this rite by going through these details one at a time.

First, the participation of women in the *samakuy* divinations of the potato sowing represents a significant departure from the maize sow-ing divinations, where only men took part. Whereas women were exempt from the entire deathly process surrounding the maize sowing, their 'salvation' is now at stake in the divinations of the potato sowing. One reason for this might be that women are closely linked with pota-toes in Andean thought. There are places in the Andes where people baldly state that potatoes are living, sentient females (see Allen 1988: 172).[4] As potatoes are interred then, so by extension are women, and this would make them subject to the *samakuy* divination. Although this may be acceptable as a first approximation, it does not explain why men also take part in the divinations of the potato sowing. The potato sowing cannot be opposed to the maize sowing as women are to men, since men participate in both divinations. Rather we have a cumulative transformation whereby women are subsumed by a deathly process that had previously only managed to engulf men.

The representation of 'salvation' by the number three develops this notion of cumulation. As Harris (1982: 62) suggests, the number three is an indicator of completeness in Andean symbolism. I would argue more specifically that the totality designated by the number three is a synthesis of the symmetric duality of men and the asymmetric duality of women and men.[5] In the previous chapter, we saw how *yanantin*, in which a woman passes two horns of corn beer to a man, who, in turn, passes one of them on to another man, involves the conversion of the asymmetry between a man and a woman into the symmetry of a pair of men. A cast of three characters, one woman and two men, is necessary to embody these two states of being. We also saw that this symmetric duality of men represents a productive principle based on *ayni* and the equalization of souls on death, whereas the asymmetry of woman and man represents a conjugal principle of appropriation, which corresponds to the asymmetry that exists between *alma* and *ánimo* in life. This second, asymmetric principle was engaged only as a background condition in the maize sowing, first in the unstressed gender complementarity of the work party, then as a point of departure for the reduction of men's souls to symmetry in work. This pattern changes, however, with the full participation of women in the divinations of the potato sowing, which seems to suggest that the asymmetric principle of conjugal appropriation has now been subsumed by the deathly dynamics of the growing season. This shift is perhaps appropriate now that the household is expending its last reserves of seed into the ground in a final act of sowing, and is holding nothing back from the productive order of the rainy season. Thus, the number three signifies the total commitment of the household, both as a unit of labour and as a unit of property holding, to a regime of collective production that is now reaching its zenith.

Finally, we must address the significance of cutting tatters from people's clothes as 'fertilizer' when they fail to 'save themselves' in the potato sowing. Here, the contrast is with the collection of rotting vegetable matter in the maize sowing, which suggests again that the process of death has arrived much closer to home, shifting from plants to people. The collection of tattered bits of clothing as 'fertilizer' in the potato sowing might also refer to the clothes that attract the *alma* back to this world on All Saints' and the Day of the Dead. Instead of being washed and preserved to act as a link between the *alma* and its living kin, however, these bits of clothing are mutilated, at first unintentionally by use over time, and then purposefully by the 'son-in-law's' blade during the rite. When these tatters are then interred as a de-individuated assemblage that is part of an agricultural offering, they effectively negate and even reverse the role played by clothing in the vigils of All Saints' Eve. Instead of remaining intact and aboveground to draw the dead back, these bits of clothing follow them into their underground world. Therefore, the interment of these scraps of clothing develops the emphasis on collectivization and cutting individualized kinship links with the dead initiated by the *Paqpako*. However, one might also argue that as part of an agricultural offering, these anonymous tatters of clothing are meant to draw equally anonymous life-forms like potatoes towards the surface of the earth, in a 'return' modelled on that of the *alma* during All Saints' and the Day of the Dead. In the previous chapter, we saw that the apparently trivial homonym that connects clothes (*p'acha*) and earth (*pacha*) was recast into a motivated relationship by the ritual correspondences between funerary clothes washing and irrigation. In the potato sowing, clothes (*p'acha*) are interred in the earth (*pacha*) in a way that might suggest a similar contiguity between the *alma* and the potato.[6] The following local beliefs justify such an equation of the potato and the *alma.*

People in the Antabamba Valley take the growth of especially large potatoes, particularly those few that begin to assume a human or animal form, as a sign that the owners of the field in which they grew will soon die. This belief is remarkable for the explicitness with which it poses the possible transformation of human life into the underground life of the potato. As a life-form, the potato is attributed the power to assume a nearly human form, and rob its erstwhile owners of life in the process. Thus, the potato is like a human *alma* in an underdeveloped, shrunken, subterranean form: precisely the form in which the dead exist. Indeed, we have already encountered the idea that the dead exist as *ch'uño,* freeze-dried potatoes whose moisture has been wrung from them by the alternating heat and cold of the land of the dead. Like the dead, potatoes may lead an underground life of modest proportions, but it is normally a passive existence, and any unusually vigorous growth can be achieved only at the expense of the living.[7]

A second, but equally significant aspect of this belief is the way it poses this unusual growth as a threat to the life of the owners of the field. Instead of simply recapitulating the 'work as death' theme from the maize sowing, this belief extends deathly breakdown to the proprietors of the domestic economy. By extension, women are included in the *samakuy* divination of the potato sowing because they are the prototypical (if not exclusive) representatives of the proprietorial aspect of the household. If both labourer and proprietor are now undergoing this deathly metamorphosis, then it is significant that the potato sowing, unlike any other task in Huaquirca's annual cycle, is done by work parties that complete several people's plots in a single day and are, therefore, characterized by a less rigid division between owners and workers. This inclusiveness is further reflected in the communal tenure of the *laymi* zone, as opposed to exclusive right in the terraces below town, and suggests that the levelling and collectivizing mission announced (but not accomplished) during All Saints' and the Day of the Dead may now be approaching practical realization.

By the middle of December, after the last of the potatoes have been sown, and most have begun to sprout, it is time for the guardians (*laymi kamayoq*) appointed in the meeting after Santa Rosa to establish residence in the fields, where they will live until the end of May, making sure that animals do not wander in and destroy people's crops. As mentioned in Chapter 2, these guardians, along with the water judges, are the only remnants of the *varayoq* system of traditional commoner authority that once existed in Huaquirca. True to that tradition, each *laymi kamayoq* has a staff of office made of black palm wood, complete with an inset silver band, but these staffs are supposed to be shorter than the ones that belonged to the old offices.

Before moving to the *laymi*, each guardian must build a hut there, and bring down the crosses that also guard the *laymi*'s crops, along with a handful of soil from the fields. The guardians take both crosses and soil across the valley to be blessed with holy water by the padre in the church of Antabamba, and then return to the plaza of Huaquirca, where they are met by a crowd of well-wishers, both commoners and notables. What follows was described to me as 'the send-off of the *kamayoqs*' (*despedida de los kamayoq*): a milling about in which the *kamayoqs* are presented with food, cane alcohol, and clothing by those who can spare it, as a gesture of gratitude for the service they are about to perform for the entire community. Although I never witnessed this event, I was told that it invariably involves the consumption of copious amounts of alcohol, and that the *kamayoqs* rarely, if ever, depart for the *laymis* at the end of the afternoon, but usually end up drinking well into the night. It is only the following day, and with a terrible hangover, that the guardians begin their solitary vigil in the alpine zone.

Second Hoeing

The second hoeing of maize (*kutipa*) begins in late November, reaches a peak around Christmas, and tails off by mid-January. By then, the rains have generally become frequent and heavy, and people hope to perform this task on a sunny day, so that weeds will dry up and die immediately, and work will progress without interruption, since a deluge will send people running for cover under the bushes and trees at the side of the field. Thus, after providing the usual morning meal to those who will be working that day, the woman of the sponsoring household may attempt to prevent rain by taking some coals from the hearth outside, burning some rubber on them, and wafting the fumes towards the local mountains, while invoking the names of the *apus* (mountain spirits) associated with them. Perhaps the burning rubber stimulates the stench and heating associated with death, thus reversing the process by which an excess of water is being driven into this world. Another altogether more lighthearted measure against too much rain is for a member of the work party to grab a guinea pig from the kitchen floor while the morning meal is being served and hold its forepaws between thumb and index finger to make it 'dance' on its hind legs. The comic relief of this act was often enhanced by the magico-religious rationale of preventing rainfall.

The motives for the second hoeing are much the same as those for the first: to remove weeds and pile soil at the base of the plants, which are now 60–100 cm tall and much more robust, but are also more vulnerable to being blown over by the wind. Less care is now needed with the hoes, but it is much more difficult to see the spaces between the plants from which to haul soil, since the men have their heads in or just on top of the plants, in the crouched position from which they operate their tools. It is also more difficult to maintain the herringbone alternation from left to right with each new drag of the hoe. The women also have more work, since the weeds have grown at a pace with the maize in competition for sunlight. They form teams that go ahead of the men, and aid their vision by clearing out the weeds. When the men have finished an area, the women will also collect and remove the weeds uprooted by the hoes. In spite of this cooperation, it is during the *kutipa* that I heard the men belittle women's work in the fields most vociferously.

The breaks from work during the *kutipa* feature the same seating arrangements and forms of corn beer distribution (including *yanantin*) that have been described earlier. They also have distinctive *quena* tunes. At the end of the final period of work, there is a modest but distinctive rite known as the *sara p'ampa* (maize burial). Maize plants that have been accidentally uprooted during the day's work are collected in a poncho and taken to a shallow pit, about fifty centimetres deep, that has been excavated for them. In the town of Antabamba, there is a particular spot on each parcel of land known as the *qoturipata* (place or terrace of stockpiling), where this rite is always performed. This spot is supposed to be particularly fertile and productive as a result. In Huaquirca, it does not seem that the same place is necessarily used from year to year, or that any increase in fertility is expected. Nonetheless, someone will assemble a *coca k'intu* (three unblemished leaves of coca superimposed, dark side up) and place it at the bottom of the pit. Just as a body is brought to the grave in a poncho, so the maize stalks are lowered into the pit. Those who care to pour libations of corn beer on the plants do so and then use their hoes to cover the pit. In certain ways, the act is comparable to the ritual planting that takes place at the end of the *samakuy* divinations of the sowing, since both include a *coca k'intu* offering and both may be performed on the same spot in the field. However, the location of the ritual planting during the sowing is sometimes a matter of debate, in a way that the location of the *sara p'ampa* is not. The notion of sowing as an interment that renews life is confirmed here, now in the reinterment of the casualties of that regenerative process. Again, the ancient patterns of human burial on the terraces and in the *laymis* do not seem so remote.

The return to town from the *kutipa* proceeds slowly, the men playing flutes and the women sometimes singing. As with the sowing, people may wait for the whole group to congregate on the road just outside town before entering it, to achieve maximum impact.[8] Those close to the sponsors of the work party will return to their house to continue drinking, singing, and playing the flute until late at night. It is in the *kutipa*, more than any other agricultural task, that people seem most inclined to continue drinking after the day's work is done. On any given night in Huaquirca at this time of the year, several such sessions will be in progress. As the night wears on, flute music becomes more sporadic and the singing more meandering and disjointed, until people either pass out or find their way home, attempting to make music in the process. Since the *kutipa* is the last major work that needs to be done on the maize until the harvest, it is hardly surprising that people would want to celebrate its completion.

Christmas

By the time Christmas arrives, the first hoeing of the maize and the potato sowing have been completed, and the *kutipa* is in full swing. Rainfall is usually abundant, and from now on, agricultural tasks do not overlap with the same intensity, leaving more days to dedicate to other activities. On the afternoon of 24 December, there is an abrupt break in the continuum of agricultural work for four days of celebrations in the Antabamba Valley,[9] one that heralds the coming period of decreasing productive expenditure. Not only are the Christmas festivities of the Antabamba Valley quite singular within the Andean context,[10] they are undoubtedly the most enjoyed event of the year, one that people describe as a great spectacle and a welcome diversion from work. Christmas in Huaquirca is also an event of considerable symbolic complexity, however, and this is part of its entertainment value.

The main attraction of Christmas consists of four days of dancing the *wayliya*, the combined march and song that we have already encountered during the return from the fields after maize sowing. This time, however, the *wayliya* itself is the focal act, and not an adornment of a labour process. Again, only men dance, but now in troupes under the auspices of religious devotions, each with a sponsor (*carguyoq*). Like the sponsor of an agricultural work party, the sponsors of the troupe provide food and drink for the dancers throughout the festivities (cf. Sallnow 1974: 135). There are three sponsorships for the Christmas *wayliya* in Huaquirca: *Taytaq*, *Mamaq*, and *Exaltación*. However, only two of these sponsorships will be occupied in a given year. In 1981, *Taytaq* and *Mamaq* were activated, whereas in 1982, the two troupes were *Taytaq* and *Exaltación*. I was told that *Taytaq* represents the Father, *Mamaq* the Mother, and *Exaltación* the Christ-child. Each of these sponsorships is further associated with a date during the dry season, though there is no obligation to provide festivities then. It is said that *Taytaq* corresponds to Corpus Christi, which marks the end of the harvest in June; that *Mamaq* corresponds to the Virgin of the Assumption (15 August), the patron saint of Huaquirca; and that *Exaltación* corresponds to the Exaltation of the Holy Cross on 14 September, when the sowing begins. Once assumed, each of these sponsorships lasts three years, and demands considerable expenditure by the sponsor. As we have seen, *Taytaq* and *Mamaq* have fields that their sponsors can cultivate, but this is not so with *Exaltación*. Between *Taytaq* and *Mamaq* there is said to be 'more rivalry,' whereas *Exaltación* is sometimes called an 'emergency sponsorship,' which is why *Taytaq* and *Mamaq* form the ideal pair of the three combinations of two possible.

On the afternoon of 24 December, costumed men begin to arrive at the house of the sponsor they have agreed to dance for. Ideally, the costume should consist of a pair of high leather riding boots, trousers with military braid running down the outside seam of each leg, a white shirt, a felt sash draped over the neck and secured at the waist by a broad felt cummerbund bedecked with mirrors, a mask of fine wire mesh (painted with pink skin, blue eyes, black hair, and a moustache), brightly coloured nylon handkerchiefs that cover the entire neck and head except for the face, and, finally, a straw hat with three peacock feathers sewn into the hatband at the front. For lack of money, many of these items may be improvised by the dancers, but there is an explicit aspiration towards uniformity, and the idiosyncrasies of some costumes may be criticized with reference to these ideals.[11] Several people suggested to me that these costumes represent 'Spaniards,' even though this notion remains wholly undeveloped by the performance.[12] I was struck by how these costumes correspond in every detail to how people describe the *apus* (mountain spirits) in other contexts, but when I offered this counter-interpretation it was always rejected, at times with evident concern.

After an hour or so of drinking at the houses of the respective sponsors, the two troupes set out to dance in the plaza. Each troupe is composed of two parallel columns of men, with the tallest and best dressed at the front, and the rest arranged in descending order of stature towards the back of each column. This ordering creates a lateral symmetry between the two columns, as they march about four metres apart. Between the two columns and about mid-way down them is an uncostumed fiddler who plays alternate stanzas of the *wayliya*. When the violin's stanza is over, the men will all but stop marching, as the two columns turn to face each other and sing:

> *wayliya wayliya wayliya*
>
> *wayliya-hiya wayliya*
>
> *wayliya-hiya wayliya*

This completed, the violinist resumes his tune, and the men their march. The men at the front of each column (the *punteros*) introduce periodic changes in the tune and mood of the *wayliya*, but otherwise, this basic pattern is repeated again and again as the troupes parade around the plaza, keeping out of each other's way for the most part. The two troupes make no attempt to coordinate their respective alternations between singing and marching, and studiously ignore each other in an attempt to convert their own performance into the exclusive focus of the event.

After about an hour of this dancing on the afternoon of 24 December, an image of the Christ-child is removed from the church by the sponsor of either *Mamaq* or *Exaltación* (but never *Taytaq*). The two troupes then begin the ascent to the Niñupata ('place of the Christ-child,' a small chapel above the neighbourhood of Huachacayllo, see Figure 5), their sponsors leading the way, one of them carrying the image of the Christ-child in his arms. During this ascent, the troupes exchange the lead several times, as the two columns of the leading troupe part, and allow the other troupe to pass through the middle into the lead. The image of the Christ-child is put in the chapel, and the two troupes dance on the small, flat clearings to either side of this building, surrounded by hundreds of onlookers. The dancing goes on until dusk, when the troupes file down the steep path into town, exchanging the lead as in the ascent, and retire to the homes of their respective sponsors where they are fed and given more drink, before going to bed early.

The dancers arise before dawn on the morning of 25 December, and are fed before continuing the *wayliya* back up to the Niñupata. Again, the two troupes dance on either side of the chapel before returning to town exchanging the lead. This time, however, women who have helped the sponsoring household prepare food and drink carry the image of the Christ-child down by turns and return it to its normal place in the church. This schematic enactment of the birth of Jesus is further developed through the use of the term *pastor* ('shepherd') to refer to the dancers, and the association of the sponsorships with members of the holy family.[13] Once the figure of the Christ-child is back in the church, the two troupes perform the *wayliya* in the plaza until noon, when the padre from Antabamba arrives in his pickup truck to give a mass, which is interrupted by intermittent blasts of gunpowder let off close to the church. After the mass, the padre performs baptisms while the troupes continue the *wayliya* for a short time in the plaza, before eating lunch. Later in the afternoon, the troupes parade through the neighbourhood of their sponsor, visiting homes that have children, where they will dance briefly and be served cane alcohol for the courtesy of their visit.

By 5:00 in the afternoon, the troupes reassemble in the plaza to dance, and their sponsors set up tables to serve them drink at opposite ends of the plaza on the wall closest to the church. In what turns out to be the last of these breaks, the men are served a cup of *pito* and a cup of corn beer each by the women helping the sponsoring household. This pair of cups is not *yanantin* since the contents of each cup differs from that of the other, and the same man drinks both. When the men get up to resume the *wayliya*, they leave their masks and hats with their wives, or another trusted person, which indicates that the culminating battle (for which the *wayliyas* of Huaquirca and Antabamba are notorious) is not far off. As the troupes cross and recross the plaza, their mutual interference becomes more systematic, their marching and singing more spirited. Finally, the two troupes meet head-on, the lateral symmetry of each troupe now compounded in the dimension of depth, as the two front rows of tall men confront each other, with a graduation towards the shortest at the back of each troupe (see Figure 15). Tension builds up in a standoff that may last up to ten minutes, as the two sides taunt each other, singing opposite stanzas of the *wayliya*, and stomping loudly and compactly when not singing. Those at the back of each troupe crowd forward, and finally the pressure cannot be contained and a melee breaks out, scattering spectators in all directions. The two compacted troupes break up into a series of small free-for-alls of three to eight men that form and rapidly re-form, punching and kicking as they go, with no concern for the numerical mismatches that may result. Once the fight has broken loose, it quickly fans over the whole plaza. The women scream, and with older, serious-faced men, help extricate the injured from the fury of battle. Time seems to stand still, but suddenly only a few groups of men remain tumbling on the ground. Once they realize that they are alone, they break off the fight and hurriedly rejoin their troupes. A few final passes across the plaza, each troupe singing and marching exuberantly, mark the end of the day's spectacle, and each group retires to the house of its sponsor to eat and get very drunk.

There is no dancing on the morning of 26 December. After taking lunch with their respective sponsors, the troupes do a few turns of the *wayliya* around the plaza and then return to the house of their sponsors again. While these activities go on, a few troupe members leave to reap some maize from a nearby field (not the one that is associated with the sponsorship), playing the flute and tambour as they go. They bring back an armful of stalks and lay them on the table in the dining room of the sponsor. One by one, the dancers perform the *sara t'inka* (libation of the maize) by sprinkling a few drops of corn beer on the plants. A member of the troupe then dresses up as a woman by donning several layers of felt skirts (*polleras*), stuffing false breasts under a sweater, putting on a wig and a hat, and finally slinging a large jug of corn beer over the back. This dancer is know as '*Lisa*' ('impudent

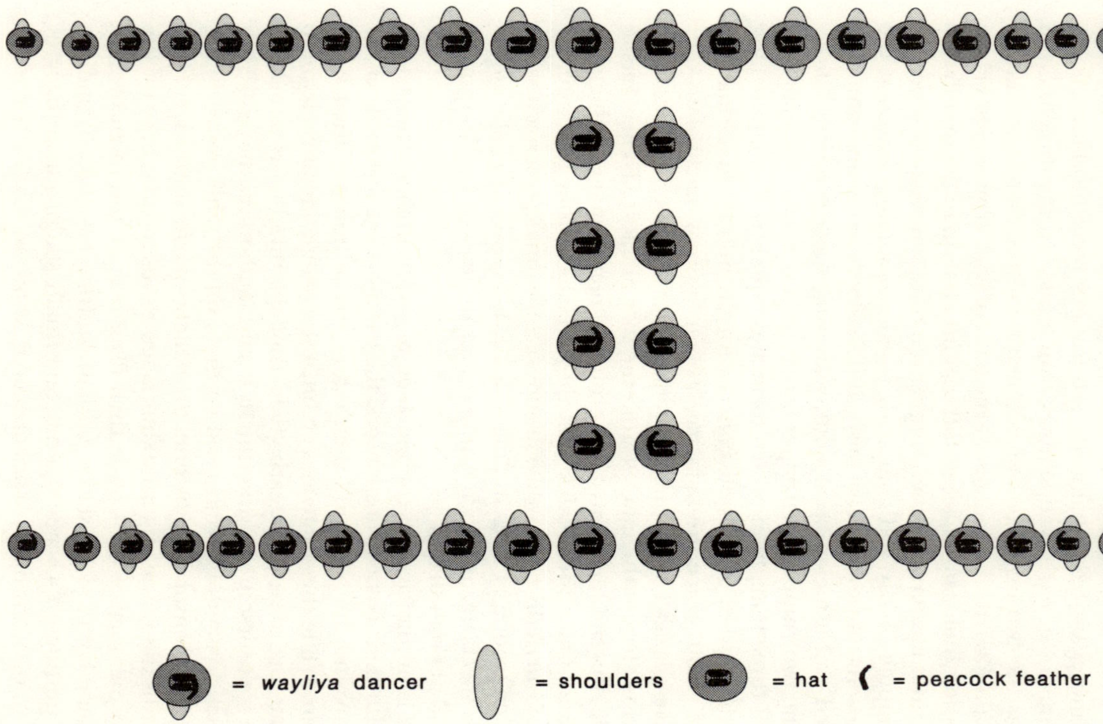

Figure 15 *Wayliya standoff*

= wayliya dancer

= shoulders

= hat

= peacock feather

one') and is always selected from the sub-category of dancers known as *layqas* (sorcerers), who speak in falsettos throughout the Christmas *wayliya*, and continually crack lewd or satiric jokes. The libated maize stalks are then arranged in bundles of two or three on the backs of the youngest and smallest members of the troupe, who are given hoes and sickles. The whole troupe then goes out to its table in the plaza without dancing.

A small group, consisting only of the *layqas*, *Lisa*, and the young boys, then sallies forth for one tour around the plaza's perimeter, in a counter-clockwise direction. In the middle is *Lisa*, surrounded by the *layqas* who jostle and knock her about as they run, shrieking in their falsettos, and trying to take the jug of corn beer from her back. About ten metres away from this main body of the procession, to the front and sides, are the boys with their hoes and sickles, performing the motions of work associated with these tools, lunging at any people or dogs that they encounter to hoe or reap them as if they were stalks of maize. On completing this round, *Lisa* then serves the whole troupe corn beer from the pottery vessel she has been carrying. The first round of corn beer is again for the maize libation (*sara t'inka*), and every dancer spills a few drops on the stalks, which the boys have returned to the table. In the second round served by *Lisa*, the dancers toast the individual members of their families by pouring a few drops on the maize in the same manner as before. A prolonged drinking break usually follows the completion of this performance by both troupes (the second of which may tour the plaza in a clockwise direction), and they do not resume the *wayliya* until later in the afternoon.

As dusk approaches, the two troupes become predictably more animated in their dancing, more belligerent, and more likely to collide. Again, this escalation of tension is broken off by a rest during which men drink both a cup of *pito* and a cup of corn beer, and leave their masks and hats with a spectator. They resume the *wayliya* with urgency and vigour, until the two troupes come to loggerheads, stomping and singing in two monolithic unities at counterpoint. With taunts and insults thick in the air, the back of each troupe begins to push forward. This time, however, the men have brought *fuetes*, braided leather riding whips with a leather-encased metal thong at the end (in the past, clubs of *lloqe* wood were also used). The fight begins with a few preliminary whip flicks from the back of each troupe. Within seconds, waves of riding whips begin to crack on the faces and shoulders of the dancers, and the fight explodes outwards, swirling through the plaza at a frenzied pace. Nonetheless, the men lean back and throw their full weight into every blow, often receiving an unforeseen lash from behind in the process. Some men stumble or are dragged off early, barely able to stand, but most carry on single-mindedly, apparently oblivious to the pain. In the middle of the fight in 1981, the two sponsors stood toe to toe, swearing and spitting at each other, whipping with unmitigated fury. Slowly, the skirmishes begin to die down, and the fight loses its massiveness and unpredictable surges. Then the men start to curl up their riding whips and retire to the table of their sponsors for some cane alcohol. Later, they will joke about having 'atoned' for their sins in this manner. After a few more turns of triumphant *wayliya* in the plaza, the troupes eat dinner at the house of their sponsor, but after this, the *wayliya* resumes, and may last well into the night.

Breakfast at the house of the sponsors on the morning of 27 December is sometimes said to mark the end of the Christmas *wayliya*, but in neither of the years that I witnessed the event did it actually conclude so soon. By noon, some members of each troupe began to parade through town again, in half costume and very drunk, but there was hardly anyone to watch them, since people have either returned to work in the fields, or to another activity out of town, such as cutting firewood. In one day, these dancers have gone from being the pride of the town to being 'a bunch of drunkards' (in the words of one notable). Some diehards will continue to drink and sing the *wayliya* in the yards in front of their houses through 28 and 29 December, but they will no longer wear costumes or dance publicly. Slowly the glow of the event wears off, and the town is again deserted during the day, and soothed with the flute tunes of the *kutipa* in the evening, as people return from the fields.

Of all the performances of the annual cycle, the Christmas *wayliya* seems the least representational at first glance. It has little to do with the Christmas story when considered as a whole, and nobody was interested in interpreting it except as a diversion from the routine of agricultural work. Indeed, the very fact that it is a break from work contributes to the sense of presence and immediacy in the performance. Above all, though, it is the endless repetition of the *wayliya* that seems to create this self-sufficiency, by refusing to proclaim anything more than its own name:

> *wayli-hiya wayliya-hiya*
>
> *wayliya wayliya-hiya*

wayli-hiya wayliya-hiya

wayliya wayliya-hiya.

In Quechua, *wayliya* means 'joy' or 'happiness,' and it is as if people achieved the state in question by endlessly repeating its name. However, this act of labelling indicates that even in its most inwardly turned and mesmerizing moment, the presence of the *wayliya* is not a matter of simple self-equivalence, but involves reference beyond the performance itself. Nor is the constant repetition of the *wayliya* without an aspect of sequential development, since there is a progression through various moods in the singing and dancing, which finally culminates in fighting: a change of state.

Above all, it is the fact that the *wayliya* is also performed in the maize sowing, and thus establishes a kind of counter-reference between Christmas and this earlier point in the annual cycle, that breaks the insularity of this performance. This counter-reference is further posited in the sponsorship of *Exaltación*, which, on the one hand, represents the Christ-child (and thus Christmas), and on the other, is associated with 14 September, when the maize sowing begins. It could be further argued that these agricultural links between the *wayliya* and *Exaltación* are themselves related. Although *wayliya* as 'joy' does deviate from the liturgical sense of 'exaltation' that might prevail in a more orthodox context, it is difficult to believe that the correspondence between the two in the triumphant contexts of the maize sowing and Christmas is entirely fortuitous, and that the two are not somehow synonymous. Nor do the connections stop here. We have already seen that like the Christ-child, maize is the mediator of human 'salvation' during the sowing, both as a means of divination in the *samakuy*, and as the object of the productive expenditure of energy to which the notion of 'salvation' refers. Thus, Christmas is not simply an opportunity to celebrate the birth of Christ (by taking his image to the Niñupata on 24 December, and returning it to the church on 25 December), but is also the appropriate occasion for the maize libation (*sara t'inka*) on 26 December. This multiple juxtaposition of the Christ-child with the growing maize ultimately suggests a certain identity between the two.

When we turn to the other two sponsorships of Christmas, this linkage between the Christ-child and the growing maize in the sponsorship of *Exaltación* is even more systematic. *Taytaq* is the Father and is associated with the celebration of Corpus Christi that takes place during the harvest, whereas *Mamaq* is the Virgin, specifically the Virgin of the Assumption, whose celebration (15 August) initiates canal cleaning. Just as the Christ-child is the product of an Immaculate Conception involving these two figures, so the sowing of maize is the product of the seed and irrigation water that they provide (see Figure 16). The two syntheses are entirely parallel, and become consubstantial by means of this generative pair.[14] This conjunction is further underlined in how both *Taytaq* and *Mamaq* have fields on which this synthesis can take place, and how *Exaltación*, that 'emergency sponsorship,' does not. Whether as growing maize or the 'joy' of the *wayliya, Exaltación* is that which is to be generated.

As with the Immaculate Conception, however, it would be wrong to overestimate the sexual nature of this process. Despite the nominal gender opposition between *Taytaq* and *Mamaq*, both troupes are composed entirely of men dressed identically and arranged in symmetric columns, suggesting the *yanantin* transformation whereby the asymmetry between women and men is resolved into an identical male pair (cf. Platt 1986: 248, 252). Mirrors, which effect a 'corrective' lateral inversion, are another way of eliminating this asymmetry (see Platt 1980: 247), and here it is significant that they should be integrated into the costumes of the dancers. The tour of *Lisa* the transvestite around the plaza, and the attempts of the *layqas* (sorcerers), with their shrieking falsettos, to seize the jug of corn beer from her back suggest a symbolic appropriation of the feminine that is centred on this crucial manifestation of female power.[15] To a limited extent, the episode may represent an appropriation of the power to embody, since following this performance, libations are poured for family members of the dancers to ensure their well-being and health. On the whole, however, the emphasis remains on the opposing process of reductive 'equalization' and energy release.

The fundamental principle of the Christmas *wayliya* is the competitive identity between the two troupes, one that is reminiscent of the competition between maize sowing teams and the notion of 'salvation' as a deathly expenditure of energy from the body. The lateral symmetry of each troupe suggests not only the *yanantin* concept (cf. Platt 1986: 245–6) but the dual formula of *ayni*, 'like for like,' which is further developed in the alternation of singing and violin music within each troupe, the alternation of verses sung when the troupes confront each other, and the changing of the lead going to and returning from

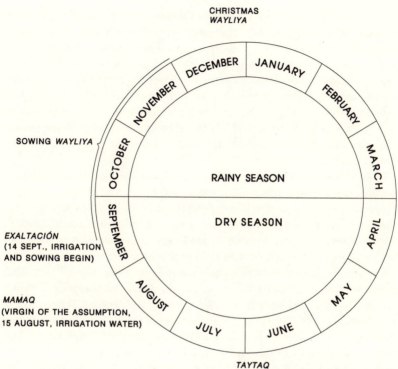

CHRISTMAS
WAYLIYA

JANUARY
FEBRUARY
MARCH
APRIL
MAY
JUNE
JULY
AUGUST
SEPTEMBER
OCTOBER
NOVEMBER
DECEMBER

RAINY SEASON

DRY SEASON

SOWING *WAYLIYA*

EXALTACIÓN
(14 SEPT., IRRIGATION
AND SOWING BEGIN)

MAMAQ
(VIRGIN OF THE ASSUMPTION,
15 AUGUST, IRRIGATION WATER)

TAYTAQ
(CORPUS CHRISTI, MOVEABLE, SEED)

Figure 16   The Annual cycle and the Immaculate Conception

the Niñupata. Even the culmination of this process in the ritual battle between the two troupes, the moment of maximum presence, is marked by *ayni*, now as a principle of revenge (see Núñez del Prado 1972: 138; Núñez del Prado 1973: 30–1), fruit of the polarization of the community into alliances with two sponsors. As the sponsor of *Taytaq* rightly observed in 1982: 'It's the fight that makes Christmas.' This fight is most spirited when it takes place between *Taytaq* and *Mamaq*, the sponsorships between which there is 'more rivalry.' Antagonism, not complementarity, is what characterizes the use of gender symbolism in this performance.

That there is something malevolent about the gender transformations of the Christmas *wayliya* is suggested by the use of the term *layqa* (sorcerer) to refer to the dancers who speak in falsettos, from whom the transvestite is recruited. The *layqas*' gender ambiguity and/or appropriation of the feminine seems linked to the deathly transformation of people into maize that is dramatized when the boys reap and hoe spectators at the front of the transvestite procession.[16] In other towns of the Antabamba Valley, where the Christmas *wayliya* does not culminate in ritual battles, people say that the troupes dance 'hard, until they urinate blood,' as if the dance generates a destructive energy that if not directed outwards, leads to an internal breakdown. This same idea is present in the name *yawar mayu* (blood river) that is given to the final phase of dancing before ritual battles in many parts of the Andes (see Ramirez 1969; Allen 1988: 61). Here, it is of the utmost significance that men drink *pito* before entering into this stage of the performance, as if they were again to come into intimate contact with the energy released on death, as during the irrigation and maize sowing. It is just such a 'total liberation of energy against the opposing moiety' (Platt 1986: 240) that results from the confrontation of the troupes in a symmetric, mutually reflecting alignment (Figure 16), one that recalls the Macha comment that both water and mirrors are 'the enemies of our *almas*' (Platt 1986: 247). Thus, it seems that the dynamic of the Christmas *wayliya* is the same as that of death: an 'equalizing' reduction of *alma* to *ánimo* that unleashes destructive energy.

As the guarantor of human 'salvation,' the Christ-child has much in common with the uncontrollable energies released by the dead (cf. Harris 1982: 65). In Huaquirca, as elsewhere, there are significant linkages between the celebrations of Christmas and those of All Saints'.[17] The return of the dead is marked by blasts of gunpowder in the fields of *Taytaq* and *Mamaq*, as if to suggest again that their 'rivalry' is inti-

mately related to a destructive release of energy on death, just as the
Christ-child is implicated in this process by the further detonation of
gunpowder during the mass on Christmas day. That it is the *Paqpako,*
that collectivizer of death and mocker of mourners, who joins *Taytaq*
and *Mamaq* in having a field, to the exclusion of *Exaltación,* shows
again that the Christ-child is a derivative of death, a monumental
release of energy that is equivalent to 'salvation,' and not to be fet-
tered with any cumbersome embodiment like a field. Whether or not
we see the *Paqpako* as a substitute for the Christ-child in this trinity of
field-holding sponsorships, there can be no denying that he performs
an indispensable preparatory labour for the celebrations of Christmas
by collectivizing and criticizing mourning on All Saints' Eve. This sets
the stage for the energetic assertion of 'salvation' during the Christmas *wayliya.*

Despite this clear continuity with the preceding part of the year and
its domination by death imagery, the Christmas *wayliya* also affirms
human life, and thus foreshadows the period of consumption to come.
For example, the visits of each troupe on the afternoon of 25 December to houses with young children is seen by their parents as a service
worthy of recompense in cane alcohol, and in no way is the destructive
energy generated by the *wayliya* felt to jeopardize the young. On the
contrary, the fact that these visits take place after the padre finishes his
baptisms in the church, and the similarity of the *wayliya* to the process
by which water is generated on death, might suggest a kind of parallel
baptism here, in which the young are socialized by controlled contact
with deathly energy. For the first time, the men eat well in a context
dedicated to the generation of energy, and thus replenish their bodies
instead of just breaking them down with 'animating' liquids. Finally,
the maize libation (*sara t'inka*) creates an important transition in focus
from the maize stalks, which are the object of the first round of libations, to the family members of the dancers, who are the object of the
second round of libations. This is the first affirmation of kinship in a
ritual context that is not qualified by the figure of a 'son-in-law,' and it
implies a transition from the emphasis on spiritual kinship in *ayni-*
based work parties (see Chapter 3) and the Immaculate Conception of
maize (as Christ) to an unambivalent affirmation of consanguinity and
carnal kinship.

In some parts of the Peruvian Andes, the Spanish word *niño* refers
not only to the Christ-child but also to 1 January, the New Year (see
Adams 1959: 194–5; Valderrama and Escalante 1980: 263). This was

the date when political authorities traditionally changed office. Intriguingly, the most powerful notables of certain areas are also called *niños* (Fuenzalida 1970a: 38), perhaps because of their habitual assumption of office on this day. The inauguration of district-level authorities in Huaquirca now takes place every other year on 1 January, and is celebrated with a certain amount of drinking by the notables, but before their elimination in 1947, the *varayoq* (see Chapter 2) were replaced every year on this date. After receiving their staffs of office from the outgoing authorities, the incoming recruits would parade through the streets of Huaquirca with troupes of men behind them, playing flutes and drums, alternating between the melodies of the *kutipa* (second hoeing of maize) and those of Carnival (Centeno 1949: 22–3). Although this event takes place during the *kutipa*, it points ahead in the year towards Carnival.

The *niño* as political authority also explains why men should dress up as 'Spaniards' that look suspiciously like mountain spirits during the Christmas *wayliya*, since the latter are, as we shall see in Chapter 7, very much the cultural model on which political authority is understood. Up to this point, we have come across only four mountain spirits (*apus*), Qoropuna and Solimana associated with death and the west, and Sawasiray and Pitusiray associated with maize and the east. In many ways, their symmetric opposition recalls the structure of the dance troupes, in which each *apu* could be seen as the head of a column confronting its opposite number. These mountains form an axis that grounds the regional hierarchies of lesser apus, which will be discussed in Chapter 7. It is also in the light of the *t'inkas* that we can understand the ritual battle of the Christmas *wayliya* as a kind of blood sacrifice by which the parallelism and confluence of life and death are disrupted, and a measure of autonomy won, but this point cannot yet be clarified. For now, the main point is that in pushing the reduction of life to its breaking point in the deathly symmetry of the ritual battle, the Christmas *wayliya* reiterates and completes the phase of the annual cycle that has been described in the past two chapters at the same time as it begins to point towards a period in which consumption, sacrifice, and political authority come to the fore. It also accomplishes this transition in a major performance that is a break from work in the fields instead of being integrated into it, and thus initiates a separation of work and ritual that will increase in the phase of the year to come.

6

Carnival and the Harvest

By the middle of January, the second hoeing of the maize is virtually complete, and people begin to turn their attention to their cattle. This is the heart of the rainy season, when natural pasture is most abundant, and the cows are producing more than enough milk to feed their calves. As the month wears on, commoner families begin to send members up to the grazing lands (*vaquerías*) to milk the cattle and make cheese. Notable households begin to receive a steady stream of cheeses from their servants (*vaqueros*) permanently stationed on their privatized cattle estates above town. By the end of January, whole commoner domestic groups may leave their houses in town for weeks at a time to go live on the grazing lands, where they drink milk and whey, and eat a milk-based maize meal porridge (*mazamorra*) and cheese. Huaquirca remains half deserted throughout February. This is a time of relative relaxation from work, during which consumption comes to the fore.

Each commoner household has its informal grazing territory on a fallow sector of the sectoral fallow fields (*laymis*). The focus of this territory is a small thatched hut (*chuklla*) with a stooped entrance, oval floor plan of about two by three metres, and a cramped interior in which it is impossible to stand upright. At meal times and during heavy rains, people crouch shoulder to shoulder in its dark interior, and at night, they line the bare earth floor with sheep skins and curl up together under blankets to sleep in groups as large as six. In the morning, the skins and blankets are stowed around the perimeter of the hut: there is simply no question of any permanent functional divisions of space. It is in these huts that the notables' *vaqueros* live for most of the year. Two or three such huts may congregate together on particularly lush hillslopes, since tenure is communal, and nobody has the right to deny others access. In such cases, each household nonetheless works independently, using separate corrals and different areas of the hillside for grazing. Generally, the trend is towards an even dispersal of huts across the landscape, as with the houses of the pastoralists of the upper *puna* zone. Indeed, many contacts between valley and *puna* people are renewed at this time of the year. Notables do not tend to spend as much time with their cattle at this point in the year due to their general dislike of the *puna*, but those with holdings of more than eighty head usually build stone-walled, thatched houses on their estates, similar in size and layout to a commoner's house in town, in which to stay during their tours of inspection.

A typical day on the grazing lands begins early in the morning when the calves are let out of the hut or enclosure in which they have spent the night. They are driven onto one side of the hill, whereas the cows and bulls are driven onto another, so that the cows and calves are separated by the hut in the middle and cannot nurse. Women and children are usually responsible for this task (cf. Skar 1982: 153) and combine it with others, such as fetching drinking water and firewood. By late morning, the hillside reverberates with bellowing cows and bleating calves, both converging on the hut and anxious to nurse. The calves are herded into a corral, and the children release them one at a time to bolt towards their mothers. As the calf suckles, the woman milks the cow, each trying to outdo the other. The process is repeated until all of the calves have been released and all of the cows milked. Sheep's intestines are put in the buckets of milk earmarked for cheese to start the curdling process. The rest of the milk is set aside in the hut or served immediately with toasted grains of maize (*kancha*). During the early afternoon, the women continue making cheese, compressing ever further the curds that are separating from the whey, until finally a large ball of fresh cheese emerges, which is taken from the bucket to be put in a straw mould and compressed between flat stones where it will continue to release whey throughout the afternoon. After milking, the cows and calves are again separated to graze on separate parts of the hill, but before dark, the women and children herd them back to their respective corrals by the hut. In the evening or on the following morning, the cheese is taken from the mould and either consumed directly or put on a rack above the hearth to smoke dry into a delicious hard cheese that is virtually imperishable. Depending on the household's circumstances, these cheeses may be sold for cash, bartered for meat, or stored for consumption at other times of the year.

Men do very little work on the grazing lands, and often leave for days at a time to sell or barter cheese, to arrange and participate in work parties for the potato hoeing (*papa hallma*), or simply go visiting in the *puna*. The potato hoeing takes place from mid-January to mid-February. Like other agricultural tasks done by *ayni*, it requires the preparation of corn beer, and the purchase of coca and cane alcohol. Thus, the woman of the sponsoring household must return to town five or more days before the work party to make the corn beer and give it time to ferment. Often the rest of the household follows her down, and will remain until the day following the work party. Depending on its distance from the potato fields currently under cultivation, the hut on the grazing lands may or may not be an appropriate place for a man to live during the potato hoeing, but since this task requires few workers, and has no competition from other agricultural tasks, it need not cause long absences.

A day of potato hoeing begins with a morning meal at the house of the sponsors in town, although several workers may join the work party in the fields, coming directly from their huts in the grazing land. The largest work party that I saw for this task consisted of six men and three women, and the smallest consisted of only two men and a woman. Each man takes his hoe to the bottom of a furrow aligned with the slope of the hill and begins to work up it, drawing soil to the ridges (*surcos*) on either side of the furrow, on which the potatoes are planted. This deposited soil accentuates the ridge in relation to the furrow, covers over any weeds, and gives support to the growing potato plants. When many people are present, a minimal division of labour occurs. One or two men may work ahead of the hoers, loosening the soil in the furrows with a footplough. Women may follow behind the hoers with small picks, removing weeds that show through the loose soil piled onto the ridges. The ease and speed with which this work is carried out depends greatly on the density of the weeds, which diminishes notably towards the upper limit of *laymi* cultivation. As on all other agricultural working days, there are two long breaks for drinking cane alcohol and corn beer, and chewing coca. Usually, the potato hoeing is complete by the time Carnival arrives in February or early March, but this timing is not sanctioned by notions that cultivation of the crops past Candlemas (2 February) is detrimental to their growth, as has been reported elsewhere (Buechler and Buechler 1971: 11).

Carnival

Carnival in Huaquirca is said to begin on *Comadres* Thursday and last for two weeks, although in my experience its temporal boundaries are far from precise. Two activities mark the duration of Carnival: (1) playful ambushes and fights on the street involving water, stale urine, cow dung, and flour (to be thrown in the eyes); and (2) the *t'inka* rites that each household performs on its grazing land, which will be the subject of the next chapter. The distinctive melodies and rhythms that mark Carnival throughout the Andes may also continue beyond this two-week period. *Puqllay* or 'play' is the constant refrain at this time of the year, a word that enters many Carnival songs, and labels the entire Carnival period in some places (see Flores 1979: 90). Carnival disperses slowly and unevenly, with the satiation of the desires for enjoyment, rest, and consumption that come to a peak in these two weeks. Instead of ending with a sharp transition into privation, such as Lent, Carnival in the Andes is primarily a first fruits ceremony (see Harris 1982: 57) brought on by the ripening of the maize, the abundance of milk and meat on the grazing lands, and the anticipation of even more relaxation and consumption to come. In Huaquirca, Carnival is difficult to interpret as a period of ritual licence because neither Lent nor Easter are subsequently observed. Perhaps the only thing that might qualify as a Lent-like 'backlash' against Andean Carnival is the return to agricultural work when it is over. Breaking ground is the final task of the rainy season, and it is one of the most strenuous tasks of the annual cycle. Finally, what is most noteworthy about Carnival in Huaquirca is the way it makes a celebration of consumption and first fruits into a celebration of notable power and privilege. This linkage becomes clear when we turn to the two central days of Carnival: the Sunday and the Tuesday following *Comadres* Thursday.

By Carnival Sunday, there have already been three or four days of exuberant water fights in town. Many households will have sponsored a *t'inka* for one of their categories of livestock, and most will have at least attended someone else's rites. Those who are in town will probably have spent some time on the grazing lands relaxing. The first sign that anything special is going to take place on this day comes in the morning, when men associated with the sponsors of the two banquets that are to happen later in the day arrive at the plaza dragging a tree that they have cut down in the wooded areas close to the river. The men dig a hole in the middle of the plaza and plant the trunk of the tree upright in it. This tree is known as the *yunsa*, and is decorated with paper streamers (*serpentina*), sweets, bottles of beer and wine, and balloons full of water, all strung from its branches. About 1:00 in the afternoon, people begin to congregate at the home of one of the sponsors (*carguyoq*) of the banquets that will take place that afternoon. Unlike all other events described in the annual cycle thus far, this event belongs exclusively to the notables. They and only they are both sponsors and guests. Commoners participate only as domestic servants, hired musicians, and passive spectators.

The banquet takes place in the little-used, long, dark dining room that every notable aspires to have, complete with plastered walls and family portraits. Those poorer notables whose house compounds do not include such dining rooms will serve the banquet outdoors, but are subject to embarrassment should the event be interrupted by rain. Tables are set up end to end so that as many as fifteen people may sit on either side. At the head of the table sits the sponsor. Dozens of different bottles of beer, wine, alcohol, and liqueur are arranged in a line running down the centre of the table. These bottles are woven together by a dense mesh of paper streamers bearing printed messages such as: 'May you never forget me' and 'You are my only hope / Alone I go in the world.' Large quantities of specially prepared *chicha de jora*, a corn beer distinct from that served in the fields, are also served. This ideal of culinary diversity is expressed by the somewhat mythical standard of the 'Banquete de las Doce Potajes' (Banquet of the Twelve Courses) established in bygone days, when it is said that people still knew how to sponsor *fiestas*. In a formal speech before the meal, the sponsor is likely to bemoan the divisiveness of the town's *vecindario* (i.e., the notables), in a tacit admission of the petty rivalries that exist within the assembled company, and propose a return to old-time values as a remedy, as symbolized by the banquet. Indeed, tension is an integral part of these meals, and complements their formality to accentuate the sense of distinctiveness already inherent in an event that assumes the exclusion of ninety-five per cent of the local population. Bottles are opened, glasses are filled, and toasts are proposed as the children of the sponsor and his commoner servants bring on course after course: soup, beef in a peanut and chili sauce, chicken and noodles, spiced pork, apple pastry, etc. A notable feature of these meals is that they contain the first fresh maize cobs of the year and the first beans, both served as a matter of principle, even if they are not ripe. No sooner does the banquet fall back on its alcoholic component than the second sponsor arises from his or her seat to invite the assembled guests to remove to his or her house for a second banquet. A certain amount of debate about how soon to do this may follow, which is often traceable to the rival factions among the notables, but eventually the second banquet is also consumed.

Between 3:00 and 4:00 in the afternoon, the notables emerge from the house of the second sponsor, bloated and slightly drunk, to make for the plaza, carrying with them an axe and the remaining alcohol from both banquets. The sponsors pour alcoholic libations on the axe as the rest of the notables choose partners of the opposite sex who do not live in the same household. A band comprising two notables playing guitar and charrango, two commoners playing flutes, and another commoner playing a drum launches into Carnival music while the notables dance around the tree that has been planted in the plaza (*yunsa*) holding hands in one big circle. The musicians stop at regular intervals, and a pair comes to the tree, both to take a few chops with the axe, while the rest drink. With every break in the music, another couple takes a turn with the axe; thus, the re-felling of the tree is drawn out over two or more hours.

The *yunsa* dancing is interrupted throughout by Carnival games, which often threaten to take over completely. As someone looks in one direction, flour will be thrown into his or her eyes from another. Balloons full of water come crashing into the circle of dancers at regular intervals, and people leave to give chase just as often. The men may begin to drag the women through the mud around the plaza, and the latter retaliate by slinging mud back, or sneaking up from behind and slapping it into the faces of their defilers. People steal each other's supplies of flour and more chases ensue. Some commoners watch the proceedings from a distance, sitting on the steps of the church, silently and somewhat forlornly. Perhaps they will be served a glass of the notable's corn beer, or be forced to duck inside their ponchos like turtles to avoid flour thrown at their eyes, and perhaps they will not. Only as the *yunsa* is about to be felled does it begin to re-emerge as the centre of attraction. Each couple now begins to measure its blows more circumspectly, knowing that if they fell the tree they must sponsor next year's banquets. Some continue to strike hard, showing their willingness, whereas others make only token efforts. Meanwhile the notable women sing:

Que corten,	Let them cut,
que corten,	let them cut,
que corten la yunsa,	let them cut the yunsa,
la yunsa,	the yunsa,
la yunsa,	the yunsa,
de los carnavales.	of Carnival.

Once the *yunsa* is felled, the dancing ends, but those who want to keep on drinking and playing Carnival games will retire to the house of one of the newly designated sponsors for the coming year. The following day, Monday, features more water fights.

On Tuesday, the commoners celebrate Carnival. Early in the afternoon, the guardians of the two *laymi* sectors under cultivation, who are known as *kamayoqs*, return to town for the first time since their festive send-off in early December. Each *kamayoq* sets up a table in the plaza from which female helpers serve cane alcohol and corn beer in abundance to all of the commoners who have come down from the grazing lands. The men bring flutes and drums (*tinyas*) and form several small clusters near each table to play Carnival tunes. Even though each of these groups plays the same tune, they are all out of phase with the others, resulting in a cacophony that can only be described as wilful. This lack of coordination results from the way the musicians continually drift in and out of groupings as they play. Women circulate through the flux of musicians, serving more corn beer and cane alcohol, occasionally breaking into a song whose constant refrain is *puqllay* ('play'). Two women stand out from this meandering group of people by the brilliance of their clothes and their energetic dancing, which they punctuate with the crack of a sling. These are the wives of the *kamayoqs*. From time to time, men may attempt to dance with them for a few minutes. The women respond by lashing out at the men's legs with a sling until they retire and leave the women to continue alone at opposite ends of the plaza, which they do all afternoon, well after people have started to disperse.

The *kamayoq* mingles among the musicians, serving cane alcohol and passing out a few potatoes to every participant. He also paints three parallel coloured bands on each cheek of those who give him material assistance in sponsoring this event. Since, in theory, all commoners are supposed to serve as *kamayoq* once in their lifetime, many may choose to do so when their material fortunes are at a low ebb to minimize the inconvenience that living in the *laymi* creates when also trying to cultivate valley land. As a result, many *kamayoqs* cannot afford to sponsor this spectacle on their own, or even with the assistance of others, in which case they do not come down from the *laymis*, but will be visited there by friends and well-wishers instead. In years of abundance, however, the two *kamayoqs* will not only be present in the plaza, but may even use slings to hurl potatoes, apples, or peaches at each other from their respective tables. Nonetheless, there is no developed polarization of people between the *kamayoqs*, or hostility, as during Christmas. Rather, musicians and onlookers pass freely between both tables, and many commoners spend most of the time sitting on the steps of the church, mid-way between the two, receiving drinks and socializing with people helping both sponsors. Notables were entirely absent from this event in both of the years I witnessed it in Huaquirca. With an hour left before sundown, the celebration begins to break up, allowing people to return to the grazing lands. Finally, the wives of the *kamayoqs* stop their dance with the sling and the musicians retire. This is the last orchestrated public manifestation of Carnival, although water fights and *t'inkas* may continue for another ten days.

The opposition between 'Notable Sunday' and 'Commoner Tuesday' is fundamental to Carnival in Huaquirca, and colours the activities and images that are specific to each event with more than a tinge of class. First, it is of the utmost significance that this cameo appearance of the notables in the performances of the annual cycle should be to inaugurate the coming period of consumption and private appropriation with their banquets, which are effectively first fruits ceremonies for maize and beans. Carnival is generally a first fruits ceremony and an opportunity for displays of wealth throughout the Andes, even in areas that lack a localized class relation between notables and commoners. Where such local differentiation exists, as it does in Huaquirca, it falls to the notables to play the part of the extravagant consumer-proprietor. Despite the fact that there is no longer an official prohibition on the consumption of green maize, as there was under the Incas (Murra 1978: 46), it is only after 'Notable Sunday' that people begin to eat fresh ears of maize from their fields; thus, the banquets of this day have an authorizing function in which the status of the notables as rulers plays a part. Similarly, the cutting of the *yunsa* is a widespread element of Andean Carnival (see Tomoeda 1982: 283–9), and may be carried out by commoners in towns that lack notables (see Stein 1961: 261), but tends to be performed by the notables where the two classes co-exist (e.g., Montoya 1980: 255). Although other interpretations of the act are certainly possible, the felling of the *yunsa* most clearly depicts the end of a period of growth, which could be taken as a foreshadowing of the harvest, especially in a first fruits ceremony. Again, it is highly appropriate that the notables should be the ones to push the annual cycle ahead to this culminating phase of appropriation.

If 'Notable Sunday' seems determined to bring about the seasonal reversal generally associated with Andean Carnival (see Harris 1982: 60), then 'Commoner Tuesday' would seem to prevent this transition. The whole performance is like an exaggerated break from work in the fields, featuring extended consumption of corn beer, and music turned riotous. Explosive cracks from the slings of the *kamayoqs'* wives and potato fights between the *kamayoqs* suggest, again, the generation of uncontrollable energy through symmetric duality, as in the Christmas *wayliya* and the growing season in general. The way the *kamayoqs'* wives whip the legs of the series of men that try to join in their dance seems to reject the formation of a couple, with its asymmetric duality, which is the very basis of the notable event on Sunday. Here, it is significant that the two common sponsors are always men, whereas the two notable sponsors will always be a man and a woman, because it is a couple that chops down the *yunsa*. Thus, a symmetric duality of men (*yanantin*) characterizes the aspect of Carnival that maintains continuity with the growing season ('Commoner Tuesday'), whereas the rupture into private appropriation ('Notable Sunday') is marked by the asymmetric duality of man and woman, an association that will hold throughout the dry season. Given the links between flute music and rainfall established in the previous chapter, however, it is above all the musical assault of 'Commoner Tuesday' that affirms the rainy season in the face of the notables' attempt to cut it off on Sunday. The reason for such a massive .solicitation of further rainfall will become clear when we turn to the task of breaking ground in the *laymis*, which follows Carnival in the annual cycle.

The commoners of Matapuquio, who only recently escaped the domination of a local *hacienda*, also seem to use Carnival as a pretext for a univocal affirmation of the rainy season. This is expressed in a pronounced parallelism between Carnival and All Saints' in Matapuquio. On both occasions, people bring the crosses that protect various fields and paths to the graveyard, where they proceed to eat and drink, invoke the ancestors, and take part in ritual battles (Skar 1982: 232, 235). During Carnival, a tree is also planted and decorated here, but is given the name *malki*, which refers only to 'tree' in modern Quechua, but once included seeds and ancestors in its purview (see Duviols 1979: 22). Instead of cutting this tree down, men attempt to climb its greased trunk (Skar 1982: 242). This refusal to fell the tree is quite unusual within the Andean context (see Tomoeda 1982: 284–6), and states an unwillingness to sever the link with the dead and the growing season, an interpretation that is reinforced by the counter-reference between All Saints' and Carnival in Matapuquio.

The situation is more complex in Hualcán, a settlement of feral *mestizos* turned commoners, which falls under the political domination of the District of Carhuaz and its notables. Again, crosses are brought down from the fields and other places that they protect to be cleaned, repaired, taken to mass in Carhuaz, and then given a festive wake, complete with the prayers of a specialized *rezador*, much as on All Saints' (Stein 1961: 262, 269–70). After the *yunsa* has been felled in the plaza on Tuesday, crosses associated with the graveyard and the plaza are planted near where it stood (Stein 1961: 270). Certainly the forms of collective mourning appropriate to All Saints' and the growing season are observed here, but as Stein (1961: 269) notes, the downward movement of crosses into town is associated elsewhere with Santa Cruz on 3 May and the beginning of the harvest (e.g., Isbell 1978: 145–51). This is a straightforward case of seasonal contradiction, as in Huaquirca, except with a tighter fusion of opposing tendencies. It also transposes the observances of human death onto the death of the crops, which will soon take place during the frosts of April.

On closer inspection, even the class-divided observances in Huaquirca, which at first glance seem to align the notables entirely with the phase of appropriation and the commoners entirely with production, also reveal certain internal contradictions. As a first fruits ceremony characterized by the asymmetric duality of male and female, 'Notable Sunday' inaugurates the consumption of maize and broad beans. However, these crops are consistently associated with symmetric duality in the divinations of sowing and death, and their interrelation is sometimes represented by the image of Sawasiray and Pitusiray, twin peaks sharing a single base. 'Commoner Tuesday' solicits further rainfall, and is structured by the identical male pair of *yanantin*. Yet the sponsors of the event are the guardians of the potato fields, who give away uncooked potatoes, which embody asymmetric duality and the number three, as we observed in the divinations of the potato sowing. In other words, the associations of these crops during the growing season run counter to the contexts they find themselves in during Carnival. Following Bourdieu (1977: 105–6, 141–2), one could say that this contradiction simply shows the futility of trying to cumulate and totalize the various uses of a sign into a fixed meaning. On the other hand, what better way to signal an end to the growing season than by consuming maize and beans, and the symmetrical principle of growth that they represent; and what better way to sustain it than by having a ritual battle with uncooked potatoes, denying their consumability and asymmetry by employing them in a generation of energy through symmetry and breakdown? At a point in the year when a change in emphasis from production to consumption is taking place, the disjunction between these crops and their Carnival contexts is one way of expressing transition, and negating prevailing frames of reference.

It is quite possible for this tendency towards internal contradiction in Carnival to engulf even those aspects of the event whose meaning seemed most secure and stable. For example, we have already interpreted the felling of the *yunsa* as the symbolic termination of the growing season. Tomoeda (1982: 288–9), however, interprets this same act through a series of Amazonian myths that relate the origin of cultivated plants to the felling of a tree, myths that Tomoeda links to those of the gluttonous fox (see Chapter 3) by arguing that both portray the origins of agriculture in an act of disjunction and dispersal. Although Tomoeda discusses the felling of the *yunsa* outside the context of the annual cycle, the obvious place to enact the origins of agriculture would be at the beginning of the sowing. Here, it is worth recalling the apparently gratuitous attack on the wooded lands of Huaquirca, described in Chapter 3, to provide the sponsors of the Virgin of the Assumption (15 August) and Santa Rosa (30 August) with enormous quantities of firewood. Similar practices have been reported for Carnival (Montoya 1980: 255). Therefore, it seems that the transitions into and out of the growing season are both marked by a ritual assault on trees. As a result, the felling of the *yunsa* can be read as either the termination or the initiation of the growth cycle of the crops. Only the seasonal context of the felling of the *yunsa* in Huaquirca suggests termination, but this does not rule out initiation.

Carnival is not a contradictory event in all regions of the Andes. Among the Laymi, for example, Carnival unproblematically enacts the end of the rainy season (Harris 1982: 57), just as in Matapuquio it unproblematically extends the rainy season. This event becomes complicated when the moralities of production and appropriation each lay claim to the same content, instead of following a pattern of segregation and personification in local class relations, or the suppression of one morality in favour of the other. Finally, however, it is of the greatest significance that a first fruits ceremony should be the occasion of the reversals and contradictions documented here. These are indications that despite their necessary unity, there really is a tension between production and consumption in Huaquirca's annual cycle, and that transition between them is not easily managed. This tension will become even clearer in the remainder of this chapter, and it is only in the *t'inka* rites to be discussed in Chapter 7 that anything like a resolution of the contradiction between production and appropriation will emerge.

Ground Breaking

The final task of the annual cycle performed through *ayni* is ground breaking in the *laymi* sector that is to be sown with potatoes the following year. This chore is known as the *barbecho* (Spanish), or the *chaqma* (Quechua, often Hispanicized as *chaqmeo*). Ground breaking generally occupies all of the month of March, but may begin in late February and continue into early April: it follows Carnival, but precedes the end of the rains. The purpose of this task is to plough under all of the vegetation on the hillside that is to be sown with potatoes the following November, so that all of this wild growth dies during the intervening dry season. Abundant rainfall is necessary to soften the ground and allow sods to be cut by footploughs and overturned. Thus, the task comes to an abrupt halt with the onset of frosts and the dry season.

As usual, the working day begins with a meal at the house of the sponsoring couple, which may start as early as 6:30 in the morning to accommodate the increased travel time to a particularly remote *laymi* sector, and the customary hour or more that each worker takes to tend to his own affairs between the morning meal and setting off to work. Often, people ride horses to work at this time of the year to spare themselves the strenuous climb into the *puna*. Early in the morning, the man of the sponsoring household borrows steel blades (*rejas*) for the footploughs of his workers, loans he must repay on the basis of *ayni*. Since not all commoners can afford to own this component of the footplough, it is up to the sponsors to provide it for them, which sets a generalized circulation of steel blades in motion, alongside that of labour days.

Work gets under way once everyone has arrived at the plot to be worked, has had a few cups of corn beer, and has received some coca leaves from the sponsors. Starting from the bottom right-hand side of the plot (when facing uphill), men form teams of two footploughs each, and begin to cut furrows up the slope in a staggered order, so they do not get in each other's way. Plunging their footploughs into the ground in a vigorous driving motion initiated from the right leg, and then following through with a second hop to drive the blade deeper, the men jointly pry up a sod (about fifty centimetres square), which a woman or man working with them overturns to one side of the furrow. The men cut a second sod, which is overturned to the other side of the furrow, while they take a step uphill and repeat the procedure again. Advancing up the hill in this way, the team cuts furrows and piles sods on either side to form ridges about a metre apart, in which potatoes will be planted the following November. As a rule, there will be more women and men without footploughs to turn the sods than teams of footploughs present at the work party, so those turning sods take turns working with the teams, and wait in a line at the bottom of the plot. Where the *kikuyu* grass is particularly thick, typically in the lower half of the *laymis* (e.g., 3800–4000 m above sea level), the system of ground breaking in furrows and ridges may not be sufficient to kill it off, and here it is common for the entire area under cultivation to have its sods cut and inverted.

This work is particularly strenuous, and after five minutes, the men working the footploughs may already have sweat dripping from the end of their noses despite the cold, damp, and windy conditions that prevail in the *laymis* at this time of the year. The two breaks from work feature the usual consumption of corn beer, cane alcohol, and coca, but there is no longer any flute playing, though there may be anxiety that an early end to the rains could cut the task short before it is completed. There is a sense of pressure about this task that is a significant departure from previous agricultural work, and this, along with the cold and the rain, shortens the breaks. Even casual conversation is difficult to maintain for the men in the footplough teams because of the exertion of the work, and to a certain extent this affects the breaks as well. The only thing resembling a 'ritual act' that I observed during ground breaking was the woman of the sponsoring household taking a pinch of earth from the first sod she overturned and putting it in her mouth with the coca she was chewing, an act that was repeated by other women with soil from the same sod. What is most notable about this task in comparison with others is the degree to which such gestures are unelaborated, and how closely it comes to being unmitigated hard work.

At another level, however, ground breaking enacts literally what the felling of the *yunsa* only hints at: a levelling of wild growth that marks the end of the rains, but points ahead to the beginning of the next cycle of growth. Indeed, in several ground-breaking sessions that I attended, people put considerable effort into uprooting saplings and collecting firewood during breaks from work, both of which fit neatly into the *yunsa*/firewood complex discussed earlier. Given the notions of seasonal reversal between the worlds of the living and the dead mentioned in Chapter 4, the very act of inverting sods and pointing their wild growth downwards might almost seem a way of inverting the seasons, and shutting off the rains. This time, however, it is the commoners who effect this change under the sign of *ayni*, not the notables in a context of festive consumption. The fact that ground breaking is also the beginning of the next year's agricultural cycle reinforces the relation between the felling of the *yunsa* and the origins of agriculture, something that would remain paradoxical had we not followed on from Carnival into this next phase of the annual cycle.

Crop Theft and Property Consciousness

During March, when people are breaking ground in the *laymis*, the maize grows to full maturity on the terraces, and figures in every evening meal, whether it is boiled and eaten on the cob or grilled on the coals of the oven to make what is locally known as *cheqche*.[1] Household members make trips to the fields every few days to check the crops and to bring more fresh cobs home. By early April, the first frosts have usually come and killed the maize, and rainfall is becoming scarce. This finishes ground breaking in the *laymis*, and leaves people with little to do but watch over their crops. There are still some minor tasks to do, such as cutting vines that intertwine the maize stalks and threaten to drag them to the ground. This work is done by the household itself, without recourse to larger work parties based on *ayni*. Once the hard frosts set in by late April, the vibrant green of the maize quickly retracts into a withered yellow, revealing the browns and reds of the soil. As people wait for their crops to dry and lose weight for transportation during the harvest, they become increasingly, even constantly, concerned with the very real danger of crop theft (cf. Stein 1961: 55).

Crop theft has been widely reported in Andean ethnography,[2] and it is a cultural fact that is every bit as predominant at this time of the year as cooperation was during the growing season. Of course, livestock rustling (see Orlove 1973) and theft from houses are also common, but they can take place at any time of the year, and they do not have the same predictability or massive incidence as crop theft. Although losses of fifty to one hundred percent have been reported in some parts of the Andes (see Stein 1961: 55; Burchard 1980: 608), the pattern common in Huaquirca is one of small raids at night by one or two people, which rarely net more than five per cent of the crop in a single strike. These raids may be preferentially directed towards the notables and rich commoners (cf. Burchard 1980: 613), but everyone is vulnerable. As of April, most households construct or repair small huts on their main plots of terraced land, from which a member will guard the crops at night (cf. Gade 1970: 8–11). Although most households find it impossible to maintain strict vigilance, by May the paths out of town to the fields seem better travelled at night than during the day. People who had been linked in a harmonious effort of collective production short weeks ago now eye each other with suspicion. Even the most closely watched fields are likely to suffer some losses, but rarely is vigilance so lax as to allow losses of more than twenty per cent.

Previous explanations of crop theft have focused on scarcity and treat it as a symptom of improper land use (e.g., Gade 1970: 5–6, 12–13). Lacking any absolute standard to decide what is and is not proper land use in the Andes, I suggest that crop theft is best evaluated against the patterns of legitimate appropriation it violates. Here, an interesting tension emerges. While the crops are not consumable and exist only as an object of labour, the generalized exchange of *ayni* labour creates an implicit social recognition of individual property rights. Once the crops become consumable, individual property rights require the exclusion of other people, and a retreat from collectivity. However, it is impossible to suppress the previous period of collective production entirely, and theft is one way of asserting it during the emergent phase of private appropriation. As a first approximation, generalized crop theft results neither from unmediated biological need nor some inexplicable social pathology. Rather, it is an outcome of conflict and transition between two incompatible ways of asserting property rights in Andean culture, which are embodied in two seasonal regimes of social practice.

The ways in which Andean people rationalize and respond to crop theft confirm and develop this basic point. Since the onset of the heavy frosts that kill the maize generally corresponds to Easter, people say that both the earth and God die during Holy Week, and that it is permissible to steal crops at this time because God does not see.[3] This correspondence of the death of maize to the death of Christ confirms the link between the two that was established in the previous chapter. It also indicates in the strongest possible manner that the moral order of cooperative Christianity, expressed primarily in relations of *compadrazgo*, is linked to the growing period of the maize, and comes to an abrupt end with its 'crucifixion' by frost. From this time on, a kind of amoral appropriation comes to the fore, of which theft is one expression. This is the amorality of sorcery, not precultural need. Discovery of a theft is inevitably a matter of great trauma, as shown by Stein's (1961: 166) descriptions of people retiring to darkened rooms and wrapping themselves in blankets. In Huaquirca, people attributed crop theft, like sorcery, to the 'envy' that the aggressor feels towards the victim. This sorcery is foreshadowed by the *layqas* of the Christmas *wayliya*, who illicitly harvest flowering maize, and try to impersonate women. In the following chapter, I will show that sorcery also pervades the *t'inkas*, and is an important dynamic of appropriation in them. Although Andean people clearly want to enjoy the fruits of their labour as property, they recognize that they do so under a different moral framework than that which orchestrates the cooperation of the growing season.

Not only are people liable to rob each other's fields at this time of the year, but so are their cattle, which have grazed the natural pastures of the *puna* lean by now and wander down into the valley knowing that there will be plenty of rich fodder if only they can breach the stone walls that protect the terraced maize fields. Any animals that are caught in the act, and there are usually several per day, are taken to the communal animal pound (*coso*), which does a roaring business collecting fines from the owners, who are identified by the brand on the animal's hide. The owners are inevitably petulant about having to pay, no matter how much of someone else's crops their animals may have eaten, and usually protest that the animal was unfairly rounded up on the paths by people who are simply jealous of them. People call these animals '*daño*' (damage) even before they have broken into the fields, because even the least enterprising animal will find its way through the fences and into the maize if left on its own for more than a few hours. Often, people may lose more of their crop to animal intrusion than to human theft, and in particularly severe cases may even hold the animal for ransom until its owner pays compensation, especially if the plaintiff is a notable.

During this period of heightening property consciousness, marked by an almost institutionalized disregard for the rights of others, another round of *t'inkas* takes place in Huaquirca. This time, the rites are held exclusively in honour of cattle and San Marcos, who is said to look after them. San Marcos' day in the liturgical calendar is 25 April. For about a week following this date, people will hold *t'inkas* on their grazing lands in the *puna*, as during Carnival. Elsewhere in the Andes, celebrations are common on or around Santa Cruz (3 May), in which crosses that guard the fields are decorated with produce and taken down to the church in town for blessing, including a series of wakes of the sort that may happen during Carnival (see Brush 1977b: 165–6; Isbell 1978; 145–51; Buechler 1980: 61). This downward movement of the crosses is an indication of the incoming harvest, as Isbell (1978: 150–1) argues, and as we have already established in Chapter 3. It also underlines, yet again, the connection between Christ and the crops.

Harvest

In Huaquirca, the harvest usually begins in mid-May, but it can be postponed if the maize has not yet dried fully in the sun (for ease of storage and lightness for transport) or scheduled to take advantage of a full moon that would allow working at night. Communal regulations forbid individuals to harvest their crops whenever they want, although they do allow the removal of small quantities of produce for immediate consumption. Instead, the fields are grouped into large harvest sectors, each of which receives an opening date in a communal assembly. As of this date, all those who own land in the sector start harvesting at once in a frantic rush, with little or no help from other households, who are similarly engaged. Arguedas (1968: 45) describes this pattern for Spain, and it is an integral part of the land tenure system described in Chapter 2, also of Spanish origin. There are two *laymi* sectors, one sown with potatoes, and the other under second-year crops. The harvest sectors of terraced land consist of the large block of 'private' land around Pomache, on the one hand, and 'lands of the community' on the other (see Figure 17). The sequence is always as follows: the 'private' lands around Pomache, the *laymis* under potatoes, the *laymis* under second-year crops, the smaller *laymi* circuits of the *puna* of Huaquirca, and, finally, the terraced 'lands of the community.' What the assembly must decide are the particular opening dates for each sector. Two or three possible dates are proposed before the assembly breaks down into a bedlam of factions, each frantically shouting a date and trying to recruit others to the cause. Individuals decide according to the amount of time they need to complete the harvest in one sector before the opening date in the next. Any two people may find themselves shouting in unison for a given date in one sector, and in opposite camps for the next, trying to drown each other out. The summation of these various self-interests is taken by vote for each new entry date, and the one to find the most backers wins. In 1982, the following dates were assigned: 10 May, Pomache; 15 May, *laymis* under potatoes; 25 May, *laymis* under second-year crops; 30 May, *laymis* of the *puna*; 12 June, 'lands of the community.' The long delay between the final two dates was to accommodate Corpus Christi, in theory, although the event is no longer celebrated in Huaquirca.[4]

It is not clear to me why the harvest needs to be this tightly regulated. When I asked why fixed dates were necessary, the first answer I usually got was that without them there would be more crop theft. Yet it is just as possible to argue that these rules create even more theft by imposing excessive waits for opening dates. A second answer was that pack animals transporting the produce of those to harvest first would trample the crops standing in other people's fields. Of course this might occur, but it could easily be prevented. What this rationalization shows, however, is the lack of trust that prevails among people once the crops are consumable. A breakdown of interhousehold cooperation is all but inscribed in the communal regulation of the harvest, since it forces everyone to complete their work in a much shorter interval than any of the tasks of the growing season, where *ayni* prevails. Those found guilty of jumping the entry date in a given harvest sector are given a healthy fine (in relation to commoner levels of monetary income: S/. 4,000). Rumours and accusations of such violations abound.

Thus, the harvest is undertaken in a manner that approaches the extreme of every household for itself. As Skar (1982: 141–2) observes, every household member may work well into the night for up to a

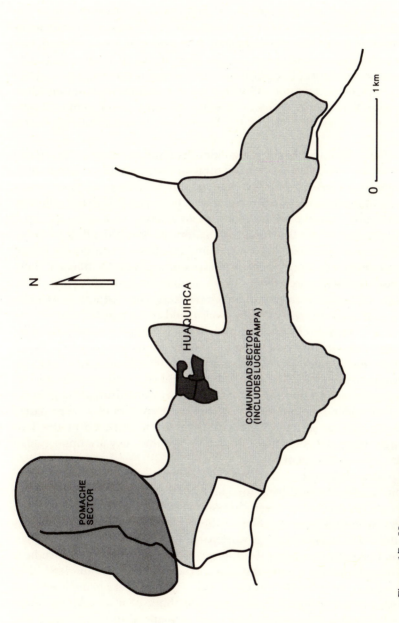

Figure 17 Harvest sectors

week to complete the task. Many families actually camp out in the fields for the duration of the harvest, and do not even leave a member behind to guard the possessions of their house in town. A family may feel considerable pressure in the task if the next opening date approaches before they finish work in the sector currently open, since they assume that people will steal any crops that they are not busy harvesting. For a large household that need not worry about its own labouring capacity, however, the harvest can be a very pleasant occasion.

There are ways of recruiting extra-domestic labour for the harvest even if most people are occupied on their own land. For example, godchildren (*ahijados*) are expected to help their godparents (*padrinos*) in some way during every agricultural task, but it is at this time of the year that godparents who are normally lax are likely to demand help, and it is very difficult to refuse them, no matter what the godchild's own obligations may be. There are always some families that do not have land in the sector currently open, or not very much land. Members of these households will make themselves available to those with particularly large holdings, which cannot be harvested on time without extra help. These people are recruited by *mink'a*, and receive one *arroba* of produce for every day's work they provide. This is approximately 11.5 kilograms in theory, but is in fact a traditional volume measurement based on the maximum capacity of a *lliqlla* cloth tied around the shoulders. By any standard of calculation, this payment represents a much higher level of remuneration for labour than is provided during the growing season under relations of *ayni*.[5] Therefore, owners of a large parcel may quietly curse their *mink'ays* during the harvest, no matter how much they need their help, since they feel that they are opportunists who take advantage of them.

Although I cannot absolutely swear that *ayni* does not take place among households during the harvest, the very question struck many people in Huaquirca as odd. Not only is the hurried time frame of the harvest entirely uncongenial to the principle of delayed reciprocity implicit in *ayni*, but no large work parties are convened during the harvest. Furthermore, this is the one agricultural task for which corn beer is not prepared for consumption in the fields (cf. Urton 1981: 26). Thus, the harvest does not follow the etiquette that normally governs work parties, probably because people think of it as a family affair, even if non-kin do in fact help. Conceptually, if not empirically, the harvest remains a task that each household performs on its own. This is why any demand for extra-domestic labour is met through invoking dormant kinship ties. For these reasons, I find it surprising that other scholars mention *ayni* during the harvest.[6]

The task of dehusking (*deshoje*) maize cobs coincides with the opening of a harvest sector. Before the opening date, the owners usually cut and pile stalks of maize. They take considerable care to see that the stalks are well piled so that the dehusking can proceed as efficiently as possible. Husks are ripped from the cob with the aid of a pointed stick, and the cobs pile up in front of the worker until they fill a *lliqlla* cloth, at which point they are taken to a central collecting point for the entire parcel. The normal daily output per *mink'ay* is ten to twelve *lliqllas* full of cobs, so the central pile does not grow very quickly. Once the dehusking is completed, the cobs are loaded into large sacks of coarse-spun llama wool (*costales*), which hold five *arrobas* each (fifty-five to sixty kilograms). These are sewn shut across their narrow mouths, and then loaded and lashed onto donkeys, mules, horses, and/or llamas that transport them back to town. In town, the sacks are unloaded in the family's storeroom (*despensa*). After several such trips, the process is completed.

The potato harvest effectively begins before the opening dates, when the guardian of the *laymi*, who has been living there since early December, selects the best ridge (*wacho*) from every plot of land that has been opened and digs potatoes out of it as recompense for the service that he has provided for all who have sown there. The guardians may even harvest their own potatoes before the opening date in some cases without anyone objecting because it is generally recognized that they prevent the sort of theft in the *laymis* that is endemic on terraced land; therefore, they have a certain moral authority. Potatoes are dug out of the ridges with picks by loosening the soil on either side of the plant and then pulling on its dried stem and roots until the tubers come up. If potatoes were not sown in ridges, this process would be much less efficient, but it is still common for a dried stem to break when it is pulled, which means that one must swirl around in the soil with the pick looking for potatoes to come up one by one. By the time of the potato harvest, the ground has been baked hard by the sun, and in digging up the ridges, people dislodge large clods of earth. These are used to make an igloo-like dome that serves as an earth oven for making *watia* (baked potatoes), which when eaten with cheese, is the classic meal of the potato harvest. Again, people may need *mink'ays* to complete the potato harvest on time, and the standard payment is also the full carrying capacity of a *lliqlla* cloth, which is said to be two *arrobas* (twenty-three kilograms).[7] Because potatoes are denser than maize, it is possible to get eight *arrobas* into each sack instead of five. The total output per *laymi* plot (*chaqmana*) varies between ten and forty such sacks, according to the area opened, its fertility, and losses to the various blights that affect potato production in the area. Before the arrival of *kikuyu* grass, when much larger areas were cultivated, the notables claim to have regularly harvested fifty to sixty sacks per year, and in exceptional years eighty, which they would freeze-dry and sell as a component of their muleteer commerce. Now, most households in Huaquirca have trouble making do for a whole year with their potato harvests.

The Antabamba Valley is one of the few areas in modern Peru that still meets the need for pack animals during the harvest by means of a traditional arrangement between the agricultural peasantry in the valleys and the pastoralists in the alpine zone, who may come from as far away as the Departments of Arequipa and Ayacucho to provide llamas for crop transport. This arrangement has been the subject of two excellent studies by Concha (1971, 1975). Llamas can carry about half the load of a mule or horse, but their number more than makes up for their relative weakness as beasts of burden. For every ten sacks they carry from the fields into town, the *llamero* keeps one as a charge for his service. Each of these animals has a bell of a given pitch fixed around its neck, and during the harvest in Huaquirca, their movement sounds like a wind chime. The enclosed courtyards of the notable compounds in Ñapaña may temporarily house troupes of twenty to thirty llamas, as do the more open yards around the house clusters of Huachacayllo and Champine. The owner of the troupe is given food and lodging at the house of the family whose crops he transports, for the duration of the work. Often, these are long-standing relationships that are renewed every year, perhaps with additional forms of barter for herbs from the *puna*, etc. *Llameros* who lack such contacts in a given town will simply wait around by the path leading out to the fields for someone to engage their services. With the endemic problem of livestock rustling in the area, few people can afford to keep enough horses, mules, and donkeys for the requirements of the harvest; thus, valley people claim that they are more dependent than ever on the *llameros*.

Once the harvest is completed, and sometimes even during the dehusking, the owners' cattle will be brought into the terraced fields to eat the dry husks and stalks as fodder. The cattle and horses will spend the greater part of the dry season on the terraces, according to the grazing rights described in Chapter 2. There is nothing that could be called a straightforward public celebration of the harvest in Hua-quirca or the other towns of the upper Antabamba Valley, despite the one-day break in the harvest schedule for Corpus Christi, which once may have been such an event. The mood following the harvest is more one of relief than festivity. Men occupy themselves with dry season tasks, such as making adobe bricks and sawing eucalyptus planks for house repair and construction, whereas the women spin wool and weave blankets, ponchos and *lliqllas*. Many days in July are spent simply sitting around in the yards drinking in small groups, and few of the projects mentioned above are pursued for more than a few days running without a day of drinking '*por gusto*' ('for fun,' 'for its own sake'). Only by the end of July does this period of relative relaxation give rise to the public expressions of Santiago and the *Fiestas Patrias* discussed in Chapter 3.

7

The *T'inkas*

The *t'inkas* are by far the most complex rites that occur in the annual cycle of Huaquirca. Similar rites take place throughout the Andes under a variety of names.[1] In Quechua, the verb *t'inkay* means to sprinkle or libate, and refers not only to these complex rites, but also to the simpler acts that precede every Andean drinking session, in which alcohol is sprinkled on the ground, is flicked with the fingertips into the air towards important mountains, or has its fumes blown towards them. Although such simple libations are included in the rites to be described here, burnt offerings and blood sacrifice are actually their featured events. Therefore, what is of interest about the use of the term *t'inka* to refer to these rites as a whole is how it highlights the restoration of fluids to the mountains. Bearing in mind the aquatic vital force provided by the dead throughout the rainy season, I would argue that these 'libations' are an *ayni* debt of the living.[2]

In the previous chapter, we saw that valley people perform separate *t'inkas* for their cattle and horses during Carnival and Santiago, and that their cattle also receive rites on San Marcos (see Figure 18). Pastoralists who live above Huaquirca also perform separate *t'inkas* for their sheep, llamas, and alpacas during Carnival and Santiago. Within recent memory, they also sponsored a third round of these rites on San Andrés (30 November), although this practice is now defunct. Although there is local variation in the timing of these rites throughout the Andes, the most common pattern among agriculturalists features one round of *t'inkas* at the beginning of the period of private appropriation (Carnival) and another in anticipation of the resumption of collective production (Santiago, or in early August). There are some significant exceptions, however, particularly among pastoralists.[3] Although people usually say that they perform these rites for the well-being and fertility of their animals, the *t'inkas* also acquire considerable agricultural significance because of their position within the annual cycle, and the relation to rainfall noted above. This conjunction goes some way towards explaining the paradox noted by Quispe (1969: 10) and Skar (1982: 165) that the most elaborate rituals in predominantly agricultural areas are those connected to herding. We will see that the *t'inkas* have a powerful totalizing tendency, one that draws many other concerns into their immediate focus on livestock. Similarly, these rites are the most developed expression of the phase of consumption and private appropriation in the annual cycle, but they also express the unity between that phase and the collective production of the growing season in a larger whole. The location of the *t'inkas* on the two main transition points of the year, and in the dry season, further suggests this totalizing function. It is no exaggeration to say that these are the most important rites in the annual cycle, and in Andean culture as a whole.

Once a household sets a date for a *t'inka*,[4] the woman must prepare corn beer, and buy cane alcohol and coca, while the man notifies close kin, friends, and neighbours in the grazing lands. Although the *t'inkas* take place outside the context of labour in the fields, they nonetheless use the agricultural work party as a kind of organizational form, so that people may attend each other's rites in *ayni* or *yanapa*, and the unfolding of the rite is punctuated by periods of rest (cf. Quispe 1969: 25, 67).

Around noon on the day of the rite, the animals are rounded up into a corral near the hut on the grazing territory.[5] Next, the sponsors take some preliminary measures to prevent sorcery against their animals, usually before guests begin to arrive. The most basic procedure is for the man to light a thick-wicked candle (of the sort used in church devotions) and circumambulate the corral counter-clockwise ('to the left') three times while reciting the credo.[6] Meanwhile, the woman of the sponsoring household grinds separate piles of white and yellow maize into a flour called *llampu*. Small quantities of this flour figure in the various offerings of the ritual, but its primary function is to protect the ritualist's paraphernalia (*mesa*) from sorcery. Therefore, one must never run out of this flour during the rite. Once the rite is over, the paraphernalia must be amply sprinkled with *llampu* before it is bundled up. Elsewhere, this flour is used during the circumambula-

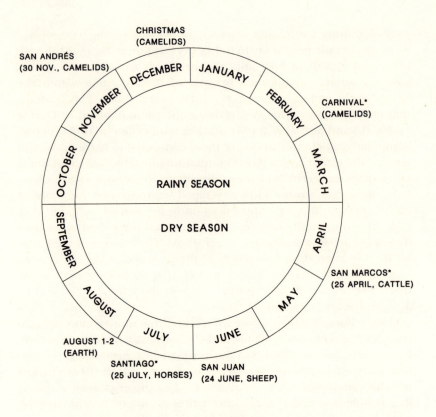

CHRISTMAS
(CAMELIDS)

SAN ANDRÉS
(30 NOV., CAMELIDS)

DECEMBER JANUARY

NOVEMBER

CARNIVAL*
(CAMELIDS)

FEBRUARY

OCTOBER

MARCH

RAINY SEASON

SEPTEMBER

DRY SEASON

APRIL

SAN MARCOS*
(25 APRIL, CATTLE)

AUGUST

MAY

SEPTEMBER

JULY JUNE

AUGUST 1-2
(EARTH)

SANTIAGO*
(25 JULY, HORSES)

SAN JUAN
(24 JUNE, SHEEP)

*denotes *t'inka* observed in Huaquirca
(animal association is strict only in the case of San Marcos)

Figure 18   Seasonality of the *t'inkas*

tion, and to absorb dangerous power during the rite, procedures that fit well with what I observed in Huaquirca.[7]

Having taken these precautions, the man of the sponsoring household begins to unpack a cloth bundle in the corral. The outer covering of the bundle is a rectangular carrying cloth (*lliqlla*), which the man lays out flat on the ground, revealing a mound of smaller cloth bundles and plastic bags. This carrying cloth and its contents are known as the *mesa*. Intermediate Quechua pronunciation of the Spanish vowels *e* and *i* gives *mesa* two possible meanings. As *mesa* (table), the cloth becomes a surface for the construction of offerings called *platos* (servings, plates), and thus establishes a clear sense of consumption. As *misa* (mass), however, this consumption is marked as symbolic sacrifice, and given a Christian significance. This sense of mass is reinforced by the title of '*cura*' ('priest') assumed by the man of the sponsoring household for the duration of the rite, or in the case of the notables, by the cowherd servant,[8] who constructs and burns the offerings. Thus, *mesa* refers to both the active and the objective side of the rite at once. The *mesa* takes an orientation when the priest places three stalks of maize along one of the long edges of the rectangular cloth. Often, bean stalks will be interspersed among them as well. Elsewhere in the Andes, three crosses serve the same purpose (Quispe 1969: 65, 1984: 612; Isbell 1978: 160), a practice that further underlines their connection to these crops, and the identification of the crops with Christ. The agriculturalists of the upper Antabamba Valley often orient their *mesas* towards the west, whereas the pastoralists orient theirs towards the east, as do ritualists elsewhere in the Andes (see Quispe 1969: 26; Casaverde 1970: 231).

As the guests begin to arrive, the 'priest' begins to gather dry cow dung as fuel for the fire on which burnt offerings will be made. The first offering consists of incense, along with red and white carnations, which are taken from their respective bundles on the *mesa*, wrapped in a dried maize husk, and then burned by the sponsoring couple on the dung fire as, with doffed hats, they mutter prayers in a rapid but barely audible tone. This offering is to '*Nuestro Alto*' (God on High), and is made to obtain his permission to continue with the rite proper.[9] Holding their hats in one hand, the sponsoring couple give all non-kin present an arm's-length embrace, thanking them for coming, and asking '*licencia*' (permission) to perform the rite.

Next, the 'priest' clears a space at the centre of the *mesa*, moving the bundles of paraphernalia to the edges and towards the top, and lays

out as many as four horizontal rows of three dried maize husks each
(see Figure 19a). These are the 'plates' or 'courses' that will be served
in the rite, but may simply be called husks (*panqas*) as well. From the
various bundles of paraphernalia at the top of the *mesa*, the 'priest'
puts the following ingredients in each husk: three coca leaves, incense,
flour and grains of white and yellow maize, *chamán* leaves, red and
white carnations, bits of crab-apple or peach, growing maize and beans
(during Carnival), llama chest fat (*pechuwira*), and scrapings from a
collection of coins, bills, various metallic rocks, seashells, and deer's
hooves. Each individual husk 'serving' is tied shut and then lashed to
the other two husk bundles on every horizontal row. Finally, each horizontal of three husks is bound together with the rest to form one big
packet (see Figure 19a).

This composite packet of offerings is returned to the centre of the
mesa, which people now begin to approach in successive pairs. The
men go to the lower right-hand corner of the *mesa* and the women to
the lower left. Married people generally go with their spouses as partners, but this conjugal model is not so rigid as to prevent pairs of the
same sex from going to the *mesa* when unequal numbers of men and
women are present. The woman of the sponsoring household hands a
large gourd or wooden cup (*q'ero*) of corn beer and a small one of
cane alcohol to both members of the pair. A previously chosen non-
consanguineal friend of the sponsoring couple begins to fulfil his role
as 'son-in-law' (*qatay*) by nominating a particular deity or object of paraphernalia for which the pair will pour libations and make invocations.
Once the 'son-in-law' has named this entity, each pair must come forward in turn to pour libations, make toasts, and drain their cups until
all present have done so. The 'son-in-law' then names a new deity or
ritual object and the process repeats itself. Thus, the development of a
t'inka consists of an additive sequence of rounds of drinking dedicated
to various sources of power. To describe the inner workings of the rite,
I will go through a sequence of rounds that actually took place at one
particularly short *t'inka* I attended. The entities libated and invoked in
this sequence are all stock-in-trade for these rites, but it should be
emphasized that they form only a core group that would be amply supplemented in a more elaborate rite. Furthermore, each *t'inka* has its
own unique sequence of rounds determined by a dialogue between
'priest' and 'son-in-law' as the rite progresses.

Virtually every *t'inka* that I attended had its first round dedicated to
an entity known as *pachamama*, which I would translate as 'earth

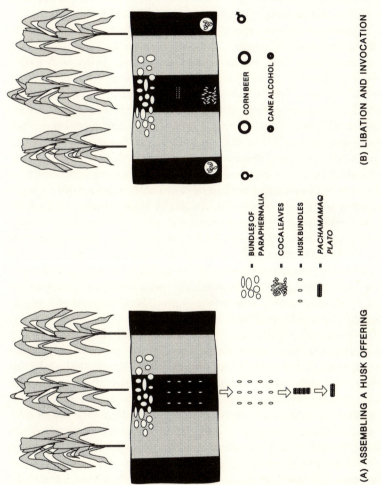

BUNDLES OF PARAPHERNALIA

COCA LEAVES

HUSK BUNDLES

PACHAMAMAQ PLATO

CORN BEER

CANE ALCOHOL

(A) ASSEMBLING A HUSK OFFERING

(B) LIBATION AND INVOCATION

Figure 19   Uses of the *mesa*

source,' and interpret as the particular spirit of a named or occupied place, here, the grazing territory.[10] As the 'priest' places the composite bundle of husk offerings at the centre of the *mesa*, the 'son-in-law' simply announces: 'We will libate *pachamama*.' With a sprig of leaves, each member of each pair that comes to the *mesa* sprinkles a few drops from each cup onto the husk offerings, all the while muttering such standard phrases as: '*Pachamama*, holy earth.' Next, the 'son-in-law' demands somewhat officiously: 'What do you invoke?'[11] and threatens to whip the toaster with a switch if he or she is not prompt. A typical response would be 'I invoke *t'año*,'[12] the latter being one of many ritual names for cattle. The 'son-in-law' interjects: 'May it come, may it come!'[13] as the invocation continues 'From Phukawasi, also from Ch'aynawiri,'[14] both of which are particular grazing territories other than the one where the rite is taking place. The 'son-in-law' and all of the assembled company respond emphatically: 'May it just come, may it just come!'[15] as the person who made the invocation first drains the cup of corn beer and then the cup of cane alcohol, places the cups rim down on a small pile of coca leaves at the lower central part of the *mesa*, and picks them up again to see if any leaves have stuck. If there are many coca leaves, the 'son-in-law' shouts: 'It just came!' and the sponsors thank the person profusely. If there are few or no coca leaves, the 'son-in-law' observes: 'Your adhesion didn't come.'[16] When the 'son-in-law' removes the leaves from each set of cups and puts them in dishes at either side of the *mesa* (see Figure 19b), the next pair comes to the table to repeat the process.

Once everyone present has come to the ritual table to pour libations, make invocations, and drink, the 'priest' and 'son-in-law' take the composite packet of husk bundles that has been libated to the fire and burn it. This composite bundle is called the *pachamamaq plato* (serving of *pachamama*) because it was constructed for the *pachamamas*, moved to the centre of the *mesa*, and libated during the round of invocations dedicated to them. As I was told on two different occasions: 'This serving is for all of the *pachamamas*.'[17] It feeds all of the localities invoked during this round.

The constant reference to spatial transfer in these invocations ('from grazing territory x, also from grazing territory y,' 'may it come, may it come,' 'it has [not] come') is key to their interpretation. Elsewhere, comparable invocations are seen as requests to the spirits of the animals on other grazing territories to come to the one on which the rite is being performed (Valderrama and Escalante 1976: 184–5;

Quispe 1984: 621). Adhesion of coca leaves, the classic Andean divinatory medium, indicates by mimesis that the spirits invoked have also in
some sense 'stuck' to the locality where the rite is taking place, and
can be expected to augment prosperity there. Thus, the genuine
thanks expressed by the sponsors when someone does manage to
make many leaves adhere. The necessity of non-kin from other grazing
territories at these rites derives from their ability to invoke the spirits
of faraway places. Through their knowledge of ritual names[18] and elo-
quence, they can summon sources of power and make them adhere, if
they are attending out of good will. Yet this is necessarily a kind of sorcery directed at the more successful grazing territories and their spirits (*pachamamas*); hence, the elaborate procedures at the beginning of
every rite to ensure that one's own animals are not bewitched, and the
request for 'permission' from God and the assembled company to
indulge in what is essentially a selfish and even evil act of appropriation. At one level, it is true that the presence of non-kin in these rites
does lend legitimacy to the proprietary claims of the sponsoring
household (cf. Quispe 1969: 102), as in the practice of *ayni*. However,
there is a crucial deviation from the *ayni* model in the way one territory's gain becomes another's loss in the spatial transfers posited by
these invocations. Here, property becomes an exclusive, zero-sum
affair, as during the period of crop vigilance and theft extending from
Carnival to the harvest. Although the principle of cooperation is not
entirely absent from the *t'inkas*, and is even a necessary part of them, it
is nonetheless subordinated to private appropriation. As a result, non-
kin attending these rites may be labelled '*peones*' (Quispe 1969: 26;
Tomoeda 1985: 287), and their presence is best understood on the
hierarchical model of *mink'a*, immediate consumption for services
rendered, as is typical when limited cooperation is needed to realize
an act of private appropriation.

In these rites, the imagery of marriage also provides a model for the
redistribution of animals across the landscape. When people come to
the *mesa* in pairs to make invocations, conjugality provides the model
for the desired influx and 'adhesion' of vital force to the locality where
the rite unfolds. However, it is the 'son-in-law' who orchestrates this
process, and his presence is a reminder that the hosts must offer a
daughter, however figuratively, to ensure the ritual services of non-kin.
Thus, marriage signifies not only adhesion but also dispersal. Nor is
this redistribution entirely symbolic. In Huaquirca, *t'inkas* are a standard occasion for parents to publicly proclaim that specific animals

will be inherited by their children when they marry. Elsewhere these rites have been mentioned as a forum for pledging animals to new owners, sometimes including non-kin (see Quispe 1969: 32; Morissette and Racine 1973: 174). Thus, through the imagery of affinity, these rites attempt to portray the accumulation of circulating animal wealth as something that will be undone when their children marry, and the herds are divided and dispersed. In this way, accumulation acquires a different representation that is morally acceptable, and counterbalances the model of sorcery described above.

The next round of the particular *t'inka* that we are following was dedicated to a set of three figurines representing the cattle in whose name the rite was being performed. The 'priest' fashions such figures from a mixture of llama chest fat and maize flour, sometimes adding coca seeds for hooves. Figurines made of yellow maize flour will be slightly larger than those made of white maize flour, and a figurine of one of these colours will be flanked by two of the other inside a dried maize husk: either YwY or wYw.[19] This offering is called *kallpa*, which means 'force' or 'vitality' in Quechua. Several times I was told that these figurines represent the vital force of the animals. As with virtually every offering assembled on the *mesa*, this one stresses the number three, but in a particularly interesting way that gives us insight into the Andean trinity formula. Two of its members are identical in size and colour, suggesting the subsumption of the symmetric dual principle of *ayni* to a central element. Following Lévi-Strauss (1958: 151), this pairing could be seen as a special case of concentric duality, but Harris' (1986) derivation of the trinity from asymmetric duality, particularly that between men and women, was especially well illustrated by an incident that took place at one *t'inka* I attended. In the drunken enactment of animal copulation that sometimes breaks out, complete with satiric squealing (see also Quispe 1969: 75; Isbell 1978: 161), the 'priest' had two women kneel down like flanking figurines, while he repeatedly thrust into the space between them. Thus, the notion of *kallpa* or vital force may well be linked to sexuality, and the avowed magical role of the *t'inka* in stimulating animal reproduction.[20] Alternatively, a female informant interpreted a configuration of two small white figurines flanking a central yellow figurine as a cow and two calves. Despite their different emphases, both interpretations of *kallpa* stress animal fertility.

The 'son-in-law' puts the husk bundle containing the *kallpa* figurines at the centre of the *mesa* and announces that it will be libated, thus initiating another round of sprinklings, invocations, and toasts. Usually, participants wish the hosts an increase in their herds, invoking the ritual names of the animals in question and the names of people who own large numbers of them. These people are invoked in the same manner as grazing lands that are particularly abundant in the desired animals, that is, 'from Maxi Castillo, also from Magín Barrientos.' Again, these invocations seem to posit a spatial transfer of property from the person mentioned to the sponsor of the *t'inka*. Once everyone has come to the ritual table to libate the *kallpa* figurines, they are usually burnt on the fire, as with the 'plates' from the previous round.

As a mode of offering, burning involves a dispersal of substance through fumes, much as simple libations may be made to the mountain spirits by blowing vapours from a bottle of cane alcohol towards the peaks. In certain areas of the Andes, people say that the dead and the mountain spirits can only ingest vapours and emanations, not solid substances (Oblitas Poblete 1978: 47–8), and that these emanations are the ethereal essence of offerings, called *sami* (Núñez del Prado 1970: 114; Allen 1988: 49–50). These notions accord well with the form of the burnt offering. Furthermore, if the *t'inkas* are meant to restore the fluids extracted from the dead during the rainy season, then the burnt offering in this world would invert the process of desiccation that the *alma* undergoes in its journey to Qoropuna, and its vapours would include water destined for the land of the dead.

The burnt offering's emphasis on dispersal seems to run directly counter to the process of invocation, which attempts to concentrate the bounty of diverse grazing lands on the territory where the rite takes place. Burnt offerings appear to negate the accumulative ends of the *t'inka*, especially when they consist of figurines that are supposed to represent the vital force of the animals concerned. Thus, it is significant that the ashes of burnt offerings are sometimes interred on the territory where a rite occurs (Dalle 1969: 146; Casaverde 1970: 146). Although I never witnessed the act, I was told that when people are particularly anxious to increase their herds, they may resort to a practice known as 'lineage' or 'origin'[21] whereby six *kallpa* figurines are interred in a special hidden recess in the corral wall, or a subterranean niche lined and covered with stone slabs: installations that have been widely reported throughout the Andes.[22] Interred offerings are often called 'payments' (*pagos*) in the Andes, although interment can also be designated by the verb *samay*, which, as we have seen, describes the invocation of the spirits of other grazing territories. Thus, interred offerings can be seen as outwardly directed 'payment' and a means of fixing inflowing fertility. This is further reflected in the complex relation of semantic identity and opposition that exists between *sami* (the dispersed ethereal essence of offerings) and *samay* (the principle of invocation).[23] At the bottom of this situation lies the paradox of sacrifice, the calculated loss that brings increase, a dynamic that, as we shall see below, characterizes other aspects of the *t'inkas* as well.

The next round of the particular rite we are following was dedicated to *sawasira/pitusira*. This couplet forms the ritual name for maize, and refers to the complementary principles at work in its growth, as we saw in Chapter 4. During this round, dried cobs of yellow and white maize are moved to the centre of the *mesa* and receive libations. These are usually the same cobs whose grains were used in the husk offerings; thus, they may be partially stripped. Sometimes, however, *sawasira/pitusira* is represented not by the complementary duality of white and yellow maize, but by a single bifurcating cob, consisting of two ears joined at the base. This corresponds particularly well to the mountains of Sawasiray and Pitusiray, twin peaks deriving from a common base, from which the ritual names of maize are taken. There are other cases where ritual names of crops or animals coincide with those of the mountain spirits from which these beings are thought to originate,[24] and these cases show how ritual names may be closely linked to the spatial transfers that the invocations attempt to cause. An additional embodiment of *sawasira/pitusira* is the interspersed arrangement of maize and bean stalks at the head of the *mesa* (see Figure 19). As Wallis (1980: 251) notes, this couplet also represents the principles of vegetative growth in general. Some invocations that I heard during rounds of drinking dedicated to *sawasira/pitusira* also made use of the ritual name of the potato: *santo roma*.[25] In the nearby Department of Cotabambas, *santo roma* is the ritual name for maize (Dalle 1971: 65), whereas *sawasiray* is a ritual name for potatoes (Valderrama and Escalante 1976: 183). Clearly, inversions and other changes of referent are quite conceivable for these terms, which stand for relations of generative opposition within the plant world at least as much as they do for particular crops in themselves. Indeed, the presence of maize and beans on the *mesa* (also potatoes in the rites of pastoralists) is at best only partly on their own behalf.

My adoptive 'mother' once asked me of the maize and bean stalks at the head of the ritual table: 'Son, do you know why we put these here? It is because we have many calves.' When I then asked: 'Is it because the plants are growing too?' she agreed heartily. Thus, the *sawasira/pitusira* model of generative complementarity in agriculture metaphorically promotes the growth of young animals (cf. Tomoeda 1985: 294–5). Those who treat the *mesa* as a literal representation of Andean ecology (e.g., Flores 1977: 227–8; Custred 1979: 389–90) clearly misunderstand the symbolism of these rituals.[26] Although I do not deny the agricultural significance of these rites, the most important point is that it remains oblique, and is mediated by a primary concern for animal fertility. This is further demonstrated by the use of maize to prevent and initiate sorcery in these rites,[27] and as a component of burnt offerings. Ironically, the pastoralists of the Antabamba region, who do not grow maize, regularly use not only the white and yellow maize that figures in the offerings of valley people, but black and red maize as well. Because they own many more animals than the agriculturalists, they must make better offerings. Nothing could better demonstrate that serving maize in these rites is not a simple reflex of cultivating it for a living, but is a response to the imagined tastes and needs of *pachamamas* and mountain spirits. It is the ownership of animals that causes a proliferation of agricultural products in these rites. By the same token, agricultural concerns are mediated through the animals, a dynamic that ultimately leads to sacrifice.

The next round in the particular *t'inka* followed here was dedicated to a miniature yoke of bulls (*yunta*) carved in wood. Since this was a rite held for cattle (*waka t'inka*) sponsored by an elderly couple, many wishes and invocations made for them called for the birth of a pair of bull calves that would be strong, tame, and compatible as a team, to cut down on the amount of *ayni* work that the old man was obliged to do. Again, owners of particularly good teams of bulls figured heavily in the invocations.

In other *t'inkas* that I attended, similar rounds of libation were dedicated to stone amulets known as *kantas* (probably from the Spanish '*encanto*': 'spell' or 'enchanted object') or *illas*. These are invariably objects found by the 'priest,' sometimes in a supernatural encounter. These *kantas* are said to resemble a particular category of livestock or crop, and are known by a variety of names throughout the Andes.[28] Sometimes they may also be large rocks that are part of the landscape, and come to life as animals only on the night of a full moon (cf. Roel Pineda 1965: 27; Núñez del Prado 1970: 91) to fecundate the herds of the particular territory on which they are located, or to indicate a change in the weather by a 180 degree change in orientation. They are often said to be the animals of the mountain spirits (see Núñez del Prado 1970: 91; Isbell 1978: 151), which transform into amulets when they are approached in the fog (cf. Flores 1977: 220–1). A man told me of how, as a youth, he was travelling through the high *puna* around Mt Supayco on a foggy day around Carnival. He lost his way in the mist at one point and came upon a lake in which three white alpaca calves were swimming. Being lost, young, and a valley-dweller unversed in these matters, he continued to the grazing territory he was meaning to visit and told people there what he had seen. Aghast, they explained that the animals were *illas*, and that he should have tried to lasso them out of the water, for he could have become a highly successful herder of alpacas. In other cases, mountain spirits may give these amulets directly to people, as happened to the grandfather of a notable school-teacher who was attending a seance with the Apu Phakusuri. To assuage this notable's scepticism, Phakusuri gave him three *kantas*, which rapidly increased his cattle to 100 head. Then the father of my schoolteacher informant somehow lost the *kantas*, and ever since, the herd has been in decline due to rustling, disease, and poor reproduction, to the point where it now numbers fifty head. The schoolteacher told me that he has seen enough now to believe that the herd will never prosper until the *kantas* are recovered, and that he was seriously considering the offer of a local diviner to find them for the price of a yearling calf. This story illustrates well the universal function of these amulets in conserving and ensuring the reproduction of herds.[29]

Kantas may appear singly, and not in threes, as they do in these stories, but their resemblance of *kallpa* figurines in size and shape makes these amulets especially likely to occur in trinities. So pronounced is this resemblance that in certain areas, terms such as *kanta* and *illa* refer to the perishable figurines (see Arguedas 1956: 244; Tomoeda 1985: 285), not just amulets. This conflation is entirely understandable given their common involvement in animal reproduction. Several times people told me that a *kanta* 'is just the same as the *ánimo*' of whatever it represents (cf. Gow and Gow 1975: 147, 150). Similarly, the notion of *kallpa* after which the perishable figurines are named denotes 'vital force,' a notion entirely akin to that of *ánimo*. However, the sense of *ánimo* involved here does not exclude ideas of embodiment normally associated with the *alma* (see Arguedas 1968: 340; Flores 1977: 224), rather, it includes them as a part of the more general concern with sexuality and fecundity. Thus, even where some importance is placed on a division of amulets into two categories that might be interpreted along the lines of *alma* and *ánimo* (see Gow and Gow 1975: 150; Flores 1977: 217–28; Oblitas Poblete 1978: 223–4), they never become completely differentiated or independent of each other. All of these amulets are supposed to make the invocation of livestock spirits from other grazing territories more effective. One account even suggests that these amulets force the local mountain spirits to repeat the invocations made at the *mesa*, which would virtually ensure the proposed transfers of vitality (Gow and Gow 1975: 148–50). Perhaps the most significant difference between *kallpa* figurines and these amulets is the much greater ability of the latter to fix animal abundance to a particular territory.

The next round in the sequence of libations we are following was dedicated to *potosí*, the antique coin and assemblage of more recent coins and bills that were scraped into the husk bundles offered to the *pachamamas*. Now, the 'priest' moves the bundle of money to the centre of the table, as the 'son-in-law' announces: 'We will libate *potosí*.' An invocation that I heard during this round was: 'I will invoke golden *mesa*, silver *mesa*, for your money, from the Agrarian Bank, also from the Gibson Bank,'[30] punctuated by the standard interjections of the 'son-in-law.' In two *t'inkas* I attended, all of the non-kin present contributed coins to the *potosí* bundle of the sponsoring household during this round of invocations (see also Tomoeda 1985: 291).

In a comparable rite among pastoralists in the Province of Cailloma, Arequipa, Wallis (1980: 251) describes burnt offerings for a coin known as *potosí*, which he interprets not just as cash, but also the commodities that can be bought with it. Oblitas Poblete (1978: 228–9, 241) describes Callawaya amulets known as *potosí*, *Cerro de Potosí* (Mt Potosí: site of a famous colonial silver mine), and *qena qellona*, all of which are meant to attract and accumulate money (among other things), especially from banks in the latter two cases. It seems that the coin known as *potosí* in Huaquirca has the same function as these Callawaya amulets, and might justifiably be seen as an amulet itself. In many parts of the Andes, antique coins share the name *illa* with the animal amulets that we encountered in the last round of invocations (see Lira 1944: 273; Oblitas Poblete 1978: 178, 224). Therefore, *potosí*, the antique coin, exercises the same attracting and binding influence on money as *kantas* do on animals, and when both share a common generic name like *illa*, we may begin to suspect that the domains of money and animals may not be entirely discrete in Andean culture. The first indication of this connection is that Andean shopkeepers also use the offerings and amulets of agrarian rites (see Stein 1961: 315; Oblitas Poblete 1978: 236–40; Nash 1979: 136), but the most telling point is that the latter are partly constructed on a monetary root metaphor. Thus, interred offerings are widely known as 'payments' (*pagos*),[31] and the stone-lined recesses in which they are deposited may be known as 'safes' (*cajas*), which are further covered with stones known as 'lock and keys' (Quispe 1969: 34–7, 1984: 613; Isbell 1978: 158). Since these offerings promote animal fertility, we may surmise that fecundity is not merely 'like' monetary abundance, but actually requires 'payments,' a point that will emerge with increasing force below. So while it is entirely plausible to interpret coin scrapings in burnt offerings as a way of providing the deities with cash (e.g., Bastien 1978: 145), this should not rule out the possibility that money, like maize before it, is present at least as much for the benefit of the animals as it is on its own behalf. Therefore, we must ask how it might act as a model for animal abundance.

Oblitas Poblete (1978: 244) accounts for the magical value of the antique coin as follows: 'With the passage of time, and from having passed from hand to hand, it has come to attain an extraordinary magical virtue for attracting money, for maintaining capital intact, for attracting jewels, precious metals, etc.' This emphasis on previous circulation is surely correct, but equally important is the fact that the coin has been withdrawn from circulation and is now an amulet; indeed, that it is incapable of further circulation because of its antiquity.[32] A comparable circulation of animals is posited by the invocations. Their vital force can be called from various grazing territories to the one where the *t'inka* is unfolding, where it is fixed by amulets. The idea that these amulets represent the ancestors of the animals (Favre 1967: 125; Yaranga 1979: 705) runs entirely parallel to the antiquity of the coin, and creates a similar air of precedent and tradition. Thus, when people contribute money to the *potosí* bundle of the sponsors, they show its ability to attract and fix circulating wealth and vitality.[33]

The next item to be moved to the centre of the *mesa* and receive a round of libations was a cloth bundle containing the stones from which powder was abraded into the husk offerings made earlier for the *pachamamas*. These stones also have the generic name of *mesa*, and sometimes they are kept in the same bundle as *potosí*, the antique coin, and form a single assemblage of objects. Even when they are kept separate, *mesa* stones and antique coins are not absolutely separable at a conceptual level, as the invocation 'golden *mesa*, silver *mesa*' in the round dedicated to *potosí* indicates. Some of these stones are highly metallic, and people say that ritualists on isolated estates in the *puna* find golden nuggets that are the 'bullets' of Santiago the Lightning Bolt (a figure not entirely distinct from the mountain spirits). The names of specific *mesa* stones in Huaquirca reflect the notion that they should be sources of gold and silver, even when their appearance belies it.[34] Most of the ritualists with whom I discussed the matter felt that each *mesa* stone represents a different sort of animal within the species for which the rite is performed. Some suggested that each *mesa* stone might impart particular qualities, such as strength, robustness, endurance, courage, and so on, but were reluctant to enumerate these direct magical correlations, which leads me to suspect that this notion is secondary to a more basic pattern of diversity and complementarity grounded in the constant reference to gold and silver.

The notion that these *mesa* stones enter into the makeup of the animals is particularly well displayed in rites for horses (*caballo t'inka*) in the Antabamba Valley. When the round of libations dedicated to the *mesa* stones is complete, horses are brought into the ceremonial corral three by three to have their manes and tails sheared. The 'son-in-law' takes some coals from the fire for burnt offerings and puts them on a slab of shale for transport. Then he sprinkles incense on the coals, and walks from horse to horse, wafting smoke into the nostrils of each. Meanwhile, the 'priest' takes a combination of *mesa* stones, or the bundle containing the antique coin, and rubs each animal on the chest with it and then above each hoof. Some ritualists breathe harshly on the stones or coin bundle each time before rubbing with it, a gesture that seems to unite the apparently unrelated meanings of *samay* as 'exhaled air' and 'transferred vitality.' Only on completion of these acts are the horses sheared. A similar massage of the animals with 'crude gold' and 'crude silver' has been reported elsewhere as part of a sequence of acts designed to stimulate their fertility (Isbell 1978: 161). Here, precious metals appear to be an inseparable and indispensable component of the body's vitality.

Also included with the *mesa* stones in the same bundle may be scallop (*mullu*) and conch (*ch'uru*) shells, deer's hooves, and *wayruro* beans, all but the latter of which are scraped into the husk offerings. One ritualist gave hooves the obvious magical function of imparting sure-footedness to the animals, and although I never heard anything to confirm the pre-Columbian function of shells as an offering to stimulate rainfall (see Murra 1975: 257–8), this possibility would support an agrarian interpretation of the *t'inkas* as 'libations' that restore the fluids spent during the rainy season. One 'priest' told me that *mesa* stones are 'especially for the mountains.' This subordinates the narrow magical goal of animal reproduction, upon which these stones also bear, to a more general restitution to the mountain spirits of what they have come to lack during the growing season. Here, the alimentary and the financial metaphors that structure *t'inka* offerings share the common theme of replenishment. Thus, not all *mesas* represent a component of the ideal animal or herd, and even those that can are part of the 'servings' and 'payments' that people offer to the *apus* ('lords,' i.e., mountain spirits). In this sacrificial nexus, consumption, tribute, and fertility become highly interdependent, and the metallic and the organic are wholly intertwined.

At the end of this round of libations, the 'priest' emptied the coca leaves from the now-full dishes on either side of the ritual table (see Figure 19b) into two separate maize husk bundles. These are known collectively as the *samakuyoq plato* (plate of the invokers) and were each burned. Although I never pressed for any commentary on this offering, its name suggests that it might be dedicated to those present at the rite, not to the various entities that have been successfully invoked. Unlike the other burnt offerings, the *samakuyoq plato* is not the object of a round of libations and invocations, but is burned as soon as it is assembled.

Away from the *mesa*, the woman of the sponsoring household began to serve corn beer to all of those assembled as the 'priest' set about constructing a new set of husk offerings with essentially the same ingredients as the earlier 'serving' for all of the *pachamamas*. Since the next round of libations was to be dedicated to an offering to the Apu Phakusuri, the 'priest' made sure that the husk bundles' contents were 'according to the preference and taste' of that mountain. Still, the standard three coca leaves, flour and kernels of white and yellow maize, incense, white and red carnations, llama chest fat, scrapings from the *mesa* stones, and *potosí* were all included. Again, the number of bundles offered is variable, but is always a multiple of three. According to the size of his herds, each ritualist offers a traditional number of bundles to a given mountain spirit. Those agriculturalists who own only a few animals may offer just three bundles, those with many may offer up to twelve. Pastoralists will offer dozens of bundles to many different mountain spirits or groups of mountain spirits. Since their flocks are large, their connection with the mountains is more intimate, and their 'payments' are necessarily higher as a result. Before a *t'inka,* any ritualist who wants to know if the traditional content and quantity of his offerings are still adequate may consult the mountains through a simple yes/no coca leaf divination, which answers his specific questions. One man whose *t'inkas* I regularly attended told me that the Apus Phakusuri and Utupara generally demand twelve husk bundles of him, and occasionally request small changes in their contents, whereas other mountains only want six bundles from him.

An offering made to the mountain spirits is sometimes called an *alcanzo plato* ('serving of the handing over'). The verb *alcanzar* describes all burnt offerings, and not just those dedicated to the mountain spirits, and it emphasizes the tributary nature of the offering.[35] The only significant difference between the *alcanzo plato* and the *pachamamaq plato* described earlier is that the *alcanzo plato* generally includes a special horizontal row of three bundles, always placed at the top of the *mesa,* called the *t'ika plato,* or 'flower serving' (see Figure 20). This row of husks does indeed contain as many different wildflowers as are available at the time, and bits of any fresh fruits, maize, or beans. The husks may include coca leaves, various sorts of dried maize, and incense, but they specifically exclude such non-vegetative components of normal offerings as llama chest fat and scrapings from the *mesa* stones. It is tempting to view the 'flower serving' as a specifically agricultural offering, given the role that white and yellow flowers play in marking water given off by the dead for agricultural purposes in this world (see Chapter 4), and the fact that the *t'ika plato* often has its own round of libations, separate from that of the *alcanzo plato.* However, one of my best informants depicted it in the tributary idiom of the *alcanzo:*

> The flower plate is given to the most important mountains. It's like serving a big meal, something extra, to the authorities, while the lower bundles are for the plebeians, that is, for the mountain spirits of less value. 'Town Council' is the name of the highest ranking mountain, and it [the *t'ika plato*] is like serving a glass of champagne to the prefect.

Here, Phakusuri, as the mountain spirit to whom the round was being directed, would act as 'Town Council' for the spirits of lesser peaks and localities under his sway. This dual division of mountain spirits into those of greater and lesser rank is extremely common throughout the Andes,[36] as is the tendency to model their interrelations on political and administrative structures. Thus, the sphere of influence of the tallest peaks is greater than that of those peaks that are shorter, which leads to a hierarchical incorporation of the latter by the former, out of which regional 'councils,' 'directorships,' and 'capitals' emerge (see Favre 1967: 140; Earls 1969: 68–70; Isbell 1978: 59, 151). Indeed, the title *apu* (best translated as 'lord'), by which these spirits are known, was once borne by the rulers and administrators in the early colonial period.

In the Antabamba Valley, as in most parts of the Andes, the mountain spirits are still thought of as rulers and owners of the territories they overlook (cf. Earls 1969: 67). When they appear in human form, it is generally as a blonde, blue-eyed man dressed as a *hacendado* or notable of the old school.[37] So literally do the *apus* emulate these secular authorities that many accounts refer to them simply as *gringos* or *mistis* (e.g., Gow and Condori 1976: 52; Fuenzalida 1980: 161). Perhaps their most typical activity in human form is the payment of tribute in gold and silver up the administrative chain of command, using vicuñas and other wild creatures as beasts of burden (see Morote Best 1956b: 293; Casaverde 1970: 142–3; Gow and Condori 1976: 45). In one account, these tribute networks are said to culminate in the president's office in Lima, and to provide the Peruvian state with its revenue (Earls 1969: 69–70). As Earls (1969: 70) notes, special machines inside the mountains convert the offerings of these rites into the gold and silver collected in these tributary hierarchies. Much the same idea is present in the categorical insistence on *mesa* stones as sources of gold and silver. Here, the full tributary significance of the *alcanzo* as a 'handing over' or 'rendering up' becomes clear, and reveals the political dimension of the *t'inkas* in something of its true magnitude.

At no point, however, does the integration of the mountain spirits into power hierarchies remove them from limited divisions of labour, in which each takes charge of a certain sort of livestock or crop. On the contrary, the power of a mountain is typically expressed through its position in a hierarchy of agrarian responsibilities. For example, the two most important *apus* in the Antabamba region are Supayco, source and 'owner' of all alpacas, and Suparaura, source and 'owner' of all cattle (see Figure 21). Stories portray Suparaura as Supayco's son-in-law, who continually tries to rustle his father-in-law's alpacas, animals

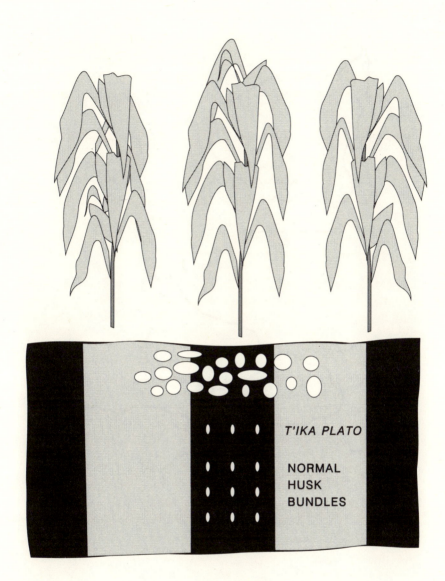

Figure 20   *Alcanzo plato*

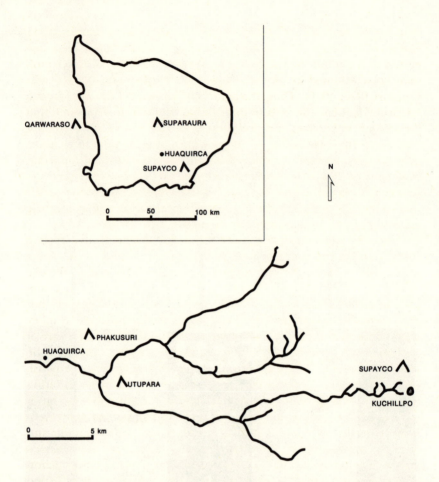

Figure 21 Local and regional mountain spirits

that are emblematic of Supayco's superiority. Just as mountains in charge of camelids outrank those in charge of cattle, it has been suggested that mountains assigned to particular crops are of lower rank than those assigned to animals (Núñez del Prado 1970: 82; Gow and Condori 1976: 40–1). Thus, the agrarian functions of the *apus* form a hierarchy that corresponds to their political power. If we assume that the idiosyncratic tastes and preferences attributed to each mountain (see Favre 1967: 129) indicate its position in the division of agrarian labour within a regional group, then offerings become an important indication of the particular niche each mountain occupies. Several valley ritualists explained to me that even the political rank of the *apus* is determined by the offerings that people give, and is not an intrinsic feature of the mountain itself, like its height.

Since offerings modify the character of the mountains that receive them, ritualists can negotiate with their imaginary rulers, whose power would otherwise be absolute. Here, the hierarchical and qualitative aspects of the offering work together in an important way. For example, the *t'ika plato* confers an honour upon a local mountain spirit, but also pushes it towards a very specific agricultural function. In other parts of the Andes, particular mountains are nominated to take care of a given year's agricultural production (Martínez 1983: 92), and the *t'ika plato* would be a very apt means of implementing such a responsibility. Many valley ritualists rank *kallpa* figurines as a higher offering than the *t'ika plato*. Agreement on this point was not universal, but it was confirmed by the way more distant and important *apus* were invoked in the round for *kallpa* figurines. Again, the mountains and offerings associated with livestock reproduction outrank those associated with agriculture. Those mountains in charge of the reproduction of wool-bearing animals require an even higher offering: *sullu* (dried fetus, preferably of vicuña, but often of llama or alpaca). Agriculturalists in Huaquirca feel that they have neither the ritual knowledge nor the need to make fetus offerings, but for the pastoralists, such offerings figure in every *t'inka* as a matter of course.[38] Here, the prestige of wool-bearing animals in the hierarchical division of labour among *apus* is reflected in the greater potency of this offering, although the fetus also specifies what the ritualist wants: new animals. This cutoff point in the continuity of offerings between agriculturalists and pastoralists in the Antabamba region corresponds to a change from the burnt offering to interment or immersion in a body of water, the two methods by which pastoralists offer fetuses.

The next round in the sequence that we are following was dedicated to Pukarumiyoq, the particular grazing territory on which this rite occurred. The offering of husk bundles libated in the name of the Apu Phakusuri during the previous round remained at the centre of the ritual table. Now it received libations in the name of Pukarumiyoq, a subordinate *apu* in the 'Town Council' headed by Phakusuri. An invocation I remember from this round was '*qorikiraw, qolqekiraw*' ('cradle of gold, cradle of silver'). This depicted the corral where the rite took place as such a cradle, and a source point for the new animal life solicited in the *t'inka*. This notion is borne out by the special ceremonial corrals that have been mentioned in the literature (Favre 1967: 124; Flores 1977: 233; Quispe 1984: 611), which invariably include repositories covered and lined with stone for interred offerings. These repositories are often thought to be where new animals are born into the grazing territory (Martínez 1983: 94). In the *puna* of Huaquirca, these ceremonial corrals often occur around springs, another place where animals are thought to enter into this world (see Gow and Gow 1975: 142; Flores 1977: 219; Bastien 1978: chap. 10). The belief that young animals emerge from subterranean, aquatic sources would explain why people offer the mountains dried fetuses by interment and submersion. Although the agriculturalists of the Antabamba region may not possess ceremonial corrals or make such powerful offerings, the cradle imagery of their invocations suggests that they expect their modest place spirits or *pachamamas*, such as Pukarumiyoq, to provide animals on a similar basis, if less abundantly. Once this round of libations was finished, the husk bundles were duly burned on the special fire in the corral.

The next round of libations was dedicated to the *qocha* (lake), namely the vessel from which corn beer is served during the rite. This vessel is not the collectively drunk cup of corn beer, also called *qocha*, that appeared in the maize sowing (see Chapter 4). Again, however, there is a clear connection between alcoholic libations and reservoirs of water. In several rites I attended, seashells were moved to the centre of the *mesa* and libated during this round, either with the vessel of corn beer or instead of it. This substitution further suggests the magical connection between shells and water mentioned earlier. Nonetheless, invocations frequently included the ritual name for corn beer, *ashwa*, and not esoteric terms related to water such as *aguay uno*[39] (Arguedas 1956: 238–40) or *elemento* (Gow and Condori 1976: 60–1). Two different ritualists whose *t'inkas* I attended had stone amulets named *queso* (cheese), which they moved to the centre of the *mesa* during rounds dedicated to the *qocha*. This amulet is supposed to promote milk production in cows. Thus, the image of the lake covers the propagation of milk, not just corn beer and water. Again, items and images that have no intrinsic connection to the animals may become models of abundance for them.

It is a particularly close connection with the mountain spirits that gives the image of the lake this polyvalent connotation of abundance. Stories that I heard in the Antabamba region mentioned that the local mountains have lakes at their inner core, often equated with the *apus'* testicles. These stories also treat above-ground lakes and reservoirs as the abodes of *apus*.[40] The regenerative powers of this water are unmistakable. For example, there is said to be a lake high on the flanks of Utupara, the most important local *apu* for the towns of Huaquirca, Antabamba, and Matara. Those who live at the foot of the mountain say that this lake is the heart of Utupara, and that its water is very sweet and salutary to drink. Some add that the head engineer of the Utupara mines, when he looks into this lake with his binoculars, can see a golden puma and a silver vicuña in its depths. From this lake, the famous golden bull (*qori toro*) of Utupara is supposed to have emerged, before ramming a hole in the side of Phakusuri and re-emerging from Pumaqocha (the 'wild lake' of Chapter 4), and going on to Malmanya and Cusco. In short, this lake periodically expels wild metallic life-forms. Judging by the number of Sonqoqochas (Heart Lakes) that one sees on any map of this part of the Andes, this concept must be reasonably common.

These fertile lakes contrast notably with the Map'a Mayo in that they nurture animal and human life. Metallic animal embodiments precipitate from them, not just the wild disembodied energies released from the land of the dead. By accumulating this water in lakes, the mountains seem to domesticate the volatile energy it brought from the land of the dead. Affirmations that such water represents the blood or sperm of the *apus*[41] suggest that the mountains do indeed convert this pure energy into a living substance. Here, the image of the lake follows that of the *kallpa* or vital force figurines, where energy is no longer opposed to embodiment, as during the growing season, but encompasses it. Because of this transformation, the local and regional *apus* provide a crucial mediation between the living and the dead, and help drive the cycle that connects them. By creating new life-forms out of disembodied energy, they reveal a profoundly female dimension to their male-dominated androgynous identity.

The final round of libations in all of the *t'inkas* of the Antabamba Valley, including the one we have been following here, is called 'farewell' (*kacharpari*). In rites for cattle and horses performed by agriculturalists, the 'priest' prepares a potion to libate the animals at the end of this round. First, he pours corn beer into a double-necked pitcher or two separate wooden cups, then he adds scrapings of the *mesa* stones, *potosí*, shells, and deer's hooves, bits of fresh crab-apple, peach, beans, and maize, and any available wildflowers, especially red and white carnations. Although people still come to the table in pairs to drink during this round, they no longer invoke deities or objects of power, but simply propose toasts. When all have finished, a pair of women, including the woman of the sponsoring household, take maize stalks from the head of the *mesa* and the vessels of the specially prepared potion, and proceed to splash the animals with it, striking them with the stalks in the process, so that they will leave the corral. Sometimes the pair of women will disperse the people at the *mesa* in the same way.

The 'farewell' round of the rites performed by pastoralists in the *puna* of Huaquirca is different. Instead of preparing a potion and splashing it on the animals, this round features the interment (in a special stone-lined niche of the 'altar' in the corral where the *t'inka* takes place) of a double-necked pitcher of water previously filled from Lake Kuchillpo at the foot of Mt Supayco, along with pieces ceremonially cut from the young animals' ears, coca leaves, and llama chest fat. Every year, the water in the double-necked pitcher is renewed at Kuchillpo, and the remains of the previous year's offerings are removed from the niche. This interment of water clearly enacts the pattern of a subterranean domestication of the wild energy of water into fertility that has just emerged from the discussion of the concept of *qocha*. Alternatively, ear-cuttings may be deposited into a spring associated with the corral, instead of the niche in the 'altar.' Both modes of offering ear-cuttings are called *rinripaqana*, and comparable practices occur elsewhere (Quispe 1969: 35, 1984: 613).

More than one *t'inka* that I attended had to be stopped before completion due to the advanced drunkenness of the 'priest' and participants. In these cases, the rite would simply be finished on the following day when hangovers wore off. Indeed, many rites devolved into moments of drunken uncertainty shared by 'priest' and 'son-in-law' over whether they had forgotten to give a round of libations to an important entity. An offering to such forgotten forces, the *huchuy alcansucho*, is actually institutionalized in some areas (Roel Pineda 1965: 31). Problems of omission aside, however, the developmental sequence of a *t'inka* cannot fail to have at least some coherence because of the interplay, overlap, and redundancy of the various entities that receive rounds of libation. Thus, thematic developments from one round to the next can be found in the *t'inkas* of all but the most incompetent of Huaquirca's ritualists. Skilful practitioners combine thoroughness with a sequence that dramatically underlines the particular result they wish to achieve from the rite. Yet in the end, I must join Stein (1961: 248) in insisting that in these rites, 'feelings of holiness are uniquely blended with feelings of abandon.' Whatever coherence these rites possess is not elaborated in an atmosphere of contemplation, let alone one of fervour, respect, and fear, as Casaverde (1970: 146) would have it.

As the *t'inka* is ending, pairs of men may begin to play flutes, sometimes accompanied by another man with a drum (*tinya*), and the women may sing. The *t'inkas* of Carnival have their own special song, the refrain for which is '*hermano paisano*' ('brother countryman'). Those of Santiago also have special songs, although it is said that they are falling into disuse. Another tune, the *waka t'inka*, may be played at any time of the year when there are rites for cattle. It is accompanied by a circle dance in which people hold hands and take short rapid steps in a single direction. Before guests leave a *t'inka* in the late afternoon, there may be a prolonged period of music, dancing, and drinking to send them on their way. These celebrations after the rite proper can become so lively, especially among the pastoralists above Huaquirca, that people decide not to disperse, but to go 'visiting' neighbours who did not attend the rite. They arrive at the door, singing and dancing, and demand to be served any cane alcohol that might be on the premises. In the *t'inkas* of Santiago, which the agriculturalists perform on the terraced maize lands where their cattle and horses are grazing at that time of the year, everyone leaves at once in a group that makes its way towards town, dancing and singing. As in the *wayliya* that will take place during the maize sowing in September and October, there is a pause on the outskirts of town to collect stragglers, thereby making as unified and impressive an entrance as possible.

An additional *t'inka*, beyond those routinely performed during Carnival, San Marcos, and Santiago, takes place whenever an animal dies a

violent death due to predators or being struck by lightning. Such kill-
ings are taken to be the work of the *apus*, or agencies closely associated
with them such as *michiq* ('herder': a cross between a puma and a condor that preys on calves) or *Santiago el Rayo* (Santiago the Lightning
Bolt), who kills animals from the sky with his golden bullets. Animals
that are killed by lightning are buried 'just like people,' and I was told
that it would be unthinkable to eat them because of the pervasive taste
and smell of iron that permeates their carcasses,[42] although this taboo
does not hold elsewhere (see Roel Pineda 1965: 29). When a calf
belonging to my adoptive 'father' was killed by lightning several years
ago, he went to an oracular medium (*pongo*) to arrange a seance in
which various local *apus* were summoned and asked who was responsible. Finally, Phukawasi, the spirit of my father's grazing territory,
owned up, and said that he had 'sold' the animal because the offerings
he was receiving were inadequate. From that time on, my father has
made offerings with greater care and elaboration, and he claims that
his cattle have increased notably. It seems in retrospect that the *apu*
was drawing him into a closer relation by killing his calf, thereby initiating a sacrificial escalation of higher 'payments' for greater prosperity. Indeed, the interment of an animal killed by lightning can be seen
as a kind of 'payment,' and the metallic smell of the carcass as evidence that precious metals were extracted from it during the 'sale.'
Elsewhere in the Andes, lightning strikes establish permanent sites for
ritual offerings (see Bastien 1978: 69; Harris 1980: 80; Platt 1986: 254).
They are also thought to pursue pregnant women and cause twins
(Yaranga 1979: 702; Bourque and Warren 1981: 112). This emergent
link between the violent discharge of electrical energy and organic fertility is confirmed in the derivation of the name *illa* for reproductive
amulets from the archaic Quechua name for lightning, *illapa*. Finally,
the pastoralists above Huaquirca consider San Andrés (30 November)
to be a particularly dangerous day for lightning strikes, perhaps
because they recently abandoned it as the date for a third round of *t'inkas* during the year.

Nonetheless, the pastoralists of Huaquirca still maintain a very
intense interaction with the *apus*, and no description of the *t'inkas* in
this area would be complete without going another level beyond the
fetus offering, which already sets them apart from agriculturalists, and
into sacrifice proper. On the day before *Comadres* Thursday during Carnival, pastoralists from throughout the headwaters of the Antabamba
and Vilcabamba Rivers converge on Lake Kuchillpo in the high *puna*

of Huaquirca. Two men come from each *estancia* on horseback, bringing with them their *mesa* and a young alpaca from their herds. Hundreds of stone 'altars' are scattered on the ridge above the western
shore of the lake, facing Mt Supayco and the rising sun, and each is
associated with a particular *estancia*. The pair of men set about making
dozens and dozens of husk offerings of the sort described earlier.
Those who brought alpacas tie their legs and slit their throats, catch-
ing all of the blood in a basin. They then cut through the animal's ribs
and extract its throbbing heart (see Nachtigal 1975: 136 and Miller
1977: 197–201 for detailed descriptions of this method of sacrifice).
One of the men, elegantly dressed and mounted on a horse, takes the
heart and gallops off to deposit it in the lake, ideally while it is still
beating. I was told that some ritualists tie a stone to the heart to ensure
that it sinks immediately. Most of the blood collected from the sacrifice is poured into a niche in the stone 'altar' that is specially designed
for such 'payments' (cf. Nachtigal 1975: 136), although some of it may
be mixed with cane alcohol and drunk by the ritualists (cf. Quispe
1969: 72). The flesh of the animal is roasted, and every last scrap must
be eaten before returning home. Furthermore, all of the bones, down
to the most insignificant, must be saved and burned. 'Fines' are meted
out to those who lose them. In the afternoon, people begin the return
journey to their grazing lands, a trip that may take many hours. On
arrival, they are supposed to spend the entire night making and burning more husk offerings, and to continue into the next day, when they
round up their animals and perform a *t'inka* like the one already
described. I should emphasize that I did not see these sacrifices performed, but am relying on the accounts of those who have, including
some pastoralists who live near Kuchillpo.

The heart offering adds little that is new at a thematic level, but displays quite dramatically the sacrificial nature of the entire *t'inka* complex of which it is a part. We have already seen that the niches and
springs into which fetuses are deposited are supposed to be the
sources from which new animals emerge, and this belief also applies
here, because of the association of Kuchillpo with the Apu Supayco,
'owner' of alpacas (see also Gow and Gow 1975: 149). The offering of
the palpitating organ further confirms the notion that the lake is the
heart of the mountain as well. Nor is it entirely surprising that the
range of offerings considered here should culminate in abortion and
sacrifice, becoming more efficacious as the degree of violence associated with them increases. The *t'inkas* clearly treat animals as a privi-

leged mediator between people and *apus*. This is true even among agriculturalists, whose substantive debt to the mountains derives mostly from the growth of the crops, but is settled in rites that are ostensibly for their relatively few animals. One explanation of this use of animals is that through the identification of the maize with Christ, the harvest is turned into a kind of 'crucifixion,' much as for the Kabyle it is a murder, which is simply extended and enacted more explicitly in the sacrifice of animals (see Bourdieu 1977: 133–5; cf. Frazer 1890). Yet it is also as if people are trying to interpose animals between themselves and the revenge of the crops, in the remarkably unmediated cycle of life and death described in Chapters 4 and 5. This principle of sacrificial substitutability also holds when people are on the threshold of a more intensive relationship with the *apu*, as indicated by an animal struck by lightning instead of a direct attack on the ritualist. When the *apus* and/or *pachamamas* are 'hungry' due to inadequate offerings, they may still seize human organs, and so cause the serious condition of *hallp'asqa* ('earthed'), but this can be cured by the 'payment' of a fetus. Thus, animals represent a kind of buffer zone in a system where life appears as a limited good, whose increase in one place demands a loss in another (Bloch and Parry 1982: 7–9). Undoubtedly, this is why the disappearance of animals is a sign of the end of the world in Andean thought (see Flores 1977: 234). As a result of these diverse impulses towards sacrifice, the consummate image that the *t'inkas* provide for the emergence of new life from old is the palpitating heart wrenched from the maternal body, a supernatural Caesarean birth won from a bloody death.

Particularly successful herders are thought to owe their prosperity to an even more effective offering, that of a daughter as a concubine to the local mountain spirit (Favre 1967: 133–4; Fuenzalida 1980: 162). Sometimes this may take the form of an exchange of *illas* (which increase the family's herds) for sex (Morissette and Racine 1973: 174), or a semi-conjugal relation between *apu* and woman, a relation that no man dares violate (see Isbell and Roncalla Fernandez 1978: 440). Although the sexual voracity of the *apus* is hardly confined to women (see Earls 1970: 91; Martínez 1983: 95–6), its stereotypical manifestation in Huaquirca was during the *qhashwa* dances of bygone days, where they would take the form of tall, good-looking *mistis*, to seduce and impregnate a woman. Illegitimate children are still jokingly explained as the result of such encounters (cf. Earls 1970: 87–8). In some areas, this notion is so systematically developed that women are

said to draw the spirits of particular grazing territories into human kinship systems (the term *apu* can mean father's father's father's father in
Quechua), and even to give birth to new mountain spirits, thus mediating their descent hierarchies (cf. Favre 1967: 123; Earls 1969: 68,
1970: 91). Therefore, it would appear that just as the *apus* are interested in aborted fetuses and extracted organs as potential life-forms,
so they are also interested in the reproductive and embodying capacities of women. Thus, these unions of women and mountain spirits
extend the sacrificial dynamic by which the desired influx of animal
fertility can be achieved only by a calculated loss, which is now portrayed as that of a daughter in marriage.

Even in the less efficacious offerings of agriculturalists, the imagery
of affinity is already subsumed by the logic of sacrifice. Outsiders
invoke the spirits of other grazing territories in an attempt to fix them
to the locality, but the one who orchestrates this process is called the
'son-in-law.' Just as the sponsors must make offerings to the spirits
invoked, so they must also give up a daughter, however figuratively, to
ensure the ritual services of non-kin. Elsewhere, Harris (1982: 65)
reports a similar conceptual merging of affines and mountain spirits.
Since both offerings and imaginary daughters are posed as counter-
balancing payments for animal fertility, they acquire a kind of structural equivalence that is lived out when herders begin to keep a
daughter in virginal seclusion for the local *apu*. Although only a few
people go this far, the imagery through which the *t'inkas* are conducted makes such practices permanently conceivable. Of course, one
reason why more herder's daughters are not converted into living
offerings to the *apus* is the profound ambivalence towards sharing that
characterizes these rites. The accumulative ends that serve as a rationale for bringing in 'affines' are undercut by the thought of giving
wives to them, so it is not surprising that there should also be a movement towards agnatic exclusivity and/or incest in the performance of
these rites.[43] Yet the lure of a more intensive and prosperous relation
with the *apu* exerts a pressure to supersede these limits through sacrifice.

The point at which sacrificial substitutability begins to break down is
when the landscape is modified through the construction of terraces,
tunnels, roads, bridges, railways, churches, and above all, mines. Many
authors report that human sacrifices take place when such works are
initiated because they 'bother' the mountain spirits.[44] Whether or not
such sacrifices are actually made, any 'accidental' deaths on the job

can be attributed to the anger or the hunger of the *apus*. It is probably because these works damage the generative surfaces of the mountains, and constitute a direct violation of them, that they must be stabilized through a restitutive organic 'payment.' Once again, we encounter the principle of an indissoluble link between the organic and the inorganic that was established in the *t'inkas*, now in the more precise form of a metaphorical equivalence of the mountain and the human body (cf. Bastien 1978: chap. 3), whereby the violation of one requires the violation of the other.

To stress only the symbolic equivalence and shared substance of mountains and human bodies, however, is to miss the undeniable element of hierarchy that exists between *apus* and people. In these rituals, the life of the mountains takes precedence over that of individual animals and people. Sacrifice is not an egalitarian relationship, but it does involve notions of connectedness, mutuality, and responsibility within a hierarchical whole. These characteristics make sacrifice an appropriate model of legitimate political power. Furthermore, there is little doubt that when Andean commoners use tributary imagery to describe how the *apus* assimilate their sacrificial victims, and hold that the mountains form elaborate administrative hierarchies, they are understanding the general preeminence of the *apus* in specifically political terms. Indeed, the mountain spirits are 'the' model of political power that emerges from the annual cycle. They are the commoner alternative to the notable vision of political order enacted in the *Fiestas Patrias* (see Chapter 3). It may seem that there is an insuperable gulf between this sacrificial understanding of politics and Western democratic individualist traditions, at least at the level of theory. In the following chapter, however, I will argue that the matter is not quite so clear cut, particularly when we turn to how notions of sacrifice developed in the *t'inkas* have been deployed in concrete historical actions by commoners.

8

Conclusions

With the presentation of the annual cycle now complete, let us summarize what it has taught us about production, appropriation, and political power in towns like Huaquirca, and apply this to the question of class formation. On the one hand, we have seen that production and appropriation exist in a state of contradiction. The relations of *ayni* that characterize the period of collective production are thoroughly negated by the appropriation of their product, in a manner that reflects the transgressive nature of notable rule, at least as it existed during the *gamonal* era. On the other hand, we have seen how the *t'inkas* depict a less antagonistic totality of production and appropriation under the sign of legitimate political power (the *apus*), one in which the principle of cooperative production is maintained in the process of appropriation, and not simply violated by it. Clearly, an important question to discuss here is the difference between contradiction and hierarchical totalization as basic dynamics in the political economy of the annual cycle.

Once this discussion of the annual cycle is complete, I will show how it contributes to the structural understanding of rural Andean society sketched out in the first two chapters. I will also prove the historical relevance of this analysis by turning to the autonomous commoner political movements of the period 1956–79, and showing that they frequently made use of the *t'inka* complex to assert their rights to the land, and their relation to the state. By drawing on the preceding analysis of the annual cycle, I will show why the *t'inkas* became appropriate vehicles of political action, and relate these findings to the existing historiography of these peasant movements. Thus, the main goal of this chapter is to show that what we have learned from the annual cycle really does tell us something about the structure of rural Andean society, and the recent political activity of commoners as a class. This connection should further justify the political economic interpretation of Andean annual cycle rituals undertaken here, and bring out additional dimensions in their symbolism. Finally, I will discuss what this analysis implies about the guerrilla war that has been going on in Peru since 1980.

Contradiction of Production and Appropriation

One of the most basic points emerging from the previous chapters is that the annual cycle of work and ritual does not take place through a uniform or homogeneous set of social relations. Commoners oscillate between the practice of *ayni* during the growing season and *mink'a* during the dry season. Only the notables hold to the proprietary format of *mink'a* throughout the year. The fact that commoners do not conduct production and appropriation according to the same social principles suggests that the separation between these two phases of activity is not simply seasonal, but also moral.

Ayni, the giving and receiving of similar labours across household boundaries, is the relation that orchestrates the productive effort of the growing season. Although *ayni* tends to be represented as an exchange of working days, especially male working days (cf. Malengreau 1980: 510), we know that it is actually the provision of corn beer by women that is crucial to recruiting a work party at this time of the year, and not the accumulation of labour 'credits' in an exchange system. On closer inspection, however, we discovered that when women provide men with corn beer during work parties, they do so according to the notions of *maña* and *yanantin*, which reinstate precisely the idea of an exchange of similar labours that was beginning to appear problematic. Thus, it seems that *ayni* categorically suppresses the ongoing necessity of consumption, and this is the key to its economic and cultural significance. It creates a domain of production that is opposed to one of consumption, and underpins the ritual focus on work that takes place during the growing season. The fact that *ayni* comes to a halt once the crops become consumable further proves its productivist character within the broader context of the annual cycle. Indeed, it is only against the backdrop of *ayni* that we can understand why this part of the year is so dominated by the ritual imagery of death.

Like *ayni*, death is a domain of anti-consumption: the *alma*'s journey to Qoropuna begins with the burning of food and clothes, and the emphasis on the ingestion of burning foods, or dung and ashes (Arguedas 1956: 266) in the afterlife points towards the breakdown and shrinkage of the *alma*, as energy is extracted from it and returned to the world of the living as water. The most graphic illustration of this reduction of the *alma* is its return as a fly on All Saints', that is, in the same form that the *ánimo* departed from the body on death, indicating an equalization of 'big' and 'little' souls. Labour power is extracted from the human body in a similar process of reduction and equalization of souls set in motion by the consumption of corn beer, which 'animates' the worker. Therefore, death becomes a cultural model for labour done through *ayni*. Most growing season rituals focus on the image of an identical (usually male) pair, which fuses the 'like for like' formula of *ayni* with the symmetry of souls on death, to form a single complex. From this perspective, *ayni* ceases to be an optional or contractual relation among individuals, and becomes part of a much broader process oriented by the 'work as death' metaphor, one in which the like derivation of labour power and water makes the growth of the crops a matter of *ayni* between the living and the dead.

The circulation of men across household boundaries, or their substitution for each other within their conjugal relationships, is an important aspect of the equalizing dynamic that underwrites both death and *ayni*. This circulation shows that men work out of a desire for women, and the female product of corn beer. It also shows that the female-dominated framework of conjugal appropriation (both sexual and economic) provides the structure within which men are momentarily equalized through general circulation. Relations of *compadrazgo*, and the incest prohibition accompanying them, direct this cooperation away from sexual sharing and towards the mutual recognition of property rights through labour. This same intervention of Christianity to spiritualize the process taking place under the sign of *ayni* is evident in the equation of the *niño* with maize, and its ability to embody the explosive energy released by death. Thus, the Christ-child becomes the object of the entire growing season, which reaffirms the Christian nature of *ayni* cooperation. Thus, commoners can see *ayni* labour as morally right, a kind of Christian sacrifice that makes them better people than the notables. By extension, when *ayni* orchestrates a socialized recognition of individual household rights to 'communal' land, it creates what commoners consider to be a morally superior kind of property.

There can be little doubt that this moral dimension to the generalized exchange of *ayni* labour offers a strong basis for commoner class identity, and little surprise in the fact that *ayni* is everywhere the practice that separates commoners from notables. One need look no further than this to understand the full moral import of the commoners' condemnation of the notables for being work-shy (see Casaverde 1970: 238; Arguedas and Ortiz 1973: 227; Montoya 1980: 226). The problem with this moral stance, however, lies in the particular concept of work from which it derives. If *ayni* is about the suppression of consumption, sexuality, and, ultimately, life itself, then it is something that rulers can simply decide to do without. Thus, the historical succession of ruling classes in the Andes have never bothered to dispute the organization of *ayni* with commoners the way they have the ownership of land. To the extent that *ayni* orchestrates a work-based commoner class identity, it also promotes a transgressive strategy of rule, in which rulers distinguish themselves from the ruled precisely by violating the prohibitions connected to labour (see Bataille 1933: 74). This violation lay at the heart of *gamonalismo*, as we saw in the first two chapters of this book. By establishing work-based egalitarian class identity for commoners, *ayni* engenders resistance to notable domination, but it also provokes further acts of violence from notables, who thus prove their distinction from commoners, and their cooperative social values. In both of these ways, *ayni* is a key element of local class structure.

Carnival Sunday marks the point in the year when maize loses its status as an object of production and becomes an object of consumption and appropriation. The notable banquets on this day are effectively first fruits ceremonies, and the felling of the *yunsa* further develops the break with the growing season. It is no accident that the notables terminate the growing season, and inaugurate a phase of the year concerned with property, since they are *propietarios* in both a legal and a stereotypical sense. Here, the literature that stresses the foreignness of the notables to the communities in which they live (e.g., Isbell 1978: 70; Ossio 1978a: 10) must be significantly qualified: in their willingness to consume the object of agricultural production, the notables effect a transition in the annual cycle that the commoners seem particularly reluctant to bring about. The exteriority of the notables to the moral universe of *ayni* is a symptom of the contradiction between production and appropriation *within* Andean culture, a contradiction that creates the need for oppressive, appropriating 'foreigners,' and upholds the myth of the conquest as the origin of modern social relations in the Andes.

Although agricultural work continues after Carnival, the focus of ritual shifts to consumption, and after ground breaking in the *laymis*, *ayni* gives way in exhaustion, leaving each domestic group to tend the ripening crops in its own fields. The fact that *ayni* disintegrates once the crops become consumable proves that it is subordinate to the paramount goal of domestic appropriation. April initiates a crescendo of property consciousness, which rises through the period of vigilance, theft, and accusations to culminate in the frantic rush of the harvest. Crop theft is one way of continuing to assert the communal morality of the growing season under the changed circumstances of the dry season. It also helps to vanquish the period of Christian cooperation that has prevailed during the growing season, just as the maize is 'crucified' by frost at Easter. It is only a short step from routinized crop theft to the ritualized invocation and capture of the vital force of animals from other grazing territories in the *t'inkas*. When ritualists invoke the spirits of other grazing territories, they are merely exercising their skill, but when they protect their own territory against similar attempts by other ritualists, they are preventing sorcery. Nothing could better demonstrate the vision of limited good that prevails during the dry season. There can be little doubt that the *t'inkas* overstep the function of legitimating property that Quispe (1969: 102) has rightly given them, and thrive on the intent to appropriate what belongs to others. The *t'inkas* could well be seen as the cultural basis of the widespread and ruinous practice of livestock rustling in the Andes, and of the artistry with which it is performed in some areas. These unsavoury acts show that commoners are quite capable of following the notables' lead into a period of amoral appropriation modelled on sorcery, and of repudiating the previous period of Christian cooperation once its object becomes consumable.

Despite the force with which appropriation emerges as a social value at this time of the year, it is not simply an end in itself, but also restores certain relations of hierarchy that have been reduced to symmetry by the productive expenditure of the growing season. This restoration is particularly obvious at the level of the individual male labourer, whose *alma* needs to be built up through consumption after its productive depletion during the growing season. Central to this process is the hierarchical relation of *mink'a*, in which the appropriating owner rewards the labourer in food. Within the conjugal unit, the transfer of crops from field to *despensa* during the harvest renews the dominance of women, since their conversion of crops to food can command the labour of many men, and is the irreducible basis of the *mink'a* relationship (cf. Skar 1982: 216). This inferiority of the male labourer within the framework of domestic appropriation is the means by which *mink'a* can be writ large into a class relation, like that which prevails between notables and commoners in Huaquirca. Here, we arrive at a second asymmetric unit, the polity dominated by a ruler, where it is worth noting that even during pre-Columbian times, *mink'a* was the relation by which work was carried out for local rulers (see Fonseca 1974: 91). It is also likely that *mink'a* lies at the root of traditional Andean labour tribute, which is distinguished from its instrumentalized modern counterpart by the wining and dining of workers by the state (see Murra 1980: 98). Through their work, men recognize the sovereignty of women within the household and rulers within the polity, in return for which they secure the consumption that restores a healthy asymmetry of souls within their own bodies after their deathly reduction to symmetry during the growing season. Restoration of asymmetry to the life of the individual during the dry season is further developed by the tendency for marriages to take place then, as discussed in Chapter 3.

From a labourer's perspective, *mink'a*, like the *t'inka* sacrifices, represents a calculated loss of self in the recognition of authority, in return for a renewal of life through consumption. The main difference is that the ritualized consumption of the *t'inkas* goes beyond the simple restoration of the body to a welling up of new life within it, that bursts forth as a throbbing organ in sacrificial birth. However, this difference is merely a matter of degree. What is remarkable about *mink'a* and the *t'inkas* is the extent to which they share the same thematic concerns with the regeneration of individual life, conjugality, and the recognition of authority, and unite these three asymmetric domains in the same interdependent sacrificial nexus. Although *mink'a* and sacrifice may not be as closely interwoven in particular episodes of the annual cycle as are *ayni* and death, their correspondence at the level of principle is just as complete.

Transformed by this relation to sacrifice, the private appropriation secured by *mink'a* now seems to restore a generalized asymmetry that brings health to the individual person, fertility to the domestic group, and legitimacy to relations of property and sovereignty within the political unit. Thus, the *t'inkas* represent appropriation not only as theft and violation of *ayni* morality, but also as something much more positive, which creates health, fertility, and harmony at many interconnected levels. This morally positive treatment of appropriation does not completely supersede the earlier negative view, but it does suggest that a kind of totalization results from the contradiction between collective production and private appropriation within Andean culture. These two antagonistic moralities do not merely remain locked in static opposition to each other, but give rise to something that partially transcends them. Let us now attempt to specify the nature of this totality.

Totality of Production and Appropriation

The first indication of a totality emerging from the contradictory phases of the annual cycle arises in moments of transformation and transition. As we saw in the analysis of the Christmas *wayliya*, an act that begins as an extreme manifestation of the growing season's symmetric duality becomes, when pushed to its limits, a kind of blood sacrifice that prefigures the *t'inkas* of the dry season, and their concern with political hierarchy. Although this does not annul the evidence of contradiction in the annual cycle presented above, it displays a measure of continuity that makes movement between opposing phases a matter of transformation, and not just truncation. Without this continuity, there would be nothing cyclical about the annual cycle. Starting from the symmetric male pair (*yanantin*) in the growing season, in which men are the victims of productivist death, and women are spared because of their reproductive capacities, the ripening of the crops brings a change in emphasis away from productive expenditure towards consumption and a welling up of life, which expresses itself in the asymmetry of *alma* and *ánimo*, woman and man. The crowning moment of this welling, regenerative asymmetry is the sacrificial birth of the palpitating heart from the victim-mother in the *t'inkas*. This may be an image of fertility fulfilled, but it is also a separation comparable to that of big soul and little soul on death. Thus, excessive ritual consumption not only completes the asymmetric phase of the annual cycle, but returns it to its point of departure in death, as with the myth of the fox discussed in relation to house rethatching. At this point, the continuity between sacrifice and death as organizing themes of seasonal practice becomes clear. Yet seasonal transformation is achieved not solely by means of this continuity, but also by following an ascendant tendency through to its breaking point, where its opposite number takes form in the ruins that result. In sum, the annual cycle involves both dialectical transformation and structural continuity, and each must be considered when discussing its totalizing dimension.

Of particular significance here are several tripartite images, which seem to resolve the symmetric duality of production and the asymmetric duality of appropriation. The first of these images occurred during the potato sowing, where the result of three represented 'salvation' in the *samakuy* divination. This trinity retains the male/male symmetric dual formula (*yanantin*) that comprised 'salvation' in the earlier divinations of the maize sowing, but adds to it male/female asymmetry, resulting in a tripartite representation. It is in the *t'inkas*, however, that the Andean trinity formula predominates. Here, the first example is the three stalks of maize that are put at the head of the *mesa* (see Figure 22). In the *puna*, where 'altars' are used with the *mesa*, a stone slab replaces the three maize stalks as an orientation marker, but preserves the trinity formula in a raised peak that slopes to two shoulders, a pattern that is also present in the profile of a house roof, and the related image of the mountain (see Figure 22). The same configuration of a raised centre flanked by two subordinate elements occurs in the *kallpa* figurines. On a more skewed basis, it is also present in the organs that the *apus* are most likely to seize from the body (see Figure 22). These may be appropriated as a triad (heart and lungs), or separately, to correct an imbalance (heart and testicles). In all cases, the productive principle of symmetry is conserved, but subordinated to a central and hierarchically superior element taken from the asymmetric dualities just discussed, namely the *alma* in the body, the woman in the household, or the ruler in the political unit.

On closer inspection, however, some tripartite imagery displays a slightly different structure from that outlined above. There are cases where the central, superior element is 'small' and male, whereas the subordinate symmetrical elements are 'big' and female. For instance, we saw in the previous chapter how the three *kallpa* figurines offered to the mountain spirits may sometimes take the form of two large yellow figurines flanking a small white one. One important meaning of this configuration was acted out when the 'priest' had two women kneel down on the ground side by side, and simulated animal copulation by climbing on top of them and thrusting into the space between them. A similar female symmetry occurs in the 'farewell' round of the *t'inkas*, when a pair of women disperse the animals, and in the dancing of the guardians' wives during Carnival. This female '*yanantin*' can be taken as the counterpart of that which occurs among men during the growing season, and is linked to the reductive generation of labour power. Only in the *t'inkas*, with their emphasis on reproduction, this

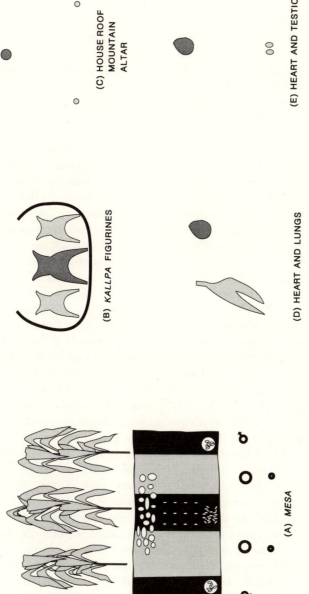

Figure 22   Tripartite imagery

(A) MESA

(B) KALLPA FIGURINES

(C) HOUSE ROOF
MOUNTAIN
ALTAR

(D) HEART AND LUNGS

(E) HEART AND TESTICLES

reduplication of women seems to be about the swelling up of new life to the bursting point of (sacrificial) birth, a process that is the opposite of that undergone by men during the growing season, and one in which the victims are women. If this analysis is correct, it implies that there is a seasonal alternation in how men and then women occupy the subordinate, reduplicated position in the triangle. This alternation corresponds to that between the deathly generation of labour and the sacrificial regeneration of life. Hierarchy remains constant here, as does the expression of subordination through symmetric reduplication: what varies (seasonally) is the gender coding of the basal and peak positions in the triangle.

It is no accident that most of these totalizing tripartite images occur in the *t'inkas*. In these rites, a concern for domestic appropriation predominates, but not to the exclusion of collective production, which is hierarchically subsumed in a single complex performance. Like the seasonal transformations mentioned earlier, the *t'inkas* have their paradoxical aspects, such as using the moral principle of *ayni* to recruit the services of non-kin (see Quispe 1969: 67; Morissette and Racine 1973: 174) in what is otherwise a largely amoral appropriation of other people's property through sorcery. Here, the mutual recognition of property through labour is intimately fused with the assertion of property through exclusion, in a kind of unity of opposites. A similar tension exists in the relation between people and the *apus* in these rites, where the synecdoche of 'libation' seems to indicate a restitution of the fluids spent during the growing season. This fluid exchange evokes the model of *ayni*, whereas the alimentary metaphors that inform the process of making offerings suggest the model of *mink'a*. Probably the most significant thing here, as with the comparable indeterminacy of relations of production in the house rethatching, is that people do not try to deny the complexity of the situation by proclaiming it either *ayni* or *mink'a*. The totalizing function of these rites is further expressed in their synthesis of animal, vegetable, and mineral through elaborate metaphorical connections and transformations. Part of the *t'inkas'* emphasis on the regeneration of life is a restoration of wholeness to the mountains, which is why these rites can be adapted to cure human illness as well. The fact that the *t'inkas* can be adapted for purposes outside the annual cycle suggests that they do not have an imbalanced position within it. This notion is confirmed by the timing of these rites, which is weighted towards the dry season by their predominant concern with appropriation and embodiment, but is most commonly and universally geared to the transition points in the year, Carnival and August. The totalizing powers of the *t'inka* are what makes it the most polyfunctional and most important rite in Andean culture.

Similarly, images of affinity span the entire annual cycle: the figure of the 'son-in-law' is a near-constant in the rites we have discussed. This is not to say, however, that affinity means exactly the same thing in both phases of the annual cycle. Predominant during the growing season are the labour obligations of the 'son-in-law' and his duties in death ritual. During the dry season, his presence in the *t'inkas* and in house rethatching prevents consumption and appropriation there from becoming incestuous. This legitimation is highly ambivalent, however, since it sets the dissolution of the sponsors' property in motion, and prefigures their death in the coming growing season. Thus, the growing season stresses the services and obligations of the 'son-in-law' to his wife's kin, whereas during the dry season he is primarily an inheritor of their property. These rights and duties combine in the formation and maintenance of households. Thus, the passage back and forth between the growing and the dry season can be modelled on the developmental cycle of the domestic group, whose driving principle is affinity.

The mountain spirit is another image that spans the entire annual cycle. Bastien (1978) describes at great length the role of the mountain as a central organizing metaphor in Andean culture, and the same conclusion emerges here by different ethnographic routes. First, the mountain is arguably the prototype of this triangular image of totality in Andean culture. Although the same pattern of a ruling element raised over two symmetric elements of a productive base is echoed in the house roof and the organs of the body, these are but microcosms of the mountain. Furthermore, as participants in the productive process and consummate appropriators, the mountain spirits embody and unify the two seasonal phases of commoner social life. We know from their various regional titles, and from their mythical exploits, that the *apus* are thought of as both condors and hawks, carrion eaters and predators, a contrast that maps onto the seasonal alternation between the imagery of passive death and the imagery of sacrifice. Thus, the *apus* incorporate both the energy given off by the *alma* on death and the ability to create new lives by violent extraction of organs from a living body in sacrifice. As appropriators of both the pure, disembodied male energy of death and the female impulse towards embodiment (the sacrificial offering), the *apus* emerge as essentially androgynous, even hermaphroditic, characters. Through their connection to affines in Andean culture, and as recipients of triadic offerings in the *t'inkas*, the mountain spirits emerge as the culmination of all of these impulses towards totality.

The emergence of these hierarchical totalities significantly alters (but does not eliminate) the contradiction between collective production and private appropriation discussed earlier. Even Andean commoners, who define themselves as a group primarily through the exchange of *ayni* labour, recognize that production cannot be an end in itself, and must ultimately find its reason for existence in consumption and appropriation. If they did not, there would be no seasonal break in social relations of the sort documented here for the period between Carnival and the harvest. Yet this same seasonal break retains the contradiction between collective production and private appropriation, even while resolving it into hierarchy at another level. The totality that emerges from the annual cycle, therefore, is a dialectical one, not a flat system in which every element has a stable function or a definite positional value. Although the morality of *ayni* is subordinate to private appropriation, it still remains antithetical to it, and provides a basis from which to criticize it. Thus, seasonal contradiction generates the hierarchical totality of the annual cycle, but is not resolved by it.

Sacrifice, Class, and History

Any general assessment of the annual cycle as class discourse must address both its contradictory and its hierarchical dimensions. However, the contradictory aspects of the annual cycle are undoubtedly the ones that most directly create a sense of class. Although commoners participate in both collective production and private appropriation on a seasonal basis, they realize that notables do not, and that the practice of *ayni* during the growing season sets them apart as a social group. This is evident in the way they criticize notables as being 'lazy' people who lack the 'tenderness to work' for others. It is also clear in the way commoners cede the first fruits celebrations of Carnival to the notables, and in so doing allow them to initiate the coming period of private appropriation. The contradiction between production and appropriation in the annual cycle feeds directly into the sense of class division between commoners and notables in rural Andean towns like Huaquirca, and gives it nuanced cultural expression.

I take the most generic aspect of class formation to be this polarization of workers and owners into distinct social groups. Of course it is true that commoners appropriate and notables produce, but what makes the distinction between them class-like is the way commoners identify with and culturally elaborate their role as labourers, and notables their role as appropriators. Beyond this elementary distinction, there are several other familiar aspects of class in this situation. First is hierarchy. Commoners' identification with labour marks their social subordination, whereas notables' identification with appropriation expresses their ruling status. As in other class societies, a hierarchical distinction between appropriation and labour generates and reflects social hierarchy. Within this globally hierarchical arrangement, however, there is an elaboration of egalitarianism from the subordinate position, here as *ayni*. This egalitarianism is articulated around the subordinate activity of agrarian work, and primarily by commoner men. It is less developed among commoner women, and particularly problematic in relations between commoner women and men, since these verge on the relation of *mink'a* that characterizes the hierarchy between notables and commoners. Thus, among commoners there is a tension between an egalitarian class identity, which is predominantly male and grounded in field labour, and domestic life, which is female dominated, and relatively more proprietorial and hierarchical in orientation. Similar contradictions exist in Western working-class life, and are the result of a comparable attempt to construct a social identity around a narrow, productivist notion of labour.

However, there are obviously many significant differences between the sense of class that emerges in Andean towns like Huaquirca and the theories of class that have developed in Western trade unions, political parties, and universities since the nineteenth century. Our sense of class took form around possessive individualist notions that have a long genealogy and very pervasive hold on our culture (see MacPherson 1962; Dumont 1986). In particular, the Marxist conviction that class is, above all, a matter of economic exploitation can be traced to the notion that the individual worker is, or at least should be, owner of his or her person, and, by extension, his or her labour power. It is from this perspective that the extraction of surplus-value appears as an exploitative violation of the rights of the self-owning individual. Although not all Western class discourse derives from economic liberalism as transparently as this, there can be no denying that our sense of class has been profoundly shaped by the peculiarities of capitalist individualism and economism. When we take these latter traits as what is essential to class, as most Marxists and Weberians do, then it is not surprising that we fail to find class outside Western industrial settings.

Rural Andean class discourse is often unrecognizable as such to us because most of it occurs in the idioms of 'race' and agrarian ritual. Although Andean notions of 'race' are linked to Western individualism (cf. Dumont 1970), the rituals of the annual cycle are not. Initially, nothing could differ more from possessive individualism than the endless emphasis on death and sacrifice that we have encountered in this annual cycle. Instead of emphasizing the autonomous individual as a supreme social value, these rituals seem to subordinate individual lives to the well-being of the land, and its hierarchy of mountain spirits. Hierarchical assimilation, not freedom or self-realization, is the paramount value here. It is particularly difficult for us to see how a sense of class based on such assumptions could lead commoners to defend their interests, let alone contest the broader organization of society. Victimization, not resistance, would seem to be the most likely stance for commoners to adopt. Therefore, I think it particularly worthwhile to focus on the hierarchical aspects of the annual cycle, and to show that (contrary to our expectations) they can, indeed, articulate a culture of opposition.

Hierarchy involves not just a distinction between the dominant and the subordinate, but also a logical and substantive connection between them, such that neither could exist without the other. In the Andean case, this connection is expressed materially through sacrifice and libation, acts that simultaneously constitute the power of the mountain spirits and the dependency of commoners. Within this explicitly hierarchical discourse, distinction is realized through interconnection, thus the weak still have a claim on the strong. However, the opposite is true of possessive individualism, and related notions of 'race.' Here, distinction proceeds through separation and the essentialization of difference. It follows that when commoners assert that they are connected to the ultimate holders of power through sacrifice, they are not simply upholding hierarchy, but implicitly subverting notable ideas of 'racial' distinction. For sacrifice asserts precisely the substantive connection between rulers and ruled that local notions of 'race' attempt to deny. Thus, hierarchical subordination provides a peculiarly appropriate way of resisting the specific idiom of domination to which commoners have been subjected. Rather than look for familiar battle cries of individual dignity and liberty, we must be prepared for a mode of class struggle that accepts hierarchy, and proceeds to make use of it by attempting to reconstitute and assimilate 'alien' powers from below.

The potentially subversive character of hierarchy depends largely on how we understand the mountain spirits as idealized ruler-proprietors in a sacrificial relation with commoners. Since the *apus* commonly take on the human form of rich *mistis*, we must ask whether the totality they represent is simply the sum total and sacralized reinforcement of actually existing notable rule, as Zorilla (1978: 123) suggests. After all, this would accord well with the domination of the Andean trinity formula by its central, hierarchically superior element, associated with appropriation and power. Furthermore, just such an equation emerges from the words of one of Arguedas' informants: 'The mountain spirit is ferocious, he can suck out one's heart while one is asleep ... just as the powerful man, the man with lots of money is ferocious' (Arguedas 1956: 235–6). Commoners frequently extend this sacrificial understanding of wealth and power to account for their domination by non-Andean people within the national arena (see Gose 1986). Furthermore, they do so with accuracy and insight. The idiom of sacrifice amply reflects commoners' historical experience of victimization by the *gamonales*, and like the myth of the conquest, it represents power relations through an imagery of blood and violence.

However, the praxis of commoners in the annual cycle also posits the *apu* as something more than notable power as it actually exists in society. It would be wrong to emphasize only the subordination of Andean commoners to the imagined appetites of their rulers, and the tendency towards violent domination that undeniably results. Although these tendencies exist, and sometimes predominate even in the *t'inkas*, we have already seen several instances where they cannot completely rid themselves of a grounding in cooperation (e.g., symmetry, affinity). This is no less true of the *t'inka* complex in its broadest implications than it is in matters of detail. Furthermore, the very notion of a sacrificial rejuvenation of power implies a certain recognition of the victim, which opens the possibility of further negotiation through the development of ritual skill. From the preceding chapter on the *t'inkas*, we have already seen that commoners expect to be able to convert the vast disparity in power between themselves and the mountain spirits into a relation of cooperation and mutual sustenance through the most elaborate of their rituals. Often, this expectation leads individual commoners, or entire communities, into an especially intimate relation with a particular mountain spirit who becomes their benefactor and guardian. Far from viewing their connection to the mountains as a purely oppressive one, commoners usually discuss it with optimism, and hope to prosper from it. This attitude, in turn, encourages commoners to be critical of notables, as the following vignette (in all its triviality) will show.

During the Christmas *wayliya* of 1981, a drunken commoner approached me and demanded, with a sweeping gesture of his arm that led from the edge of the plaza, where some notable ex-residents of Huaquirca on holiday from Lima had congregated, to the centre of the plaza, where the dance troupes were marching in full-throated *wayliya*: 'How would these little lawyers know how to dance? What are they worth?'[1] With a similar amount of drink under other circumstances, this man might still have ridiculed the orientation of the notables towards professional success on the national scene. But there was a certain euphoria and confidence with which he did so on this occasion that was seldom present in other outbursts of notable-baiting by drunken commoners that I heard in Huaquirca. Besides a great deal of alcohol, I attribute this confidence to the spectacle of commoners dressing up like *apus* and marching in a formation that bears the symmetric duality of *ayni*. Instead of imposing a blind compliance, the figure of the *apu* seems to act as a kind of standard here, against which the contemptibility of the current regime and its 'little lawyers' stands fully revealed. Indeed, the very fact that commoners can dress up as *apus* and dance, even if they stop short of claiming to represent them, contributes to the feeling that the *apus* are 'like us' (Flores 1979: 77), and suggests that they are an image that commoners can take hold of to empower themselves.

To assess the extent to which this is actually the case, we must turn to contexts of political struggle, and see what becomes of the *apus* within them. When we turn to those extraordinary times in recent history when commoners seized the political initiative from notables, we discover that many commoner movements deployed various elements of the *t'inka* complex, and relied on the guidance of the mountain spirits (via oracular mediums) in their attempts to win recognition of communal rights to the land from the Peruvian state. Far from orchestrating a capitulation or self-immolation in the face of power, the mountain spirits and their associated rites have consistently been a rallying point against *gamonal* domination. This evidence must be interpreted in the light of what we know about the *t'inkas* and the mountain spirits from the annual cycle. It also provides us with an invaluable pragmatic test of that analysis in historical contexts outside the 'cyclical time' of the annual cycle, where the political stakes were extremely high. By discussing Andean peasant movements, we can thus fine-tune and extend the 'structural' insights about class gained from the annual cycle.[2]

The cult of the *apus* has never stopped commoners from trying to defend themselves against the power of the *gamonales*, which it allegedly sacralizes. The literature on peasant movements in the Andes since the late nineteenth century, too vast to cite here, shows that commoners have no reliable predisposition to accept notable rule. Even Antonio Trelles, one of the most notorious and cruel *gamonales* in the entire Department of Apurímac, was unable to definitively intimidate the peasants of the Pincos Valley, who captured him and killed him in 1910 (Skar 1982: 246). Like so many Andean peasant movements before and after it, this one met with momentary success at the local level. It lasted long enough to allow the killing of the most oppressive notables before troops arrived to massacre the insurgents. During the Chayanta uprising of 1927, the Macha captured and killed their local *hacendado*, devoured his flesh, and offered his bones to one of their most important mountains (Langer 1990: 239). According to Platt (1983: 66), the Macha decided that the *hacendado* no longer enjoyed the mountain's backing; hence, he should be returned to it as an offering. Here again, it seems that the mountain spirit did nothing whatsoever to uphold this *misti*'s power, but acted instead as a standard by which he could be judged and found wanting.

This incident from the Chayanta rebellion shows that the sacrificial understanding of power developed in the annual cycle can be mobilized in political action. Similarly, the act of libating a community's stone boundary markers, repeated annually in many parts of Peru and Bolivia, can also be invoked in land occupations or border disputes with neighbouring communities (see Custred 1979: 382; Rasnake 1988: 246). The ritual battles that take place in many areas of Bolivia and southern Peru between Christmas and Corpus Christi have also been interpreted as sacrificial offerings of blood that renew communal claims to the land (see Platt 1987a). As Platt (1986: 239–40) argues, it is but a short step from this sort of ritualized quasi-military event to a more strategic use of community mobilizations and offerings for purposes that go beyond the normal purview of the annual cycle, such as regaining lost communal lands. For example, Necker (1982: 261–2) mentions animal sacrifice, coca offerings, and communal labour (*faena*) during the land occupations in Puno during the late 1970s.

These offerings are appropriate in an act of repossession, as is the collective labour by which commoners have traditionally obliged the state to recognize communal tenure (Chapter 2). There can be little doubt that commoners use libation and sacrifice to claim rights on their own behalf, even as they recognize the sovereignty of the state. In the annual cycle, the *t'inkas* also use libation and sacrifice to legitimate property and recognize authority. Clearly, this ritual strategy has been transposed from the annual cycle onto specific political conjunctures.

The importance of the *t'inka* complex in political action becomes even clearer and more dramatic when we turn to the land occupations of the period 1958–64, by which many communities throughout Peru attempted to regain land expropriated from them by *haciendas*. In retrospect, these occupations were the high-water mark of the peasant movement in Peru during the twentieth century. Yet what is often misunderstood, particularly by those most anxious to classify these movements as 'revolutionary' in an orthodox sense (e.g., Kapsoli 1977: chap. 4), is how political consensus and strategic decision-making were orchestrated by leaders who acted as mediums of the mountain spirits, and thereby recruited them to the cause of the land occupations. This process has been described for both Cusco (Núñez del Prado 1970: 105; Gow 1980: 287; Gow 1982: 200–1) and Cerro de Pasco (Rivera Pineda 1980): the two areas of greatest commoner militancy at the time. Undoubtedly, there is still much that we do not know about the oracular leadership of these political movements. If anything, it is surprising that we know as much as we do. However, it seems that especially in Cerro de Pasco, the scheduling of land occupations was decided in consultations with the mountain spirits, as commoners attempted both to assert their claim to the land and avoid military and vigilante repression (Rivera Pineda 1980). A similar use of coca divinations to determine the tactics of the Andahuaylas land occupations of 1974 has also been reported (Labrousse 1985: 96). At several politically crucial moments, commoners have deployed the *t'inka* complex at its most powerful and esoteric level, that of oracular mediumship. In the decisive moment, commoners saw the mediums as their most trustworthy leaders, and the mountain spirits they gave voice to as the most powerful manifestations and advocates of their cause. Far from being just so much 'pre-political' mumbo jumbo, the mountain spirits (and the everyday practices that supported them) defined the politics of these situations.

Clearly, the political function of the *apu* cannot be consigned to the oblivion of a 'millenarian period' of peasant struggle that was supposed to have ended in 1930 (according to Kapsoli 1977: chap. 2). Nor does the intervention of the mountain spirit imply any retreat from the strategic realities of the 'revolutionary' struggle, only a way of framing them through consultative seances and coca leaf divinations. By using these cultural forms to interrogate the political conjunctures in which they found themselves, the protagonists of these movements, however implicitly, also transposed their own ritual framework on the resolution of these conflicts. These hegemonic manoeuvres are especially clear in the sacrificial offerings that took place during land occupations, since as we saw in the previous chapter, these offerings allow the reconstructing from below of the very powers that assimilate them. More than just a demand of recognition and justice from the state, these offerings also presupposed that such revindications should take place through an Andean framework. Not surprisingly, this aspect of the 1956–64 movements went largely unnoticed, misunderstood, and unrecognized by the rest of Peruvian society. This blindness only emphasizes once again that the *apus* do *not* sacralize actually existing power relations, but represent instead an attempt to reconstruct them on a different basis.

Again, an understanding of how the *apus* are constructed in the routinized context of the annual cycle contributes greatly to our understanding of their political significance. Because the mountain spirits represent the very land that commoners have struggled for, they naturally become rallying points for political action. As archetypal landowners and political authorities, the mountain spirits differ from the *gamonales* in predicating their dominion on the fertility of the land. Each *apu* has a specific role in an agrarian division of labour, which corresponds to its rank in an administrative hierarchy. Thus, the mountain spirits embody both the commoner world of agrarian labour and the notable world of political power, just as they totalize the principles of collective production and private appropriation at work in the annual cycle. By including the principle of collective production, the mountain spirits revindicate and elevate the social position of commoners in relation to the existing order. They represent not just the central, predominant element, but also include the symmetric principle of production at the base of the triangle formula, upon which the principle of rule must rest if it is to be legitimate. It is out of an awareness that power is necessarily based in cooperation, and not just transgression, that commoners turn to the mountain spirits for help, especially when their very existence is at stake. This is why a superficial reading of the *apus*, one that equates them with the *mistis* they resemble, is misleading. The mountains assume a substantive link with the notables in their appearance and status as rulers to put the force of an alternative conception of power on them, one that is grounded in a recognition of the sacrificial victim, and the symmetric base of the Andean trinity formula. This is a relation of whole to part, a kind of synecdoche in which the mountain (momentarily) appears as a *misti* without fully becoming one. Thus, the *apus* emerge most emphatically as a totality in the sense of an encompassing cultural framework not identical to the actually existing social order, and reveal the indispensable political function of cultural constructs that operate in this manner.

In reviewing the use of annual cycle imagery for political ends beyond its normal context in the fields, we have seen a consistent selectiveness in which the mountain spirits (and *t'inka* rites dedicated to them) come to the fore at the expense of virtually everything else. Surprisingly absent is the complex of imagery centred on *ayni*, given the role that this practice plays in defining local class boundaries between commoners and notables. There are many reasons for this absence, some of which we have already touched on. The *ayni*-oriented imagery of the growing season does not fully address the issue of property, which is really what was at stake in the peasant movements discussed here. To be sure, the horizontal solidarity of direct producers was the basis of political action in all these cases, but what made these movements militant was precisely that they projected this productivist solidarity into the realm of property to contest the ownership of the land. From a base in the symmetric duality of *ayni*, these movements can be visualized as pushing 'upwards' into the hierarchical domain of property, giving rise to the triangular sign of the mountain spirit, that idealized ruler-appropriator who contains, but also surpasses, the principle of productive cooperation. Thus, the hierarchical idioms of Andean culture do not guarantee a politically docile peasantry. On the contrary, they have often become a vehicle for articulating opposition.

No matter how important the *apus* may be as vehicles of political revindication for the Andean peasantry, the fact remains that they are not recognized as such by the states in which they live. This non-recognition raises the question of how commoners have managed to press their claims in a larger society that operates under a different legal framework. Without necessarily abandoning their own cultural framework of meaning and right, commoners have nonetheless managed to act intelligibly within national law, and have actually placed a great deal of faith in it. For example, most of the commoner political mobilizations in Huaquirca described in Chapter 2 used Peruvian law to articulate their objectives. Although it is possible that Andean ritual forms may have been deployed in the boundary dispute with Sabayno in 1945, and the occupation of Lucrepampa in 1960, none of my informants remembered them as an important part of these actions. Furthermore, there is little doubt that commoners have generally preferred legal to more militant forms of conflict resolution. Since the middle of the colonial period, commoners have attempted to settle their land disputes with *haciendas* through litigation, and have resorted to land occupation only as a last resort (cf. Hobsbawm 1974; O'Phelan 1983: 76, 79). The communities of the upper Antabamba Valley, as in other parts of Peru (see Matos Mar 1951: 71, 115; Hobsbawm 1974: 124–6), have zealously conserved their colonial titles in anticipation of the need for such litigation.

Initially, we are confronted with a discrepancy between two regulative frameworks that commoners have employed in political action: one that is 'Andean' and derived from annual cycle rituals, the other that is 'national' and codified in Peruvian law. Although the commoners of Huaquirca (and other Andean localities) certainly punctuate their ordinary working lives with annual cycle rituals, they differ from the peasants of Cusco and Cerro de Pasco in having abandoned them in favour of national law when it came time for serious political action. This discrepancy between 'Andean' and 'national' frameworks is both an internal characteristic of specific commoner movements in places like Huaquirca, and a matter of divergent political response among different Andean peasantries.

A number of interesting issues arise from the fact that the commoners of Huaquirca deployed national law instead of their annual cycle rituals in overt political action. First, we see that the historical record of commoner political activity in Huaquirca is no guide to the political economic culture they have created in everyday life. This is a problem for those, like E.P. Thompson, who adopt a strictly historical approach to class on the assumption that people will transparently reveal their commitment to a particular vision of their social order through political action over time. With this formula, we would never detect how annual cycle rituals powerfully orchestrate everyday life in Huaquirca.[3] Nor would we discover how the protection of property rights informally established through *ayni* labour was the underlying motive of many of the legal actions described in Chapter 2. In short, this discrepancy is a reminder of the poverty of the legally codified views of society that predominate in the historical record, and of the need to pay attention to informal regulative processes.

Conversely, this discrepancy further demonstrates the need to qualify the regulative view of ritual adopted at the outset of this study. It suggests that annual cycle rituals structure social action in Huaquirca only up to a certain point, beyond which other regulative frameworks take over. Not all rituals count as law, even though law is highly ritualized. This underlines the basic objection to regulative understandings of ritual. Because many rituals are non-discursive and image-oriented, they are ill-suited to firmly direct other activities, and are not an infallible guide to social action. It is hardly surprising that people would abandon them for a harder, more codified regulative framework in situations of heightened political conflict. Alternatively, one might argue that as conflict becomes more immanent, the rituals that address it must become more authoritative and prescriptive. Thus, the annual cycle rituals are driven into the background because their non-propositional multivocality renders them inappropriate.

These points can be summarized by arguing that the annual cycle rituals of Huaquirca's commoners are a subordinate discourse. This subordination implies that the annual cycle rituals are seldom historically visible, and that they lack the privilege of law, despite their regulative efficacy. Rather, they work behind the scenes, lending order and meaning to the lives of a subordinate class/ethnic group, but lack the authority to establish binding claims on more powerful outsiders. Given the agrarian character of these annual cycle rituals, it is hardly surprising that they are not politically dominant. They are the rituals of a peasantry, not a ruling elite. Arguably, they would have to be completely reworked from another social position before they could be anything other than a subordinate discourse. Nonetheless, we have already seen that these rituals figured conspicuously in some of the most militant commoner movements of the twentieth century. If the ritual traditions discussed in this book are a subordinate discourse, this does not mean that they have lead to surrender. Not only have they regularly produced insubordination, but their regulative legitimacy has been openly asserted in many peasant movements. In short, they are capable of at least a limited degree of hegemony. It is an open question whether commoners are a subordinate group because they have organized their lives around a ritual discourse that is inherently subordinate, or if their rituals become a subordinate discourse because commoners are a subordinate social group.

Beyond arguing that Andean annual cycle rituals are less authoritative than Peruvian law, we have yet to explore the difference between them. It is all too easy to assume that the two differ from each other as religious fantasy to legal reality, tradition to modernity, or one bounded culture to another. These synoptic formulations must be replaced with a more careful examination of similarities and differences, which does not automatically impute dichotomy or incommensurability. This is especially necessary when the same group of people makes use of both idioms, as have the commoners of Huaquirca. Until we know exactly what the difference consists of, there is no point in offering sociological or historical explanations of why one Andean peasantry acted through national law and another through its own ritual tradition. We will not know what we are trying to explain.

Ironically, it is Hobsbawm (1959), author of the pernicious distinction between 'pre-political' and 'political' movements, who has most seriously questioned the difference between ritual and legal discourse in the Peruvian case. He shows that even the most flamboyantly ritualized land occupations were often an outgrowth of claims based on title, and that they did not represent a disregard for the rule of law as much as an attempt to speed up litigation. Indeed, Hobsbawm (1974: 124) has actually portrayed the 'Andean' trappings of these movements as part of an entrenched 'legalism' that characterizes the Peruvian peasantry. Far from being opposed to each other, he suggests that the two are, in fact, complementary. Following his lead, I propose to look for interaction and accommodation between the deployment of the t'inka complex in land occupations, and recourse to national law. In the process, we must continue to rethink the dichotomy between 'reform' and 'revolution,' 'modern' and 'millenarian' political movements that seems entirely unproblematic to many writers on peasant politics.

First, Andean 'legalism' is not of a bureaucratic sort, but took its distinctive form under the varayoq system of communal authority (see Chapter 2) in which particular functions of social control always carried particular ritual obligations (cf. Montoya 1980: 205–6, 250–1). There is good reason to suspect that law enforcement and ceremonialism are more overtly and consciously integrated in Andean culture than they are in our own. Thus, the simultaneous presence of 'legalism' and 'millenarianism' during land occupations. Indeed, both of these terms are somewhat prejudicial, since they arbitrarily isolate and reify specific aspects of what may be, from an Andean point of view, a unified process of social regulation. There is no good reason why recourse to the law should represent a fundamentally different strategy from sacrificial offerings to the mountain spirits. Not only do both discourses regulate the distribution of property in the Andes, they do so through the mediation of a transcendental political authority. After, all, the mountain spirits are thought to form administrative hierarchies that parallel those of the state.

At a more specific level, there is evidence that Andean ritual traditions have attempted to encompass national law. During commoner struggles against the *gamonales* of the Hacienda Lauramarca in Cusco, the Apu Ausangate is said not only to have issued strategic directives to oracular mediums, but also to have acted as a lawyer on behalf of the peasantry (Gow 1980: 287; Gow 1982: 200). In other areas of Cusco, peasants made offerings with juridical names like 'lower appeal' to mountain spirits thought to act as judges, before entering into what we would recognize as 'real' litigation in court (Roel Pineda 1965: 27). Finally, the previously mentioned sacrificial immolation of a *hacendado* during the Chayanta rebellion of 1927 was preceded by an elaborate trial of other *hacendados* that meticulously observed the ritual forms of Bolivian national law (see Langer 1990: 230–8). Evidence such as this plays havoc with any polar treatment of national law and Andean ritual, and suggests that from a commoner perspective, the two are not mutually exclusive options.

Although annual cycle rituals and national law may be compatible as regulative discourses, this does not necessarily alter the hierarchical relationship between them, or their ethnic coding. Like the mountain spirits who appear as rich *mistis*, national law remains dominant and foreign, but capable of being harnessed from below through sacrifice. By bringing national law within the purview of their own sacrificial traditions, commoners have attempted to make contact with an actually existing form of power, to use it effectively, and put the pressure of an alternative discourse upon it. The dynamic of the Andean triad is particularly relevant here: a powerful and initially foreign peak is sustained by a symmetric and quintessentially Andean base. In the process, the foreignness of national law, like the whiteness of the *apu*, is assimilated and reworked from below. Thus, commoners' use of Peruvian law actually extends their own ritual framework as it covertly encompasses the foreign. This strategy is particularly appropriate for a subordinate social group practising a subordinate discourse, who nonetheless refuse to concede their definitive 'racial' inferiority.

It follows from this analysis that a dichotomy between Andean and national cultures may be equally suspect from an Andean point of view. We know from the work of Mallon (1983) and Manrique (1981) that an alternative national project was launched in all seriousness by Peruvian commoners during the War of the Pacific (1879–83), and that similar developments were occurring in Bolivia at the same time (Platt 1987b). Similarly, the Peruvian flag constantly figured in the land occupations of 1958–64 (see Hobsbawm 1974: 127), but not necessarily as a gesture of compliance to the actually existing state. Rather, we know that during these years Andean people came to see themselves as the only true 'Peruvians' (Ortiz 1973: 166). There is every reason to suspect, Hobsbawm (1974) and Bonilla (1987) notwithstanding, that the Andean peasantry has not neglected the nation-state as an object of political action in favour of 'localism,' but that, on the contrary, they have often attempted to reorient nationalism, only to be thwarted by the uncomprehending parochialism of criollo society (and Western social science). Although reports of plans to restore the Inca empire during the so-called 'millenarian period' of the peasant movement (1919–30, see Kapsoli 1977: chap. 2) are often dismissed as pure folly or *gamonal* paranoia, they deserve to be taken seriously, and rethought as part of an ongoing alternative national project (cf. Platt 1987b: 319–20). Perhaps they were nothing more than a slightly more aggressive variant of this general strategy of equating national identity with the Andean, one that would not, after all, have been out of line with the growing influence of *indigenismo* on the political scene of 'official' Peru at the time.

Thus, it is safe to conclude that Andean 'legalism' is compatible with the ritually generated framework of meaning and right discussed in this book, and the 'millenarian' strand of the peasant movements that have arisen from it. This compatibility derives primarily from the fact that annual cycle rituals regulate matters of labour, property, and political power in a quasi-legal way and, therefore, have something of the same function as national law. What prevents this compatibility from being understood by non-Andean people is their predisposition to perceive these rituals as mere folklore, a tendency that has been exacerbated by ethnicity theory, and often culminates in overt racism. Far from proposing a barbaric challenge to national law, however, the quasi-legal framework developed by commoners in the annual cycle has consistently intervened on the side of a strong central state, and against the 'localist' sovereignty of the *gamonales*. When we consider the Peruvian peasant movements of the 1880s, and the periods 1919–30, and 1956–64, the upholding of national law and sovereignty against internal and external threats was a crucial motive in every case. Despite the outward difference between national law and the annual cycle rituals described here, there has been a significant overlap in purpose and considerable *de facto* cooperation between these two forms of social regulation. Indeed, to the extent that there has ever been rule of law in the Peruvian countryside, it has largely been underwritten by the parallel ritual framework of commoners.

The democratic importance of these subordinate, para-legal ritual traditions has become increasingly clear since 1958, as individuals of varying Leninist persuasions have managed to implant themselves in Andean land occupation movements, and have occasionally realized their ambition of providing 'leadership' within them. Although the role played by such militants cannot be completely dismissed (cf. García-Sayán 1982: 197), their inability to understand or work within the idioms of Andean culture has limited their effectiveness. Often, these people overestimate their own contribution simply because it is the only thing they can really understand. For example, during the Andahuaylas land occupations of 1974, certain Maoist militants made significant organizational contributions, but were not invited to meetings on the eve of planned actions, during which commoners performed coca leaf divinations (see Labrousse 1985: 96). We have already seen the role played by divination and oracular consultation in such movements, and it is undoubtedly the persistence of these forms that is responsible for commoners' conviction that their communities and their leaders remain the instigators and protagonists of these actions, despite the presence of the organized left (cf. Labrousse 1985: 98). Naturally, the Leninist analysis has been that if they are to be effective, the 'spontaneous' struggles of the peasantry require centralization through the traditional Western 'class organizations' of trade union and political party. Their response has been to promote forums like the Peasant Confederation of Peru (CCP). Although this organization has genuinely attempted to learn from local mobilizations and provide a venue in which lessons can be passed on (cf. García-Sayán 1982: 195), the fact that it lacks even the most feeble ties with vast areas of the Peruvian Andes means that in practice it has often served more as a recruiting ground for Leninist sects than as a truly organic out-growth of the commoners' existence as a class (see Montoya 1982: 283–7). The failure of the CCP's attempts to orchestrate and coordi-nate land occupations during the late 1970s seems to bear consider-able relation to its remoteness to commoner reality (see Labrousse 1985: 98). Conversely, Andean ritual forms appear to have helped commoners maintain their own agenda despite repeated attempts of the organized left to take over their political movements.

With the return of Peru to formal democracy in 1980, the elected right-wing government was met with a guerrilla campaign led by the Maoist party, *Sendero Luminoso* (Shining Path). This confrontaion quickly led to militarization of the Department of Ayacucho, and neighbouring areas of Huancavelica and Apurímac, including, sporad-ically, the Antabamba Valley.[4] The conflict deepened and spread to other areas of Peru in 1985, and has involved massive human rights violations (primarily by Peruvian counter-insurgency forces), includ-ing the death of nearly 30,000 people at the time of writing, the major-ity of them non-combatant commoners. Although the 'armed struggle' was never a focus of my research, it formed an important backdrop against which it was carried out, and a significant reason to study commoner traditions of political action. The autonomy of peas-ant movements from the organized left during the period 1956–79 in Peru, and their truly popular character, is best seen in the distinctive cultural forms that they took. By the same token, the absence of any-thing resembling these forms in the post-1980 armed struggle is the true measure of the political usurpation that *Sendero* has committed against commoners. There is no doubt that it represents a new, and much more devastating, phase in the ongoing attempts of the Leninist 'vanguard' to hijack commoner politics. Although a detailed analysis of *Sendero Luminoso* is beyond the scope of this book,[5] several specific comments are in order.

First, it is a well-documented fact that the origins of *Sendero Luminoso* were in the San Cristóbal de Huamanga National University of Ayacu-cho (see Labrousse 1985: 111–14; Degregori 1990). Most of its mili-tants in the early phases of the armed struggle came from the petty bourgeoisie of Ayacucho and the notability of the rural towns in the university's catchment area of the Departments of Huancavelica, Ayacucho, and Apurímac. *Sendero* also recruited successfully among the many students from such backgrounds who were denied post-sec-ondary education by the limited capacity of the university system (see

Labrousse 1985: 115). The origins of *Sendero* in the school system are evident in many ways, some of which connect with this ethnography. For example, the red flag rituals that *Sendero* militants perform in jail would be at home in any rural school and, above all, in the *Fiestas Patrias* discussed in Chapter 3. The ritualized, formulaic quality of 'Gonzalo thought,' the ideology that *Sendero* presents as the science of armed struggle, also reflects the rote learning and unquestioned deference to the teacher that prevail in most rural schools. Stylistically and organizationally, *Sendero* is a direct outgrowth of the rural education system and, by extension, of notable culture in small Andean towns. However, *Sendero* also represents a crisis in education, and the unrealistic hope that it could completely transform rural society away from *gamonalismo*. As the national economy became increasingly unable to absorb educated provincial youth, the process of social reconstruction that had taken place in previous decades was frustrated, and even began to reverse itself. Degregori (1989, 1990: 211–17) has astutely analysed *Sendero*'s theatrical mass killing of commoners as a kind of neo-*gamonalismo*. It is only from the class position of the notability that *Sendero* could assume an inalienable right to politically represent commoners, and subject them to such 'disciplinary measures.'

From the standpoint of rural class relations, *Sendero Luminoso* is not a revolutionary movement, but a reversion to the myth of the conquest. Like the *gamonales* before them, *Sendero* militants discover their ultra-revolutionary identity through redemptive violence. This violence was always implicit in the myth of the conquest, but now it is explicit in 'Gonzalo thought,' the science of armed struggle. The war between *Sendero* and the government is a not a 'peasant war' of commoners against the *misti* state, nor is it an outbreak of 'Andean millenarianism' (see Poole and Rénique 1991). If it were, we would see some continuity with the commoner traditions of political mobilization discussed above. There is no mistaking that *Sendero*'s program derives from the rituals of the school, and not those of the field. Cultural expression identifies the social interests at stake in the current war in Peru. Furthermore, the intensity of this war shows just how much the neo-*gamonales* of *Sendero* will sacrifice to assert the power of a mode of expression they learned in school. As in the myth of the conquest, commoners are the main scapegoats in the current war between *Sendero* and the army. They continue to represent an inferior other whose degradation and slaughter ritually constitutes a separate and more powerful 'racial' identity for their violators. The crisis that drives this conflict is primarily about how to maintain 'racial' distinction in a pauperized economy: It is not a crisis of commoner culture or its representation by anthropologists, as some have suggested (e.g., Starn 1991; Mayer 1991). Far from proving that cultural difference and cultural analysis are obsolete, this war shows how fundamental they remain.

By the second half of the 1980s, *Sendero*'s membership and arenas of activity were increasingly less confined to the rural Andes. Nonetheless, the class structure of small Andean towns like Huaquirca remains key to understanding why such a violent political movement should arise out of the highland school system. Against this backdrop of renewed *gamonal* violence, it becomes abundantly clear why commoners have consistently used their regulative rituals to buttress and extend the influence of national law, instead of challenging it. Given their long historical experience of violent, extra-legal rule, 'revolution' looks decidedly like the bad old days. By backing a strong central state, and subordinating their own regulative framework to it, commoners have attempted to distance themselves from *gamonal* violence. Nonetheless, the imagery of death and sacrifice pervades their rituals. Although these ritual idioms have a long genealogy in Andean culture and, therefore, cannot be explained solely with reference to the present, they must tell us something about commoners' experience of the modern era; otherwise, they would not have persisted into it. Among other things, the imagery of death registers a highly ambivalent experience of work as both a limited affirmation of equality and a loss of life, whereas the practice of sacrifice confirms a bloody experience of property and political power. There can be no doubt that these cultural forms accurately and insightfully portray the starker realities of commoner life. Because death and sacrifice remain agrarian idioms, however, they also express the hope of winning a degree of prosperity and security from a history of violent domination. If, for the time being, this attempt has failed, then it only shows that the nation-state and its social order cannot be maintained exclusively from below forever. Although commoners have been attacked (and in some places, decimated) during Peru's dirty war, their way of life has not been discredited by it. Can the same be said of the schools?

Epilogue

The most basic thing I hope to have shown in this book is that the rituals of the annual cycle in Huaquirca are more than so much 'ethnic' folklore. When restored to their practical context, these rituals can tell us much about politics and economics as commoners practise and experience them. Although this Andean understanding of political economy differs from our own in many important ways, it is not so totally alien as to appear incoherent or defy translation. In its own way, Andean culture distinguishes social practices and relationships that are very comparable to labour, property, and political power in our own society. Furthermore, it creates a configuration of hierarchical relations among them that gives rise to our familiar reality of class. It is not necessary to deploy Western analytical categories, such as 'surplus labour,' to discuss class in the Andes, since it is constructed through local notions of *ayni*, sacrifice, and the myth of the conquest, which are the true keys to the social relations in question. Thus, I join E.P. Thompson in affirming the importance of culturally constructed experience in discussing class formation, but do not oppose this to a 'structural' understanding of class, since the 'structures' in question come from Andean ethnography, not academic sociology or primers on 'the basic concepts of historical materialism.' Not only is it ethnographically necessary to proceed through local categories, but this also shortens the leap into discussions of actual political conduct, since we can treat a figure like the mountain spirit as an integral part of the social relations under negotiation, and not just an 'ideology' that is extrinsic to them. Finally, this interpretive approach allows a greater appreciation of commoners as agents in Andean history, since it shows how, in their rituals, commoners have created not a narrow peasant utopia, but a regulative framework that sustains the national life of Peru.

Notes

Preface

1 See also Stein (1961: 227), Núñez del Prado and Bonino Nievez (1969: 59–60), Bourricaud (1970: 193), Flores (1974: 189), Malengreau (1974: 187), Isbell (1978: 73), Ossio (1978a: 17), and Montoya (1980: 202–3).

2 Fonseca (1974: 88) notes the asymmetric nature of *mink'a*, and its potentially exploitative character has been mentioned by Carter (1964: 49), Fonseca (1974: 91), Mayer (1974: 47), Malengreau (1980: 515), Orlove (1980: 118), and Sánchez (1982: 182).

3 See also Stein (1961: 230), Arguedas (1968: 335), Mayer (1970: 120), Montoya, Silveira, and Lindoso (1979: 26), and Montoya (1980: 68).

4 See also Adams (1959: 83), Stein (1961: 232), Fuenzalida (1970a: 40), Isbell (1978: 83), Ossio (1978a: 18), Montoya, Silveira, and Lindoso (1979: 26), and Montoya (1980: 68).

5 See also Stein (1961: 232), Quispe (1969: 55), Earls (1970: 76), Fuenzalida (1970a: 53), Flores (1974: 191), and Ossio (1978a: 22).

Chapter One: Introduction

1 See Mayer and Zamalloa (1974: 79), Brush (1977a: 140–1), Guillet (1979: 153–7), and Sánchez (1982: 167).

2 The following authors have noted the symmetric and egalitarian nature of *ayni*: Núñez del Prado (1972: 136), Fioravanti (1973: 122), Fonseca (1974: 87–8), and Malengreau (1974: 185). This is clearly an important reason why *ayni* is not practised between notables and commoners, and why it so strongly defines the latter as a group.

3 This is particularly important to note in the case of Andean 'wage labour,' whose peculiarity, from a comparative perspective, is that the host always provides the worker with food and drink, as in any Andean work party, a point that Stein (1961: 110), Fioravanti (1973: 123), Brush (1977b: 106), and Malengreau (1980: 506) have all noted. Thus, the wage does not represent the cost of the reproduction of labour power, as it would in a truly capitalist economy.

4 Unlike most ethnographers of the Andes, I do not treat wage labour and the use of money as a distinctive feature whose absence defines all other Andean relations of production (negatively) as 'reciprocity.' Rather, I argue that wage labour is encompassed by, and subordinated to, the more properly Andean axis of *ayni* and *mink'a*.

5 The crucial issue here is whether the rituals in question are merely empty conventional forms or whether they have a more intrinsic connection to the process of class formation. Nash certainly does not demonstrate that the symbolic details of the rites she describes have any bearing on matters of political economy. In the end, she offers little more than the functionalist argument that ritual promotes work force solidarity at the point of production (Nash 1979: 159, 161). Why this solidarity should be achieved through ritual, specifically sacrifice, and have an insurrectionary character instead of a corporate leaning is not explained. By emphasizing the 'semiological unity' and 'transformational continuity' of the miners' sacrifices with those of the peasantry, Platt (1983: 48) comes some of the distance towards meeting these objections, but again falls short of demonstrating any real connection between these rites and the issues involved in class formation.

6 See Stein (1961: 226), Bourricaud (1970: 187), Mayer (1970: 114, 124), Isbell (1978: 20), and Skar (1982: 75, 224).

7 See Urbano (1976: 146–8), van den Berghe and Primov (1977: 127), Montoya (1982: 273), and Skar (1982: 76).

8 See (Isbell 1978: 10), Ossio (1978a: 21), Albó (1979: 484), Harris (1980: 86), and Rasnake (1988: 44).

9 Most ethnographers of rural Andean society agree that class is a purely economic reality associated with the market (e.g., van den Berghe 1974a: 129, 1974b: 140; Isbell 1978: 22; Montoya, Silveira, and Lindoso 1979: 153). Around this Weberian mean, there may be the occasional oscillation towards a more Marxist emphasis on the relations of production (e.g., van den Berghe 1974a: 121, 125; van den Berghe and Primov 1977: 4) or an American 'stratification' theory emphasis on education (e.g., van den Berghe and Primov 1977: 136, 259), but in general, the underlying economism is left intact.

10 Having learned much from Thompson on this and other points, I should
   also note where I disagree with him. First of all, he still sees class formation
   as something that begins with an economically determined raw experience
   of class-in-itself, which is subsequently transformed into the consciousness
   of class-for-itself as people realize what their situation is, and come to
   define themselves 'in class ways' (see Thompson 1963: 11, 1978a: 147,
   1978b: 298–9, 1978c: 20). This, along with his related willingness to negotiate with the formula that 'social being determines social consciousness'
   (Thompson 1978c: 17, 20), clearly tends to reduce class formation to a
   kind of quiz question with a 'correct' answer, despite his protestations to
   the contrary (Thompson 1978a: 150). Behind this lies a refusal to let go of
   the structural definitions of class he has so eloquently criticized, and a
   refusal to allow that the very political economic facts that class revolves
   around might already be culturally constructed from the very beginning,
   instead of as a revolutionary afterthought (cf. Sewell 1990). To be fair, in
   his practice as an historian, Thompson (1978a: 149–50, 1978b: 276, 356,
   1978c: 20–1) certainly does provide us with some wonderfully incisive
   analysis of how 'the relations of production' can become an object of cultural struggle, not a primitive point of departure, and this occasionally carries over into his theoretical pronouncements. In spite of what his
   'Marxist' critics often maintain, however, and perhaps because of their
   endless accusations of 'culturalism,' Thompson tends to take a very orthodox position on the economic point of departure for the process of class
   formation, and generally confines the role of culture to determining how
   such structurally generated experiences will be handled at the level of
   political action (cf. Meiksins Wood 1982). In short, Thompson initiates a
   break with a causal, economic determinist view of class, and a move
   towards a more interpretive position, but he is reluctant to complete
   either, at least as a theoretician. I agree with Sewell (1990: 69) that what is
   missing here is a greater emphasis on class discourse and its ability to selec-
   tively shape experience. The 'culturalist' tone of this study is intended to
   address that problem.

Chapter Two: 'Race,' Property, and Community

1 See the '*Expediente Sobre la Completa Desmoralización Eclesiástica en Aymaraes*,'
   1841, Archivo Arzobispal del Cusco, and Raimondi's (1874: 226) description of ruined churches in Totora-Oropeza. Note that a priest is mentioned
   as a resident of Huaquirca in the 1838 document '*Provincia de Aymaraes-
   Matrícula de los Individuos Poseedores de las Tierras Soberantes de Comunidades
   ...*,' Fondo de Tesorería Fiscal, Aymaraes Doc. 4, Archivo Departamental

del Cusco, but fails to appear in a similar document from 1872 (*'Marjesi de los Terrenos Soberantes de Comunidad de la Provincia de Aymaraes ...,'* Fondo de Tesorería Fiscal, Aymaraes Doc. 8, Archivo Departamental del Cusco).

2 This neighbourhood is marked by a fierce rivalry between two surname groups, the Huachacas and the Pumacayllos. Perhaps the most important reason for the emergence of Barrio Alto as an alternative name for the neighbourhood was that the Pumacayllos could not stand it bearing the name of their foes. Nonetheless, the name Huachacayllo does seem to be patterned on Pumacayllo, and my guess is that it took hold as the dispute between these families grew, perhaps as late as the turn of this century, and is not a direct outgrowth of the pre-Columbian *ayllu* form. A colonial census from 1689 does mention an *ayllu* named after D. Martín Vachaca, a *kuraka*, but it contained only a few Huachacas within it (see Villanueva 1982: 407–8), whereas many others were scattered throughout the remaining six *ayllus* that existed in Huaquirca at that time. Whatever these *ayllus* were, they were clearly not groups united on the basis of surnames. That two of these *ayllus*, including one named after D. Martín Huachaca, were also present in the neighbouring town of Matara (Villanueva 1982: 392–3) shows that they were not necessarily localized groups either. On the basis of this information alone, direct historical transmission of the *ayllu* form can be ruled out as the process by which this neighbourhood came to exist. It is possible that the one Pumacayllo mentioned in the 1689 census (Villanueva 1982: 412) may have been the first in the area, since he was classified as an *Indio Forastero* ('Foreign Indian,' a category of tribute collection that admittedly was sometimes more accurate about the amount of land held by an individual than their place of origin). In any case, one Pumacayllo would hardly have been in a position to feud with scores of Huachacas, so this phenomenon must have developed later. Even as late as 1826, there were no males bearing the surname Pumacayllo in Huaquirca (see *'Aymaraes de Indígenas 1826,'* Fondo de Tesorería Fiscal, Aymaraes Doc. 1, Archivo Departamental del Cusco). In all probability, this rivalry, whose origins many people in Huaquirca would place in time immemorial, is a development of the nineteenth century.

3 In the 1689 census, an Ayllo Chambini is mentioned, but it did not include any Aiquipas (Villanueva 1982: 409–11), while the latter were concentrated in an *ayllu* bearing the Spanish name Guzmán (Villanueva 1982: 399–401). Since the Ayllo Chambini may not have been a localized group corresponding to the modern neighbourhood of Champine, it is still quite possible that some or all of the Aiquipas may have lived in this area, but the chances are that it was the eighteenth century land grant from Zola y Castillo that

brought about their residence here. Once again, the relation between pre-Columbian *ayllus* and modern neighbourhoods appears to be at best a weak one.

4 This pattern has been reported by Adams (1959: 87), Fuenzalida (1970a: 53), Isbell (1978: 71), Ossio (1978a: 10), and Fioravanti-Molinié (1986: 349).

5 Comparison with other ethnographies is difficult here because most either do not give figures, or fail to distinguish between cultivated land in the valley and that in the lower *puna*.

6 Stein (1961: 37) mentions domestic holdings consisting of over twelve parcels and Isbell (1978: 72) gives a range of up to fifteen to twenty. This extreme fragmentation probably reflects the predominance of inheritance over the purchase of land, unlike the situation in Huaquirca.

7 In other areas, investigators have reported landholdings that were more differentiated than those I observed in Huaquirca (e.g., Fioravanti 1973: 122; Isbell 1978: 51, 72; Montoya, Silveira, and Lindoso 1979: 63; Montoya 1980: 54). Again, I must note that the problem with these studies is that they do not specify what sort of land, under what sort of tenure and what sort of use, is included in these figures: distinctions that this chapter will show to be of considerable significance.

8 Consider the hypothetical case of two parental households, each with 0.75 ha of land on the eve of a marriage between their children. If each were to cede 0.25 ha to help establish their children in an independent household, the resulting three domestic groups would each have 0.5 ha, at best the bare minimum necessary for autonomous existence. Any remaining children would receive no land at all in their *dotaciónes*. What this situation seems to indicate is that domestic holdings are less a matter of the number of mouths to feed (since this does not change significantly until the new couple has older children) than of the expenses of running an autonomous household, such as sponsoring work parties. It is not enough to have a harvest that simply feeds household members, since the very process of agricultural labour that produces the harvest demands a significant redistribution of domestic food supplies from those who sponsor work parties to those who work in them. If, true to the letter of *ayni*, there were equivalent exchanges of labour days, the overall effect would be one of cancellation, but this is precisely what notables refuse to do, which means that their share of the agricultural work in Huaquirca is shifted en bloc to the commoners, who will work on other people's land. As we will see, those commoners who manage to run an independent household are already well along in avoiding the need to work for the notables. Some of these com-

moners receive more days of labour than they give, and give more food and drink than they receive, in a system of generalized exchange that keeps poor commoners from starving, and rich commoners from completely renouncing all labour on other people's property, as the notables have. It is in this sense that running an 'autonomous' household implies a complex relation to a broader community, one that cannot be reduced to ratios between individuals and amounts of land among affines.

9 Here, calculations must proceed (somewhat artificially) based on the fact that small amounts of maize were bought and sold within Huaquirca during 1982 at a rate of S/. 3000 per *arroba* (11.5 kg), mostly to assuage the hunger of the shopkeepers from Puno. Given that the harvest from an average sized valley holding in a normal year is approximately 1500 to 1800 kg of maize, its theoretical monetary worth would be about S/. 390,000 to S/. 470,000 per year before expenses, whose monetary calculation would be no less problematic. Compare this to the annual rent of S/. 5000 and selling price of S/. 500,000 that I know was paid for one such field in 1982, and the obvious is underscored: the buying and selling of land does not take place under market conditions (cf. Ossio 1983: 35). Previous studies, in their eagerness to demonstrate capitalist penetration, have reported a long-standing 'market' in valley lands without bothering to undertake this sort of calculation, and are almost certainly misleading (e.g., Montoya, Silveira, and Lindoso 1979: 25). Since those who rented or sold their land had, in every case I knew of, migrated from Huaquirca to an urban centre, the relatively small payments they received (in market terms) might be understood as a compromise between two generally recognized principles that conflict in the case of migrants: on the one hand, use rights to valley land are supposed to be exclusive; on the other, they are supposed to be tied to residence in Huaquirca. The various rights and restrictions that comprise property in this zone will be discussed in the text. What is important for now is that the buying and selling of land does not necessarily indicate the sort of unfettered, absolute right of property that capitalism tends to promote and presuppose.

10 Terms varied from S/. 10,000 to S/. 40,000 per year during my residence in Huaquirca.

11 This theft does not necessarily work against the notables in the long run, and could even be seen as part of a structural pattern that keeps herders dependent on their patrons. A particularly revealing example concerns a *vaquero* who stole and butchered the cow of the mother-in-law of his patron's brother. She discovered him trying to bury the hide and went immediately to her son-in-law's brother, who had no choice but to repay

the damage. The amount, however, was used to extend the *vaquero*'s period of servitude for another few years, which would, in turn, aggravate the motivation to steal further. Since herders are tied to a particular locality by their responsibilities, and are not professional rustlers with networks of *compadres* spanning several valleys, they cannot easily get rid of stolen animals, and are very likely to get caught. Another example concerns a young commoner who broke into a store in Huachacayllo and made off with a large tin of cane alcohol, only to pass out in the street shortly afterwards, still clutching the incriminating evidence. After a few days in jail, the justice of the peace offered to pay the cost of the alcohol to the shopkeeper in return for a year of the commoner's service on his estate in the *puna*, an offer that the offender could not refuse. Therefore, theft could be seen as a recruitment mechanism for debt peonage. In discussing theft by commoners, however, I would not want to deny that some notables are involved in animal rustling, which seems quite probable in the Antabamba region, and has been reported elsewhere as a part of the overall complex of *gamonalismo* (Skar 1982: 246; Poole 1988).

12 An extreme case involves a young man from the *puna* who received no pre-inheritance from his parents when he married the daughter (and oldest child) of a relatively wealthy commoner from Ñapaña, one of the few who owns land in both the valley and the *puna* like the notables. Probably as a result of the extreme disparity of wealth between these two families, the young couple went off to tend her father's sheep and alpacas in the *puna*. This situation differs from servitude to the notables only in the relatively liberal amount of valley produce they receive from her parents, and a yearly payment in animals instead of cash, which might one day serve to establish an independent household. This yearly payment was beginning to look slightly theoretical, however, given that no animals had been turned over after three years' service.

13 This proviso has occasionally been extended to the occupation and reappropriation of unused land left by migrants. During my residence in Huaquirca, there was at least one case of a resident using a piece of valley land owned by a migrant whose kin were unable or unwilling to make the squatter pay rent. This had been going on for three years, and I heard people say of the squatter: 'It's almost his already.' Yet the ultimate weakness of these corporate restrictions on individual tenure, and related notions that ownership rights must be asserted through residence and labour, is demonstrated by the failure of the land occupations of 1960 (described in the text), which effectively established that relatively powerful commoners have the right to exclude others from cultivating land that they own, but

do not bother to cultivate themselves. Thus, in Huaquirca today, where access to valley land is an acute problem for many young commoners, there are abandoned terraces used only for grazing during the dry season.

14 This same situation has been noted elsewhere in the Andes by Brush (1977b: 116), Isbell (1978: 49), Montoya, Silveira, and Lindoso (1979: 90), Montoya (1980: 292), and Skar (1982: 163). Prior to expansion of the local state in the Antabamba Valley during the past few decades, when there was virtually no regular salaried work to be had, cattle were also the principal source of cash income for the notables, and were the main factor in their economic differentiation from the commoners. Several notable house-holds still rely on the sale of cattle for most of their income.

15 Considerations such as these make the notion that the Andean community is an autonomous, self-determining entity that chooses not to participate in the market (e.g., Isbell 1978: 19, 21, 168) as inaccurate as the opposing view, criticized in note 9 above, that there is a 'market' in land to be found there. Surely, the point is that the commodity form plays a subordinate role in the organization of rural Andean society, not that it is absent. Romantic positions, such as that adopted by Isbell (1978), reflect the extreme economism of dependency theory in that both attribute an unwarranted significance to relatively isolated acts of commodity exchange.

16 This property is named Huaylla-Huaylla, and consists of 5.15 ha. It is enclosed and irrigated by the canal bearing the same name as the estate, a highly anomalous practice on land at this altitude (4000 m). This estate was owned by a notable, but was part of the only expropriation of land that took place in Huaquirca during the agrarian reform of 1969–75. The land had been bought in 1944 from seven individuals, all of whom must have sold their *laymi* holdings in the sector from which the estate was carved. On being returned to communal tenure by the expropriation of 1975, this land was not reintegrated into the *laymi* system, but lay fallow until 1982, when it was effectively parcelized, each commoner receiving a minute amount of land to cultivate.

17 Huaquirca's rich pasturelands have always been coveted by notables from Antabamba in particular. Not only do a few of them still have *estancias* in the remote *puna* of Huaquirca (around Mt Supayco, the ritual significance of which will be discussed in Chapter 7) but some will even turn their cattle loose in Huaquirca's communal grazing lands, and claim the right to pay the Peasant Community of Huaquirca for access to them. Similar arrange-ments have been reported elsewhere (Montoya 1980: 239). Although the Community seemed to feel that this was an infringement, it did not refuse

this forced rental of its pastures, so this practice may have some customary legitimacy.

18 The most important reason why the law cannot be applied is that it assumes the existence of a communal authority with a mandate to redistribute all land under its jurisdiction as if it were *laymi* land. Although there are persistent rumours of communities that still have annual redistributions of land, or did until recently (e.g., Arguedas 1968: 331; Fuenzalida 1970b: 238–9; Malengreau 1980: 533–4), what is never specified is what sort of land. There are no reports that specify a communal redistribution of valley land, and without such an arrangement, rental and sale become virtually the only way of coordinating the developmental cycles of the ensemble of domestic groups in the community, given the inadequacy of inheritance mentioned in note 8 above. To suppress the sale and rental of land in Huaquirca would also be to suppress the developmental cycle of its domestic groups; thus, nobody has ever attempted to apply the law.

19 The general pattern of privatized valley land and communal access to the grazing lands of the *puna* has been reported by Malengreau (1974: 179) and Isbell (1978: 38), whereas Matos Mar (1964: 73, 119) and Ossio (1983: 46) speak of private agricultural use right in general, without distinguishing between valley and *laymi* tenure. Nonetheless, Ossio (1983: 47) reports similar use of enclosure to define traditional 'private' property and notes that its absence in the fallow potato fields is taken as an indication of communal control. Skar (1982: 144) reports that such enclosed parcels of valley land are called *michkas*. Montoya (1980: 53, 294) notes the enclosure of valley land in Puquio, and along the banks of the Pampas, Pachachaca, and Apurímac Rivers. Arguedas (1968: 202–3, 330, 332) reports the retention of collective grazing rights to the stubble left from the harvest on definitively parcelized valley land, and that the latter prevails in Puquio and the Andes in general. All of this seems to concur with what I have described for Huaquirca. Although Mishkin (1964: 144–6) reports the conversion of '*ejido*' (communal grazing land) into private agricultural land in the community of Kauri, he presents this as a deviation from the general pattern in the area, which also seems to conform to the model given here.

20 In this regard, Fuenzalida (1970a: 71) is entirely right to argue that the archaism of the 'Indian' is, in fact, largely a Hispanic archaism. Furthermore, one could suggest that modern Andean 'Indians' are in this sense closer to the Iberian peasantry than to their pre-Columbian ancestors (Stein 1961: 12), a point developed at length by Arguedas (1968) in a pro-

vocative study that subsequent 'ethnicity' theory has been compelled to ignore.

21 This is particularly the case when an opposition party controls the district, as was the case with the United Left during my residence in Huaquirca. Officials of Popular Cooperation, the agency in charge of labour tribute projects for the ruling Popular Action party, continually visited Huaquirca to inspect and harass local officials, and to accuse them of 'communism.' Out of fear that these charges would be boosted to 'terrorism' (often as good as a death sentence in the political climate of the time), community and district officials in Huaquirca ended up carrying out government tributary policy virtually to the same degree as was the case elsewhere.

22 During the Velasco period (1969–75), commoners were appointed to positions such as mayor and governor for the first time. In the municipal elections of 1981, several commoners ran for alderman, some successfully, but none for mayor. It was widely believed that the notable who won the election did so not because the commoners were convinced by the electoral program of the United Left, but because he was perceived to be the least 'abusive' of the available alternatives, an analysis that I support. In short, there still seems to be a feeling among the commoners that the post of mayor is not to be occupied by them, despite their recognition that they have an interest in who does occupy it.

23 See Fuenzalida (1970b: 224, 230–1), Grondín (1978: 21–2), and Platt (1982: 40–1). It remains to be seen exactly what this 'communal' land tenure consisted of at various times and places. In Huaquirca, for instance, a corporate title to communal land was issued by Zola y Castillo at some point in his long period of service (1720–85). However, this same colonial official granted the Aiquipas 'private' title to the lands of Lucrepampa. Furthermore, a document from 1794 lists a number of '*veci-nos*' of Huaquirca and their respective '*haciendas*,' most of which fall inside of what should strictly speaking have been communal land (see '*Expediente relativo a las fianzas q^{e}. debe dar el subdelegado del Par^{do}. de Ayma-raes D. Santiago Noboa, del R^{l}. Ramo de las Mitas de Guancavelica de su cargo*,' Archivo Departamental del Cusco, Intendencias, Gobierno, Legajo 142, 1794). This suggests something much more like the pattern I have described for the present, namely a modified form of traditional Spanish tenure. Therefore, the communality of these lands would only have been partial, and would have referred at least as much to the notional protection from the formation of true *haciendas* as it would to the actual tenure involved, which even at this point included exclusive right to small tracts (the '*haciendas*' of the document).

24 See Stein (1961: 189–90), Fuenzalida (1970b: 230), Davies (1974), and Isbell (1978: 171).

25 The list of slightly over 200 *comuneros* in Huaquirca includes the names of all males eighteen years of age or older, plus all women who run households without a man. Such women are only expected to work on certain occasions, for example, during canal cleaning (see Chapter 3), but are present at communal assemblies to represent the interests of their households. This indicates that *comunero* status is based on a number of criteria (i.e., masculinity, age, household representation) that need not all coincide to determine membership.

26 The rationale for cementing canals is to prevent water loss through seepage, but since the cement is simply poured into the existing canal, there is also a considerable reduction in volume, and some claim that less water arrives as a result. There are additional drawbacks: the 1982 agricultural season began with torrential rains and a landslide that destroyed a cemented section of a canal. This was followed by a drought when water from the canal in question was sorely missed during the month and a half that it took to solicit cement from the government and repair the damage. It became abundantly clear during this episode that Huaquirca no longer had effective control over the cemented canal, and it now depends on the state in a way that it did not when the canal remained in its previous 'rustic' condition. As for the reservoirs, they are much better regarded by those who criticize cement canals, but there were not enough of them to stop the drought of 1982–3 from ruining ninety per cent of Huaquirca's maize crop. One of the two reservoirs that had been completed when I was doing my research, after thousands of hours of unpaid labour, was already beginning to crack due to a design fault, and was never really used from the time it was built.

27 Something of the same notion was still in force in 1982, when a huge work party of forty-five people was assembled to sow the governor's maize fields. Other tasks in his fields were not so massively attended, however, so I must conclude that this large work party was an exceptional event related at least as much to the beginning of the agricultural year as the coercive power of the office in question.

28 Some commoners claim that the teachers' use of wages and increased amounts of cane alcohol and coca to attract workers have escalated the amount of these commodities that everyone has to provide to sponsor a work party. Although I do not think that labour recruitment in Huaquirca is a matter of who pays the most on an open market, there does seem to be some truth to the notion that these commodities have displaced home-

made food and drink to a certain extent as part of the immediate consumption during the working day that figures in all Andean relations of production. This is based on the accounts of older commoners who would have been working in the fields prior to the expansion of salaried work in the local schools, but I was unable to get a systematic picture of what previous standards had been (except that there was more food served in the fields), or what other factors might have entered into the changes that took place.

Chapter Three: Aesthetics and Politics in the Rituals of the Dry Season

1 People in Huaquirca translated *qatay* into Spanish as *yerno* (daughter's husband), and used the Spanish term *cuñado* for sister's husband even when speaking Quechua. In most areas of the Andes, however, *qatay* and its equivalents in the Ayacucho and Wanka dialects of Quechua (*masa/masha*) designate both daughter's husband and sister's husband, and might be better glossed as 'wife-receiver' (cf. Earls 1970: 101; Custred 1977: 123; Webster 1977: 39, 1981: 620; Isbell 1978: 100; Ossio 1980: 250–1; Skar 1982: 192). The focus of the term *qatay* on DH has also been reported by Quispe (1969: 14), and probably uses generational seniority to stress the superiority of wife-givers over wife-takers (see Albó and Mamani 1980: 324), although this is far from absolute. In any case, the constant use of *qatay* in ritual contexts to refer to 'outsiders' who perform essential services suggests that the term's fundamental function is to classify men as non-kin.

2 Nonetheless, Mayer (1977: 74) reports a strict, long-term calculation of labour debts and credits in house rethatching, which suggests the relations of *ayni* that others have mentioned for this task (see Adams 1959: 124; Bourricaud 1970: 191; Isbell 1978: 168). Since many of the participants in the house rethatchings that I observed had houses with tile roofs, a strict reciprocation of the same service by the sponsors on the model of *ayni* would be impossible; nor, given the life span of thatched roofs in the area, did people seem to think it possible to maintain relations of calculated equality over this labour process. Regional differences are undoubtedly involved here, but perhaps some of the ambiguity over what relations of production prevail in house rethatching are the result of its transitional position between periods of private appropriation and collective production, which are characterized by *mink'a* and *ayni* respectively. In some cases, house rethatching is said to take place on the basis of *yanapa* (Aranguren Paz 1975: 122) or *voluntad* (Mayer 1977: 69), intermediate forms where work is remunerated by consumption during the working day, as well as by an ill-defined, notional obligation on the part of the sponsor to reciprocate

somehow in the future. In my experience, these secondary forms tend to be invoked when neither the hierarchy of *mink'a* nor the egalitarianism of *ayni* can be directly and unproblematically proclaimed.

3 Elsewhere the obligations of those thus classified are much greater (see Arguedas 1968: 106; Fonseca 1974: 102–3; Mayer 1977: 71–2). In some areas, the situation is further complicated by a set of customary obligations for those classified as *lumtshuy* (or in Cusco dialect, *qhachun*), a term that designates female affines (Mayer 1977: 69–71) but has a tendency to focus on the daughter-in-law (Fonseca 1974: 99) and is thus the female equivalent of *qatay* or *masha*. For the purposes of house rethatching, however, male consanguines of the sponsors will be classified as *lumtshuys*, that is, in terms of the 'daughters-in-law' they have married, whereas female consanguines will be classified as *mashas* on a similar basis (Mayer 1977: 71–2). This suggests a transformation of the *masha/qatay* category away from 'male affine' and towards 'wife-taking group,' and that of *lumtshuy/qhachun* away from 'female affine' and towards 'wife-giving group,' an interpretation of these terms that Skar (1982: 192) and Webster (1977: 39) have proposed. Generally, the notion of 'wife-giver' seems to be designated by the Quechua term *kaka*, however. Nonetheless, it is the extreme malleability of Quechua affinal terminology that is most striking: the same terms can express a symmetric division between male and female affines at one moment and a hierarchical dominance of wife-givers over wife-takers at another.

4 Mayer (1977: 69) has suggested that house rethatching is ideally connected with marriage, and several other ethnographers have suggested that marriages involve the construction of a house as one of a series of acts that signify the union of a couple (Stein 1961: 71, 122; Buechler and Buechler 1971: 80–2; Palacios Ríos 1977: 100). There are also reports that most marriages in certain localities are confined to the period between 3 May and 8 September (Buechler and Buechler 1971: 68; Buechler 1980: 40), further suggesting an overlap between marriage and the dry season. Skar (1982: 209), however, observes that marriages are specifically prohibited in August because of malevolent winds and the imminence of the sowing. No marriages took place in Huaquirca during my stay there, nor was I able to discover if marriage is prescribed or prohibited there during particular periods of the year. Only the predominance of conjugal imagery in the main rites of the dry season, the *t'inkas* (see Chapter 7) and those of house rethatching, suggest that marriage might correspond to this part of the year, and I would not want to suggest that this association is anything more than categorical.

5 A number of authors have stressed the subordinate status of the 'son-in-law' in a manner that I find somewhat one-sided (see, for example, Earls 1970: 80; Webster 1973: 124; Isbell 1978: 114, 174; Malengreau 1980: 529; Ossio 1980: 367; Skar 1982: 192; Allen 1988: 93). As Harris (1986: 268–9) has argued, 'wife-takers' may actually enjoy a superior status to 'wife-givers,' despite the many services they owe them.

6 Here, we see how *mink'a* creates a social boundary not only by rigidifying the relation between worker and patron in the direction of class, but also by compounding this with a refusal of intermarriage. Conversely, *ayni* implies not only the generalized exchange of food and labour in the short term, but also that of spouses and property in the long term.

7 See Stein (1961: 188, 269–70), Palomino (1968: 66), Quispe (1969: 89), Urbano (1974: 44–5), Brush (1977b: 165–6), Isbell (1978: 145–7, 199), Ossio (1978: 379), and Skar (1982: 232).

8 See Fonseca (1974: 102), Mayer (1977: 72), Flores (1979: 50), and Buechler (1980: 126).

9 The connection between house and mountain spirits is dramatized in a particularly interesting way when a couple lays the foundations for a new house or occupies an already existing one for the first time. Here, it is customary for them to make particularly lavish sacrificial offerings of the sort to be found in the *t'inkas*, which centre of the legitimation of property (cf. Quispe 1969: 102), and are generally performed during the period of private appropriation leading up to the house rethatching. It is culturally appropriate to recapitulate the rites associated with private appropriation in the annual cycle at this point because the household in question is inaugurating the most central manifestation of its existence as a property-holding group: its house. In this way, a strategic rite from the annual cycle is momentarily transposed onto the developmental cycle of domestic groups, and used to underline the connection between houses and property in Andean culture. A particularly clear case of how the house spirit is metaphorically constructed on the model of the mountain involves the use of the title *condor mamani* (condor-falcon) to refer to the house spirit (see Buechler 1980: 126, Buechler and Buechler 1971: 81). This term also refers to two birds that are common embodiments of the mountain spirits and even give them their names in certain areas (for example, *wamaní* in Ayacucho). Generally, however, the house spirits should probably be seen as *pachamamas*, deities who rank lower than mountain spirits, and occur wherever there is habitation or cultivation (cf. Roel Pineda 1965: 28; Platt 1986: 238; Allen 1988: 44) or *lugarniyoq* ('place-owners,' see Oblitas Poblete 1978: 56, 114; Martínez 1983: 91). Tschopik (1951: 190–2), in what is probably

still one of the most careful works on the subject, puts house spirits at the bottom end of a hierarchy that includes the spirits mentioned above. Reports of *churos*, facilities for the interment of offerings to the house spirits (Matos Mar 1964: 65), and yearly libations and sacrifices for houses destroyed by lightning (Platt 1986: 254) further ground house rites in the sacrificial complex centred on the mountain spirits.

10 Here, there is some particularly suggestive evidence from Aymara (which was once spoken in Huaquirca): the word for 'fox,' *lari*, is also an affinal term men use to denote 'wife-givers,' especially wife's brother and mother's brother (see Bertonio 1612 bk. 2: 191; Tschopik 1951: 189; Wolf 1980: 127). I would like more evidence on *lari* as a kinship term before judging whether, or to what extent, it is cognate with the Quechua *kaka*, which might be translated as 'father-in-law' and is the reciprocal term of *qatay*, which I have translated here as 'son-in-law.' If these terms prove to be cognate, there would be an additional linguistic basis for the identification between fox and 'parents-in-law' which I am proposing. I would like to thank Olivia Harris for alerting me to the semantic field of *lari*, but take full responsibility for this (tentative) analysis of it.

11 In the celebrations of Santa Rosa, the two *alferados* provide a day of bull-fighting and a military band each, whereas these duties used to fall to separate sponsors during the Virgin of the Assumption: *terceros* provided the bullfighting and *capitanes* provided the military bands (see Centeno 1949: 10). This consolidation of most of the ceremonial obligations around two major sponsors makes competition between them the overwhelming feature of Santa Rosa.

12 Until the abolition of the *varayoq* system in 1947, the *papa kamoyoqs*, or guardians of the *laymis*, were chosen during a *faena* on a piece of church land associated with one of the sponsorships of Christmas (*Taytaq*), on which the sowing was traditionally inaugurated in September.

13 The only exception to this fixed order of access that I witnessed occurred during a drought that set in during December 1982, after irrigation would normally be over for the year. At varying points, people attempted to save their crops with irrigation water, and came to ask the water judges for permission, but no fixed rotation was observed.

14 Isbell (1978: 144) writes that *angoripa*, a high *puna* plant, 'symbolizes' the ancestors, without indicating how this relationship comes about. The proposed connection is nonetheless extremely interesting since the intimate association between these wild plants and water that is emerging here also characterizes the relation between water and the abode of the dead, as we will see in Chapter 4. In regards to the meeting of high and low, Earls and

Silverblatt (1978: 300–7) have shown in a particularly suggestive fashion that a unidirectional flow of water in a single hydraulic cycle is interpreted as simultaneously upward and downward movement in Andean thought. This is further developed by the notion of *pallqa*, a simultaneous bifurcation and confluence, used to describe canals (Earls and Silverblatt 1978: 312) and deep points of rivers where offerings are made during canal cleaning (Arguedas 1956: 245).

15 See Isbell (1978: 143), Ossio (1978b: 379–81), and Skar (1982: 225). In fact, these authors do not give clear evidence that 'the *pachamama*' is mentioned in rites of canal cleaning in Ayacucho. Furthermore, they simply assume that *pachamama* denotes a monolithic 'earth mother,' when the term is often used in a plural sense to describe the spirits of particular inhabited places (cf. Roel Pineda 1965: 28). In addition, these spirits may be androgynous or predominantly masculine in form. The idea that irrigation water represents the sperm of the mountain spirits is also somewhat problematic. In Huaquirca, irrigation water would seem to be connected to female supernaturals because of the way canal cleaning takes place between the celebrations of the Virgin of the Assumption and Santa Rosa. Furthermore, Isbell (1978: 94) notes that water is under the control of the moon, a female supernatural whose festivities have been merged with those of Santa Rosa, a key date for canal cleaning throughout the southern Peruvian Andes. Elsewhere in Ayacucho, Ossio (1978b: 381) describes the representation of water as a child, Díaz (1969: 115–6) reports an image of the Christ-child and a Peruvian flag at the head of a canal cleaning procession, and Zorilla (1978: 122) reports appearances of the Virgin and the Christ-child in association with water during canal cleaning. This imagery suggests that the Immaculate Conception might provide the most appropriate model for any notion of fertility attributed to irrigation water. To interpret this water as sperm obscures the very real possibility that a Christian opposition between the spiritual and the carnal is at work in some Andean ideas about agriculture. If water appears as the Christ-child, it has an already formed individuality associated with spiritual salvation and redemption; it cannot be treated as just an incomplete carnal substance related to biological conception, even though it may act as such in certain contexts. This discussion will be developed at greater length in Chapters 4 and 5.

16 Note that the *qhashwa* is not everywhere associated with canal cleaning: in the Bolivian altiplano, it takes place between All Souls' and Lent (Buechler and Buechler 1971: 76–7; Carter 1977: 181), that is, during the height of the rainy season. This suggests that it may be seen as part of a more continuous process of growth, and not as a single, definitive act of fertilization.

17 In Mollebamba, canal cleaning takes place on 8 September, and is accompanied by the antics of two men and their respective cohorts known as *negros* or *chacreros*, who wear straw hats, black masks, and are sometimes said to represent the black *yanaconas* who worked on coastal *haciendas* (see Adams 1959: 66 for comparable personifications). On 10 September, the celebration of San Nicolás (patron saint of Mollebamba), these *chacreros* appear at the front of a procession around the town's plaza, breaking ground with a footplough, or a plough drawn by a team of bulls, in two columns. Behind them come a variety of people impersonating *llameros* (pastoralists who use their llamas for trade and transport), *arrieros* (muleteers), miners (in blue Electroperu hard hats), teachers, and political authorities (who are allowed to give orders for the duration of the celebration). One large table, surrounded by whole trees that have been cut and brought in from the countryside, is staffed by a group of women who serve corn beer from large jugs to all who stop there. A similar spectacle has been described by Isbell (1976: 50), and the satiric representation of various social types is a common strand in festivities following canal cleaning throughout Ayacucho (see Arguedas 1956: 248–9; Isbell 1978: 141–4; Ossio 1978b: 387; Montoya 1980: 255; Manrique 1983: 36).

Chapter Four: Sowing, Death, and *Ayni*

1 Although this order was followed on Huaylla-Huaylla canal, the first field to be irrigated and sown on Totora canal belonged to the governor, and was located towards the middle of the ideal order. In other parts of the Andes, notables are also reported to override customary water distribution systems (cf. Malengreau 1974: 195; Montoya, Silveira, and Lindoso 1979: 177; Skar 1982: 138). Although this looks like yet another assertion of notable power, the matter turns out to be more complex. In Huaquirca, commoners who held religious or political *cargos* were also expected to jump their turn in irrigation, and the practice appears to be legitimate for anyone who has assumed formal duties to the collectivity, including notables. Prior to the abolition of the *varayoq* system in 1947, the first fields to be sown were connected to the sponsorship of the Christmas festivities in Huaquirca. One such field is known as *Taytaq* ('of the Father') and is located in the valley bottom at the end of Totora canal. The other is *Mamaq* ('of the Virgin'), and it lies near the beginning of Totora canal, at the top of the terraced zone. Both were sown by *faenas* organized by the water judge of Totora canal. At the time of my research, these fields were worked like any other, by the holder of the *cargo* that they are associated with.

2 In times of water scarcity, canal water may be stored in reservoirs overnight
and used to increase the amount available the following morning. Quispe
(1969: 63) notes an interesting administrative division between flowing and
reservoir water as an aspect of a complex distribution of water by *rakis*
('portions') in Huancasancos.

3 The main purpose of irrigation throughout the Andes is to lengthen the
growing season of maize (cf. Dollfus 1981: 49), not to provide a substitute
for natural rainfall. This gives it an optional character in many areas, especially in years of early rainfall.

4 Because they use footploughs, people in Huaquirca do not sow their crops
in furrows (*surcos*), unlike many areas of the Andes where the sowing is
done with a yoke and plough. Thus, their fields lack the pattern of ridges
and troughs that is so useful for subsequent irrigation. In areas where the
sowing is done in furrows, there are also reports of very particular notions
of how seeds should be distributed, for example that the basic unit of distribution for a given seed should be two parallel rows, or that wheat should be
sown into land under maize at right angles to the furrows (Skar 1982: 141).
Although there are undoubtedly good technical reasons for these practices, I would argue that they have their symbolic dimension as well. The
minimal unit of two parallel rows, for example, reflects the 'like for like'
dyadic structure of *ayni*, whereas the right-angle configuration of maize
and wheat suggests the cross, whose function it is to protect these crops.

5 Variation in the pronunciation of these names is considerable in Huaquirca: *sawasiri/pitusiri, sawasere/pitusere*, even *saywasere*. Wallis (1980: 251)
reports *sawasiri/pitusayri*, while Gow and Condori (1976: 40) report Hawa-
siray and Pitusiray as the names of the mountain peaks that these qualities
are named after. Semantic analysis of these names is difficult, but clearly
desirable. It would appear that *sawa* could be a corruption of *sara* (Quechua 'maize'), and among the many meanings of *pitu* (which will be discussed further in relation to the drink *pito*) is flour of toasted maize. I can
find no meaning for the suffix *sira*, but the Quechua verb *siray* refers to the
action of wringing a neck or slitting a throat. The suffix *siri* marks possession in Aymara; thus, *sawasiri* would mean 'having *sawa*' and *pitusiri* would
mean 'having *pitu*.' These translations seem the most probable to me. The
additional variants sort out as follows: *saywa* is boundary stone, *sayri* is
tobacco, *hawa* is outside, outdoors. I do not perceive any underlying pattern in this semantic variation and have, therefore, come to rely on the various local explications of these terms, which are, in any case, more relevant.

6 In Quechua: '*Manan qespikunchu*,' a phrase that was always translated to me
as '*No se salva*,' even though *qespikuy* can be translated as 'to liberate one's

self' or 'to give birth' (Cusihuamán 1976; Lara 1978: 201). As 'to save one's self,' *qespikuy* can refer to both the Christian metaphysical notion and the more mundane act of escaping danger. All of the evidence suggests that the first sense is most salient here.

7 These *wankas* might be interpreted as a continuation of the relations between young women and mountain spirits established in the *qhashwa* dances described in Chapter 3. In pre-Columbian times, this style of singing was associated with agricultural fertility cults centred around stone monoliths (also known as *wankas*) located in the fields (see Duviols 1979). These monoliths represented the ancestors, much as do the mountain spirits today (note that one of the meanings of *apu* is father's father's father's father). The pre-Columbian *wanka* was associated with rites of defloration (see Duviols 1979: 22), just as the modern *qhashwa* is the occasion on which mountain spirits are said to seduce and impregnate young women. Both practices appear to involve a magical attempt to transform undomesticated sexuality into agricultural fertility, and there could well be a historical connection between them.

8 See Carter (1968: 245), Duviols (1973: 158, 164), Bastien (1978: 175), Valcárcel (1980: 81), and Harris (1982: 52).

9 Lira (1944: 873) gives the following definition of *samakuy*: 'To repose, rest enjoying one's self, take rest from work or fatigue. To sleep, rest. To lie buried, sleep the sleep of death.' Only the divinatory aspect is missing here, but this seems to be covered by the term *samincha*, which is a rite of benediction in the sowing that involves divination and notions of moral conduct (Lira 1944: 875; Urbano 1976: 137–40). I join Urbano (1976: 137) and Carpenter (1992: 133) in suggesting that there is a semantic, and not merely phonetic, resemblance between these derivatives of *samay* and *sami*, primarily on the basis of the various referents of the former in the rite described here. The one major referent of the root *samay* that is not immediately present in this rite is 'breathing,' 'exhaled air,' and related notions. Across the valley from Huaquirca, however, men working in footplough teams during the sowing of the terraces of Antabamba keep up a constant alternating two-pitch yodel that echoes back to Huaquirca, and forms part of the ambience of the sowing there. Although it would be going beyond the evidence to say that this yodelling is incorporated into the sense of *samay* developed in the sowing, neither can the possibility be entirely ruled out. From Chapter 3, we have already seen a case where a ritual brings together two apparently homonymous notions (*raki-raki* as fern and many portions of irrigation water) and makes a motivated connection between them. The fusion of rest, divination, and burial brought about around the term

samakuy is only one of several similar cases that will occur in this chapter. What is of interest here is how ritual, instead of proceeding to manipulate verbal signs according to their fragmented everyday usages, seems to reopen the question of the relation of phonetic signifier to the notion signified, and deny that it is arbitrary by making the various senses designated by similar or identical sounds interact (cf. Turner 1969: 64).

10 Without claiming to have seriously studied traditional medicine in Huaquirca, it seems to me that those who cure by offerings relate their medicines much more systematically to soul concepts than those who cure by herbs. In any case, there is no standard discourse on the nature of a living person, but rather a variety of co-existing practices and ideas, any or all of which may be invoked at different times for their heuristic value, without necessarily forming a unified system.

11 In the words of Bastien (1978: 45), *alma* would be the 'life principle' and *ánimo* the 'energy principle.' In at least one area of the Andes, these qualities are given a sexual identity, and constitute a theory of conception: 'The mother gives the body, the father, life ... she provides the matter and its form; the father gives semen which is pure life, and awakens the dormant' (Ortiz 1982: 200). An additional piece of evidence linking the *alma* to the categorically feminine is the representation of Qoropuna, the mountain in whose interior the *alma* resides during the afterlife, as a woman (Roel Pineda 1965: 25). I will argue in the final section of this chapter that this reproductive model organizes the sexual division of labour in Andean agriculture to a significant extent.

12 Valderrama and Escalante (1980: 252) also mention the idea of three different souls, each with a separate fate. Ossio (1980: 260) also reports the idea that women have seven *almas* and men three. This superabundance of female souls could be related to the ability to give embodiment to new life, according to the ideas provided by Ortiz in note 11, but I was unable to determine whether or not this is so. Casaverde (1970: 188) reports the idea that women have seven *ánimos*.

13 Stein (1961: 308) reports that the wandering soul of a living person is called *upe*, which denotes deafness and dumbness, as well as general stupidity. In pre-Columbian times, the land of the dead was called *upaimarca*: 'town of the deaf and dumb.'

14 This suggests that although these soul concepts are given Spanish names, they do not correspond entirely to Christian ideas of the soul (cf. Allen 1988: 62). However, they correspond even less to the pre-Columbian soul concepts of *camaquen* and *upani* described by Duviols (1978: 136–7). Current notions of *alma* and *ánimo* probably reflect the humour-theories of six-

teenth century Spanish folk biology more faithfully than they do any
religious orthodoxy, but Bastien (1985: 596, 607) is rightly cautious on this
point.

15 This was explained to me quite poignantly by a man who had been so
accused by his affines and protested, 'I'm not a crying son-in-law' ('*no soy
waqa qatay*'), as he struggled not to openly weep over the death of his wife's
father, to whom he had been quite close.

16 See also Mayer (1977: 78), Valderrama and Escalante (1980: 250), Harris
(1982: 53), and Skar (1982: 194).

17 Harris (1982: 53) notes that consanguines of the deceased are particularly
vulnerable to attack, and this was borne out by what I was told in Huaquirca. Some people become unhinged for considerable periods of time as
a result of the death of a close relative. While I was in Huaquirca, a woman
lost her mother and then a young daughter in quick succession. For about
six months she could not work at all, and was seen every day sitting in the
streets of Ñapaña talking nonsense, usually with a group of children gathered around her and laughing. Her condition was finally diagnosed as 'seizure' by the deceased daughter, and the cure consisted of drinking a stew
made from the heads of black, white, and maroon-coloured dogs. The
basis of this cure will be partly clarified when we examine the role of dogs
in the afterlife. Shortly after drinking the stew, the woman began to participate normally in work parties, something that would have been out of the
question previously.

18 See Harris (1982: 52) and also Flores (1979: 63), who reports that an insuf-
ficiency of dirt when the grave is being filled in indicates that more people
will have to die shortly.

19 Skar (1982: 194) notes that it falls to a *qatay* (preferably daughter's husband) to pound the loose dirt on the grave with a heavy flat stone, which
further emphasizes that the corpse/*alma* is being driven downwards. Given
the role of the 'son-in-law' in death, which is concerned almost exclusively
with ensuring the departure of his 'father-in-law' from this world, it is
tempting to posit a new significance to the 'son-in-law's' placement of a
cross on the crestline of the roof once it is rethatched, based on the cross
as a grave-marker.

20 Valderrama and Escalante (1980: 235) present good evidence that this *ayni*
is not to be paid back by the *alma* itself, but by other mourners (particularly affines) when those contributing now face death. This is also the
impression that arises from Malengreau's (1974: 193) discussion of death
as an occasion of generalized exchange, in which services to the deceased
are done as *yanapa* ('help,' without expectation of strict reciprocation).

Without denying these points, I would nonetheless argue that there is a sense in which the *alma* itself returns the *ayni* of the living, particularly that which is offered in libations, by providing this world with water, a theme to be developed in the text.

21 Qoropuna is mentioned by Guaman Poma (1615: 294) as a domicile of the dead, which suggests that at least some of the elements of this tradition are of pre-Columbian origin. Other ethnographers who mention Qoropuna in this regard are Arguedas (1956: 265–6), Roel Pineda (1965: 27–8), and Valderrama and Escalante (1980). Although Harris (1982: 62–3) mentions the coastal town of Tacna as the land of the dead, and not Qoropuna, much the same set of ideas seems to be at work. The same can be said of Zuidema and Quispe's (1968) account, which is based on the ascent of an unspecified mountain. Much less easy to integrate, for reasons that will become evident, are the idea from Cajamarca that the dead go to the jungle (Arguedas 1975: 16) and Bastien's (1978: 85–6, chap. 10) report of a recycling of the dead through local mountains.

22 Irrigation in Quechua is normally denoted by the terms *qarpay* and *mallmay*. It is the extra-linguistic ritual parallelism between irrigation and clothes washing that provides a motivation to elide the phonetic difference between *pacha* and *p'acha*, and allows *p'acha t'aqsana* to be understood as 'earth washing' or irrigation. However, this is not an isolated linguistic occurrence, since I have heard *p'acha* used as a synonym for *hallp'asqa* ('earthed,' referring to a supernatural removal of heart and lungs from a living person) in Huaquirca, when in theory, it should refer only to clothes because it begins with an explosive (p'). Mannheim (1988) has provided an excellent discussion of Quechua explosives, which suggests that they are sometimes used for semantic emphasis at the expense of phonemic distinction from their non-explosive counterparts. Any systematic comparison of Quechua dictionaries will confirm that the discriminatory function of the phonetic opposition between explosive and non-explosive is by no means consistent, even within the same dialect. There are many reasons for this, including interactions between rituals and words, whereby the former (re)motivate the latter. As in the case of *samay* and *sami* discussed in note 9 above, the phonetic distinction between *pacha* and *p'acha* is elided to reinforce a metaphorical link between semantic domains created by ritual. Once again, it seems that to do justice to what is going on in these rituals, we need a theory of signification that is based on praxis, and goes beyond an emphasis on naming, classification, and even predication.

23 The inability of the soul to cross water unaided has been noted by Stein

(1961: 307), Ossio (1978b: 381), Valderrama and Escalante (1980: 259), and Harris (1982: 55).

24 See Valderrama and Escalante (1980: 259) and Harris (1982: 62). One version that I heard is that the services of the black dog have to be solicited through a white dog, who will be more favourably predisposed towards helping the *alma*. Valderrama and Escalante (1980: 258) report that the *alma* is completely devoured by the dogs in Alqollaqta, and is revived only when a white dog urinates on the resulting excrement. It would seem that in both of these cases, white dogs sustain the *alma*'s residual connection to life, whereas black dogs confirm it in death.

25 In Quechua, *lloqe* refers to the left, but is also the name of a native Andean tree from which suspension bridges were made in the Antabamba Valley up until the 1920s. Both senses of the word are incorporated in the cord, since it is spun towards the left and is the raw material for a suspension bridge. Once again, the homophony of these two words appears to be the basis of a metaphorical interaction, but one that could only come about through a specific practical implementation. The metaphorical relation between *lloqe* as tree and *lloqe* as cord spun to the left is not objectively given in the identity of the phonetic means by which these two notions are expressed, but is realized only when the cord is used to make a suspension bridge that normally would have been made from the tree.

26 See Ortiz (1973: 14), Bastien (1978: 53), Valderrama and Escalante (1980: 259), Urton (1981: 38), and Harris (1982: 62).

27 Valderrama and Escalante (1980: 259) give evidence of an inverse expansion of time: what is a year for us is barely a day in the afterlife. These complex modifications of time and space seem to be part of the transition between life and death, and indicate a reduced capacity of the dead to maintain any perspective on the landscape they must cross, which appears increasingly alien and deformed through their loss of *ánimo*.

28 Elsewhere, this ascent involves five levels (Zuidema and Quispe 1968: 367), just as there are five 'towns' mentioned here. Bastien (1978: 179) describes an ascent of three levels.

29 Arguedas (1956: 266) mentions San Francisco, whereas Valderrama and Escalante (1980: 266) mention San Pedro.

30 People I questioned in Huaquirca derived this name from the Quechua verb *wañuy* ('death' or 'to die'). The waning moon is also called *waña*, and this word also occurs in the local toponym Qochawaña, which was translated to me as 'dead lake.' In Aymara, which was once spoken in the area, *waña* means 'dry.' Since death and dryness appear to be associated in local thought, however, I take these alternative meanings to be complementary.

31 The idea that a hierarchy of special lakes controls the local supply of rainfall is also embodied in the following ritual: In times of drought, a man
skilled in the art does a tour of all of the important lakes in the *puna* of
Huaquirca, cracking his sling over them to wake them up, and taking a bottle of water from each one to pour into Taype Larqo ('canal of the mid-
point,' see Figure 10). This forced descent and distribution of water is supposed to stimulate the fall of rain (see also Yaranga 1979: 715).

32 'Jaguar' is the literal translation of *uturunku*. In many areas of the Andes,
particularly Ayacucho, this feline is only one of many manifestations of an
explosive force related to water and the subterranean, whose generic term
is *amaru* (Earls and Silverblatt 1978: 314).

33 As Isbell (1976: 50) notes, pumas are often equated with the ancestors.
Their connection with death may be retained here, since Pumaqocha is
one of the main sources of Wañaqota, that 'reservoir of death' in which
clothes are washed during funerals. Therefore, it appears that the Map'a
Mayo, and the underground streams it feeds into, form a direct cosmological link between Pumaqocha, the locally acknowledged source of rainfall,
and Qoropuna, the ultimate 'reservoir of death' (see Roel Pineda 1965:
25). Through these underground connections, the land of the dead supplies the living with water in the various localities they inhabit.

34 Arguedas (1956: 266) reports that the soups eaten by the dead are made of
ashes, and their boiled grains of maize are, in fact, llama dung, details that
suggest that the dead are to undergo a similar breakdown.

35 Harris (1980: 81) notes that this water is called *sirqa*, a name that also
applies to undomesticated animals. Here, the lack of domestication seems
to share with death not only the quality of being outside of society mentioned by Harris (1980: 83), but the related feature of hostility to the *alma*
as a principle of embodiment and moral formation.

36 An account from Kuyo Grande traces the origins of malaria to the uncover-
ing of the bones of a *condenado* in the jungle (Casaverde 1970: 204). This
further underlines the connection between *chuqchu* and death proposed
here, and suggests that there is something dangerously corrupting about
this disease.

37 This emphasis on pairing is further developed by the names for corn beer
and cane alcohol that have had toasted *quinua* flour added to them: *paresnintin aqa, paresnintin trago* (Quispe 1969: 29), where the Spanish *pares*
(pairs) combines with the Quechua particle *ntin*, which stresses unity and
totality, to connote living unity. Elsewhere, the drink that is called *pito* in
Huaquirca is known as *machka* (Isbell 1978: 57).

38 This is not to say that women do not do *ayni* among themselves. In Hua-

quirca, it is customary for women to exchange cooked food during the
Christmas festivities, for example, and this is called *ayni* (cf. Allen 1988:
75). The same also applies to the corn beer that women contribute to each
other's work parties (cf. Núñez del Prado 1975a: 395). Malengreau (1980:
510) insists that this must be regarded as non-calculated *yanapa*, and
although I would agree that this is generally the case, it is not necessarily
so. When women work in the fields, they also enter into relations of *ayni*
and *yanapa* with other women. Thus, women do practise *ayni* among themselves, but this is sometimes overlooked because less female than male
labour circulates across household boundaries, and because as producers
of food and drink, women enter into a *mink'a*-like relation with men. What
is ultimately at stake here is whether the practice of *ayni* can be defined
solely from a male perspective. To the extent that *ayni* is culturally elaborated around death imagery, it appears to be prototypically male, but there
is also a sense (perhaps a secondary one) in which it applies equally well to
services exchanged among women.
39 See, for example, Allen (1988: 78, 81). Both Núñez del Prado (1975a: 394,
398, 1975b: 624) and Skar (1982: 144) note exclusive female control of the
food supply, and that men are not allowed in the room where it is stored.
Lund Skar (1979: 453–5) presents a considerably different picture, in
which all family members have rights on the contents of the storehouse,
although these are not specified. An equally confusing affirmation of
female control of the food supply on the one hand, and the right of every
member of the domestic group to a share of the harvest on the other, can
be found in Stein (1961: 221, 128). Elsewhere, female administration of
the food supply leads to an identification of the storeroom as female (Wallis 1980: 252, 256), but rights of access are not discussed. Finally, Harris
(1978a: 31) reports that women are dominant within the conjugal unit
because they control consumption, but reports that only the kitchen is
associated with women, whereas the storehouse is associated with men
(Harris 1978a: 26), and that agricultural produce is seen as belonging to
the entire household by virtue of its joint labour (Harris 1978a: 29). This
is most definitely not the case in Huaquirca. Despite the fact that men generally outnumber women two to one in agricultural work parties, the product comes under exclusive female control once it is harvested. The
clearest expression of this is that when a man and woman quarrel, he will
not be allowed to eat at home, and will not try to assert independent access
to the food supply by cooking for himself.
40 Although it is entirely normal for a man to cook or look after children
from time to time, when I jokingly suggested, near the end of my field-

work, that I would soon have to make my own corn beer, even notables who claimed never to have drunk *laqto* could barely stifle their outrage: it was all right that I knew how to make it, but couldn't I at least find a woman to do it for me?

41 The corn beer that women spit into is known as *laqto*, and it is possible that their saliva may have some effect on the fermentation process, if only by breaking down carbohydrates to sugars. Some women, however, claim that they do not spit into the dough, and that the results are the same. In any case, the form of corn beer preferred by the notables is called *chicha de jora*, and is made from sprouted maize seeds (*wiñapu*), which give a different colour and taste to the brew.

42 In the absence of a superordinate encompassing entity like seed, the encounter of like entities in *ayni* often becomes destructive, as in the fights that break out between work parties that meet while performing the *wayliya* on the way home from the sowing. Here, *ayni* becomes a principle of revenge (González Holguín 1608: 33; Núñez del Prado 1972: 138). This is not entirely surprising, since symmetric duality, and the *yanantin* transformation by which it is achieved, represent an attack on the body.

Chapter Five: From All Saints' to Christmas

1 Apparently, several years have passed since anyone has performed the duties of *Paqpako* in Huaquirca, but in 1982, a man had announced that he would, only to be prevented from doing so by a death in his own family. There were conflicting opinions in the community about whether the sponsorship still exists, but apparently the field associated with it is still rented on a year-by-year basis, as the *cargo* goes unoccupied, without being definitively allocated to another purpose. I was told that the office of *Paqpako* is still occupied on a regular basis in the town of Pachaconas in the lower Antabamba Valley, and certainly all of the towns upstream had it as a part of their ceremonial life until recently.

2 Elsewhere, *mazamorra negra*, or porridge of black maize, is the dish that marks this event (Hartman 1973: 188). Harris (1982: 55) mentions a similar porridge of unspecified colour.

3 This sort of objection has been forcefully developed by Needham (1972), Bourdieu (1977), Rosaldo (1980), Keesing (1985), and many other writers. Although I take their point, the danger is that it will discourage any serious investigation of how cosmological notions may be implicit in ritual, conventional discourse, labour, the organization of sensory experience, etc. It may even lead to an *a priori* denial that anything like a cosmology exists, as in

Rosaldo's (1980) study, despite the abundant evidence she provides to the contrary.

4 Although I heard no such statements in Huaquirca, people there certainly did speak of the moon as being female. Since the planting of tubers is so closely tied to the waxing of the moon, the latter does provide something of a link between women and potatoes.

5 Note that I do not follow Harris (1986) or Allen (1988: 209–10) in treating triadic imagery as a direct outgrowth of asymmetric duality, but see it instead as an outgrowth of the interaction between symmetric and asymmetric duality.

6 Here, it is perhaps significant that the term *q'ala* is used to refer both to the peel of fruits and vegetables (including the potato) and, insultingly, to the notables, so as to imply that they are naked. This implicit equation of peels and clothes is particularly interesting in view of the way Andean people eat maize, beans, and potatoes, in which particular care is taken to thoroughly remove the peel, especially in the case of potatoes.

7 Both potatoes and maize are life forms that partially rival humanity, but in different ways. Maize thrives on human death, and the energetic water that is released by it. However, this is beneficial to the living, who cannot harness death in any other way than through the growth of maize, and its transformation into 'animating' substances like corn beer. Relative to water, maize is an embodying force, and thus has an *alma*-like dimension, but relative to humanity, it provides embodied energy or *ánimo*. Maize also follows humanity in its basic orientation towards the sun, and the above-ground world: even the water that it incorporates from the underground world of the dead follows a solar cycle, whereby death in the west (Qoropuna and Solimana) leads to a renewal of life in the east (Sawasira and Pitusira). Potatoes, on the other hand, come to fruition underground, and are thought to grow in phase with the waxing of the moon. Like the dead, they are diurnally opposed to the living. Because of this opposed orientation, the excessive growth of potatoes may become a direct threat to the living, and cause them to die. They are a stronger life form than maize, one that more closely resembles the human *alma*, and may even enter into a competitive identity with it. Thus, we may conclude that the potato is to maize as the human *alma* is to *ánimo*, just as Guaman Poma (1615: 336) appears to have done long ago when he wrote that habitual consumption of freeze-dried potatoes (*ch'uño*) makes one large and corpulent, but weak, whereas consumption of maize promotes a body that is small but '*animoso*' (active). This connection with cultigens is reinforced when we consider the post mortem locations of human souls: the *alma* remains underground for

the most part, like the potato, whereas the disembodied *ánimo* is expelled back into this world in the form of water, which is incorporated by maize.

8 In Cotabambas, I was told that work parties returning home from the *kutipa* may confront each other, as during their return from the maize sowing in Huaquirca. After playing their flutes in a standoff, during which tension mounts, the two troupes break into intense fighting, and then recompose themselves for the remainder of the journey home, still playing their flutes.

9 The one exception to this is in the towns of Antilla and Sabayno, where the *wayliya* does not begin until Epiphany (6 January). Since these two towns are the farthest downstream in the upper Antabamba Valley, there may be a sense in which the *wayliya* 'descends' to these towns over the twelve days of Christmas.

10 The town of San Antonio in the neighbouring Province of Grau also has a Christmas *wayliya*, even though it is supposed to be considerably different from that of the Antabamba Valley, as do the pastoralists in the intervening alpine zone. I have also heard of similar performances in the Province of Andahuaylas, but the only published account of anything remotely similar can be found in Adams (1959: 66, 188–95).

11 With the criterion of uniformity in mind, the sponsors of the Christmas *wayliya* in Sabayno used to provide their dancers with a complete outfit, and those of Antabamba used to provide masks and scarves.

12 These dances were probably introduced by the church during the colonial period, and may originally have been modelled on the Spanish *matachín*, a folk dance that enacts and celebrates the victory of Spaniards over Moors in the reconquest of Spain. This would explain the notion that the dancers represent 'Spaniards.'

13 It may be inaccurate to speak of the holy family here, since it is uncertain whether *Taytaq* represents Joseph or God the Father. Certainly, nobody with whom I discussed Christmas felt the need to clarify this sort of point. Neither can it be entirely ignored, however, since certain aspects of Christmas in Huaquirca may, indeed, be influenced by the theology of the Immaculate Conception, as I will argue.

14 Here, I do not suggest that *Taytaq* and *Mamaq* necessarily reflect male/ female relations in Andean society, since according to that model, it would be absurd for a male figure like *Taytaq* to be associated with seed. Rather, I would stress the importance of the Immaculate Conception as a model here, one that confounds and even inverts human gender relations.

15 Skar (1982: 235–6) notes transvestism as a feature of confrontations between gender-coded moieties. The only other case I encountered where

sponsorships bear the names *Tayta* and *Mama* is also enacted by a pair of men (Quispe 1969: 64), which suggests that this tension between gender difference and sameness is endemic.

16 Buechler and Buechler (1971: 84) report older boys dressing up in the clothes of dead women on All Saints', and making lewd jokes, as a representation of the dead.

17 Morote Best (1951: 79) reports a procession for the *Niño Ñakaq* ('Christ-child Slaughterer'), an image of the Christ-child that is taken to preside over dying children, in the neighbourhood of Arco, Ayacucho, on All Saints' Eve. Elsewhere, children personify the dead on this day (Buechler and Buechler 1971: 84, 97), perhaps because, like the old, they are most prone to death in this society (cf. Buechler and Buechler 1971: 84; Buechler 1980: 84), but more probably because of the idea that the *alma* shrinks on death (Oblitas Poblete 1978: 99) and loses subjective capacities in what might be seen as a reversion to childhood. Of particular interest here is the widespread Andean practice of baking bread babies (*t'anta wawa*) for baptism and subsequent consumption on All Saints' and the Day of the Dead. In some areas these babies are explicitly connected with the dead by bearing the name *aya* (cadaver, see Hartman 1973: 193–4); in others, they are treated as the body of Christ, and their consumption as a kind of communion (Bastien 1978: 185–6); or the two notions are combined, as the following song (Buechler 1980: 84) to the dead on All Saints' and the Day of the Dead indicates:

> If you are asked why you come
> Reply that you came to water the flowers
> If they ask who your father is
> Answer 'San Jose' (Saint Joseph)
> If they ask who your mother is
> Answer 'The Virgin Mary.'

This connection between the dead and the Christ-child is further underlined in some areas by another round of baking bread figurines at Christmas (Brush 1977b: 165; Skar 1982: 145).

Chapter Six: Carnival and the Harvest

1 The word *cheqche* bears a close phonetic resemblance to the Quechua word for hail (rendered as *chikchi* by Cusihuamán 1976 and *chiqchi* by Lira 1944). This phonetic resemblance was elaborated in a joke by one of my infor-

mants, who said to me in Spanish: '*vamos a hacer granizo*' as she was about to make *cheqche* using some cobs we had just brought in from the fields. To the phonetic similarity of the words involved, one can also add the similarity of referents (hailstones and grains of maize, to which might be added teeth, from the verb *cheqchiy* 'to smile'), but the conceptual basis of this joke that I would most want to emphasize relates back to the systematic connections between human souls, maize, and precipitation discussed in Chapter 4. The souls of unbaptized children are buried at night, without clothes washing or the participation of non-consanguines. The soul does not go to Qoropuna, but ascends directly to the clouds, where it is called a *limbo* or a *ch'uncho* ('savage'), and causes periodic hailstorms (cf. Ossio 1978b: 379), which are intensely harmful to the crops. If hail is caused by this premature exit from the human life cycle, and represents a destructive release of energy by an essentially amoral young *alma*, then there is a certain correspondence to how a tender ear of maize is taken from the field before it has fully dried in the sun, and baked on the coals of a fire, in a cooking process that is essentially the same as that to which the dead are subjected when water is extracted from them and sent back to this world.

2 See Stein (1961: 19), Gade (1970), Bolton (1974b: 192), Burchard (1980: 608–12), Harris (1982: 57), and Skar (1982: 141).

3 See Forbes (1870: 232), Tschopik (1951: 206), Gade (1970: 4), Aranguren Paz (1975: 131–2), and Gow and Condori (1976: 5–6).

4 In the past, Corpus Christi was an occasion for notable-sponsored banquets of the sort that still take place during Carnival (see Centeno 1949: 7). Other events may also have taken place at this time, but I was not able to reconstruct any of them from the limited questioning of older people that I undertook on the topic.

5 One way of looking at the *arroba* of maize given to each *mink'ay* is as a wage. Since the monetized value of an *arroba* of maize at this time of the year (when it is still slightly wet) is S/. 2000, it compares favourably to the wage of S/. 500 that prevails during the growing season. What makes this comparison somewhat misleading is that local wage labour always includes much better provisions of food and drink than a household will offer its *mink'ays* during the frenzy of the harvest. Another way of evaluating the payment of one *arroba* per workday during the harvest is in relation to the ratio of a total day's work put into the cultivation of a field against its yield in *arrobas*. In one field that I followed closely enough to make such a calculation, seventy workdays were spent for a yield of 170 *arrobas*: a ratio of slightly less than 2.5 *arrobas* per workday. Once the seed used to sow the fields, and to make corn beer and food for the workers is considered, this

ratio might drop below 2:1, but the fact remains that the owners of such a field benefit from this arrangement. This is the quantitative basis of *mink'a* as an exploitative social relationship, and the backdrop against which the relative advantage of workers during the harvest must be seen.

6 See Mishkin (1964: 148), Bourricaud (1970: 192), Fioravanti (1973: 122), and Skar (1982: 147).

7 Since the local cash value of an *arroba* of potatoes was S/. 1000, the standard payment for a *mink'ay* during the potato harvest was worth S/. 2000, as in the maize harvest. This apparent monetary standardization of payment in kind could be used to support the argument that *mink'a* is essentially a form of wage labour (see Carter 1964: 49; Bastien 1978: 108; Custred 1979: 387), and the more general view of Andean cooperation as a dependent manifestation of capitalism (see Guillet 1979: 157, 162–3; Sánchez 1982: 157). However, it could be equally well argued that the monetary values of the crops in question have been accommodated to the traditional measurement of the carrying capacity of a *lliqlla* cloth, so that this unit of volume represents equal monetary values of maize and potatoes. More detailed research would be needed to resolve the issue, but the danger of assuming that market forces are at work behind the 'subsistence economy' is clearly indicated by this second possibility. In other words, correspondences between monetary values and traditional units of measurement tell us nothing about which is being adapted to the other.

Chapter Seven: The *T'inkas*

1 Among the most common names for these rites are *herranza* ('branding') in the Ayacucho area, *despacho* ('dispatching') and *haywarisqa* ('handing over') in the Cusco area, and *ch'alla* ('libation,' synonym of *t'inka*) in Bolivian Quechua.

2 Quispe (1984: 622–3) emphasizes the 'reciprocity' between commoners and mountain spirits in these rites, as does Custred (1979: 383), but in a more subtle way, by pointing out a tension between symmetry and asymmetry (e.g., between *ayni* and *mink'a*) in the relations involved. Custred's point will be amply confirmed in this chapter.

3 Among those who have mentioned this basic bipolar distribution of *t'inkas* in the annual cycle are Roel Pineda (1965: 30), Favre (1967: 123), Morissette and Racine (1973: 173), Isbell (1978: 155), Nash (1979: 134–9), and Platt (1983: 54–5, 59). A more complex pattern assigns different dates to rites for different animals, in which Carnival is typically reserved for llamas and alpacas, San Marcos for cattle, San Juan (24 June) for sheep, Santiago

for horses, and 1 August for offerings to the earth. Among those who have reported partial observances of this pattern are Casaverde (1970: 126–31), Gow and Condori (1976: 82), Custred (1979: 381), and Quispe (1984: 611). Because of the rites held for cattle on San Marcos, Huaquirca partly conforms to this pattern as well. What is most noteworthy about this sequence of dates is how clearly it aligns with the dry season or phase of private appropriation in the annual cycle, as does the report that such rites are performed after the harvest (Matos Mar 1964: 70). However, Christmas has also been mentioned as a date for these rites (Aranguren Paz 1975: 108), and I suspect that among pastoralists it is quite common for there to be a third round of rites at this time of the year, as was the case in the *puna* of Huaquirca until the recent demise of the celebrations of San Andrés. Another, more anomalous report for pastoralists cites a single round of rites between December and Carnival (Flores 1977: 212). What this indicates is that among pastoralists, there is a greatly diminished tendency for these rites to be integrated into a seasonal opposition between periods of collective production and private appropriation, probably as a result of less developed interhousehold cooperation in general among herders. However, there are reports of sacrificial offerings being made before every agricultural task (Custred 1979: 382) and throughout the growing season of the potato (Gow and Condori 1976: 17–18, 40–1), which suggests that these offerings need not be seasonally opposed to a period of collective production among agriculturalists either. To a certain extent, this can be offset by the analysis of the potato developed in Chapter 5, where its constant affinity with asymmetric duality and trinity links it closely to the *t'inkas*, and sets it apart from the symmetric duality that characterizes maize and *ayni*. In the end, however, it is best to concede that the seasonal affiliation that I am proposing here is not universal, but only the most common pattern.

4 In Huaquirca, Tuesdays and Fridays are not considered inauspicious for the performance of *t'inkas*, as has been reported for other areas by Favre (1967: 128), Casaverde (1970: 231), Valderrama and Escalante (1976: 180), and Flores (1977: 212), but neither are they especially sought out, as Nash (1979: 156) describes in the Bolivian tin mines. Some ritualists may perform simple coca leaf divinations to determine whether a particular date is acceptable to the mountain spirits, but this does not appear to reach the degree of elaboration described by Valderrama and Escalante (1976: 179–81).

5 The one exception to this are the rites performed by agriculturalists on Santiago for their cattle and horses, which take place on the terraced maize

fields in the valley, where the animals graze at this time of the year. Among pastoralists, such rites are generally conducted in special ceremonial corrals (see Favre 1967: 124; Flores 1977: 233; Quispe 1984: 611), or in special rooms or residences constructed for this purpose (Valderrama and Escalante 1976: 178–9; Wallis 1980: 256).

6 See also Quispe (1969: 27) and Isbell (1978: 159). As a matter of course, pastoralists in the *puna* use a more elaborate procedure. Before a *t'inka*, the ritualist collects twelve toads and ties them into a bird's nest with a piece of cloth. Once again, the ritualist circumambulates the corral three times 'to the left,' making a sharp, dry staccato sound at the back of the throat: 'qhas-qhas-qhas ...' Alternatively, bits of *urilla* plant may be tied in with the toads, and the whole bundle is used to massage the animals in a procedure known as *morasqa*, *brujo* (sorcerer), or *desgracia* (misfortune). These bundles absorb whatever attacks are being levelled at the animals, and are abandoned in a remote area of the *puna* before the rite begins. Any animal or bird that passes over such a bundle is said to die instantly.

7 See Quispe (1969: 71, 1984: 613–14) and Isbell (1978: 156, 159). This use of maize flour to absorb dangerous energy is entirely consistent with the previously mentioned use of *pito* flour to thicken corn beer into a beverage of the same name (see Chapters 4 and 5). This suggests an interesting parallelism between the misdirected energy of the sorcerer's attack and the disembodied energy released by the dead in the form of water, one that we have already encountered in the *layqas* (sorcerers) of the Christmas *waylila*. There is at least one case where the term *llampu* is used as a generic term for sea shells (Roel Pineda 1965: 30), and not just to refer to this flour. We will see that sea shells have the magical function of stimulating rainfall in these rites. Whether as sea shell or as maize flour, the function of *llampu* is to absorb, to draw energy away from life-forms it could harm. In the rites described by Quispe (1969: 79), this maize flour is called *rit'i* (snow), an image which recalls the snow that forms on the mountains of the dead, and its colour coordination with maize.

8 This same substitution of servant for owner in the directive role of these rites has been noted by Montoya (1980: 228). As several notables told me, such a servant must be '*de maxima confianza*' (of maximum reliability) because improper use of a *mesa* can cause damage to the animals and even their owners. In cases of extended or particularly serious misuse, it can become what is known as a *mesa lisa* (wild or impudent *mesa*), which consistently kills those who use it and their family members, and the services of a particularly skilled shaman will be needed to neutralize it. Nonetheless, the degree of scepticism that most notables have about the *t'inkas* mitigates

against these considerations, and in many cases means that the servants must be particularly insistent if the rites are to be performed at all (cf. Aranguren Paz 1975: 107). Some of the most skilled ritualists in Huaquirca are cowherd servants to the notables, in keeping with the tendency towards social marginality that Favre (1967: 134) notes for oracular mediums for the mountain spirits. The latter are known as *pongos* in Huaquirca, a term that is also applied to door-servants, and tends to portray the relation between medium and mountain spirit in that light. Despite this marked gravitation towards social inferiority, people in Huaquirca consider oracular mediums to be their most accomplished ritualists.

9 People in Huaquirca seemed to feel that the Christianity of the *t'inkas* is problematic, in a way that I did not find to be true for other rites. Not only is there the preliminary offering to *Nuestro Alto*, but even those who were most certain that I approved of these rites would say things like: '*Claro que somos católicos y cristianos, y creemos en un solo Dios, pero hay que reconocer las cosas de este mundo, ¿no es cierto?, para evitar problemas*' ('Of course we are Catholics and Christians, and we believe in a single God, but it is also necessary to acknowledge things of this world, isn't it, to prevent problems'). There were many comments to the effect that the *t'inkas* are a direct historical survival from the (pre-Christian) epoch of the *gentiles*, and this was skilfully turned into a reworking of some classic Old Testament scenes by my adoptive 'mother.' As Abraham was about to make an *alcanzo* of his son Isaac, the Lord intervened to explain that henceforth, only *alcanzos* of incense and carnations would be necessary. Furthermore, she continued, Cain made *alcanzos* of putrid maize and wilted plants, whereas Abel made good *alcanzos* of sheep; thus, the distinction between agriculturalists and pastoralists in the Andes has its origin in Biblical times. Although all of this tends to include the *t'inkas* in the Judaeo-Christian tradition, it is somewhere on the far side of Christianity due to their sacrificial character.

10 The only time I heard the *pachamamas* discussed in any detail in Huaquirca was during the *t'inkas*. When I asked a woman what a *pachamama* is, she held up a pinch of soil between her thumb and forefinger, and replied 'this.' A similar identification with the soil has been reported elsewhere (Platt 1986: 238–9), but this does not exhaust the specificity of the gesture. While travelling in the *puna* above Huaquirca, I was twice warned about sleeping outdoors in corrals with 'altars,' for the *pachamamas* are likely to appear in dreams, trying to seduce the unwary. I was told to resist at all costs since 'they always take something' (i.e., castrate or rip out heart and lungs). Should I be forced to sleep in such a corral, my instructions were to cross myself, invoke the holy trinity, and eat a tiny pinch of earth from the

floor of the house connected to the corral, but above all, to pour libations for the *pachamama* without fail every time and at every place I drink. Elsewhere, the kissing of dirt from the floor of the house has been reported as a means of appeasing a dwelling spirit known as the *condor mamani* (Buechler 1980: 56), and ingestion of a pinch of soil has been cited as a means of avoiding supernatural attack (Manya 1969: 137; Oblitas Poblete 1978: 38, 95). Here, I would argue that the pinch of soil does not represent the earth in general, but the spirit of a particular habitation or grazing territory (cf. Roel Pineda 1965: 28; Malengreau 1980: 493).

11 In Quechua: '*Imata samanki?*' This translation of *samay* as 'to invoke' can also be found in Tomoeda (1985: 286), who describes similar rituals in the neighbouring Province of Aymaraes. The most common dictionary definitions of *samay* are 'to rest,' 'to be buried,' and 'exhaled air' (Lira 1944: 874). Clearly, the latter is significant in the context of invocation.

12 In Quechua: '*Ñoqa samasaq t'año.*'

13 In Quechua: '¡*Hampuchun, hampuchun!*'

14 In Quechua: '*Phukawasimanta, Ch'aynawirimantapas.*'

15 In Quechua: '¡*Hampullachun, hampullachun!*'

16 In Quechua: '*Manam hampusqachu k'askullayki.*'

17 In Spanish: '*Este plato es para todos los pachamamas.*' Note that these entities are represented as being both plural and masculine here.

18 Ritual names are a common feature of these rites, and are often secret (cf. Platt 1983: 54) or at least idiosyncratic enough that one has to rely on the knowledge and creativity of other people to make sure that enough of them are brought to bear on the entities concerned to compel them to come to where the rite is taking place. I suspect that the principle involved is a kind of correspondence of the ritual name to the *ánimo* of the entity concerned, which exerts a kind of involuntary influence on it. In any case, among the ritual names I encountered in Huaquirca were *t'año* for cattle, *castaño* for horses, *castellano* for sheep, *qarwaraso* and *hachuski* for alpacas, *waswa* and *hayuncha* for llamas, *lázaro* and *michiq* for dogs, and *ashwa* for corn beer.

19 Note the continuity of the symbolism of yellow and white from the discussion of death. In both cases, yellow marks the larger soul or figurine, and white the smaller. Unlike the context of death, however, the emphasis here is not on splitting and duality, but rather on asymmetry, growth, and trinity.

20 This concern is also displayed when people bring young animals to the *mesa* and give them rehearsals in copulation (see Quispe 1969: 28, 71, 1984: 614; Isbell 1978: 161). Roel Pineda (1965: 31) describes a young

male animal placed between two females, like the 'priest' and the two women above.

21 The Spanish terms are *linaje* and *origen*. For Roel Pineda (1965: 26) and Yaranga (1979: 713), *linaje* connotes human ancestry, not that of the animals. In Huaquirca, however, I only heard of the notion in relation to this particular offering. Some ritualists in Huaquirca actually keep locks of hair from the tails of various bulls that they and their forefathers had owned, and duly give them rounds of libations. This suggests another way that notions of descent may be brought to bear on the animals in the context of the *t'inka*. However, it may be forced to rigidly differentiate between what pertains to people and what pertains to the animals in these rites, given the constant use of metaphor and high degree of identification between people and animals (cf. Quispe 1969: 91).

22 In the *puna* of Huaquirca, these niches are set into 'altars' made of piled stone, which are present in ceremonial corrals, and other sites where *t'inkas* are performed. Bastien (1978: 57–8) reports similar 'earth shrines' without giving their Callawaya name, whereas Favre (1967: 124) and Fuenzalida (1980: 163) give the name *allpapa sonqon* ('earth's heart'), and Quispe (1969: 34–7, 1984: 613) and Isbell (1978: 153, 158) mention stone-lined niches known as 'safes' (*cajas*), whose covering slabs are called 'lock and keys.' Flores (1979: 78) describes similar cylindrical niches called *pikota*, whereas Martínez (1983: 94) mentions shrines called *juturi* that not only receive offerings, but are thought to be the point from which new animals are born onto the grazing territory, a point that will be discussed more fully. As was mentioned in the discussion of the *pachamamas* in note 10 above, these shrines or 'altars' are constantly blamed for causing human sickness through the invisible extraction of hearts, lungs, or testicles, and are very likely where the place spirit/*pachamama* of each estate is localized, as both an extractive and reproductive force.

23 There are several facets to the semantic unity of *samay* and *samiy*: first, *samay* as 'exhaled breath' corresponds closely to *samiy* as the essential aroma of a given substance; second, *sama(ku)y* as divination overlaps fully with *samiy(a)* as ritual counting (see Roel Pineda 1965: 31–2; Urbano 1976: 137–8) and/or destiny (Urbano 1976: 138–9); third, *samay* as interment relates to the class of offerings called *pagos* ('payments'), whose assembly may include a procedure known as *saminchay* (Urbano 1976: 137); and, finally, *saminchay* as a rite of seed libation during the sowing (Urbano 1976: 137) corresponds to the *t'inka de semilla* described in Chapters 4 and 5, a constituent act of which is the *samakuy* divination. Opposition between these two terms arises only around the tendency towards dispersal in *samiy*

(as ethereal essence of offerings), and the contrasting sense of influx and concentration of vitality in *samay* (as invocation and interment, but not as exhaled breath).

24 For example, *qarwaraso* is used as a ritual name for alpacas in the Antabamba region, but it is the name of a very important mountain spirit in the nearby Province of Lucanas, Department of Ayacucho.

25 The use of *santo roma* ('Holy Rome') as a ritual name for the potato must be read as a sacrilegious pun at one level, based on the fact that *el papa* is the pope and *la papa* is the potato, and consisting of a transference of the dignity of the former onto the latter.

26 This is particularly true of Custred (1979: 385–6, 1980: 197), who imputes an 'indexical' function to the items on the *mesa*, such that each stands for the class to which it belongs; for example, corn = corn, coca = coca, wool = wool, fat = animal products. Custred (1979: 385, 387, 1980: 197) does not derive these equivalences from local exegesis or practice, but rather his own belief that the 'symbolic status' of the items in question must be determined by (his view of) their value as scarce resources in an attempt to control the environment. Next, these 'symbols' are submitted to a contrived 'syntax' of the rite (Custred 1979: 383–4). Here, the *a priori* models of linguistics and cultural ecology combine to substitute themselves for any investigation into the processes of reference actually at work in the rite. Maize does not stand for itself, as we have already seen, nor does coca stand for itself, since I was often told to chew it in order that the cattle might find pasture in the months to come (cf. Tomoeda 1985: 295), nor wool for itself, since it is an offering that is commonly expected to give rise to a whole animal (see Isbell 1978: 154; Montoya 1980: 204). Only by allowing that offerings have a metaphorical status, not an 'indexical' one, can we realize that carnations might be present not so that the hills be covered with flowers, but because they can be converted into animals (Casaverde 1970: 184; Gow and Condori 1976: 52), or that *kallpa* figurines may not only represent the vitality of the animals, but also act as a sacrificial substitute for a human being (Favre 1967: 131).

27 We have already encountered this in the case of the maize that is ground into *llampu*, but it is also considered a wise precaution to keep a cob of *kutisara* ('return maize') amid the paraphernalia on the *mesa*. This is a variety of maize whose grains have pointed tips that curl over backwards towards the cob, and has the property of deflecting any witchcraft back towards its originator in a like manner. White maize is sometimes referred to as 'witches' maize,' probably because of its affinity with the *ánimo* or vital

force of the animals that is being summoned so frequently by *t'inkas* on other grazing territories.

28 Among these names are *inya, inlla, inkaychu, enqaychu, enqa, khuya, hut'u, hispa, sepja*, and *conopa*; see Roel Pineda (1965: 26), Delgado de Thays (1965, cited in Quispe 1969: 99), Arguedas (1968: 340), Gow and Gow (1975: 150), Flores (1977), Oblitas Poblete (1978: 223–4), and Fuenzalida (1980: 166).

29 See Roel Pineda (1965: 27), Casaverde (1970: 146), Núñez del Prado (1970: 90), Gow and Gow (1975: 148), and Flores (1977: 218).

30 In Quechua: '*Ñoqa samasaq qori mesa, qolqe mesa, platanankichispaq, Banco Agrariomanta, Banco Gibsonmantapas.*'

31 See Arguedas (1956: 245), Morote Best (1956b: 297), Favre (1967: 129), and Flores (1979: 78).

32 One ritualist whose *t'inkas* I regularly attended had a colonial coin dating from 1787, and several coins of comparable antiquity are held by other 'priests' in the community. Even those who do not own such a prize coin will at least have one from an earlier part of this century. Oblitas Poblete (1978: 239) even mentions old British pound sterling coins serving an amuletic function in modern Bolivia. What unites all of these coins is that they have been withdrawn from circulation by the state, and it would appear that the longer ago this happened, or the farther away the origin of the coin, the more efficacious in the role of *potosí*.

33 Wedding guests make similar contributions of money to the couple in many parts of the Andes (see Quispe 1969: 62; Carter 1977: 200; Isbell 1978: 121; Buechler 1980: 120–5; Ossio 1980: 304). These contributions are virtually identical to those that take place in *t'inkas*, and express similar hopes that the young couple will become a centre of wealth and fertility.

34 Common names for *mesa* stone in Huaquirca are *qoripunta* (golden point), *qolqepunta* (silver point), *urpiminta* (Spanish *oro pimienta*, fool's gold), *allpaqori* (earth gold), *acero* (steel), and *solimana*. One of the reasons that I was never able to pin down specific referents for these names was that they have little or no descriptive value for the stones that they are applied to, which include yellow and red sandstone, various grey and black vitreous rocks, laminar quartz, granite, and various high-grade silvery ores. Only in the case of *solimana*, which always seemed to be a piece of white chalk or limestone (consistently attributed the power to prevent sorcery against the animals), did I find any constant relation between title and object. Similar emphasis on 'crude gold' and 'crude silver' can be found in Fuenzalida (1980: 166) and Isbell (1978: 155–6), whereas Casaverde (1970: 228–9) reports a number of ingredients for offerings that are conceived in terms

of an opposition between gold and silver, and are thought to be sources of these metals.

35 Despite its apparent derivation from the Spanish *alcanzar, alcanzo* cannot be found in any Spanish dictionary, and Urbano (1976: 136) argues convincingly that it is the result of an attempt to translate the Quechua verb *hayway* ('to hand over') into Spanish as a noun. The continuing use of the verb *hayway* to refer to these offerings (see Casaverde 1970: 225; Aranguren Paz 1975: 104; Flores 1977: 212) is perhaps the most compelling reason for limiting the possible translations of *alcanzo* to 'handing over.' This considerably limits the multivocality of *alcanzar* in Spanish, and highlights the tributary nature of these offerings, as Custred (1979: 380–1) has rightly emphasized. However, *alcanzo* is also used to describe the seizure of human hearts and lungs by the mountain spirits (Morote Best 1956b: 291), even though this act is more commonly designated by terms such as *hallp'asqa*, or *chuqalli* (Favre 1967: 130). Such seizures are especially likely when people have not been making adequate offerings to the mountains, or have trespassed on their inner sanctuaries. Here, it seems that the sense of 'drawing near' present in the Spanish *alcanzar* might be particularly relevant, as the mountains subsume and engulf the body of the ritualist. This suggests, by way of contrast, that one of the major goals of Andean sacrifice is to prevent the mountain spirits from 'drawing near,' to keep them at bay and avoid a bloody communion with them (cf. Evans-Pritchard 1956). Thus, the practice described by Isbell (1978: 157) of 'gaining advantage' over the mountain spirits through lower-level offerings is probably a defensive measure, a means of ensuring that ritualists themselves are not taken advantage of by the mountain spirits. It seems that the tension in this sacrificial relationship is expressed through a spatial metaphor neatly inscribed in the verb *alcanzar*, whereby one 'hands over' to avoid a 'drawing near.'

36 See Arguedas (1956: 235), Roel Pineda (1965: 27), Favre (1967: 122), Earls (1969: 69), Núñez del Prado (1970: 82), Morissette and Racine (1973: 171), Gow and Condori (1976: 40), and Oblitas Poblete (1978: 114–15). Sometimes mountain spirits of lower rank are known by names such as *awki* (e.g., Núñez del Prado 1970: 82), and are thought to be less benevolent than the *apus*, and more closely connected to agriculture than herding. I suspect that reports that *pachamamas* are connected to agriculture and mountain spirits to herding (e.g., Quispe 1969: 102; Morissette and Racine 1973: 175) are actually part of this same pattern of more local spirits being in charge of crops, and those of broader regional significance overseeing animals.

37 Although the mountain spirits generally appear in this form, they may also

appear as women or children with either black or white skin (see Earls 1969: 67; Morissette and Racine 1973: 170; Gow and Condori 1976: 38, 96, 98). I was told that when the *apus* appear as notable men, one must be especially wary, since this is the form in which they are most likely to seize organs from people. Yet they also assume a number of non-human forms, such as condors (as the title *mallku* suggests) and hawks (as the title *wamaní* suggests), and may even manifest themselves 'as a fire that issues from the stones and launches itself into the air' (Earls 1969: 67). Perhaps it is their ability to transform themselves and the offerings that are submitted to them that should be most emphasized.

38 Agriculturalists in Huaquirca do make fetus offerings (in a rite called *kutichiy*: 'to replace') to cure the condition known as *hallp'asqa*, whose classic symptom is a nasal haemorrhage, thought to result from the seizure of heart and lungs or testicles by the *apus/pachamamas*. Usually, they will have to obtain the offering from a *puna* ritualist, whom they will already have consulted to make the diagnosis in the first place. The awe with which many valley people hold this offering was well expressed by one of my favourite informants: 'Fetus is the highest offering that there is, it's like paying a doctor in dollars.' This medical use of fetus offerings is common elsewhere (e.g., Oblitas Poblete 1978: 45, 58), but as might be expected, it is also for the creation of new lives (see Nash 1979: 123). In the Cusco area, it forms a standard part of prepackaged offerings that can be bought, known as *despacho grande* and *medio despacho* (Casaverde 1970: 225) or *mesa grande* and *mesa chico* (Dalle 1969: 140). This would tend to suggest that not everywhere is the ritual knowledge to make a fetus offering considered to be as great as it is in Huaquirca.

39 This combination of the Spanish and Cusco Quechua names for water would be redundant if it did not find a reflection in the duality of liquids that are used in these libations: corn beer and cane alcohol. It is as if the internal contrast in this couplet between a clearer, lighter, and more alcoholic member with one that is darker, denser, and less alcoholic, replicates the union of distinct, but compatible, elements along the lines of *alma* and *ánimo*. The same might also be said of concoctions of sacrificial blood and cane alcohol that may be drunk in these rites (see Quispe 1969: 72, 1984: 614). Arguedas (1956: 244) mentions a preparation of corn beer, cane alcohol, and wine that is called *agua florida*, in which trinity once again results from asymmetric duality. Certain springs in Lucanas are held to well forth this same concoction of alcoholic drinks, now boiling hot (Arguedas 1956: 228). What all of these carefully prepared libations suggest is that we are no longer dealing with the dangerously corrosive water of the rainy sea-

son and its disembodied destructive energy, but fluids that combine tendencies towards both energy and embodiment. The image of 'florid water' captures this rather well, as does that of the 'lake,' which calms the wild waters of the rainy season, and almost seems to begin their fermentation into the alcoholic libations that are now being given these aquatic names.

40 Isbell (1978: 59) reports that the *wamanís* of Ayacucho are not simply mountain spirits but those of lakes as well. This appears to be true to at least a limited extent in the Antabamba region as well. In the town of Antabamba, for example, the reservoir named Wansoqocha is said to have an 'owner' who appears as a rich cattle-buyer from Cotahuasi. Although I never heard Wansoqocha described as an *apu*, he clearly looks like one. Furthermore, it seems that a mountain may be reduced to its watery essence, as is illustrated by the following story about Supayco, the most important *apu* in the region. One day, Supayco has designs on seducing Willkarana, another mountain spirit, and leaves his alpacas with Kuchillpo, his younger brother, to set off on this mission. While Supayco is gone, his arch-rival Suparaura arrives and overpowers Kuchillpo to steal a large number of alpacas. When Supayco returns to discover this, he is so furious that before setting out in pursuit, he smacks Kuchillpo across the face so hard that he turns into a lake. This is Lake Kuchillpo at the foot of Mt Supayco, which is a very important ritual site.

41 See Arguedas (1956: 239), Isbell (1978: 143), Ossio (1978b: 379–81), and Skar (1982: 225).

42 Here, the idea seems to be that the lightning-strike actually injects the carcass with a greater metallic content than usual, which is why it can be taken, despite the immediate losses involved, as a sign that the *apus* are attempting to confer greater wealth on the animal's owner. Further examples of this are iron-like odours and white blotches on the skin (mentioned by several informants regarding animals killed by lightning) that characterize ritualists who have been given special powers by lightning-strike (see Roel Pineda 1965: 29). Again, it would seem that the metallic smell in question might be taken to have a causal connection to the transfer of ritual power. Ritual collections of coins of the sort associated with the notion of *potosí* are thought to give off a similar powerful odour, called *waspi* (Isbell 1978: 121, or *huapci*, see Urbano 1976: 136). Furthermore, a comparable smell is associated with buried treasures (*tapados*) in the Antabamba area. An informant once told me that the Apu Utupara had met him high on the grazing lands at the top of the mountain and, after embracing him, told him to dig in a certain spot on the flank of the mountain, where the man and some friends returned with shovels at

night. As they dug, they uncovered a skunk with a tail of glowing coals, but its smell overcame them with sleep, and when they awoke the next morning, it was gone. After a short period of digging fruitlessly, they realized that the skunk was an *illa* which they should have captured immediately if they were to find the treasure. This same smell of the skunk has been reported for graveyards where a being known as the *kharisiri* (or *ñakaq*) extracts fat from the bodies of the dead (Oblitas Poblete 1978: 123), and suggests that their bodies might also be a source of buried metallic treasure. This is confirmed by Roel Pineda (1965: 28), who writes that *surimana* (Solimana) is not only considered to be the final abode of the dead in Chumbivilcas, but that it 'has much gold and much silver, that is to say, it has 'potosí' which is wealth.' This generative relation between death and precious metal is the conceptual basis of the entire tributary aspect of Andean sacrifice. As a final note, it is interesting that those who have been given the powers of a *pongo* by lightning-strike, and the consequent impregnation of their bodies with metal, are attributed the power to converse with the dead in the seances that they perform (this is particularly so in the town of Pachaconas in the lower Antabamba Valley), and in some areas are even thought to have the power to make 'payments' that will restore them to life (Flores 1979: 80). Here, it seems that metal forms an important link between *pongos* and the dead.

43 Although the commoners of the Antabamba region are in good company when they insist on the presence of classificatory male affines at all *t'inkas* (see Roel Pineda 1965: 32; Quispe 1969: 28; Earls 1970: 101; Valderrama and Escalante 1976: 180; Isbell 1978: 158), there are also places where all outsiders are definitely excluded (see Favre 1967: 134; Flores 1977: 213). Where this is so, it is often accompanied by an almost fanatical level of secrecy concerning the location of niches for interred offerings (see Matos Mar 1951, cited in Quispe 1969: 98; Favre 1967: 124), and prohibitions against non-kin seeing ritual paraphernalia (see Delgado de Thays 1965, cited in Quispe 1969: 99; Dalle 1969: 140; Flores 1977: 214). Even where 'affinal' presence is institutionalized, interment sites may be treated with a kind of agnatic exclusiveness according to Isbell (1978: 162). Imaginary marriages of daughters to local mountain spirits can be seen as part of this pattern when the latter are considered to be agnatic ancestors of a territory's owners. Under these circumstances, the *apu* can be reincorporated into the property-holding group from generation to generation as a perpetual 'son-in-law' in a pseudo-affinity that never represents a dispersal of the power of the locality.

44 For example: Favre (1967: 131–2), Núñez del Prado (1970: 76), Vallée and Palomino (1973: 14), Aranguren Paz (1975: 123), Velasco de Tord (1978: 197), and Ortiz (1980: 85).

Chapter Eight: Conclusions

1 '*¿Acaso estos abogaditos saben bailar? ¿Que valen?*'
2 Inevitably, there are methodological problems with this exercise. The political movements to be discussed did not occur in Huaquirca, and it will always be debatable whether conclusions drawn from the annual cycle in one area of the Andes are commensurable with fragmentary information on political mobilizations from another. Lan (1985) avoided these problems by doing research in an area where a major political movement had already occurred, but even his exemplary study assumes a degree of cultural homogeneity among the areas that participated in the movement. Such assumptions are inevitable in the use of ethnographic methods to explore broader historical events: the question is whether they are empirically justifiable, not whether they can be avoided. A related issue is whether Andean peasant class identities are local in nature, or based on a broader sense of shared culture and experience. These are important questions to which some provisional answers have already been offered (see Albó 1979; Platt 1983). No definitive answers will be possible until we know much more than we currently do about the range of variation in rural Andean culture. However, I would not have cited so many authors in this work if I did not perceive some fundamental similarities between what they describe and what I experienced in Huaquirca. To put the argument conservatively, if the commentary on production, property, and political power embodied in Huaquirca's annual cycle helps us understand political actions taken elsewhere in the Andes, then presumably it is more than a purely local phenomenon.
3 Thus, I contend that class must be described synchronically if we are not to miss politically marginalized forms of expression. To concentrate on the heroic (or cowardly) making of history is to invite this sort of oversight. Ethnographic methods, which are content to explore the cyclical grind of everyday life, can tell us much more about the experiential reality of class than Thompson's attempts to redeem and transcend class through historiography.
4 Several months prior to my fieldwork in Huaquirca, there was a bout of *Senderista* activity in the neighbouring town of Antabamba. Slogans were painted over several prominent buildings in town, and the rickety wooden

door was blown off the Banco de la Nación. Shortly afterwards, five school-teachers and several students from the secondary school in Antabamba were arrested on charges of 'terrorism.' After almost two years in jail without trial, all but one of the students were released. Rumour had it that the real mastermind behind *Sendero*'s activities in the Antabamba Valley was a university student from the town of Mollebamba, who died in *Sendero*'s spectacular assault on the jail of Ayacucho in March 1982. While the army kept a close eye on the area through the end of 1981, and extorted a pack of cigarettes from a schoolteacher on the truck that first took me into the area, there were no further incidents of guerrilla or state terrorism in the Antabamba Valley during my stay there. Nearby areas, including the town of Chalhuanca, were repeatedly affected and occupied, however, and the possibility of being swallowed up in the conflict was a constant source of worry and speculation among notables and politically aware commoners.

5 See Labrousse (1985: chap. 5), Degregori (1990), Gorriti (1990), Palmer (1992), and Poole and Rénique (1992) for useful discussions of *Sendero*.

Glossary

Note that the language affiliations of the following words are given on etymological grounds, and are somewhat artificial given the high degree of lexical interaction between Quechua and Spanish in the southern Peruvian highlands.

alferado Spanish: primary sponsor of a community-wide religious celebration.

allacho Quechua: digging stick.

alma Spanish: soul that records body form and survives in afterlife.

alma mayor Spanish: major or large soul, usually synonymous with *alma.*

alma menor Spanish: minor or small soul, usually synonymous with *ánimo.*

altarero Spanish: minor sponsor who provides an altar during a community-wide religious celebration.

ánimo Spanish: soul that provides vitality, senses, and animation.

apaq Quechua: dead souls that reside in the graveyard and arise to take the souls of the dying.

apu Quechua: lord, generally in reference to the mountain spirits.

aya taki Quechua: funerary song.

ayla Quechua: dance performed after canal cleaning.

ayni Quechua: the advance and return of similar labours or products, particularly in agricultural cooperation among households.

barrio Spanish: neighbourhood.

cabildo Spanish: town council.

capitanes Spanish: minor sponsors who provide music during community-wide religious celebrations.

cargo Spanish: sponsorship.

carguyoq Hispanicized Quechua: sponsor.

chawpi samay Quechua: rest of the mid-point, second break in a work party.

chicha Spanish: corn beer.

cholo Spanish: person of 'Indian' background.

chuqchu Quechua: malaria, shivering.

ch'uspa Quechua: small woven wool bag for coca leaves.

comadre Spanish: co-mother, godmother of one's children.

compadrazgo Spanish: spiritual co-parenthood.

compadre Spanish: co-father, godfather of one's children.

comunero Spanish: commoner, holder of common land.

Comunidad Campesina Spanish: Peasant Community.

condenado Spanish: condemned one, soul that commited heinous sins in life.

conscripción vial Spanish: road conscription, a government project initiated under President A. Leguía (1919–30).

costumbre Spanish: custom, ritual.

espíritu Spanish: spirit.

estancia Spanish: ranch, herding estate.

Exaltación Spanish: a sponsorship of the Christmas festivities in Huaquirca, associated with the Christ-child.

faena Spanish: communal labour obligation or tax.

Fiestas Patrias Spanish: Celebrations of the Fatherland.

gamonal Spanish: violent, domineering small rural landowner.

gamonalismo Spanish: an act or order of violent domination perpetrated by a *gamonal.*

grama Spanish: grass.

grameo Spanish: grass-removal session.

hacendado Spanish: an owner of large landed property.

hacienda Spanish: a large landed estate.

hallma Quechua: the first weeding of a crop.

hamank'ay Quechua: a white, daffodil-like flower.

herranza Spanish: branding.

ichu Quechua: coarse bunch grass of the alpine zone.

illa Quechua: amulet used to attract money or animals in ritual.

indigenismo Spanish: a political philosophy that glorifies the Indian as the cultural basis of national identity.

indio Spanish: Indian.

jornal Spanish: wage labour.

kallpa Quechua: vital force, animal figurines connoting this idea.

kamayoq Quechua: guardian of fields; foreman in charge of project.

kanta Quechua: amulet used to attract animals in ritual.

kikuyu Spanish: imported grass with creeping subterranean root.

kuraka Quechua: elder, hereditary local political authority under colonial and Inca regimes.

kutipa Quechua: return; the second weeding of a crop.

laqto Quechua: a variety of corn beer prepared by spitting into dough.

laymi Quechua: a sectoral fallow field in the lower alpine zone.

layqa Quechua: sorcerer; a category of dancer in Christmas festivities in Huaquirca.

Lisa Spanish: impudent one; transvestite dancer in Christmas festivities in Huaquirca.

llant'akuy Quechua: cutting and collection of firewood.

lloqe Quechua: left (hand); an Andean species of tree; a cord composed of one strand of white wool and another of black both woven counterclockwise.

Mamaq Quechua: of the Mother or Virgin, a sponsorship of the Christmas festivities in Huaquirca.

maña Quechua: request; a serving of one cup of corn beer; something that lacks its pair.

mesa Quechuized Spanish: a ritual table, its paraphernalia, and the offerings constructed on it; metallic stones used for ritual purposes.

mestizaje Spanish: racial mixture.

mestizo Spanish: métis, person of mixed blood.

mink'a Quechua: work remunerated in food and drink.

mink'ay Quechua: one who works for food and drink.

misti Quechuized Spanish: person of mixed or white race, powerful other.

pachamama Quechua: earth mother or earth source, a minor place spirit.

p'acha t'aqsana Quechua: clothes washing.

Paqpako Quechua: official community mourner of All Souls' and the Day of the Dead.

phatawa Quechua: boiled cobs of previously dried corn.

pito Quechua: corn beer thickened with flour of toasted maize.

pitusira Quechua: a spirit of plant growth.

potosí Quechua: antique coin used in ritual.

propietario Quechua: tax-paying property owner.

puna Quechua: alpine zone.

qatay Quechua: son-in-law, wife-taker.

qhashwa Quechua: dance performed after canal cleaning.

qheshwa Quechua: warm valley land.

quena Quechua: flute.

querendores Spanish: those who care.

quinua Quechua: chenopodium: a native grain of the Andes.

runa Quechua: human being.

samakuy Quechua: to rest one's self; sowing divination ritual.

sara p'ampa Quechua: maize burial, a weeding ritual.

sawasira Quechua: a spirit of plant growth.

Taytaq Quechua: of the Father, a sponsorship of the Christmas festivities in Huaquirca.

tercero Spanish: minor sponsor who organizes bullfights during a community-wide religious celebration.

t'inka Quechua: libation, ritual featuring burnt offerings or blood sacrifice.

vaquería Spanish: cattle grazing territory.

vaquero Spanish: cowherd servant.

varayoq Quechua: staff-holder, communal authority.

vecino (notable) Spanish: (notable) resident.

wanka Quechua: women's sowing song.

wanu Quechua: fertilizer.

wasichakuy Quechua: house rethatching.

wayliya Quechua: dance performed during maize sowing and at Christmas in Huaquirca.

yanantin Quechua: an identical, symmetric pair; in Huaquirca, a serving of two cups of corn beer.

yanapa Quechua: help; labour sharing without strict calculation.

yarqa faena Quechua: canal cleaning.

yunsa Quechua: tree ceremonially felled during Carnival.

References

Adams, R.N. 1959. *A Community in the Andes: Problems and Progress in Muqui-yauyo*. Seattle: University of Washington Press.

Adorno, T. 1973. *Negative Dialectics*. New York: Continuum.

Albó, J. 1979. '¿Khitipxtansa? ¿Quienes Somos? Identidad Localista, Étnica y Clasista en los Aymaras de Hoy.' *América Indígena* 39/3: 477–527.

Albó, J., and M. Mamani. 1980. 'Esposos, Suegros y Padrinos entre los Ayma-ras.' In E. Mayer and R. Bolton (eds.), *Parentesco y Matrimonio en los Andes*, 283–326. Lima: Pontificia Universidad Católica del Perú.

Allen, C. 1988. *The Hold Life Has: Coca and Cultural Identity in an Andean Com-munity*. Washington: Smithsonian.

Anderson, B. 1983. *Imagined Communities: Reflections on the Origin and Spread of Nationalism*. London: Verso.

Aranguren Paz, A. 1975. 'Las Creencias y Ritos Mágico-Religiosos de los Pas-tores Puneños.' *Allpanchis* 8: 103–132.

Arguedas, J.M. 1956 [1964]. 'Puquio, Una Cultura en Proceso de Cambio.' In J.M. Arguedas (ed.), *Estudios sobre la Cultura Actual del Perú*, 221–272. Lima: Universidad Nacional Mayor de San Marcos.

– 1968. *Las Comunidades de España y del Perú*. Lima: Universidad Nacional Mayor de San Marcos.

– 1975. *Formación de una Cultura Nacional Indoamericana*. Mexico: Siglo XXI.

– 1976. *Señores e Indios: Acerca de la Cultura Quechua*. Buenos Aires: Arca/Cali-canto.

Arguedas, J.M., and A. Ortiz. 1973. 'La Posesión de la Tierra, Los Mitos Post-Hispánicos y la Visión del Universo en la Población Monolingüe Quechua.' In J. Ossio (ed.), *Ideología Mesiánica del Mundo Andino*, 226–236. Lima: Igna-cio Prado Pastor.

Bastien, J. 1978. *Mountain of the Condor: Metaphor and Ritual in an Andean Ayllu.* St Paul: West Publishing Co.

– 1985. 'Qollahuaya-Andean Body Concepts: A Topographical-Hydraulic Model.' *American Anthropologist* 87/4: 595–611.

Bataille, G. 1933 [1979]. 'The Psychological Structure of Fascism.' *New German Critique* 16: 64–87.

Bertonio, L. 1612. *Vocabulario de la Lengua Aymara.* Juli.

Bloch, M. 1989. *Ritual, History and Power: Selected Papers in Anthropology.* London: Athlone.

Bloch, M., and J. Parry. 1982. 'Introduction: Death and the Regeneration of Life.' In M. Bloch and J. Parry (eds.), *Death and the Regeneration of Life*, 1–44. Cambridge: Cambridge University Press.

Block, A. 1974 [1988]. *The Mafia of a Sicilian Village, 1860–1960: A Study of Violent Peasant Entrepreneurs.* Prospect Heights: Waveland Press.

Bolton, R. 1974a. 'Tawanku: Vínculos Intermaritales.' In G. Alberti and E. Mayer (eds.), *Reciprocidad e Intercambio en los Andes Peruanos*, 153–170. Lima: Instituto de Estudios Peruanos.

– 1974b. 'To Kill a Thief: A Kallawaya Sorcery Session in the Lake Titicaca Region of Peru.' *Anthropos* 69: 191–215.

Bolton, R., and C. Bolton. 1976. 'Concepción, Embarazo y Alumbramiento en una Aldea Qolla.' *Antropología Andina* 1: 58–74.

Bonilla, H. 1987. 'The Indian Peasantry and "Peru" during the War with Chile.' In S. Stern (ed.), *Resistance, Rebellion, and Consciousness in the Andean Peasant World (18th to 20th Centuries)*, 219–231. Madison: University of Wisconsin Press.

Bonilla, H., and K. Spalding (eds.). 1971. *La Independencia del Perú.* Lima: Instituto de Estudios Peruanos.

Bourdieu, P. 1977. *Outline of a Theory of Practice.* Cambridge: Cambridge University Press.

– 1984. *Distinction: A Social Critique of the Judgement of Taste.* Cambridge, Mass.: Harvard University Press.

Bourque, S., and K. Warren. 1981. *Women of the Andes: Patriarchy and Social Change in Two Peruvian Towns.* Ann Arbor: University of Michigan Press.

Bourricaud, F. 1970. '¿Choloficación?' In F. Fuenzlida et al., *El Indio y el Poder en el Perú*, 183–198. Lima: Instituto de Estudios Peruanos.

Brush, S. 1977a. 'Kinship and Land Use in a Northern Sierra Community.' In R. Bolton and E. Mayer (eds.), *Andean Kinship and Marriage*, 136–152. Washington DC: American Anthropological Association.

Brush, S. 1977b. *Mountain, Field and Family.* Pittsburgh: University of Pennsylvania Press.

Buechler, H. 1980. *The Masked Media.* The Hague: Mouton.

Buechler, H., and J. Buechler. 1971. *The Bolivian Aymara.* New York: Holt, Rinehart and Winston.

Burchard, R. 1980. 'Exogamia como Estrategia de Acceso a Recursos Interzonales: Un Caso en los Andes Centrales del Perú.' In E. Mayer and R. Bolton (eds.), *Parentesco y Matrimonio en los Andes,* 593–616. Lima: Pontificia Universidad Católica del Perú.

Carpenter, L. 1992. 'Inside/Outside, Which Side Counts? Duality-of-Self and Bipartization in Quechua.' In R. Dover, K. Seibold, and J. McDowell (eds.), *Andean Cosmologies through Time: Persistence and Emergence,* 115–136. Bloomington: Indiana University Press.

Carter, W. 1964. *Aymara Communities and the Bolivian Agrarian Reform.* Gainesville: University of Florida Press, University of Florida Monographs (Social Sciences) 24.

– 1968. 'Secular Reinforcement in Aymara Death Ritual.' *American Anthropologist* 70/2: 238–263.

– 1977. 'Trial Marriage in the Andes?' In R. Bolton and E. Mayer (eds.), *Andean Kinship and Marriage,* 177–216. Washington DC: American Anthropological Association.

Casaverde, J. 1970. 'El Mundo Sobrenatural en una Comunidad.' *Allpanchis* 2: 121–244.

Centeno, A. 1949. 'El Servicio del Varayoq en el Distrito de Huaquirca.' Unpublished ms. available in the series *Monografías de Geografía Humana* 12: 31. Archivo Departmental del Cusco, Cusco.

– 1960. 'Esquema Prehistórico e Histórico de la Provincia de Antabamba.' Doctoral thesis in Letters, Universidad Nacional Mayor de San Agustín, Arequipa.

Chevalier, F. 1963. *Land and Society in Colonial Mexico.* Berkeley: University of California Press.

– 1970. 'Official *Indigenismo* in Peru in 1920: Origins, Significance, and Socioeconomic Scope.' In M. Mörner (ed.), *Race and Class in Latin America,* 184–196. New York: Columbia University Press.

Clifford, J. 1981. 'On Ethnographic Surrealism.' *Comparative Studies in Society and History* 23/4: 539–564.

Concha, J. 1971. 'Los Pueblos Pastores del Sur del Perú (y las Relaciones Económicas con los Agricultores).' Bachelor's thesis in Anthropology, Universidad Nacional Mayor San Antonio de Abad, Cusco.

– 1975. 'Relación entre Pastores y Agricultores.' *Allpanchis* 8: 67–101.

Cusihuamán, A. 1976. *Diccionario Quechua Cusco-Collao.* Lima: Ministerio de Educación/Instituto de Estudios Peruanos.

Custred, G. 1974. 'Llameros y Comercio Interregional.' In G. Alberti and

E. Mayer (eds.), *Reciprocidad e Intercambio en los Andes Peruanos*, 252–289. Lima: Instituto de Estudios Peruanos.

– 1977. 'Peasant Kinship, Subsistence and Economics in a High Altitude Andean Environment.' In R. Bolton and E. Mayer (eds.), *Andean Kinship and Marriage*, 117–135. Washington DC: American Anthropological Association.

– 1979. 'Symbols and Control in a High Altitude Andean Community.' *Anthropos* 74/3–4: 379–392.

– 1980. 'The Place of Ritual in Andean Society.' In B. Orlove and G. Custred (eds.), *Land and Power in Latin America: Agrarian Economics and Social Process in the Andes*, 195–209. New York: Holmes and Meier.

Dalle, L. 1969. 'El Despacho.' *Allpanchis* 1: 139–154.

– 1971. 'Kutipay o Segundo Aporque del Maíz.' *Allpanchis* 3: 59–65.

Davies, T. 1974. *Indian Integration in Peru: A Half Century of Experience, 1900–1948*. Lincoln: University of Nebraska Press.

Degregori, C. 1989. *Que Difícil es Ser Dios: Ideología y Violencia Política en Sendero Luminoso*. Lima: El Zorro de Abajo Ediciones.

– 1990. *Ayacucho 1969–1979: El Surgimiento de Sendero Luminoso*. Lima: Instituto de Estudios Peruanos.

Delgado de Thays, C. 1965. *Religión y Magia en Tupe (Yauyos)*. Lima: Publicationes del Museo Nacional de la Cultura Peruana, Serie Tesis Antropologicas 2.

Deverre, C. 1980. *Indienes ou paysans*. Paris: Le Sycomore.

Díaz, A. 1969. 'La Antinomía Andina: Latifundio-Comunidad.' *América Indígena* 29/1: 89–141.

Dollfus, O. 1981. *El Reto del Espacio Andino*. Lima: Instituto de Estudios Peruanos.

Doughty, P. 1967. 'La Cultura, La Bebida y el Trabajo en un Distrito Mestizo Andino.' *América Indígena* 27/4: 667–687.

Dumont, L. 1970. *Homo Hierarchicus*. Chicago: University of Chicago Press.

– 1986. *Essays on Individualism: Modern Ideology from an Anthropological Perspective*. Chicago: University of Chicago Press.

Duviols, P. 1973. 'Huari y Llacuaz: Agricultores y Pastores. Un Dualismo Prehispánico de Oposición y Complementariedad.' *Revista del Museo Nacional* 39: 153–191.

– 1978. 'Camaquen, Upani: Un Concept Animiste des Anciens Péruviens.' In R. Hartman and U. Oberem (eds.), *Estudios Americanistas* 1: 132–144. Bonn: Collectanea Instituti Anthropos, vol. 20.

– 1979. 'Un Symbolisme de l'Occupation, de l'Aménagement et de l'Exploitation de l'Espace.' *L'Homme* 19/2: 7–31.

Earls, J. 1969. 'The Organization of Power in Quechua Mythology.' *Steward Journal of Anthropology* 1: 63–82.

– 1970. 'The Structure of Modern Andean Social Categories.' *Steward Journal of Anthropology* 2: 69–106.

Earls, J., and I. Silverblatt. 1978. 'La Realidad Física y Social en la Cosmología Andina.' In *Actes du XLIIe Congrés International des Américanistes*, vol. 4, 299–325. Paris.

Evans-Pritchard, E. 1937. *Witchcraft, Magic and Oracles among the Azande.* Oxford: Oxford University Press.

– 1956. *Nuer Religion.* Oxford: Oxford University Press.

Favre, H. 1967. 'Tayta Wamani: Le Culte des Montagnes dans le Centre Sud des Andes Péruviennes.' In *Colloque D'Études Péruviennes*, 121–140. Publications des Annales de la Faculté des Lettres, n.s. 61. Aix-en-Provence: Éditions Ophrys.

– 1970. 'Evolución y Situación de la Hacienda Tradicional de la Región de Huancavelica.' In Matos Mar, J. (ed.), *Hacienda, Comunidad y Campesinado en el Perú*, 105–138. Lima: Instituto de Estudios Peruanos.

Favre, H. 1971. *Changement et Continuité chez les Mayas du Mexique.* Paris: Anthropos.

– 1980. *L'État et la Paysanerie en Mesoamérique et dans les Andes.* Ivry: Équipe de Recherche sur les Sociétés Indiennes Paysannes d'Amérique Latine, Document de Travail 16.

Fioravanti, A. 1973. 'Reciprocidad y Economía de Mercado.' *Allpanchis* 5: 121–130.

Fioravanti-Molinié, A. 1986. 'The Andean Community Today.' In J. Murra, N. Wachtel, and J. Revel (eds.), *Anthropological History of Andean Polities*, 342–358. Cambridge: Cambridge University Press.

Firth, R. 1939. *Primitive Polynesian Economy.* London: Routledge and Kegan Paul.

– 1967. *The Work of the Gods in Tikopea.* 2nd ed. London: Athlone.

Flores, J. 1973. 'La Viuda y el Hijo del Soq'a Machu.' *Allpanchis* 5: 45–55.

– 1974. 'Mistis and Indians: Their Relations in a Micro-Region of Cusco.' *International Journal of Comparative Sociology* 15/3–4: 182–192.

– 1977. 'Aspectos Mágicos del Pastoreo: Enqa, Enqaychu, Illa y Khuya Rumi.' In J. Flores (ed.), *Pastores de Puna: Uywamichiq Punarunakuna*, 211–238. Lima: Instituto de Estudios Peruanos.

– 1979. *Pastoralists of the Andes: The Alpaca Herders of Paratía.* Philadelphia: Institute for the Study of Human Issues.

Flores, J., and Y. Nájar. 1980. 'Un Aspecto del Parentesco de los Pastores de la Puna Alta.' In E. Mayer and R. Bolton (eds.), *Parentesco y Matrimonio en los Andes*, 481–491. Lima: Pontificia Universidad Católica del Perú.

Fonseca, C. 1974. 'Modalidades de la Minka.' In G. Alberti and E. Mayer
(eds.), *Reciprocidad e Intercambio en los Andes Peruanos*, 86–109. Lima: Instituto
de Estudios Peruanos.

Forbes, D. 1870. 'On the Aymara Indians of Bolivia and Peru.' *Journal of the Ethnological Society of London* 2: 193–305.

Frazer, J. 1890 [1922]. *The Golden Bough* (abridged edition). London:
Macmillan.

Friedlander, J. 1975. *Being Indian in Hueyapan: A Study of Forced Identity in Contemporary Mexico.* New York: St Martin's Press.

Friedrich, P. 1965. 'A Mexican Cacicazgo.' *Ethnology* 4: 190–209.

Fuenzalida, F. 1970a. 'Poder, Raza y Etnia en el Perú Contemporáneo.' In
F. Fuenzalida et al., *El Indio y el Poder en el Peru*, 15–87. Lima: Instituto de
Estudios Peruanos.

– 1970b. 'Estructura de la Comunidad de Indígenas Tradicional. Un Hipótesis
de Trabajo.' In J. Matos Mar (ed.), *Hacienda, Comunidad y Campesinado en el
Perú*, 219–263. Lima: Instituto de Estudios Peruanos.

– 1980. 'Santiago y el Wamaní: Aspectos de un Culto Pagano en Moya.' *Debates
en Antropología* 5: 155–188.

Gade, D. 1970. 'Ecología del Robo Agrícola en las Tierras Altas de los Andes
Centrales.' *América Indígena* 30/1: 3–14.

García-Sayán, D. 1982. *Tomas de Tierras en el Perú.* Lima: Desco.

Geertz, C. 1973. *The Interpretation of Cultures.* New York: Basic Books.

Gellner, E. 1983. *Nations and Nationalism.* Ithaca: Cornell University Press.

González Holguín, D. 1608. *Vocabulario de la Lengua General de todo el Perú Lla-
mado Lengua Qqechua o del Inca.*

Gorriti, G. 1990. *Historia de la Guerra Milenaria en el Perú.* Lima: Editorial Apoyo.

Gose, P. 1986. 'Sacrifice and the Commodity Form in the Andes.' *Man* 21/2:
296–310.

– 1988. 'Labour and the Materiality of the Sign: Beyond Dualist Theories of
Culture.' *Dialectical Anthropology* 13/2: 103–121.

– 1991. 'House Rethatching in an Annual Cycle: Practice, Contradiction, and
Meaning.' *American Ethnologist* 18/1: 39–66.

Gow, D. 1980. 'The Roles of Christ and Inkarrí in Andean Religion.' *Journal of
Latin American Lore* 6/2: 279–298.

Gow, R. 1982. 'Inkarrí and Revolutionary Leadership in the Southern Andes.'
Journal of Latin American Lore 8/2: 197–223.

Gow, R., and B. Condori. 1976. *Kay Pacha.* Cusco: Centro de Estudios Rurales
Andinos 'Bartolomé de las Casas.'

Gow, D., and R. Gow. 1975. 'La Alpaca en el Mito y el Ritual.' *Allpanchis* 8: 141–
164.

Gramsci, A. 1971. *The Prison Notebooks.* New York: International Publishers.

Grondín, M. 1978. *Comunidad Andina: Explotación Calculada.* Santo Domingo: Unidad de Divulgación Técnica, Secretaria de Estado de Agricultura, Republica Dominicana.

Guaman Poma, F. 1615 [1980]. *Nueva Corónica y Buen Gobierno.* Mexico: Siglo XXI.

Gudeman, S. 1986. *Economics as Culture.* London: Routledge and Kegan Paul.

Guillet, D. 1979. 'Reciprocal Labour and Peripheral Capitalism in the Central Andes.' *Ethnology* 19/2: 151–167.

Harris, O. 1978. 'Complementarity and Conflict: An Andean View of Women and Men.' In J. La Fontaine (ed.), *Sex and Age as Principles of Social Differentiation*, 21–40. London: Academic Press.

– 1980. 'The Power of Signs: Gender, Culture and the Wild in the Bolivian Andes.' In C. MacCormack and M. Strathern (eds.), *Nature, Culture and Gender*, 70–94. Cambridge: Cambridge University Press.

– 1982. 'The Dead and the Devils among the Bolivian Laymi.' In M. Bloch and J. Parry (eds.), *Death and the Regeneration of Life*, 45–73. Cambridge: Cambridge University Press.

– 1986. 'From Asymmetry to Triangle: Symbolic Transformations in Northern Potosí.' In J. Murra, N. Wachtel, and J. Revel (eds.), *Anthropological History of Andean Polities*, 260–279. Cambridge: Cambridge University Press.

Hartman, R. 1973. 'Conmemoración de Muertos en la Sierra Ecuatoriana.' *Indiana* 1: 179–197.

Hobsbawm, E. 1959. *Primitive Rebels.* New York: Norton.

– 1974. 'Peasant Land Occupations.' *Past and Present* 62: 120–152.

Isbell, B.J. 1976. 'La Otra Mitad Esencial: Un Estudio de la Complementariedad Sexual Andina.' *Estudios Andinos* 12: 37–56.

– 1978. *To Defend Ourselves: Ecology and Ritual in an Andean Village.* Austin: University of Texas Press.

Isbell, B.J., and W. Roncalla Fernandez. 1978. 'La Ontogénesis de la Metáfora: Juegos de Adivinanza entre Quechua-Hablantes Vistos como Procedimientos de Descubrimiento Cognitivo.' In *Actes du XLIIe Congrés International des Américanistes*, vol. 4, 435–462. Paris.

Kapsoli, W. 1977. *Los Movimientos Campesinos en el Perú: 1879–1965.* Lima: Delva Editores.

Keesing, R. 1985. 'Conventional Metaphors and Anthropological Metaphysics: The Problematic of Cultural Translation.' *Journal of Anthropological Research* 41/2: 201–217.

Kertzer, D. 1988. *Ritual, Politics and Power.* New Haven: Yale University Press.

Labrousse, A. 1985. *Le Réveil Indien en Amérique Andine*. Lausanne and Paris: Éditions Pierre Marcel Favre.

Lan, D. 1985. *Guns and Rain: Guerillas and Spirit Mediums in the Liberation of Zimbabwe*. London: Curry.

Langer, E. 1990. 'Andean Rituals of Revolt: The Chayanta Rebellion of 1927.' *Ethnohistory* 37/3: 227–253.

Lara, J. 1978. *Diccionario Castellano-Queshwa Queshwa-Castellano*. La Paz and Cochabamba: Editorial Los Amigos del Libro.

Leach, E. 1964. *Political Systems of Highland Burma*. 2nd ed. London: Athlone.

Lévi-Strauss, C. 1958 [1963]. *Structural Anthropology*. New York: Basic Books.

– 1964 [1969]. *The Raw and the Cooked*. New York: Harper and Row.

Lewis, G. 1980. *Day of Shining Red*. Cambridge: Cambridge University Press.

Lienhardt, G. 1961. *Divinity and Experience*. Oxford: Oxford University Press.

Lira, J.A. 1944. *Diccionario Kkechua-Español*. Tucuman.

Lund Skar, S. 1979. 'The Use of the Public/Private Framework in the Analysis of Egalitarian Societies: The Case of a Quechua Community in Highland Peru.' *Women's Studies International Quarterly* 2: 449–460.

MacPherson, C.B. 1962. *The Political Theory of Possessive Individualism*. Oxford: Oxford University Press.

Malengreau, J. 1974. 'Comuneros y "Empresarios" en el Intercambio.' In G. Alberti and E. Mayer (eds.), *Reciprocidad e Intercambio en los Andes Peruanos*, 171–205. Lima: Instituto de Estudios Peruanos.

– 1980. 'Parientes, Compadres y Comuneros en Cusipata (Perú).' In E. Mayer and R. Bolton (eds.), *Parentesco y Matrimonio en los Andes*, 493–536. Lima: Pontificia Universidad Católica del Perú.

Malinowski, B. 1925 [1954]. 'Magic, Science and Religion.' In B. Malinowski, *Magic, Science and Religion and Other Essays*, 17–92. Garden City: Doubleday.

– 1935 [1965]. *Coral Gardens and Their Magic*. Bloomington: Indiana University Press.

Mallon, F. 1983. *The Defense of Community in Peru's Central Highlands: Peasant Struggle and Capitalist Transition 1860–1940*. Princeton: Princeton University Press.

Mannheim, B. 1988. 'The Sound Must Seem an Echo to the Sense: Some Cultural Determinants of Language Change in Southern Peruvian Quechua.' *Michigan Discussions in Anthropology* 8: 175–199.

Manrique, N. 1981. *Campesinado y Nación: Las Guerillas Indígenas en la Guerra con Chile*. Lima: Centro de Investigación y Capacitación.

– 1983. 'Los Arrieros de la Sierra Central durante el Siglo XIX.' *Allpanchis* 21: 27–46.

Manya, J. 1969. '¿Temible ñakaq?' *Allpanchis* 1: 135–8.

Mariátegui, J.C. 1971. *Seven Interpretive Essays on Peruvian Reality.* Austin: University of Texas Press.

Martínez, G. 1983. 'Los Dioses de los Cerros en los Andes.' *Journal de la Société des Américanistes* 69: 85–115.

Matos Mar, J. 1951. *La Ganadería en la comunidad de Tupe.* Lima: Instituto de Etnología de la Facultad de Letras de la Universidad Nacional Mayor de San Marcos, Publicación 2.

– 1964. 'La Propiedad en la Isla de Taquile.' In J.M. Arguedas (ed.), *Estudios sobre la Cultura Actual del Perú*, 64–142. Lima: Universidad Nacional Mayor de San Marcos.

Mayer, E. 1970. 'Mestizo e Indio: El contexto Social de las Relaciones Interétnicas.' In F. Fuenzalida et al., *El Indio y el Poder en el Perú*, 87–152. Lima: Instituto de Estudios Peruanos.

– 1974. 'Las Reglas del Juego en la Reciprocidad Andina.' In G. Alberti and E. Mayer (eds.), *Reciprocidad e Intercambio en los Andes Peruanos*, 37–65. Lima: Instituto de Estudios Peruanos.

– 1977. 'Beyond the Nuclear Family,' In R. Bolton and E. Mayer (eds.), *Andean Kinship and Marriage*, 60–80. Washington DC: American Anthropological Association.

– 1991. 'Peru in Deep Trouble: Mario Vargas Llosa's "Inquest in the Andes" Reexamined.' *Cultural Anthropology* 6/4: 466–504.

Mayer, E., and C. Zamalloa. 1974. 'Reciprocidad en las Relaciones de Producción.' In G. Alberti and E. Mayer (eds.), *Reciprocidad e Intercambio en los Andes Peruanos*, 66–85. Lima: Instituto de Estudios Peruanos.

Meiksins Wood, E. 1982. 'The Politics of Theory and the Concept of Class: E.P. Thompson and His Critics.' *Studies in Political Economy* 9: 45–75.

Miller, G. 1977. 'Sacrificio y Beneficio de Camélidos en el Sur del Perú.' In J. Flores Ochoa (ed.), *Pastores de Puna: Uywamichiq Punarunakuna*, 193–210. Lima: Instituto de Estudios Peruanos.

Mishkin, B. 1964. 'Posesión de la Tierra en la Comunidad de Kauri, Quispicanchis.' In J.M. Arguedas (ed.), *Estudios sobre la Cultura Actual del Perú*, 143–149. Lima: Universidad Nacional Mayor de San Marcos.

Montoya, R. 1980. *Capitalismo y No Capitalismo en el Perú: Un Estudio Histórico de su Articulación en un Eje Regional.* Lima: Mosca Azul Editores.

– 1982. 'Identités Ethniques et Luttes Agraires dans les Andes Péruviennes.' In L. Briggs et al., *De l'Empriente à l'Emprise: Identités Andines et Logiques Paysannes*, 267–300. Paris and Geneva: Presses Universitaires de France/Institut Universitaire d'Études du Developpement.

Montoya, R., J. Silveira, and F. Lindoso. 1979. *Producción Parcelaria y Universo Ideológico: El Caso de Puquio.* Lima: Mosca Azul Editores.

Morissette, J., and L. Racine. 1973. 'La Hiérarchie des Wamaní: Essai sur la Pensée Classificatoire Quechua.' *Recherches Amérindiennes au Québec* 3/1–2: 167–188.

Mörner, M. 1978. *Perfíl de la Sociedad Rural del Cuzco a fines de la Colonia.* Lima: Universidad del Pacífico.

Morote Best, E. 1951. 'El Degollador.' *Tradición* 2/4/11: 67–91.

– 1953. 'Cabezas Voleadoras.' *Perú Indígena* 4/9: 109–124.

– 1956a. 'La Zafa-Casa.' *Cultura* 1: 13–30.

– 1956b. 'Espíritus de Montes.' *Letras* 56/7: 288–306.

Murra, J. 1975. *Formaciones Económicas y Políticas del Mundo Andino.* Lima: Instituto de Estudios Peruanos.

– 1978. *La Organización Económica del Estado Inca.* Mexico: Siglo XXI.

– 1980. *The Economic Organization of the Inca State.* Greenwich: JAI Press.

Nachtigal, H. 1975. 'Ofrendas de Llamas en la Vida Ceremonial de los Pastores.' *Allpanchis* 8: 133–140.

Nash, J. 1979. *We Eat the Mines and the Mines Eat Us.* New York: Columbia University Press.

Necker, L. 1982. 'À Propos de Quelques Thèses sur l'Indianité.' In L. Briggs et al., *De l'Empriente à l'Emprise: Identités Andines et Logiques Paysannes*, 241–266. Paris and Geneva: Presses Universitaires de France/Institut Universitaire d'Études de Développement.

Needham, R. 1972. *Belief, Language and Experience.* Chicago: University of Chicago Press.

Núñez del Prado, D. 1972. 'La Reciprocidad como Ethos de la Cultura Quechua.' *Allpanchis* 4: 135–154.

– 1975a. 'El Rol de la Mujer Campesina Quechua.' *América Indígena* 35/2: 391–401.

– 1975b. 'El Poder de Decisión de la Mujer Quechua Andina.' *América Indígena* 35/3: 623–630.

Núñez del Prado, J. 1970. 'El Mundo Sobrenatural de los Quechuas del Sur del Perú a través de la Comunidad de Qotobamba.' *Allpanchis* 2: 57–119.

Núñez del Prado, J., and M. Bonino Nievez. 1969. 'Una Celebración Mestiza del Cruz-Velakuy en el Cusco.' *Allpanchis* 1: 43–60.

Núñez del Prado, O. 1973. *Kuyo Chico: Applied Anthropology in an Indian Community.* Chicago: University of Chicago Press.

Oblitas Poblete, E. 1978. *Cultura Callawaya.* La Paz: Ediciones Populares Camarlinghi.

O'Phelan, S. 1983. 'Tierras Comunales y Revuelta Social: Perú y Bolivia en el Siglo XVIII.' *Allpanchis* 22: 75–91.

Orlove, B. 1973. 'Abigeato.' *Allpanchis* 5: 65–82.

– 1980. 'Landlords and Officials: The Sources of Domination in Surimana and Quehue.' In B. Orlove and G. Custred (eds.), *Land and Power in Latin America: Agrarian Economics and Social Process in the Andes*, 113–127. New York: Holmes and Meier.

Ortiz, A. 1973. *De Adaneva a Inkarrí*. Lima: Retablo de Papel.

– 1980. *Huarochirí, 400 Años Después*. Lima: Pontificia Universidad Católica del Perú.

– 1982. 'Moya: Espacio, Tiempo y Sexo en un Pueblo Andino.' *Allpanchis* 20:189–207.

Ossio, J. 1978a. 'Relaciones Interétnicas y Verticalidad en los Andes.' *Debates en Antropología* 2: 1–23.

– 1978b. 'El Simbolismo del Agua y la Representación del Tiempo y el Espacio en la Fiesta de la Acequia de la Comunidad de Andamarca.' In *Actes du XLIIᵉ Congrès International des Américanistes*, vol. 4, 377–395. Paris.

– 1980. 'La Estructura Social de las Comunidades Andinas.' In *Historia del Perú*, tomo 3, 203–377. Lima: Mejía Baca.

– 1983. 'La Propiedad en las Comunidades Andinas.' *Allpanchis* 22: 35–59.

Palacios Ríos, F. 1977. 'Hiwasaha Uywa Uywatana, Uka Uywaha Hiwasaru Uyusitu: Los Pastores Aymaras de Chichillapi.' Magisterial thesis in Social Sciences, Specialty in Anthropology, Pontificia Universidad Católica del Perú, Lima.

Palmer, D. (ed.). 1992. *Shining Path of Peru*. London: Hurst and Company.

Palomino, S. 1968. 'La Cruz en los Andes.' *Amaru* 8: 63–66.

Platt, T. 1982. *Estado Boliviano y Ayllu Andino: Tierra y Tributo en el Norte de Potosí*. Lima: Instituto de Estudios Peruanos.

– 1983. 'Conciencia Andina y Conciencia Proletaria: Qhuyaruna y Ayllu en el Norte de Potosí.' *HISLA: Revista Latinoamericana de Historia Económica y Social* 2: 47–73.

– 1986. 'Mirrors and Maize: The Concept of *Yanantin* among the Macha of Bolivia.' In J. Murra, N. Wachtel, and J. Revel (eds.), *Anthropological History of Andean Polities*, 228–259. Cambridge: Cambridge University Press.

– 1987a. 'The Andean Soldiers of Christ. Confraternity Organization, the Mass of the Sun and Regenerative Warfare in Rural Potosi (18th–20th Centuries).' *Journal de la Société des Américanistes* 73: 139–191.

– 1987b. 'The Andean Experience of Bolivian Liberalism, 1825–1900: Roots of Rebelion in 19th-Century Chayanta (Potosí).' In S. Stern (ed.), *Resistance, Rebellion, and Consciousness in the Andean Peasant World, 18th to 20th Centuries*, 280–323. Madison: University of Wisconsin Press.

Poole, D. 1988. 'Landscapes of Power in a Cattle-Rustling Culture of Southern Andean Peru.' *Dialectical Anthropology* 12/3: 367–398.

Poole, D., and G. Rénique. 1991. 'The New Chroniclers of Peru: U.S. Scholars and Their "Shining Path" of Peasant Revolution.' *Bulletin of Latin American Research* 10/2: 133–191.

Poole, D., and G. Rénique. 1992. *Peru: Time of Fear.* London: Latin America Bureau.

Primov, G. 1980. 'The Political Role of Mestizo Schoolteachers in Indian Communities.' In B. Orlove and G. Custred (eds.), *Land and Power in Latin America: Agrarian Economics and Social Process in the Andes*, 153–163. New York: Holmes and Meier.

Quispe, U. 1969. *La Herranza en Choque Huarcayo y Huancasancos.* Lima: Instituto Indigenista del Perú, Serie Monografica 20.

– 1984. 'La "Chupa" : Rito Ganadero Andino.' *Revista Andina* 2/2: 607–628.

Radcliffe-Brown, A. 1952. *Structure and Function in Primitive Society.* London: Routledge and Kegan Paul.

Raimondi, A. 1874. *El Perú*, volume 1. Lima: Imprenta del Estado.

Ramirez, J. 1969. 'La Novena del Señor de Qoyllur Rit'i.' *Allpanchis* 1: 61–88.

Rasnake, R. 1988. *Domination and Cultural Resistance: Authority and Power among an Andean People.* Durham: Duke University Press.

Rivera Pineda, F. 1980. 'Los Dioses de la Guerra: La Mediación del Hirca, La Mishkipa y las Revelaciones en las Luchas Campesinas de Pasco, 1955–1962.' Unpublished ms.

Roel Pineda, J. 1965. 'Creencias y Prácticas Religiosas en la Provincia de Chumbivilcas.' *Historia y Cultura* 2: 24–32.

Rosaldo, M. 1980. *Knowledge and Passion: Ilongot Notions of Self and Social Life.* Cambridge: Cambridge University Press.

Sahlins, M. 1976. *Culture and Practical Reason.* Chicago: University of Chicago Press.

Sallnow, M. 1974. 'La Peregrinación Andina.' *Allpanchis* 7: 101–142.

Sánchez, R. 1982. 'The Andean Economic System and Capitalism.' In D. Lehmann (ed.), *Ecology and Exchange in the Andes*, 157–190. Cambridge: Cambridge University Press.

Sapir, D. 1977. 'The Anatomy of Metaphor.' In D. Sapir and C. Crocker (eds.), *The Social Uses of Metaphor*, 3–32. Pittsburgh: University of Pennsylvania Press.

Sewell, W. 1990. 'How Classes are Made: Critical Reflections on E.P. Thompson's Theory of Working-Class Formation.' In H. Kaye and K. McClelland (eds.), *E.P. Thompson: Critical Perspectives*, 50–77. Philadelphia: Temple University Press.

Skar, H. 1982. *The Warm Valley People.* Oslo: Universitetsforlaget.

Smith, G. 1989. *Livelihood and Resistance.* Berkeley: University of California Press.

Smith, W.R. 1889 [1969]. *Lectures on the Religion of the Ancient Semites.* New York: Ktav Publishing House.

Starn, O. 1991. 'Missing the Revolution: Anthropologists and the War in Peru.' *Cultural Anthropology* 6/1: 63–91.

Stein, W. 1961. *Hualcán: Life in the Highlands of Peru.* Ithaca: Cornell University Press.

Tamayo, A. 1947. 'Breve Estudio Monográfico de la Provincia de Antabamba.' *Lunarejo* 2: 31–67.

Tambiah, S. 1985. *Culture, Thought, and Social Action.* Cambridge, Mass.: Harvard University Press.

Taussig, M. 1987. *Shamanism, Colonialism, and the Wild Man.* Chicago: University of Chicago Press.

Thompson, E.P. 1963. *The Making of the English Working Class.* New York: Vintage.

– 1975. *Whigs and Hunters.* Harmondsworth: Peregrine.

– 1976. 'The Grid of Inheritance: A Comment.' In J. Goody, J. Thirsk, and E.P. Thompson (eds.), *Family and Inheritance: Rural Society in Western Europe, 1200–1800,* 328–360. Cambridge: Cambridge University Press.

– 1978a. 'Eighteenth-Century English Society: Class Struggle Without Class?' *Social History* 3/2: 133–165.

– 1978b. *The Poverty of Theory and Other Essays.* London: Merlin Press.

– 1978c. 'Folklore, Anthropology and Social History.' Brighton: Studies in Labour History Pamphlet 5.

– 1981. 'The Politics of Theory,' In R. Samuel (ed.), *People's History and Socialist Theory,* 396–408. Boston: Routledge and Kegan Paul.

Tomoeda, H. 1982. 'Folklore Andino y Mitología Amazónica: Las Plantas Cultivadas y la Muerte en el Pensamiento Andino.' *Senri Ethnological Studies* 10: 275–306.

– 1985. 'The Llama is My *Chacra*: Metaphor of Andean Pastoralists.' In S. Masuda, I. Shimada, and C. Morris (eds.), *Andean Ecology and Civilization,* 277–299. Tokyo: University of Tokyo Press.

Tschopik, H. 1951. *The Aymara of Chucuito, Peru.* New York: Anthropological Papers of the American Museum of Natural History, vol. 44, pt. 2.

Turner, V. 1969. *The Ritual Process.* Chicago: Aldine.

Tylor, E.B. 1871 (1903). *Primitive Culture.* 2 vols. 4th ed. (rev.). London: J. Murray.

Urbano, H. 1974. 'La representación andina del tiempo y del espacio en la fiesta.' *Allpanchis* 7: 9–48.

– 1976. 'Lenguaje y Gesto Ritual en el Sur Andino.' *Allpanchis* 9: 121–50.

Urton, G. 1981. *At the Crossroads of the Earth and the Sky: An Andean Cosmology.* Austin: University of Texas Press.

Valcárcel, L. 1980. 'La Religión Incaica.' In *Historia del Perú*, tomo 3, 75–202. Lima: Mejía Baca.

Valderrama, R., and C. Escalante. 1975. 'El Apu Ausangate en la Narrativa Popular.' *Allpanchis* 8: 175–184.

– 1976. 'Pacha T'inka o la T'inka a la Madre Tierra en el Apurímac.' *Allpanchis* 9: 177–192.

– 1978. 'Mitos y Leyendas de los Quechuas del Sur del Perú (Apurímac, Cusco).' *Debates en Antropología* 2: 125–135.

– 1980. 'Apu Qoropuna (Visión del Mundo de los Muertos en la Comunidad de Awkimarca).' *Debates en Antropología* 5: 233–264.

Vallée, L., and S. Palomino. 1973. 'Quelques éléments d'ethnographie du "ñakaq".' *Bulletin de L'Institut Français d'Études Andines* 2/4: 9–19.

Van den Berghe, P. 1974a. 'Introduction.' *International Journal of Comparative Sociology*, 15/3–4: 121–131.

– 1974b. 'The Use of Ethnic Terms in the Peruvian Social Science Literature.' *International Journal of Comparative Sociology* 15/3–4: 132–142.

Van den Berghe, P., and G. Primov. 1977. *Inequality in the Peruvian Andes: Class and Ethnicity in Cusco*. Columbia and London: University of Missouri Press.

Velasco de Tord, E. 1978. 'La K'apakocha: Sacrificios Humanos en el Incario.' In M. Koth de Paredes and A. Castelli (eds.), *Etnohistoria y Antropología Andina*, 193–199. Lima: Museo Nacional de Historia.

Villanueva, H. 1982. *Cuzco 1689: Economía y Sociedad en el Sur Andino*. Cusco: Centro de Estudios Rurales Andinos 'Bartolomé de las Casas.'

Wallis, C. 1980. 'Pastores de Llamas en Cailloma (Arequipa) y Modelos Estructuralistas para la Interpretación de su Sociedad.' In R. Matos (ed.), *El Hombre y la Cultura Andina*, tomo 3, 248–257. Lima: Actas y Trabajos del III Congreso Peruano.

Warren, K. 1978. *The Symbolism of Subordination: Indian Identity in a Guatemalan Town*. Austin: University of Texas Press.

Webster, S. 1973. 'Native Pastoralism in the South Andes.' *Ethnology* 12: 115–133.

– 1977. 'Kinship and Affinity in a Native Quechua Community.' In R. Bolton and E. Mayer (eds.), *Andean Kinship and Marriage*, 28–42. Washington DC: American Anthropological Association.

– 1981. 'Interpretation of an Andean Social and Economic Formation.' *Man* 16/4: 616–633.

Wolf, F. 1980. 'Parentesco Aymara en el Siglo XVI.' In E. Mayer and R. Bolton (eds.), *Parentesco y Matrimonio en los Andes*, 115–135. Lima: Pontificia Universidad Católica del Perú.

Wright, E. 1985. *Classes*. London: Verso.

Yaranga, A. 1979. 'La Divinidad Illapa en la Región Andina.' *América Indígena* 39/4: 697–720.

Zorilla, J. 1978. 'Sueño, Mito y Realidad en una Comunidad Ayacuchana.' *Debates en Antropología* 2: 119–124.

Zuidema, R. 1983. 'The Lion in the City: Royal Symbols of Transition in Cuzco.' *Journal of Latin American Lore* 9/1: 39–100.

Zuidema, R., and U. Quispe. 1968 [1973]. 'A Visit to God: The Account and Interpretation of a Religious Experience in the Peruvian Community of Choque-Huarcaya.' In D. Gross (ed.), *Peoples and Cultures of Native South America*, 358–374. New York: Doubleday.

Index

144, 148, 152–3, 159, 161, 168,
170, 179–81, 202, 229–32, 234–5,
239, 244, 248, 255, 280–1, 285

Taytaq (Christmas sponsorship), 141,
158, 160, 165–6, 168–9, 269, 271,
282–3
theft, 13, 39, 49, 57, 184–8, 190, 201,
229–30, 260–1
t'inka (libation and sacrificial ritual),
xiii, 13, 78, 84, 91, 98, 101, 110–12,
149, 161, 163, 165, 169–70, 174,
182, 186–7, 194–25, 229–32, 234–
6, 239–40, 242, 244, 247, 267–8,
285–97
tribute: labour (*faena*), 18, 57–61,
95–101, 230, 241, 264, 269, 271;
sacrificial, xiii, 13, 210, 212, 224

valley land, warm. *See qheshwa*
vaquería (grazing territory), 49–50,
171–3
varayoq (staff-holder), 61–2, 155,
170, 247, 269, 271
vecino. See notable

velorio. See wake
violence, xi, 19–20, 66, 221, 224, 235,
252–3
Virgin of the Assumption, 91–5, 98,
102, 158, 166, 181

wake (*velorio*), 117–18, 121–2, 142–3
wanka (song), 111, 140, 151, 273
wanu (fertilizer), 110, 113, 135, 151,
153
wayliya (song and dance), 111–12,
158–70, 179, 186, 219, 231, 240,
280, 282, 287
whites ('race'), 18–20, 53, 64, 69

yanantin (pair), 135–6, 138, 144,
148–9, 152, 156, 160, 166, 179–80,
226, 231–2, 280
yanapa (help, form of reciprocity),
8–9, 266, 275, 279
yarqa faena. See canal cleaning
yunsa (Carnival tree), 174–81, 184,
228